Understanding Aging: A Multidisciplinary Approach

Understanding Aging: A Multidisciplinary Approach

Edited by

MARIAN G. SPENCER, R.N., M.S., C.A.G.S.

Associate Professor of Nursing
Coordinator, Gerontology Program for Community Health Nursing
Boston University School of Nursing
Boston, Massachusetts

CAROLINE J. DORR, R.N., M.S.

Lecturer, Metropolitan College
Boston University
Boston, Massachusetts
Supervisor, Sharon Board of Health
Sharon, Massachusetts

ACC
APPLETON-CENTURY-CROFTS/New York
A Publishing Division of Prentice-Hall, Inc.

Library of Congress Cataloging in Publication Data
Main entry under title:

Understanding aging.

1. Aging—Addresses, essays, lectures. 2. Aged—Addresses, essays, lectures. I. Spencer, Marian G. II. Dorr, Caroline J. [DNLM: 1. Aging. WT104 U54]
HQ1061.U47 301.43′5 75-12813 +1/77
ISBN 0-8385-9253-8

75 76 77 78 79 / 10 9 8 7 6 5 4 3 2 1

PRINTED IN THE UNITED STATES OF AMERICA

Dedicated to
Boston University
Gerontology Center

CONTRIBUTORS

BENJAMIN BELL, M.D.
Director, Outpatient Clinic, Veterans Administration Hospital, Boston, Massachusetts

HERBERT J. BERMAN, Ph.D.
Professor of Biology, Boston University, Boston, Massachusetts

ANDREW S. DIBNER, Ph.D.
Associate Professor of Psychology, Boston University, Boston, Massachusetts

EUGENE E. DUBOIS, Ph.D.
Executive Associate Director of Council Development, American Association of Community and Junior Colleges, National Center for Higher Education, Washington, D.C.

BENEDICT J. DUFFY, JR., M.D.
Consultant on Family Services, Tri-State Regional Medical Program, Boston, Massachusetts; Lecturer on Medicine, Harvard Medical School, Boston, Massachusetts

BLANCHE FITZPATRICK, Ph.D.
Associate Professor of Economics, Boston University, Boston, Massachusetts

WALTER L. HOLCOMB, S.T.B., M.A., Ed.D.
Professor of Religious Education, Boston University School of Theology, Boston, Massachusetts

LOUIS LOWY, Ph.D.
Professor, Boston University School of Social Work; Co-Executive Director, Boston University Gerontology Center, Boston, Massachusetts

BEULA B. MARBLE, M.S.
Formerly Lecturer on Nutrition, Boston University School of Nursing, Boston, Massachusetts

M. ISABEL PATTERSON, M.S., M.P.H.
Formerly Associate Professor of Nutrition, Boston University School of Nursing, Boston, Massachusetts

CHARLES L. ROSE, Ph.D.
Assistant Director, Normative Aging Study, Outpatient Clinic, Veterans Administration Hospital, Boston, Massachusetts

F. MAROTT SINEX, Ph.D.
Chairman, Department of Biochemistry, Boston University School of Medicine; Co-Executive Director, Boston University Gerontology Center, Boston, Massachusetts

DORRIAN APPLE SWEETSER, Ph.D.
Professor of Sociology, Boston University School of Nursing, Boston, Massachusetts

ACKNOWLEDGMENTS

The miracle of education is reflected in the interaction among all individuals who are involved in the process. We are deeply grateful to each member of the multidisciplinary faculty, each student, and each guest who has participated in the study of gerontology at Boston University since 1961.

Impetus for this team effort originated within the context of nursing, where there was a felt need for greater interdisciplinary collaboration and planning among members of the health team in order to enhance life satisfaction and increase the quality-of-life chances for all persons.

We give special recognition to Ms. Catherine W. Tinkham, Chairman of the Graduate Program for Public Health Nurses; to those individuals who have served as coordinator of the multidisciplinary faculty activities: the editors, Ms. Harriet Lane, and Dr. Sara K. Archer; and to the sustaining vigilance and interest of the Boston University Council on Gerontology.

We are thankful for the excellent secretarial support of Mrs. Gertrude Smith and Mrs. Harriet Powers at Boston University School of Nursing.

PREFACE

If asked to define "aging," it is likely that most people would respond "growing old" or a synonym for this phrase. If prompted to expand on their definition, the vast majority would probably speak of the debilitating effects on body and mind generally associated with old age. Few would relate aging to the transition from infant to toddler, from child to adolescent, from teen to adult. In short, aging is popularly linked to the elderly and to negative implications. An aspect of aging that receives relatively too much attention is the retardation of the aging process and its deleterious effects. It is important to recognize that aging is a lifetime process of development, of which some aspects may be negative but many may be positive from the perspective of life's actors.

This book is a collection of individual viewpoints on a single focus: aging. It is an outgrowth of an experimental course at Boston University in which professionals from several disciplines shared their expertise and concerns related to aging. The book is organized as a series of contributions from individuals with different perspectives in order to understand aging in a greater dimension than from any one discipline. This is not meant to negate the importance of any discipline in relation to aging, but rather to document the interrelatedness of the multidisciplinary concept in the field of aging.

The content provides a theoretic framework and scientific base for students of the applied as well as the physical and social sciences. It is believed that this book will be relevant to anyone who wishes to venture into the subject of aging at any level of expertise. The book may be utilized by the more advanced student of aging to take advantage of the many source references in order to delve more deeply into the topics. The book can represent a "jumping-off point" for the beginning student in gerontology or a source of challenge or opinion refinement for the advanced gerontologist. It is possible that the nonacademic lay person could obtain valuable perspective from this volume.

This volume should be regarded as only the beginning of what will hopefully prove to be a more systematic, cooperative approach to greater understanding of aging.

Marian G. Spencer
Caroline J. Dorr

CONTENTS

Understanding Aging: A Multidisciplinary Approach

1

PROLOGUE TO AGING: SOCIETAL STRUCTURE AND THE AGED

Herbert J. Berman, Ph.D.

A society must evolve a flexible working structure adaptable to its needs if it is to function. An individual also must evolve a working structure that relates him to society and satisfies his needs, usually, however, within a framework acceptable to society. Characteristic of both of these functional structures are the processes of renewal, repetition, and, potentially, change, and evolution.

Axiomatically, the process of renewal implies the coexistence of a process of aging. It is this process as it applies to the individual, to individual with society, and to society with the aged that we wish to explore. Two simple models will be proposed, one for society and the second for the aging individual, that could serve as an elementary framework for further development. Because of the complexity of the subject, the models will of necessity be vague, yet hopefully contain sufficient detail to stimulate experimentation and evolution of the elderly and society to a better psychological, social, and economic status, and permit evaluation of the changes.

Aging—Guidelines to Its Study and to the Potential Input of the Aged to the Evolutionary Development of Society

Basic to the solution of the problems of aging and the elderly is knowledge of the nature of the aging process, especially as it applies to man, and the basic needs of the individual. Aging has been negatively defined as ". . . the deterioration of a mature organism, resulting from time-dependent, essentially irreversible changes intrinsic in all members of a species such that, with the passage of time, they become increasingly unable to cope with the stresses of the environment thereby increasing the probability of death" (Handler 1970). This definition excludes disease per se as a primary factor causing aging, while admitting that aging increases susceptibility to disease and the likelihood of a fatal outcome from a disease because of a decrease in the functional capacity and reserve of the body. Thus, atherosclerosis, diabetes, and osteoporosis are all associated with aging but are not primary causes of aging.

OBJECTIVES OF RESEARCH ON AGING

Our general objectives of research and work on the problems of aging and the aged are: (1) to produce a fuller and better life for the individual, (2) to increase his life's expectancy, (3) to modify society's attitude toward the aged from one of partial rejection and isolation to desired interaction, (4) to solve the economic problems of the aged, and (5) to integrate the aged as fully as possible into society.

Objectives of research on aging in biology and medicine are: (1) to separate and clearly define the aging process from chronic diseases associated with aging, (2) to learn how to control or prevent the associated diseases from shortening one's inherent life expectancy, (3) to determine the normal aging process in man and other species in great detail, and (4) to learn how to delay, modify, stop, or even temporarily reverse each step. In biologic research on aging, molecular engineering or biochemical modification of the genetic material may have great future application. These objectives, as they are attained, will hopefully achieve for the elderly the objectives of good health as defined by the World Health Organization: "A state of complete physical, mental, and social well-being and not merely the absence of disease or infirmity" (WHO 1946).

THEORIES OF AGING

Many theories have been proposed to explain the process of aging or a portion thereof. Most of the theories may be grouped into two major categories: that of wear and tear—the gradual destruction or loss, in varying degrees, of the normal cellular reserves in several, nonrenewable vital organs in the body, such as in the kidney, heart, and central nervous system; and those based on the genetic content—either its progressive garbling with age until the record can no longer sustain life or the expression of a terminus built into and predetermined by the genetic code. In actuality, both theories probably apply.

Objective criteria are needed to evaluate any of the numerous, more detailed theories of aging associated with the two general ones. It is generally agreed that the following criteria should be met: (1) universality—the proposed phenomenon should occur in all older members of a species and not just in a restricted number; (2) intrinsicality —the changes should be built into or inherent in all members of a species and not be a result of external influences; (3) progressiveness—the changes should develop gradually and be cumulative; (4) deleteriousness—they should result in a progressive decrease in the survival capacity of the organism (Ebert 1960).

ACTUARIAL DATA AND AGING

Actuarial data furnish a statistical correlation that relates chronologic age and frequency of death in large samples of populations. This relationship, observed first in 1825 by Gompertz, is probably based on random challenging stresses to an individual and the individual's ability to cope with them. It, therefore, is an expression of the advancement of the aging process but not necessarily part of the aging process per se.

Gompertz observed that the death rate increased logarithmically with age once adulthood is reached. This relationship (Gompertz's function, $R = R_0 e^{\alpha}$) appears to apply to all living species and probably to many types of highly ordered inanimate objects. [R = death rate at any given time or age; R_0 = death rate at any arbitrary earlier reference age; e = the base of the natural logarithms, 2.71828; t = elapsed time; and α (alpha) = a constant, the rate at which the death rate changes per unit time. α is characteristic for the species.]

The time required for the mortality rate to double varies widely from species to species—from a few days for Drosophila to about eight years for man. With improvements in health standards and increasing control of disease, the longevity of the individuals in a population increases. The Gompertz plot of mortality rate versus age shifts to the right but the slope of the line or α does not change. The α's for different species may also be the same but with the linear semilogarithmic relationship commencing at different ages. This relationship is one of the best documented and firmly established characteristics of the aging process. (This same relationship also characterizes the random rate of decay of radioactive isotopes.) Any theory on aging must account for the actuarial relationship. Two theories based on the actuarial data have been proposed: one, by Sacher (1956), is based on a Gavssian (bell-shaped) distribution of challenging rare events with which the body must cope; the other, proposed by Strehler and Milduan (1960), is based on a Maxwell-Boltzman (Poisson) distribution of the rare event (Glass 1960; Strehler 1960). In both cases, with advancing age, the body is increasingly unable to cope with these stressful events.

THE AGED—THEIR PROBLEMS AS RELATED TO THOSE OF SOCIETY IN GENERAL

It is the premise of the author that the aged share individually and collectively the same general socioeconomic problems that confront all members and subgroups of society, but in a more muted, helpless, and probably acute form. Their status in and treatment by society therefore reflects a particular society's ability and willingness to cope with what could be considered a nonessential problem area. The successful solution of the problems of the aged as individuals, and collectively as a sociologic entity, would, in turn, greatly advance the capability of society to solve problems confronting all age groups and other subdivisions. As an experimental group the elderly, therefore, provide a rich resource and challenge to society.

Societal Structure and Its Relation to the Aged

A basic understanding of the structure and function of society is most relevant to our ability to constructively cope with and solve the problems of the aged and, by so doing, of people in other age groups. In addition, a broadly based perspective of how society or civilization has developed within the above framework should provide further insight into its functional structure and future potential. It should further reinforce our ability to think broadly and creatively concerning desirable objectives and means of achieving them, as well as to evaluate more critically our present status and future progress. A most interesting series of related questions also arises from contemplations based on such a perspective: Is our civilization and society in a process of evolution? If so, will this process of development continue regardless of our activities (or lack thereof)? What is its end product? And to what extent is the end product modifiable by man?

THE BASIC WORKING STRUCTURE OF SOCIETY

Our societal structure and civilization are based on four major interacting components (Fig. 1.): (1) the *individual* with his basic needs, (2) *society* or individuals en masse and their collective needs, (3) *science and technology*, the means of society to meet its needs, and (4) *economics*, the integrating force: management of individuals en masse, available physical resources and wealth, and science and technology to meet the needs and selected goals of the society (Galbraith 1964).

The interplay of all elements in society in a varied and weighted manner determines the goals of the society and the assigned priority. These decisions are made in the political arena by the process of governance. *Politics* (the decision-making process) therefore deserves foremost attention.

Individuals. Much has been written about the basic needs of individuals. Most listings would include:

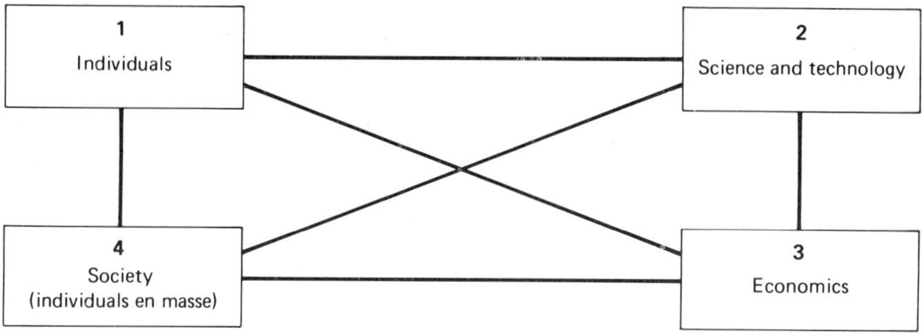

FIG. 1. A schematic of the basic fundamental structure of society.

1. A sense of individuality—a need to be recognized as an individual separate from that of a group or a statistic.
2. A sense of belonging to and being wanted by a group—an outlet for social interaction.
3. Purpose for existence and hope of achieving the goal. Once goals are attained, new ones must be created.
4. Provision of necessities (food, clothing, housing, medical care) at an adequate level.
5. A few material comforts, and elected chance to experience change in the daily routine.
6. Relief from dangerous and debilitating anxiety and tension.

These basic needs are difficult for the elderly to attain because of their status in society and in life. A successful solution here would greatly advance the solution of this problem in all other age groups. Purpose is particularly important for the aged because of forced retirement, financial penalization for further efforts to work, ostracism by the youth-oriented community with its vague but ubiquitous fear of death, general lack of goals other than those related to immediate physical needs and to family, and deterioration of their physical and mental state accelerated by lack of activity—totaling enforced disengagement from society with associated *loss* of interaction with society, loss of self-esteem, responsiveness, purpose, and even self-respect. Necessities should be given to the aged without first stripping them of past-built security, their private economic resources. Particular attention must also be directed toward relief from anxiety and tension because the aged are increasingly unable to cope with stress as a result of progressive development of physical and related psychologic handicaps.

Freedom, although highly desirable, is not considered by the author to be essential. In fact, a degree of conformity, to which we are continuously being conditioned by the mass media and education, is needed for a society to function (Skinner 1971). A balance between conformity and freedom (in its various modes and degrees) is desirable not only for the individual but also for society because the exercise of freedom tends to beget more freedom and in this capacity acts as one of the mainsprings of evolution in a society. The balance between conformity and freedom in most cases will probably be determined by economic factors and the societal structure. The increasing experience and insight that an individual gains with age are major factors conducive to an understanding of freedom, its limited availability, and obligations and responsibilities inherent in its usage.

Education, both formal and informal, molds the individual, hopefully, to fit constructively into society and at the same time to satisfy his needs and constructive desires. The following general objectives in education seem desirable: (1) chance for formal educational opportunity throughout life, (2) development of individual abilities, interests, and enterprise as opposed to uniformity and conformity, (3) development of a self-discipline in place of imposed discipline, (4) development of a spirit of willingness to work and not to reject it, (5) development of a good sense of public morality or social or civic consciousness as opposed to one-sided self-morality or self-satisfaction, (6) development of the ability and desire to make decisions and select goals for oneself as opposed to avoidance, and (7) practice in undertaking and solving problems, in sustaining one's effort until the problem is solved or goal attained, and in the development of ingenuity in problem solving.

Science and Technology. Their collective knowledge and ready application are and will be, as in the past, the determinants of society's ability to meet its physical needs. This capacity, built on language and communication, is the product of man's intelligence and endeavors—the culmination of man's single greatest attribute that sets him off from all other species on earth, the ability to accumulate and transfer ideas and knowledge and their products from generation to generation. The product of this attribute makes possible man's increasing ability and capacity to produce goods and services, and to develop new approaches in the scope and quantity needed to sustain his ever-increasing numbers. At the same time it limits his numbers and standard of living. This attribute of man has been the major determinant of his cultural and societal development to this day and in all likelihood will be the major determinant in the future. Unfortunately the future capabilities of science and technology include an increasing potential for psychologic and societal control, as well as for the well-being of the individual. This attribute of man and its ever-developing capacity faces the severe challenge of limited desirable living space, further crowding of mankind, and the limited resources on earth. We may wish that it were not so, but we are wedded to science and technology with little if any hope of a beneficial divorce. Their usage by man, as exemplified by the varied use of drugs, will determine the benefits derived and the abuses inflicted.

Science and technology today are forcing economic, social, psychologic, and political change, and in this respect have replaced biologic variation and even economic capacity, which they determine, as the factor pacing societal evolution and change. Their further development and application will, in large measure, determine the status of man's future existence. The question remains an open one: Will man subordinate science and technology to optimize his well-being? Or will he be enslaved, in varying degrees, by them in a race of numbers, and bureaucratization?

Economics. Economics is the management of our total resources. The primary goal of this management is to provide the necessities of life and therefore the means of survival of the society. Its secondary, nonessential, selected goals include nationalism with its various objectives, ideological expansionism, and the production of luxuries. Its tools are labor with its manpower and skills, all other natural resources, the intellectual capacity of the society (science and technology), and capital. Its purpose is the attainment of the most efficient output of goods and services permissible and the stimulation of their consumption.

In practice, because success is measured not only by efficient production but also by consumption and maximal profit per total output, individual management would rather and does attempt to structure and maintain society, wherever possible, so that its products or services are necessities. Furthermore, by limiting the supply (constrained rationing), individual management places the consumer in a position where he, as an individual, cannot easily protect himself, while management can, in effect, continually increase price and profit and maintain its dominance.

The management of the economy is "ideally" efficient and "readily" adaptable to change and to the integration of new phenomena including increased automation to attain the goals of maximum output per man-hour of work. To attain maximum efficiency in its operations, it usually attempts to simplify each operation and make the bureaucratic structure intimately subservient to its direction. This goal is accomplished by (1) stressing rational, logical, and clear communication; (2) organizing people under carefully defined direction, authority, and control; and (3) simplifying each operation and more minutely specializing each man so that the operation will be easier to plan, control, and direct, and the operator more easy to replace (with the ultimate objective of complete automation with computer control where applicable). The results of such operations and managerial goals on the individual worker are unfortunately deleterious, resulting in a more passive than active, more submissive than responsive employee using only shallow surface abilities in what is often a dull and boring job of limited involvement. Top management thus exercises its individualism but subjugates that of the employee. These goals of management stress the conflict between the pressure of conformity and the needs of the individual.

In contrast to its ideal efficiency and adaptability to scientific and technical change, management resists change that in any way diminishes its interests or threatens its position and power. Because of the need for management in a society and the selection of the managers (administrators) by ability and personality traits, the same types of individuals with the same production goals and mode of operation will probably be selected for managerial posts today regardless of the societal and political structure. Management, guided by economic goals, fills an essential niche in the societal structure for which as yet no suitable substitute has been found. Its goals and especially its mode of operation in an affluent society can be questioned. In a poor, developing society it may speed development and therefore be advantageous to the society but at the cost of individuality.

Society. The foremost objective of the societal structure is production of the necessities for its continued existence and growth and, where possible, a variable amount of nonessential goods and services. At present, the major factor governing the needs of society (aside from aggrandizement and perpetuation of the governing body) is population and the balance between population and the available resources. Man, like every other species on earth, has the capacity to overpopulate, and throughout most of his history, taxed the existing limits of the means for his sustenance. The main struggle of a large segment of today's world population is the day-to-day procurement of sufficient food for its continued existence.

In the past, as with all species, the population of man was regulated by three factors: war, pestilence or disease, and famine. With the advent of the industrial revolution and man's increasing ability to produce more food, goods, and services, the population started to grow. The introduction of hygiene and sanitation in Europe in the 18th and 19th centuries, resulting in the near elimination of pestilence as a restraining factor, was another stimulus to European population growth, increasing the strain on man's resources and know-how. However, at that time the European nations had new continents, including North America, into which to expand and for resources to tap. As a result, productivity increased more rapidly than population, resulting in an improvement in the material standard of living. After World War II, improvements in hygiene and sanitation spread throughout most of the other areas of the world. This development again greatly accelerated the growth of the earth's population, without, however, the availability of additional readily inhabitable land and natural resources (Dorn 1962).

To balance the effect of a decreased mortality rate, man discovered contraceptive methods, beginning with rubber, thereby separating sexual intercourse from childbearing and permitting the limitation of family size and population at will. Thus, after the factors normally governing population growth were removed, other means were made available to limit man's numbers in a voluntary manner if he so desired.

At present, the world's population is in a rapid growth phase with some limitations self-imposed by individuals and small social entities in the more advanced countries. An idea of the growth rate of the population and man's potential to continue to expand may be gleaned from the statistical data in Table 1 (Dorn 1962).

TABLE 1. ***Estimated Population of Man on Earth***

Year	Population in Billions	No. of Years for the Population to Double
Prehistoric time	0.125	—
1 A.D.	0.25	(?)
1650	0.50	1650
1830	1.00	180
1930	2.00	100
1975	4.00	45
2010	8.00	35

The data indicate that man is easily able to increase his number at an exponential rate. It is presently estimated that in many underdeveloped countries the population may double in 25 to 30 years while in some of the more advanced countries the time for doubling may range from 35 to 55 years. The significance of this old observation for man was forceably expounded by Thomas Robert Malthus in his essay on population in 1798. Malthus argued that any nation would either have to initiate and maintain institutions and customs to limit its population growth or find itself forced into a declining standard of life and a precarious balance between food, productivity in general, and population. This old conclusion is as true today as it was then. Advances in science and technology have enabled us so far to sustain an evergreater population. However, our physical resources are being increasingly taxed, depleted, and polluted. Furthermore, our growing population is exacerbating existing and developing new sociologic and psychologic strains whereby different subgroups in the society are struggling for a bigger and better portion of the economic output, power, and wealth with ever-increasing expectations, coupled with increasing impatience, in the attainment of their objectives. People vie with each other, one group with another, and one nation with another for a more favorable allocation of the limited available resources, wealth, and power. Also, if the increase in population continues, a still-to-be-reached but more acute form of conflict will arise: an increasingly tense struggle for desirable living space.

The solution to these problems is obvious: the restriction of population growth, preferably on a voluntary basis, and running the community, nation, and earth at an underpopulated level while at the same time increasing productivity. This action will apply man's resources and ingenuity not to the sustenance of an ever-increasing population but to the attainment of a higher standard and more enjoyable form of living for everyone. This solution or evolutionary step in the development of society should enable society to better treat the individual as an individual and not subordinate him as an instrument of society. The action will pose a series of old problems for man to solve but in a different form. Some of these will be examined briefly in the section on future predictions.

The Evolution of Our Society

THE IMPACT OF MAN

Man's domination of earth and the evolution of his society and culture are based on two primary factors: his intellect and the ability to accumulate its results through succeeding generations. Each generation (the cyclic or repetitive variable of society) theoretically begins its work at the frontiers reached by its predecessor. The rate of development of civilization is based on and parallels the development of four basic factors: the inceasing availability of food, water, and other necessities and resources of life; man's increasing ability to communicate, keep records, and make cross-correlations, be it in writing, verbally, electronically, or visually; the increasing availability of energy to do work; and continuously more efficient means of transportation, storage, and distribution. Man's history and the evolution of his civilization based on these four factors are concise and straightforward, and repeatedly show the dependence of their development on science, technology, and art.

Man first foraged for food as a primitive hunter and gatherer of wild, edible plant products. His total energies were almost entirely absorbed by his quest for food and the minimum necessities, permitting little specialization of labor. Fire for warmth, protection, and preparation of food and an increasing array of primitive weapons for hunting, defense, and aggression fortified his ability to exist. Gradually, on the flat grasslands, man learned how to grow, store, and distribute grain products and develop husbandry, thereby increasing the food supply and its dependability. With the development of agriculture, man gradually gave up his nomadic existence and settled in one place where the climate was warm throughout most of the year, the water plentiful, and the land fertilized each year by flooding of the river plains in a fairly predictable manner. An elite, capable of imposing its will on a growing number of "tillers of the soil," developed. As man became more secure in his food and water supply, he built towns, mainly for protection, and, as his numbers increased, cities. The ancient civilizations of the Sumerians (3500 B.C.), Babylonians (2000 B.C.), and Persians developed along the Tigris and Euphrates rivers. Other civilizations developed in the Nile Valley and along rivers in India (the Indus River) and China (the Yellow River).

The success of these civilizations depended on good agricultural practices. The population increased but the rate was slowed by epidemics, famine, and war. With the development of a more abundant and dependable food supply, man became increasingly able to free limited numbers to develop and practice speicalized skills as "artisans and men of learning." The towns and cities were, from the beginning, their selected residences. The concentration of specialized talent in the population centers fostered direct communication, interchange of ideas, and the continuous growth of specialization and knowledge. At some point in the slow development of civilization, the tempo suddenly started to accelerate. Individualism, intellectualism, and nationalism, were revived during the Renaissance (1400–1650) as the all-consuming power of the Universal State, the Holy Roman Empire, and the Universal Church faded. Inventiveness developed, resulting in the amplification of the energies expended by working man. The ability to communicate was significantly increased first by the development of a cheaper, better, and more abundant supply of paper in the early 1400s by the Moors of Spain and the manufacturers in Florence, and then by the discovery of an easy means of recording and disseminating data and ideas with movable type and the printing press (Gutenberg 1450). Somewhat later, means of creating energy (other than by the power of man, wind, water, and animals) were explosively accelerated by the development of a practical steam engine (Watt 1769), the trigger of the industrial revolution. Paced by invention of machinery, production was made more efficient in a centralized location rather than dispersed, for example, in the homes of the workers. Farmlands were also enclosed and more scientifically cultivated, forcing many people in search of subsistence to migrate to the cities where they provided cheap labor or energy. This process of specialization, abetted by production, trade, commerce, and further industrialization, feeds on itself with growth producing further growth. The simultaneous development of sanitation and methods of eliminating pestilence, the later development of antiseptic surgery, antibiotics, and means of controlling childhood diseases accelerated the rate of the population growth, mainly because more females were surviving through their childbearing years.

Today we have a close race on earth between the growth of population at an exponential rate and the ability of science and technology to provide for the increasing numbers of people.

FUTURE PREDICTIONS

Man's fate is in the hands of man alone. Based on his ability to communicate, the ever-increasing availability of energy for work, and on his sophistication in automation, the following predictions can be made:

1. Whenever a job is repetitious, it will be automated. This development will be greatly accelerated by the development of easy-to-use, reliable, automatically repaired computers and robots. The ability to transfer speech into type, type into speech, translate one language into another, and maintain massive filing systems all automatically will be developed. The net effect will be to further communications and augment scientific and technologic developments, and also to accentuate the diminishing need for labor by man and therefore the loss of purposeful jobs. Man will, therefore, have more and more leisure time.

2. Man will be forced to control his environment carefully. The objectives, first, will be to keep it fit to live in, and then to optimize it for his comfort and longevity. Enclosed neighborhoods and even cities, possibly based on the geodesic design, will be built. Public transportation will be free, efficient, and the only permissible means of transportation within the city.
3. Instant communication (by print, voice, and sight) and access to knowledge and entertainment (past and present) will be available from any one point on earth or the planetary system to any other point.
4. Energy from atomic, hydrogen, electromagnetic, and solar sources will be in surplus supply and instantly transferrable from any one point on earth (or the planetary system) to any other point.
5. Man will maintain robot colonies on the moon, neighboring planets, in space, under the oceans, and underground, and tap their resources for his use.
6. Man will regulate his population on earth on a voluntary or forced basis, or face extinction by war.
7. With the further development of computers, automation, and regulation of the population, the meaning of direct work by man, the dependence of society on it, and the essential place and preeminence of management, economics, and wealth will diminish because it should be well within man's capacity to fulfill most of his physical needs by automatic processes. However, employment will be maintained to provide a needed societal structure and to fulfill the needs of the individual. Private enterprise will be strongly sustained as a major and efficient way to satisfy the various needs of the individual, give society a varied and enriched structure, and maintain progress and create diversity. These same objectives will apply to the public sector of employment but with the additional objectives of providing employment for all and enriching the lives of the employees. Increased diversity of choice in each area of need and leisure will be developed as one means of satisfying individual needs, including the adventurousness of youth, and used as a measure for evaluating the development, evolution, and success of the society.
8. To find meaning and purpose in life, many approaches will be explored, developed, and adapted to the needs of the individual and the different age groups, especially the elderly. Probably solutions will be based on education, work, hobbies, travel, social contact, private enterprise, and the time in one's life at which labor, managerial and political responsibilities are assumed. Voluntary (or even temporary) retirement at the age of 55 or 60 will be sanctioned. However, mandatory retirement at any age will be abolished. A multi-buddy system for any one job or posi-

tion of responsibility will probably be developed, with each job filled by two or three persons on a rotating buddy basis. At least one post in each buddy team could be reserved for a person 50 years of age or older. Associate or assistant posts could be created for each political position and certain positions limited to individuals 55 years of age or older.

9. Education, necessities, and travel at more than a basic level will be free to all. Hence, hopefully conflict based on economic disparity inherent in the struggle for necessities and luxuries between individuals, social groups, and nations will be satisfied or controlled.
10. Increased and successful attention will be given to psychological understanding, training, and control of man. Development of a good sense of self-imposed restraint and consideration of others will probably be found essential in the evolution of a satisfied man.
11. Most diseases will be curable and preventable. Organ prostheses and intra- and even interspecies transplants will be widely used. Genetic material will be altered to ensure longevity and prevent piecemeal deterioration of the individual. Death will be based ultimately on disruption of the integrative function of the central nervous system.
12. The earth will not become a homogeneous population unit; instead differences will be preserved and the people will be that much richer because of the variety in their existence and the chance for each individual to savor these differences at will.
13. To further satisfy his needs, community organizations and community governance will be increasingly developed with widespread involvement of individuals and direct responsiveness to their decisions. Limitations as to the size of the community will be imposed to maximize its service and personal involvement. Each community will be an effective self-contained unit. The city and megalopolis will be divided into locally run community units. Decentralization rather than centralization of power will be favored.
14. In spite of all advances, man will prefer a simple life within a stable framework. He will make adequate use of all advances, but judiciously and in keeping with a simple existence. He will accept change as part of life but will attempt to structure his intimate home and family life to stand independent from change. He will also hope to have minimum interference in his private life by government and have the societal structure function primarily for the individual as an individual.
15. Families once again will become closely knit and will function prominently in meeting the needs of its members in all age groups. The economic pressures that now dis-

> perse the family will disappear. Differences between generations will diminish and, with regulation of the population, the family members in each age bracket will be approximately the same. With transportation for the longest trip on earth restricted mainly by psychologic and physiologic factors and approaching that of only a few hours, mobility of individuals will increase. However, the motivation will be for pleasure, adventure, and curiosity, and not for economic reasons. Even with increased travel and leisure, family roots and stability will be maintained.

All these changes, however, are predicated on man's ability to control his numbers; run the world at an underpopulated level in keeping with his psychologic needs, natural resources, and available scientific and technologic know-how; prevail as individuals; and readjust the societal structure from one dominated by economic consideration to one oriented more directly to the needs of the individual. An ever-changing judicious balance of the two will probably always exist.

The Future and the Aged

Man's scientific and technical achievements have made possible his ability to exist on earth in ever-increasing numbers. At any one time, however, his resources are limited. The choice as to how he expends them are basically twofold: he may either choose to produce and maintain an ever-increasing population at the near limits imposed by his technical and scientific ability, or he may limit his numbers and focus his limited resources on bettering the standard of living and fullness of life for the great majority. To date, he has elected to take the easier course, that of population growth.

His sociologic evolution and evolution as an individual in contrast to his technical achievements have shown little progress. Man in general tends to be self-centered and not idealistic in matters that affect or can affect him directly. His responses may have been conditioned by past and present exposure to politics, government, and economics, or possibly have not developed beyond the egocentric stage. However, many people in each generation in the past have foreseen his shortcomings and his choices and have expected more from "collective man" and his various governments.

Man can solve the problem of population strains by self-restraint and limited population growth, and the problem of shortages of goods and services by greater automation and application of computer technology carried to their logical limits. Once man decides to focus his resources on improving the standard of living for all, he will face the challenge of finding ways to make life purposeful for its members in an increasingly economically automated society, other than by daily work for sustenance. The elderly are an ideal resource with which to explore the solution to this problem and to develop a societal structure and mode of living that will have meaning and satisfaction for them and, by doing so, for all age groups.

FIRST SMALL STEPS FOR THE 1970s IN THE UNITED STATES

The elderly provide us with the means of exploring the solutions of tomorrow's problem for all of mankind today. Serious study conducted among the older members of our population would give insight and guidelines for all ages, and with less criticism than if it were conducted among younger people or different ethnic groups. After all, according to that amorphous entity, society, older people are not supposed to work, and every ethnic group has old people.

Many common problems need to be solved for the elderly and for people of all ages. For example: (1) No longer does work have the consuming role in a person's life that it once did. This is even true for young people, actually more so than for the older generation. Work hours are shorter and more time is available for nonpaid work or nonwork activities. How can a shift be made from our work-centered values to something larger and more inclusive? What may these "somethings" be? (2) Rapid change characterizes our world. Older people have lived through many changes with varying degrees of success. Could we learn something for ourselves from their experiences and thoughts regarding far-reaching change? (3) With increasing automation, fewer and fewer individuals are really needed for the production of goods and services, and those employed will have progressively less challenging, more monotonous jobs. From what sources can come dignity, status, and purpose for the individual that productive work supposedly used to supply? How can we best prepare ourselves for this eventuality? New roles and approaches must evolve. Old persons today, many of them excluded from jobs even before retirement age, offer a rich resource for research of this problem.

Education, both formal and informal, the intimate purpose and functional mode of society's structure, and the direct and purposeful involvement of the individual in them are the major keys to the solution of these problems. Also, the solution will depend greatly on our attitude to aging and what our past lives have been like. If work had been part of and not the sole purpose of our lives, more leisure time and retirement should permit greater self-fulfillment. Enjoyment of others and ourselves as we are may be the primary key to happiness in later years—an attitude, therefore, so important that it should be cultivated at all stages of life.

How else can we prepare ourselves? By living in the present, savoring it, as well as enjoying what the past has brought. By counting our blessings, not just accepting them, and by not envying the next man. By developing our own stimuli and links to the outside world. Education is an indwelling self-preparation for life, present and future.

Several small, first steps can be taken by society based not necessarily on degradation of needs but by the practicality of what can be done now.

Every person needs a certain amount of tension in life. Many have too much. For the elderly, certain reliefs from anxiety and tensions are needed because they just do not have the resources—physical, financial, or psychologic—to cope with them. Perhaps the most outstanding of these tensions is that caused by the growing gap between income and living expenses for the older person. In this respect one of the most important changes that must take place in society is an attitudinal one. No longer can the average person count on having sufficient income to live on in old age from what he is able to save or accumulate from his younger, productive, more vigorous days. A balance will have to be achieved between personal income and community service. Both will have to become a normal, accepted part of national and community budgets. Welfare must be reexamined. Assistance given to the elderly is his due, not a handout. Ways must be devised whereby a person can live with reasonable comfort and dignity despite a small personal income.

With respect to practices in the United States, the following first, small steps can help:

1. The right to earn up to two and a half times the funds provided by social security for the first five years after retirement, taxfree and without penalty, and thereafter any additional amount but with tax.
2. Experimentation with income maintenance and negative income tax.
3. Provision of adequate housing with food, with rent and food not to exceed 40 percent of the individual's social security check.
4. Development of self-contained, mixed, or predominantly "old-age" communities.
5. Provision for adequate (eg, two sets of) clothing per year at a cost not to exceed 10 percent of the individual's social security check. Clothing and food stamps with merchant's price set at cost (no profit) can be redeemable from the community government.
6. Complete rather than limited coverage of medical and nursing expenses and immediate availability of first-rate medical care.
7. Free off-rush-hour public transportation, with rush-hour transportation at a modest cost.
8. Free admission to local theatres at off-peak times.
9. Maintenance by the community of local community centers for the elderly. These centers could be at a lounge area in the local schools, libraries, and even town halls.
10. Arrangement for group travel tours at greatly reduced rates.

Additional amenities only await the ingenuity and interest of the local community, such as home care, rehabilitation programs, and halfway houses associated with local community centers for the infirm or chronically sick.

What about food? A lot is now being said about the importance of a balanced diet throughout life for all age groups. Diet will become an important component of preventive medicines in the future. An important beginning can be made with the aged.

1. Free community nutritional guidance centers can be established.
2. For those living alone and those not sufficiently ambulatory, meals on wheels can be provided.
3. Local tea rooms and coffee houses where one or two nutritious meals can be purchased at a modest rate by the elderly (but at regular rates by other age groups) can be founded. Meals can also be made available at modest cost at school kitchens and cafeterias, at the local community centers, and even in neighborhood restaurants.

What about the need of each person for a sense of individuality? Of belonging to a group and society and one's neighborhood? Do anonymity and depersonalization have to be associated with city living? With bureaucracy? With old age? Feelings of futility, loneliness, and helplessness are common reactions to the emptiness and anonymity in life and in one's relationship to a mass society, overpowering in size and complexity. Unhappiness and loneliness are persistent themes throughout history. Some degree of each can stimulate individual creativity. Too much, and the inability to cope with these feelings and the situation only heightens one's self-rejection, withdrawal, anxiety, and loss of personal esteem. We form organizations, for organizations not individuals best contend for power. Yet, throughout the history of man, the idea emerges that an individual is capable of molding his own destiny. As individuals we grope for personal commitment to goals and a philosophy of life. A first step to the solution of the needs for individuality and belonging can be made for the elderly within the community by (1) maintaining each individual's identity, (2) involving him directly in the running and managing of all services related to the elderly, (3) making each service fully responsive to his desires and not those of young management or of more remote government bureaucracy.

By providing abundant opportunities for personal distinction in a great number of diversified community services, for social meetings in a number of different community settings, greater mobility, and good home care when needed, personalization of the individual and a sense of group and community belonging should be engendered.

Government and politics cannot eliminate conflicts and needs in a society. It can only strive to mitigate and manage them in a continuously more humane and responsive way. The achievements of government and society as a whole with respect to the elderly may be judged by the sensitivity of the political arena to their needs, the involvement of the elderly in decisions affecting them, the number of desirable choices made available to the elderly, deference given to them as individuals, minimization of governmental interference in their lives, and the sensitive and fair resolution of their conflicts and problems.

References

Adams R: The origin of cities. Sci Am 203: (Sept) 153–92, 1960

Aldrich D G: World food and the population crisis. (AAA Symposium Review) Science 162:1309–1310, 1968

Braidwood R: The agricultural revolution. Sci Am 203:(Sept) 130–152, 1960

Civilization: The Past and the Future. The Athens Meeting. Organized by the Royal National Foundation. New York, Elsevier, 1965

Comfort A: The Process of Aging. New York, Signet Science Library Books, 1964

Davis K: The urbanization of the human population. Sci Am 213:(Sept) 40–53, 1965

Djerassi C: Birth control after 1984. Science 169:941–51, 1970

Dorn F: World population growth: an international dilemma. Science 135:283–90, 1962

Doty P: The community of science and the search for peace. Science 173:998–1002, 1971

Dubos R: Reason Awake. Science for Man. New York and London, Columbia Univ Press, 1970

Ebert JD: Aging and development. In Shock NW (ed): Aging: Some Social and Biological Aspects. Washington, D.C., Am Ass Adv Sci, 1960, pp 101–122

Eurich AC: Higher education in the 21st century. Atlantic Monthly 211(6):51–55, 1963

Ewald WR Jr (ed): Environment and Change. The Next Fifty Years. Bloomington, Indiana Univ Press, 1968

Galbraith JK: Economics and the quality of life. Science 145:117–123, 1964

George H: Progress and Poverty. New York, Random House, 1880

Gillette R: The limits to growth: hard sell for a computer view of doomsday. Science 175:1088–1092, 1972

Gist NP, Fava SF: Urban Society, 5th ed. New York, Crowell, 1964

Glass B: Genetics of aging. In Shock NW: Aging: Some Social and Biological Aspects. Washington, D.C., Am Ass Adv Sci 65:67–122, 1960

Glazier W: Automation and joblessness. Atlantic Monthly 210(2):43–47, 1962

Handler P (ed): Biology and the Future Man. New York, Oxford Univ Press, 1970

Huxley A: Brave New World. New York, Harper, 1932

Kahn H, Wiener, AJ: The Year 2000. A Framework for Speculation on the Next Thirty-three Years. New York, Macmillan, 1967

Life: The Struggle to Be an Individual. Part I. (The threat of anonymity) Hooper B: The problem of having too much to choose from. Life 62 (16) (Apr 21):60 (73–98)–78, 1967; Part II. The search for purpose. Life 62 (17) (Apr 28):66–79, 1967. Part III. Argyris C: We must make work worthwhile. Life 62 (18) (May 15):40 (56–68), 1967. Part IV. Bell D: A way must be found to preserve an individual's value as we evolve toward a communal society. Life 62 (19) (May 12):112–124, 1967

Meadows DH, Meadows L, Randers JO, Behrens WW III: The Limits to Growth. New York, Associates-Universe Books, 1972

Piel G: Abundance and the future of man. Atlantic Monthly 213(4):84–90, 1964
Sacher G: On the statistical nature of mortality with a special reference to chronic radiation. Radiology 67:250–257, 1956
Shock, NW (ed): Aging: Some Social and Biological Aspects. Washington, D.C., Am Ass Adv Sci, 1960
Sjoberg G: The origin and evolution of cities. Sci Am 213:(Sept) 54–63, 1965
Skinner BF: Beyond Freedom and Dignity. New York, Bantam Books, 1971
Strehler BL: Dynamic theories of aging. In Shock NW: Aging: Some Social and Biological Aspects. Washington, D.C., Am Ass Adv Sci 65:273–303, 1960
———, Milduan AS: General theory of mortality and aging. Science 132:14–21, 1960
Toffler A: Future Shock. New York, Random House, 1970

Suggested Readings

Abelson PH: (An editorial.) Limits to growth. Science 175:1197, 1972
Abrams C: The uses of land in cities. Sci Am 213:(Sept) 150–60, 1965
Allport GW: The Nature of Prejudice, abridged ed. 1958. Garden City, NY, Doubleday, 1954
Anderson B, Clark M: Culture and Aging. Springfield, Ill, C. C. Thomas, 1967
Baldwin HW: Managed news. Atlantic Monthly 211(4):53–59, 1963
Benedict R: Patterns of Culture. Boston, Houghton Mifflin, 1934
Bertz EL: Creative Aging. New York, Macmillan, 1963
Birren JE: The Psychology of Aging. Englewood Cliffs, N.J., Prentice-Hall, 1964
Blumenfold H: The modern metropolis. Sci Am 213:(Sept) 65–74, 1965
Bromley DB: The Psychology of Human Aging. Baltimore, Penguin, 1966
Burgess E (ed): Aging in Western Societies. Chicago, Univ Chicago Press, 1960
Cumming E, Henry WE: Growing Old. The Process of Disengagement. New York, Basic Books, 1961
Curtin S; Nobody Ever Dies of Old Age. Boston, Atlantic-Little Brown, 1972
Dale E: Executives who can't manage. Atlantic Monthly 210(1):58–62, 1962
Dyck AJ: Questions for the global conscience. Psychology Today 2(4). Del Mar, Calif, Communications Research Machines
Edwards VCW: Population control in animals. Sci Am 211 (Aug):68–74, 1964
Ehrlich PR: The Population Bomb, rev. ed. New York, Balantine Books, 1971
Erikson EH: Insight and Responsibility. New York, Norton, 1964
The Expanding Metropolis. The editors of Fortune, Garden City, NY, Doubleday, 1957
Ferkiss VC: Technological Man: The Myth and the Reality. New York, George Braziller, 1969
Foner A, Riley MR (eds): An Inventory of Research Findings, Vol. 1. Aging and Society. New York, Russell Sage Foundation, 1968
Fuller RB: Buckminster Fuller's World Resources Inventory. Southern Illinois University, Carbondale, Illinois, 1963
Galbraith JK: The New Industrial State. Boston, Houghton Mifflin, 1967
Greenberg M: The computers of tomorrow. Atlantic Monthly 213(5):63–67, 1964
The Growth of U.S. Population. Publ. 1279. Natl Acad Sci, National Research Council, 1965 (25 pp)
The Growth of World Population. Publ. 1091. Natl Acad Sci, National Research Council. Washington, D.C., 1963 (38 pp)

Jungk R, Galtung, J (eds): International Future Research Conference. Mankind 2000. Oslo, Universitetsforlaget; London, Allen and Unwin, 1969
Kilpatrick WH: Education and the Social Crisis; A Proposed Program. Kappa Delta Pi Lecture Ser. No. 4, 90 pp, Liveright, 1932
Leighton AC: Poverty and social change. Sci Am:21–27, 1965
Leontief WW: The structure of the U.S. economy. Sci Am:(Apr) 25–35, 1965
Malthus TR: On Population. Himmelfarb G (ed). New York, Random House, 1960
Michael DN: The Unprepared Society: Planning for a Precarious Future. New York, Harper and Row, 1968
Michener JA: The Quality of Life. Greenwich, Fawcett, 1970
Mumford L: The City in History. Its Origins, Its Transformations, and Its Prospects. New York, Harcourt, Brace and World, 1961
Packard V: The right to privacy. Atlantic Monthly 213(3):71–75, 1964
Palmore E (ed): Normal Aging. Durham, NC, Duke Univ Press, 1970
Pressey SL, Kuhlen RG: Psychological Development Throughout the Life Span. New York, Harper, 1957
Rapid Population Growth: Consequences and Policy Implications. Vol. I. Summary and Recommendation. A Study Committee Report, Natl Acad Sci. Baltimore, John Hopkins Press, 1971
Redfield R: The Primitive World and Its Transformations. Ithaca, NY, Cornell Univ Press, 1953
Rose AM, Paterson WA (eds): Older People and Their Social World; the Subculture of the Aging. Philadelphia, F. A. Davis, 1965
Rosen H (ed): Working with Older People. Washington, D.C., US Dept. HEW, 1960
Rudd J, Margolin R (eds): Maintenance Therapy for the Geriatric Patient. Springfield, Ill, Charles C Thomas, 1968
Samuelson PA: Maximum principles in analytical economics. Science 173:991–997, 1971
Shock N: Age with a Future. Copenhagen, Munksgaard, 1964
Slater PE: The Pursuit of Loneliness. Boston, Beacon Press, 1970
Solow RM: The economist's approach to pollution and its control. Science 173:498–503, 1971
Stumpf SE: The expanding new world of second-story people: a philosopher looks at aging. In Shock NW (ed): Aging: Some Social and Biological Aspects. Washington, D.C., Am Ass Adv Sci, 1960
Talland GA (ed): Human Aging and Behavior. New York, Academic Press, 1968
Teilhard de Chardin P: The Future of Man. New York, Harper and Row, 1964
Townsend C (project director): Old Age. The Last Segregation. Ralph Nader's study group report on nursing homes. New York, Bantam, 1971
Wagar WW: Building the City of Man: Outlines of a World Civilization. New York, Grossman, 1971
Wiener N: The Human Use of Human Beings. Cybernetics and Society. (Discus ed) New York, Avon, 1950

2

THE BIOCHEMISTRY OF AGING

F. Marott Sinex, Ph.D.

Modern biochemistry is rapidly removing the technologic limitations to understanding the causes of aging. What was once a question for the laboratory has become a question in national priority and social objectives. The phenomena of aging is characteristic of the life history for many species (Strehler 1962). These species are usually multicellular and eukaryotypic. That is, the cells contain a nucleus which contains chromatin and divides by mitosis. Organisms that age usually attain a finite size. Aging occurs in organisms in which populations of stem cells become differentiated and incapable of reinitiating division. In many tissues it would not appear efficient or economical for tissue to fully maintain developmental capacity and at the same time be maximally efficient in their functional task.

It is appropriate for biologists to define aging to suit their interests. A definition suitable for sociologists, economists, and social workers may not be desirable for biologists. Although the biologist wants to know why organisms decline and fail, he is less concerned with the pathologic changes brought about by disease that affect the care of the elderly subject than is the practitioner. However, it is important that the biologist suggests how lines of developing biologic investigation point to new aspects of prevention and treatment.

The fact that there is no reason for evolution to restrict aging to one particular system means that aging is, in all probability, multifaceted or pluricausal. What appears to us as failures in the human design may originate because there is little evolutionary pressure to improve the design beyond a certain point. The actual events leading to mortality in an individual are somewhat a matter of genetic and environmental chance. Although the molecular events that occur are random, the vulnerability to such events may be a genetic characteristic of the species, and highly specific (Sacher, personal communication).

Evolution would have little reason to evolve a chain with a single weak link unless there was a clear and compelling reason for the immediate destruction of the postreproductive form. In such instances, a definite path of causality might become apparent as in plants from the setting of seed to death.

As a species develops in its ecologic niche, aging may offer an advantage. The selection of the more fit individuals of successive generations may be favored by the removal of previous generations from competition for food, mates, and territory. Indeed, many forms of life are engineered in such a way that only a single reproductive cycle occurs.

The ultimate limit to the survival of a species is its ability to keep its germ line reasonably free of mutation. In a given species, extension of the period of reproduction might be expected to increase the number of recessives arising from spontaneous mutation. If the new deleterious recessives enter the germ line at a rate faster than they can be removed in subsequent generations, a compensatory shortening of the life span would result. The increase in recessives in the germ line per generation is a function of the mutation rate for egg and sperm and the length of the reproductive life.

Aging in the sense of senescence appears to be a deleterious process although this may be our frame of reference. It is probably not an extension of embryologic development, although this is a matter of opinion (Saunders 1966). Programmed cell death certainly occurs in embryologic tissue (eg, in the freeing of the wing or the arm from the body, the dissolution of finger webbing in the human, the loss of a primitive fetal kidney, and in the absorption of the tadpole's tail). Many more neurones die during embryonic development in aging of the brain.

The real biochemical limitation to the length of life is probably the chemical stability of DNA and any accompanying material of limited replacement in postmitotic tissue. Background ionizing radiation would not become limiting for a thousand years. Double strandedness confers considerable stability to DNA. Single-stranded DNA and single-stranded RNA are considerably more susceptible to spontaneous hydrolysis (Eigner et al 1961). It is, of course, not certain that all DNA in chromatin is double stranded (Crick 1971). In double-stranded DNA, cleavage of N-glycosidic bonds of purines may take precedence over spontaneous hydrolysis in determining ultimate survival of DNA. Hydrolysis occurs in this case as a sequel of the depurination (Szybalski 1967).

Peptide bonds are not stable indefinitely, particulary asparagine amide (Sinex 1960; McKerrow and Robinson 1971; Boda 1968). It is conceivable that spontaneous deterioration of histone occurs in postmitotic cells in which the replacement of histone seems to be as limited as the replacement of DNA.

After a brief discussion of mortality and life tables, we will discuss the aging of four individual tissue systems: connective tissue and blood vessel wall, the brain and the immune system. Our final discussion will deal with the search for some unifying biochemical concepts which would explain what is happening in each of these systems.

Mortality and Life Tables

The study of life tables has its attraction and disadvantages. It is easy to tell a live mouse from a dead one and the appearance of a corpse in human society is usually noted. There is a vast amount of information available in the vital statistics of the nations of the world. Age specific death rates, the death rate among survivors varies dramatically from country to country, state to state, from urban to rural, white to nonwhite, and male to female. Such variations are not trivial and unexplained geographic variations may exceed 60 percent (Sauer 1962).

We can express life tables in several ways. The most straightforward is to count the number of individuals still alive at any age. We can plot the expectation of death or we can indicate at what age most deaths occur. If we prefer a linear function, we may observe that the rate of dying among the surviving population increases exponentially with age. After the age of 35, a plot of the logarithm of the death rate in the surviving population against age is a straight line. The slope of this line, called the Gompertz function, indicates that the death rate doubles every eight and one-half years. In countries wih poor public health, high mortality in infancy and young adulthood reduces the numbers of people who become old. However, after middle age the slope approaches that found in developed countries. Modern medicine has had little effect on the life span of elderly individuals in many countries, including the United States. We have had much more success treating infectious disease, heart disease, and cancer than aging (Kohn 1971).

A life table is an expression of both the force of mortality and variance. The slope of the Gompertz function is a function of variance, either in the individual or in the environment. If everyone died at the same age, the life table would be square and the Gompertz function would become meaningless.

The life table may be thought of as being a composite of many individual life tables of those fated to die of a particular cause. The human life table is dominated by deaths from cardiovascular disease, since this is the most common cause of death. Nevertheless, many other causes of death show similar distribution.

Mortality tables are perhaps not the best way to treat the aging of individuals. Indeed they give no information about functional loss during the lifetime prior to the events leading to death. Even averages may not accurately reflect what individuals experience. This is particularly true of aging studies in which death continuously removes subjects from the sample in increasing numbers after a period of what may be acutely declining function. Reliable data can only be obtained from what is known as longitudinal study in which the aging of individual subjects is followed. In this way we can learn whether the average decline in renal function with age is occurring acutely in some individuals or gradually in most individuals. We are not misled by the observation that many persons over 90 are hypotensive. They were originally normotensive. Their hypertensive colleagues, whose blood pressures increased with age, are no longer available for measurement.

The Aging of Connective Tissue

The characteristic cell of connnective tissue is the fibroblast, although other cells, such as cells of the blood vessel walls, for example, may synthesize some of the same extracellular macromolecules. Connective tissue contains a number of extracellular elements. These include glycoproteins, acid mucopolysaccharides such as hyaluronic acid and chondroitin sulfuric acid, as well as the fibrous proteins, collagen and elastin. These extracellular elements contain much of the extracellular fluid.

The body contains large amounts of connective tissue organized in different ways, as in the dermis of the skin, tendons, cartilage, or bone, or distributed throughout other tissues (Sinex 1968). The role of connective tissues requires considerable adaptability in a young, growing animal. It must not impede the proliferation of other cellular types. In a young animal, connective tissue is often much looser and watery. When growth ceases, connective tissue organizes and contributes to the strength of the now larger adult animal. Because of the importance of these adaptations, it is not surprising that connective tissue is responsive to many endocrine hormones.

ACID MUCOPOLYSACCHARIDES

As the animals ages, there may be changes in all of these components. Some of the hyaluronic acid is replaced by chondroitin sulfuric acid which is more charged and has more compact and rodlike molecules.

The relative amount of hyaluronic acid chondroitin a, b, and c and keratosulphate is characteristic of a particular tissue and the age of the animal. In many tissues, the amount of acid mucopolysaccharide decreases with age but that which is present is more sulphated.

The replacement of hyaluronic acid by chondroitin sulphate must affect the permeability of connective tissue. Hyaluronic acid is quite space filling, like randomly coiled barbed wire. Large molecules would tend to be sieved out by hyaluronic acid during passage through connective tissue. Replacement of hyaluronic acid by chondroitin sulphate may lead to the separation of two phases, one more permeable to large molecules and the other less. Since older connective tissue tends to be more sulfated, the density of negative charge on the large molecules occupying the extracellular space increases in older animals.

Hyaluronic acid and chondroitin acid offer a convenient way for an animal to adjust the state of its connective tissue, since these substances have a higher turnover and are considerably more dynamic metabolically than collagen. Indeed, some collagen molecules are quite persistent and may last throughout the lifetime of the animal.

COLLAGEN

The principal protein of connective tissue is collagen. Large amounts of collagen are found in skin, bone, and tendon.

Collagen is an important component of the walls of blood vessels and contributes to their strength as well as to the strength of scars. Collagen is a rather stiff, elongated molecule in a triple helix. This triple helix is stabilized by the amino acid sequence -Gly-Pro-X-, that is, glycine, proline, and some other amino acid, such as alanine, repeating throughout the long sequences. Some of the proline, depending on the species and tissue, becomes hydroxylated to hydroxyproline.

Because of the stiffness and linear array of amino acid, collagen molecules form semicrystalline aggregates of considerable stability. As these aggregates are forming in the developing animal, only a portion of them may be extracted in dilute acid or buffer. As the animal matures, the amount of extractable collagen decreases. An old animal has essentially no extractable collagen, unless the tissue is first heated. At about 62 C, collagen undergoes a rather remarkable transformation (Verzar 1951). The ordered arrangement of the triple helices is lost and the previously stiff molecule appeared to be capable of considerable elastic behavior. A tendon will contract to approximately one-third of its original length and now may be stretched like a rubber band. This elastic behavior indicates that there is some sort of cross-linkage between collagen triple helices in the native state. Chemically, this cross-link seems to be formed by deaminations of lysine to adipic semialdehyde. Adipic semialdehydes then condense to form several different cross-links (Kang and Gross, 1970).

Siegel, Kagan, Franzblau, and Martin (1968), in a joint study between Boston University and the National Dental Institute, have incubated embryonic bone collagen in lysyl oxidase. Extractable two-stranded β-components form during the incubation containing both aldol and hydrolysinonorleucine cross-links. With continued incubation the extractable β-components disappear and insoluble intermolecularly cross-linked collagen appears. It would appear that intra- and intermolecular cross-links are produced by very similar reactions. Aldol formation is somewhat more characteristic of intramolecular cross-links. With time, some of aldol cross-links are reduced in vivo. As maturation proceeds, more complex condensation occurs about other aldol cross-links forming such structures as histidino-hydroxymerodesmosine.

The intramolecular aldol condensation product present in acid soluble collagen disappears during in vitro fibril formation at 37 C. During fibril formation some of the intramolecular cross-link is incorporated into histidino-hydroxymerodesmosine. In in vitro experiments, this substance begins to form after the fibril, as measured by opacity, is almost completed. Histidino-hydroxymerodesmosine originally referred to as post-histidine peak is thus characteristic of more mature tissue.

There is very little information about how the concentration of lysyl oxidase varies with age in tissue. However, the enzyme is a product of cellular activity and the rate of cross-linking may be greatest in a young animal even if the cross-link density increases throughout the life span.

The actual amount of collagen in older tissue may decrease with age, or there may be proliferation of collagen due to some stimulus, such as death of parenchynal cells, inflammation, or physical injury.

ELASTIN

In blood vessels, lung, and other tissue, a second protein appears with collagen. This protein has the property of elasticity even in its native conformation. It is thus cross-linked but not ordered in the crystalline arrays. This protein is known as elastin. In the blood vessel it carries the stress of the pulse. It moderates the force acting on the smooth muscle cells of the wall absorbing part of the energy at the peak of the pulse and transmitting it moments later, thus smoothing the pressure curve generated by the heart. The major cross-links in elastin are known. They are desmosine and isodesmosine. There is no clear-cut chemical evidence that the cross-linkage of elastin increases significantly beyond maturity.

The ultraviolet fluorescence and the yellow color are increased in elastin prepared from older animals. The importance of these observations is not clear. In older blood vessels the elastin appears less regular and the sheets of elastin that ring the blood vessel appear thinner, frayed, and slightly moth eaten. This appearance may result from the infiltration of the elastic laminae by cellular elements as well as by actual wear and tear. The elastin of blood vessels in contrast to that of the elastin of neck tendon of a cow, the ligamentum nuchae, appears to be associated with a certain amount of amorphous glycoprotein. With age, there may be deposition of hydroxyapatite crystals and cholesterol on the surface of the elastin. Plasma contains proteolytic enzymes capable of digesting elastin, although whether such digestion actually occurs in vivo is difficult to establish. The replacement of elastin in the older animal, as is the case with collagen, is limited. In an injured blood vessel, whole new intima is sometimes constructed. In contrast to collagen where shrinkage force can be elegantly and accurately followed as a function of age, no physical parameters have been followed for elastin. We do not know if elastin becomes more or less crystalline or more or less rubberlike with age (Ross and Bornstein 1971).

One of the problems has been the classical methods of purification. The methods used to remove collagen and other contaminating proteins undoubtedly denature elastin. It should be possible to develop better purification procedures, using collagenase and other enzymes. Another problem is that no adequate model of the structure of elastin has been devised to serve as a basis for comparative studies.

The statement often seen in the literature that elastin has a random conformation is probably not true. All proteins have specific amino acid sequences and as a result have a limited number of conformations of maximum stability. Mukherjee (1969) found some evidence for breakage of hydrogen bonds in ligamentum nuchae elastin during swelling with formamide.

It might be helpful to list some facts about elastin and then discuss some suppositions.

1. Elastin shows rubberlike elasticity. In balance, Hoeve and Flory (1956) showed that most of the mechanical work of stretching seems to be done against entropic factors. If new chemical bonds form on stretching, they are compensated for by breaking of bonds in other parts of the molecule or in the surrounding solvent.
2. Elastin is rich in proline and hydroxyproline. There are of the order of 124 prolines and 23 hydroxyprolines per 1,000 residues. This places some limitations on the amount of helix it can contain, since these amino acids cannot participate in alpha or pi helices.
3. Elastin is rich in glycine, over 350 residues per 1,000. This permits a number of conformations from which other amino acids are excluded.
4. Elastin cannot contain much of the collagen sequence Gly-Pro-X- or it would be digested by collagenase.
5. There is some experimental evidence that elastin has an unusual affinity for calcium ion.
6. The principal cross-links in elastin are desmosine and isodesmosine representing in mature elastin about 9 residues per 1,000. Desmosine and isodesmosine are formed by the condensation of four lysines.

Models of the structure of elastin must conform to these facts. The chains cannot be too stiff, although it does not necessarily follow that the molecule itself must stretch. Stretchability may be as much a function of weave as stretching molecules as, for example, in a nylon stocking.

Ramachadran (1967) has consistently favored a triple helical model of elastin resembling collagen and discusses the evidence for a 2.9 Å spacing in autoclaved stretched elastin. This is the spacing observed in collagen, in which three relatively extended chains having three residues per left-handed rotation are coiled about each other with a right-handed twist. Ramachadran feels that elastin would have a lower shrinking temperature than collagen because it has only half as much amino acid and considerably less polar groups available to set up strong interaction between molecules. In the Ramachadran model, elastin thus resembles a thermally denatured collagen. It would clearly make a difference as to whether the critical shrinking temperature of elastin was above or below 37 C. The sequence -Gly-Pro-X- cannot exist in elastin or it would be digested by collagenase. However, -Gly-Pro-X- is accommodated but without the same degree of stability.

Sequence studies are too fragmentary to provide much information. However, -Gly-Val-Pro-Gly- has been reported to occur with some frequency. We have built some preliminary models of this sequence with four left-handed turns per chain and four chains per helix. An essential feature of the collagen helix is that there must be three residues per turn, since the residue that faces inward toward the center of the three stranded assembly cannot be accommodated if it is not glycine. If glycine occurs every fourth residue, then there must be four residues per turn. In our model the 2.9 Å spacing per residue remain essentially the same. However it now requires 11.5 Å per turn rather than 8.7 Å. There are now two bonds to adjacent chains per four residues rather than two bonds per three residues.

Urry's (1971) model building is probably just as speculative but uses quite a different approach. His model is based on two observations: the large number of glycine residues in elastin and the apparent affinity of elastin for calcium ion. He proposes two structures for elastin, a left-handed pi helix consisting of alternating L and D residues and a modification of this structure into a series of β-turns which would complex Ca. This pi helix is possible because glycine, which has two hydrogens on the α-carbon, is at one and the same time both an L and D amino acid. A pi helix can thus be built in which glycine alternates with regular L-amino acids and in which the carboxyls and nitrogen hydrogen bonds extend up and down parallel to the helix axis. Urry's left-handed pi LD helix differs from an α-helix in that it is left handed. The conventional α-helix is right handed. Alternate carbonyls point in opposite directions rather than in the same direction as in the α-helix. The residue repeat would be 1.15 Å rather than 1.5 Å and the spacing corresponding to 5.4 Å in the α helix would be 5.1 Å. The pitch is flatter and there is a hole down the center of the helix. Out of this hole grows the second of Urry's models. By twisting glycines, the carbonyls of the glycines, the L-amino acid residues, can be brought to the inside in a confrontation that would favor coordination with calcium.

Measurements of the circular dichroism of elastin have been limited to two forms: films of coacervate and solutions of α-elastin. α-elastin is prepared by partially digesting elastin in oxalic acid. Because of its relative hydrophobic nature, elevating the temperature causes elastin to come out of aqueous solution as a coacervate.

Measurements of circular dichroism would suggest that α-elastin contains some α-helix. The molar ellipticity is low, about one-third that of L-polyglutamic acid. The sign of rotation would indicate that the predominate helices are right handed. By circular dichroism there is little indication of extended chains of the type found in collagen or of ordered random coils in which the carbonyls are perpendicular rather than parallel to the helix axis.

Torchia and Piez have carried out an interesting study of the ^{13}C spectra of native calf elastin, and found that 80 percent of the backbone carbons have short rotational times, of the order of 40 nanoseconds and that the rotational time is only reduced by a factor of two when in contact with a strong denaturant, namely 2M KCNS.

The β-turn structure postulated by Urry for coordination of calcium is more formally related to the antiparallel form of β-keratin than to the α-helix. Since antiparallel keratin is not helical, evidence must also be sought from nuclear magnetic resonance measurements and other sources for its existence.

If the stretching of elastin involves the stretchability of molecules, then the molecules must pass through a series of discrete molecular conformations as they elongate, analogous to the discrete steps that have recently been found during the denaturation of enzymes with heat.

It can be seen from this discussion that the confrontation of elastin is poorly understood and remains a difficult problem. The molecule is clearly not homogeneous and regions of the molecule may vary in conformation. Since the fibers are not well oriented in natural structure, X-ray studies of the type that elucidated the structure, collagen, silk, and wool, will never be as applicable. The precursor molecule, prior to aggregation and cross-linkage, has never been highly purified and it is not known if it exists in a crystalizable form. The precursor is present in the tissues of copper deficient hogs (Sandberg et al 1969). In copper deficiency the animals lose the ability to form the adipic semialdehyde cross-link precursor. This lysine-rich, cross-link-poor, material forms coacervates just as does α-elastin and this property is used in the partial purification of the precursor. The sequencing of such a monomer, combined with detailed X-ray crystallographic study would provide information applicable to the high polymer and represents an arduous route to the structure. At the moment, the yield of proelastin which can be obtained from copper deficient aortas is very limited.

In spite of the many problems, it would appear that improved methods for the comparison of young and old elastin will shortly be forthcoming.

Aging of Blood Vessels

The study of atherosclerosis has been dominated by the finding of cholesterol in the plaques. The preoccupation with cholesterol has obscured other lines of research including the relationship between aging and cardiovascular disease. The plaque should not be viewed as simply a bag of cholesterol, but as an abnormal proliferation of cells beneath the vascular endothelium. The fact that it contains collagen and acid mucopolysaccharide means that it is essentially connective tissue. However, there is a complication. The cells that form the plaque appear to come from smooth muscle layers of the media and to retain some histochemical evidence for their origin. The ability of these cells to acquire the functional capabilities of fibroblasts is not as surprising as it seems, since both are formed from mesenchyme (Ross and Bornstein, 1970).

In the intact blood vessel, the smooth muscle cells undergo only an occasional mitosis. If the cells are stimulated to divide in tissue culture they will, however, multiply (Jarmolyck et al 1968). It is interesting to speculate about why the mitotic activity of the mature, healthy, adult vessel remains quiescent and why in later life cells may proliferate until they close the lumen. In the young animal the aorta is growing. Both the vessel and its lumen increase in size as the tension of the wall increases, the tension being inversely proportional to the radius. When the vessel matures, further increase in tension, from hypertension, reinitiates proliferation. However, now the growth of the vessel is limited and proliferation of cells narrows the lumen. At the same time, the new cells begin to synthesize lipid. A possible factor may be levels of ATP and NADH (Wherent 1970; Baylin et al 1966; Somlyo and Somlyo 1968). We have speculated that the maximum utilization of ATP occurs in smooth muscle under optimal conditions of stretch and tension and that if pressure increases or decreases from the optimal amount, increased ATP becomes available for lipid synthesis and mitotic division.

The Central Nervous System

The aspect of aging of most concern to individuals is probably the aging of their own brain. We view the brain as the seat of our identity and our ability to cope with the world. This part of the aging process is also of greatest concern to government because inability to function in an appropriate manner in society results in the filling of nursing homes and mental institutions. With age, neurones die and glia proliferate. The number of synaptic connections decrease.

The aging of the human brain is a complex subject. It is not always easy to distinguish functional loss due to cardiovascular disease from dementia and from normal aging.

Experimental psychologists have learned many things about the elderly. The most prominent finding is that they are slower in their response. It is not clear why. Given enough time, the elderly can often perform quite well on the psychologist's test. Nevertheless, with age, an increasing portion of people show dementia. Some elderly, particularly the very old, show a noticeable decline in intelligence and the ability to care for themselves.

The lifetime risk at birth of being classified as demented in old age is small—possibly 1.8 percent for males and 2.3 percent for females. But for persons over 90 it is high, over 50 percent. The possibility of dementia is present at any age but the curve becomes markedly steeper around 55. This and many other aspects of dementia were discussed at a symposium at the University of Texas Medical Center (Gaitz 1971).

There are two kinds of dementia: acute and chronic. Acute dementia may result from a variety of causes. The clinical search must first be directed to treatable conditions. Such conditions are subdural hematoma, benign tumors, occult hydrocephalus, intoxication, infection, nutritional defects, electrolyte abnormalities, hypothyroidism, cardiac failure, and uremia. Before being incarcerated for life in a nursing home or mental institution, an elderly person should have a thorough medical examination in a general hospital. This is not always the case. Who knows how many persons are in mental institutions because they had bladder infections?

The chronic dementia are of two main types: those related to cardiovascular disease and those that are not. It is difficult to obtain accurate percentage figures. Neurologists probably see more of the later type, psychiatrists more cardiovascular. Some patients have both. The rigorousness of the screen makes a difference. Those types with a more neurologic basis are more serious and therefore relatively more frequent as milder cases are left out of the sample. The pathologist has shown that the average internist overestimates the cases attributed to cardiovascular disease.

Most knowledgeable neurologists now feel that senile dementia cannot be distinguished from Alzheimer's disease, by far the most frequent presenile dementia. Characteristic of Alzheimer's disease are senile plaques, neurofibrillary tangles, and abnormal microtubules. In addition there appear in dementia, and often in normally functioning older brains, areas of softening with large-scale cellular loss, usually the result of stroke. Another characteristic of the aging brain is the appearance of large vacuoles and dense, perioxidized proteolipid known as age pigment.

We will now discuss these separately. The senile plaques are found most often in the hippocampus and frontal cortex. They are large, 15 to 150 microns across and are conspicuous in a silver stain. They are a feature of Alzheimer's disease and are found in many older, normal brains. Senile plaques are not as plentiful as age pigment in the senile brain and occupy considerably less volume. Under low power, plaques are seen to have a core and to be surrounded by a filamentous tangle. Under the electron microscope, the core itself consists of filaments and the surrounding looser tangle is resolved into an even more tangled mass. The central core stains with congo red. It's filaments look like amyloid under the electron microscope. It is PAS positive and birefringent. It probably is indeed amyloid.

According to Terry, the plaque is initiated by the presence of sick neuronal endings (Wisniewski et al 1968, 1970). As axonal flow decreases he sees altered synapses packed with mitochondria and dense bodies. He calls these abnormal neurites. Microglia are attached to these abnormal neurites from the microcirculation and form amyloid. The final structure that results is the senile plaque. The importance of Terry's concept is that it places the primary failure within the neurone itself.

The time sequence is not clear. The formation of amyloid is suggestive of a rather long process leading to partial immune exhaustion. In the neurofibrillary tangle, there is a mad proliferation of tubules and filaments in the neuronal processes. While the normal neurotubule has a width of 240 Å in Alzheimer's disease, the senile dementias, and postencephalitic Parkinson's, an abnormal tubule appears which seems to have a narrowing every 90 Å to 100 Å. This is suggestive of a double helical structure. This type of alteration is most common in cellular processes. It is characteristic of the older brain and is associated with dementia.

Another type of tangle is found in old brain. The cytoplasm sometimes shows inclusions that consist of tangles made of 100 A filaments. Such filaments are also characteristic of human infantile neuroaxonal dystrophy, vincristine neuropathy, and sporadic motor neurone disease.

The exact relationship between normal microtubules, altered microtubules, and neurofilaments is not clear. The structure of microtubules is clearly influenced by drugs, such as colchicine and vincristine. These seem to dissociate microtubules into monomers in vitro and into filaments in vivo.

The banded structures, described by Terry, in Alzheimer's disease and senile brain may consist of a double helix. Does this originate from microtubules or is it a new class of filamentous protein? This is an important question, not only because of its theoretical interest but also because the formation and dislocation of microtubules is known to be influenced by drugs, and therefore methods of therapeutic intervention for the dementias may be suggested.

The stability of microtubules may be controlled in part by cyclic AMP whose rate of formation and destruction is strongly influenced by levels of catechol amines and CNS stimulants such as caffeine. For the first time, there may exist a physiologic link between emotion on one hand and the integrity of the brain on the other, through arousal and the maintenance of normal axonal structures.

LIPOFUSCIN

Lipofuscin is often called age pigment since larger quantities of this substance are found in older tissues. Age pigment is not as plentiful in the brain as it is in the heart because cell bodies contribute less to the total mass (Brizee et al 1968). Observation with the electron microscope and histochemical visualization of acid phosphatase, esterase, and catheptic activity suggests that lipofuscin pigment is intimately linked with lysosomes. The pigment bodies appear to contain degradation products of the lysosomes themselves, together with other lipoprotein substrates of the lysosomal vacuolar apparatus.

The appearance of age pigment is not confined to older brains. It increases in a number of situations associated with abnormal metabolism as a result of genetic defects, such as Huntington's chorea, extensive demyelination, and alcoholism. It is observed in patients with conditions as diverse as Alzheimer's disease, Batten's disease, Down's syndrome, and progeria.

The term age pigment suggests that this pigment accumulates with time and makes cells old. Although this is the more accepted way of looking at the problem, it could be equally true that aged cells make age pigment. Thus, there are reasons for wanting to know how old the actual molecules of a given deposit of age pigment actually are. Are they formed from old structural lipid or formed from relatively recent dietary lipid?

Neurologists do not view age pigment as seriously as they do neurofibrillary tangles, senile plaques, and large areas of softening because age pigment is so common that it is not considered characteristic of dementia.

What we have been discussing to date in regard to the aging of the central nervous system is rooted in classical neuropathology. These are other approaches however, based on modern neuroanatomy and biochemistry. For example, it is now becoming possible through electron microscopy to determine the number of synapses per dendrite and per cell body, and the effect of the number of available processes on the number of synapses actually made. The technique utilizes serial reconstruction of sections prepared for the electron microscope. Thick sections, stained and viewed under a light microscope, are used to assist in the reconstruction of the thin sections.

From the viewpoint of the biochemistry on aging, the nervous system offers both advantages and disadvantages. The brain is the classic postmitotic tissue. The renewal of DNA and protein, such as histone, is limited. Chemical injury induced during the passage of time in the permanent structural elements should be easier to detect in brains than in most tissue. It also seems well suited to studies of ambiguity and capacity for protein biosynthesis. Nuclei are relatively easy to prepare from brain, although there are problems as to their cell type of origin.

The life history of a brain cell resembles the life history of most cells in the body. They arise by cell division, migrate to their ultimate position, and differentiate. Sooner or later they die, either prior to or at the death of the organism. The brain differs from most other tissue in that once the migration of neurones and the differentiation is completed early in life, no further replacement occurs.

It seems probable that DNA of the brain would accumulate appreciable injury in the form of nicks and strand breaks over a lifetime. The problem of measurement of such injury is, however, most difficult since postmitotic cells cannot be labeled with isotopes.

Immunochemistry

The morbidity associated with aging is in part the result of a decreased resistance to infection. There is good evidence from studies on mice that there is a decrease in immune competence with age. It seems likely that the capacity for immunorejection of cancer is impaired as well as hypersensitivity.

First, in regards to resistance to infection. The primary response to infection is associated with the immediate production of the large IgM class of globulins. The secondary or booster response is associated with IgG globulins which normally represent 70 percent of the circulating immunoglobulin.

An animal has two classes of progenitor cells; one is genetically committed to the production of a specific antigen and the other may become committed but may also produce some other antibody. Albright and Makinodan (1966) tested the capacity of spleen cells from old and young mice to form hemagglutinins in tissue culture and when injected into previously irradiated mice. In the latter case, the injected cells colonize the spleen of the recipient animal. They found that there was a decrease in both types of progenitor cells with age in the spleens of the donor animals. There are several criticisms that can be made of these significant experiments. The cells that are scored arise as a result of severe

The results with these transferred cells were consistent with the ability of intact animals to make antibody. They found that in very old animals the capacity of mice to make antibody against foreign red cells declined dramatically. The concentration of cells capable of making antibody by the direct plaque forming hemolytic assay decreased 50 fold between 3- and 30-month-old mice. This was a measure of primary response. The cells present in the spleen capable of secondary or booster response responded reasonably well. It would appear that an older person's ability to respond to a new infection should be less than the ability to respond to an old infection.

Delayed hypersensitivity differs from the immune reaction, which produces circulating antibodies, in that it can be transferred between animals through the transfer of viable immunocompetent cells but not by sera. This type of immune resistance also becomes less vigorous with age. The older animal is more tolerant to skin grafts and to antigens injected into the skin. Part of the decreased resistance to cancer of the older individual is the result of a decreased ability to reject the tumor through delayed hypersensitivity. Adler (Adler et al 1971) discusses the possibility that the population of thymus-derived cells responsible for delayed hypersensitivity decreases with age in the spleen and are partially replaced by circulating antibody-forming cells in the marrow.

There is a remarkable increase in the incidence of cancer in adults until old age (Dorn 1958). Then the incidence decreases. Tumors promote the appearance of both circulating and the tissue antibody of the type found in delayed hypersensitivity. The latter is of most importance in the rejection of the tumor. It seems reasonable to assume that malignancy increases with age, at least in part because the rejection system fails.

Primary Causes

We have discussed aging in connective tissue, the brain, and the immune system. Can the biochemist find any unifying concepts in such diversity? It is human nature to try.

One can infer that aging involves the activity of cells and that in the older animal the cellular response made to stress is less appropriate. One might say that the information available to any older cell for an appropriate response is either absent or is garbled in transmission. Since the primary information available to a cell is coded in its DNA, DNA seems like a good place to begin a biochemical study of aging.

Injury to DNA might be visualized as double-strand breaks, single-strand breaks or nicks, and altered base pairs. Some evidence for an increased level of DNA injury in older animals has been obtained by Curtis (Curtis 1963; Curtis and Telley 1971). If the livers of old mice are injured with carbon disulfide or carbon tetrachloride, the remaining cells hypertrophy. The mitoses in these cells can be scored for chromosomal abnormalities such as missing, short, and bridge chromosomes. Such abnormalities are more demonstrable in the livers of older animals. There are several criticisms that can be made of these significant experiments. The cells that are scored arise as a result of severe injury and may not be particularly representative of mature tissue. Furthermore, while ionizing radiation is very efficient at producing chromosomal injury, it is considerably less efficient at producing life shortening at comparable levels of breaks. Therefore, it is essential to be able to measure strand breaks in other tissue, including tissue that has no potential for division by some other method. Unfortunately, as we have seen in our discussion of the aging brain, this is difficult. Chromatin is very easily injured during isolation and it is hard to know what molecular size to assign to native, uninjured DNA. In alkaline sucrose gradients, Lett finds that chromatin tends to generate 165 S DNA (Lett 1970; Klucis and Lett 1970). Unless the ultracentrifuge run is made at a low concentration of DNA, there is considerable entrapment of molecules and large error (Regan et al 1970). The runs must therefore be made with isotopically labeled DNA. However, few investigators have had the foresight to label young animals three years before they do their experiment. Better, large capacity rotors may be an answer.

Another approach is to assume that breaks increase because of failure in repair and to attempt to assay the levels of repair enzymes, polymerase, and ligase (Rose et al 1971) using synthetic polynucleotide substrates (Modrich et al 1970; Lindahl et al 1968).

Isolating tissue DNA and measuring of uptake of labeled bases with purified polymerase and ligase is probably not feasible because of some of the same isolation problems that make the direct measurement of DNA breaks so difficult.

A varient is to look at some specific region of DNA, such as that which codes for ribosomal RNA and assay it by hybridization with ribosomal RNA as now being done by Strehler. It goes somewhat against the dogma of an invarient amount of DNA per cell, but this is not really a serious objection.

Another approach is to assume that the DNA is intact but that the older cells do not have good access to the coded information (Adelman 1970). This would imply an altered state of chromatin, either in qualitative organization, for example, the amount and kinds of RNA, histone, and nonhistone protein present, or altered interaction. Investigators have found that old chromatin is not as efficient as young chromatin in serving as a template for RNA polymerase (O'Meara 1971). The dissociation of chromatin protein as a function of saline concentration varies in old and young animals. Differences can be detected between the thermal melting behavior of DNA prepared from young and old chromatin (Hahn 1970; Russell et al 1970).

In the Russell et al experiments, the amount of DNA capable of reannealing increases with age. That is, the apparent satellite DNA appears to increase. The explanation favored by Russell et al is that the amount of residual protein attached to DNA increases with age. The DNA was initially denatured in a boiling water bath at 100 C and denaturation is assumed to have been complete. The authors do not feel that the concentration of satellite would actually change.

Interpretation of this and other experiments is complicated by the fact that younger and more active cells have more chromatin protein. The extra protein is predominantly nonhistone. The presence of this protein seems to turn the DNA on rather than off. One cannot say, therefore, whether the amounts of chromosomal RNA and nonhistone protein are changing because physical interaction is changing or whether changes in physical or covalent interactions are gradually shutting off the genome. One would like to think of young chromatin as more open and breathing or opening double strands to single strands more easily. However, more evidence is needed to support such a supposition. If this were proved to be the case, it might open some areas of therapeutic application.

Not only is there the question of the proportion of the genome that is read but there is also the question of how accurately it is read. Orgel

(1970) has pointed out how error might well beget error in translation since the enzymes that synthesize RNA and protein are themselves products of such synthesis. The approach of Lewis and Halliday (1970) and Orgel is an interesting one. They must explain why the individual dies but the germ line is propagated.

In practice, somatic mutation is difficult to distinguish from irreversible changes in phenotype. Even such genetic concepts as recessiveness and dominance could apply to phenotype as well. Some changes in phenotype might not even involve the genome. Although we know a great deal about how the genetic code is copied at cell division, we know very little about accurate information required for both daughter cells to express the correct phenotype as transmitted. We believe that it is more likely that aging involves inappropriate, irreversible alterations in phenotype than conventional mutation of DNA.

Structures may fail for reasons not immediately connected with the nucleus. We do not really know whether old elastin, old synapses in the brain, or an old kidney glomeruli, can be repaired on instructions from central headquarters

Aging remains a truly challenging area of biochemical investigation. The social implications are rather awesome, and some understanding of biologic, social, and economic factors affecting the aged is essential if this rapidly developing biologic technology is to be wisely applied. The potential of future generations for better health in later years is certainly here.

References

Adelman RC: An age-dependent modification of enzyme regulation. J Biol Chem 245:1032, 1970

Adler WH, Takiguchi T, Smith RT: Effect of age upon primary alloantigen recognition by spouse spleen cells. J Immunol 107:1357, 1971

Albright JF, Makinodan T: Growth and sequence of antibody forming cells. J Cell Physiol 67:185, Supp. I, 1966

Baylin GJ, DeMaria WJ, Baylin SB, Krueger RP, Sanders AP: ATP concentration and localization of sites of apinipherme induced renal artery constriction. Proc Soc Exp Biol Med 122:396, 1966

Boda JL, Metler SL: Equilibrium constant for the reversible deamination of aspartic acid. Biochemistry 7:3404, 1968

Brizzee KR, Cancilla PA, Sherwood N, Timeras PS: The amount and distribution of pigments in neurones and glia of the cerebral cortex. J. Gerontol 24:127, 1969

Crick, F: General model for the chromosomes of higher organisms. Nature, 234:25, 1971

Curtis HJ: Biological mechanisms underlying the aging process. Science, 141:686, 1963

———, Telley J: The life-span of dividing mammalian cells *in vivo*. J Gerontol 26:1, 1971

Eigner J, Boedther H, Michaels G: The thermal degradation of nucleic acids. Biochem Biophys Acta 51:165, 1961

Gaitz C: Aging and the brain. A symposia at the University of Texas Medical Center, Houston, Texas, 1971, New York, Plenum Press
Hahn HP von: Structural and functional changes in nucleoprotein during ageing of the cell. Gerontologia 16:116, 1970
Hoeve CAJ, Flory PJ: The elastic properties of elastin. J Am Chem Soc 80:6523, 1958
Jarmolyck J, Landan J, Fritz KE, McElvene E: Aortic media explants. Exp Mol Pathol 9:171, 1968
Kang A, Gross J: Relationship between the intra and intermolecular cross-links of collagen. Proc Natl Acad Sci U S A 67:1307, 1970
Klucis ES, Lett JT: Zonal centrifugation of mammalian DNA. Anal Biochem 35:480, 1970
Kohn RR: Principles of Mammalian Aging, Englewood Cliffs, NJ, Prentice-Hall, 1971
Lewis CM, Halliday R: Mistranslation and aging in neurospora. Nature 228:877, 1970
Lett JT, Klucis ES, Sun C: On the size of the DNA in the mammalian chromosome. Structural subunits. Biophys J 10:277, 1970
Lindahl T, Edelman GM: Polynucleotide ligase from myeloid and lymphoid tissue. Proc Natl Acad Sci U S A 61:680, 1968
Makinodan T, Chino F, Lever WE, Brewen BS: Primary antibody forming activity of young and old mice with long life spans. J Gerontol 26:508, 1971a
———: Ability of old mice to undergo a secondary antibody response. J Gerontol 26:515, 1971b
McKerrow J, Robinson AB: Deamidation of asparaginyl residues as a hazard in experimental protein and peptide procedures. Anal Biochem 42:2, 565, 1971
Modrich P, Lehman IR: A simple and rapid assay of polynucleotide joining (ligase) activity by measurement of circle formation from linear desocyadenylate-desocythymodylate copolymer. J Biol Chem 245:3626, 1970
Mukherjee DP: The viscoelastic properties of elastin. Sc.D. thesis in chemical engineering. Cambridge, M.I.T., 1969
O'Meara AR, Herrmann RL: A modification of mouse lifer chromatin preparation displaying age related differences in salt dissociation and template ability. Biochem Biophys Acta, submitted in revised form, May 1971
Orgel L: The maintenance of the accuracy of protein synthesis and its relevance to aging. Proc Natl Acad Sci 67:1476, 1970
Ramachadran GN (ed): Treatise on Collagen, Vol 1. London and New York, Academic Press, 1967, p. 172
Regan JD, Setlow RB, Ley RD: Normal and defective repair of damaged DNA in human cells: A sensitive assay utilizing the photolysis of bromodesoxyuridine. Proc Natl Acad Sci 68:708, 1971
Ross R, Bornstein P: Elastic fibers in the body. Sci Am 224:44, 1971
Russell AP, Dowling LE, Herrmann RL: Age-related differences in mouse lifer DNA melting and hydroxylapatite fractionation. Gerontologia 16:159, 1970
Sandberg LB, Weissman N, Smith DW: The purification and partial characterization of a soluble elastin like protein from copper-deficient porcine aorta. Biochemistry 8:2940, 1969
Saunders JW Jr: Death in embryonic systems. Science 154:604, 1966
Sauer HI: Epidemiology of cardiovascular mortality. Am J Med Sci 7:468, 1968
Siegel RC, Kagan HM, Franzblau C, Martin GR: *In vitro* maturation of bone collagen. Isr J Med Sci 7:468, 1971

Sinex FM: Aging and the lability of irreplaceable molecules II, The amide group of collagen. J Gerontol 15:15, 1960
———: The role of collagen in aging. In Gould B (ed): Treatise on Collagen, Vol. 2, part 2. London and New York, Academic Press, 1968, p 409
Somlyo AP, Somlyo AV: Vascular smooth muscle. Pharmacol Rev 20:197, 1968
Strehler B: Time, Cells and Aging. New York, Academic Press, 1968
Szybalski W: Effects of elevated temperatures on DNA and on some polynucleotides: Denaturation, renaturation, and cleavage of glycosidic and phosphate ester bonds. In Rose AH (ed): Thermobiology. London and New York, Academic Press, 1967
Torchia DA, Piez KA: Mobility of elastin chains as determined by ^{13}C nuclear magnetic resonance. J Mol Biol 76:419–24, 1973
Urry DS: Neutral sites for calcium binding to elastin and collagen. Proc Natl Acad Sci 68:810, 1971
Verzer F: Das Altern de Kollagens. Helv Physiol Pharmacol Acta 14:207, 1956
Wherent AF: Is atherosclerosis a disorder of intramitochondrial respiration? Ann Intern Med 73:125, 1970
Wisniewski H, Shelanski ML, Terry RD: Effects of mitotic spindle inhibitors on neurotubules and neurofilaments of anterior horn cells. J Cell Biol 38:224, 1968
Wisniewski H, Terry RD, Hirano A: Neurofibrillary pathology. J Neuropathol Exp Neurol 24:163, 1970

3

THE INTERDISCIPLINARY STUDY OF LIFE SPAN*

Benjamin Bell, M.D.
Charles L. Rose, Ph.D.

This chapter presents background material for the better understanding of the complex determinants of life span. These are of two general types, intrinsic and extrinsic. The intrinsic determinants refer to factors that are transmitted genetically; the extrinsic is a residual category that may be further divided into physical-environmental and interpersonal-social. The three resulting types will be referred to as genetic, physical, and social. They do not exist actually as pure types but interact with each other in complex ways. Therefore, they must be studied through an interdisciplinary approach.

The study of life span may be approached through an analysis of its determinants and/or its consequences. The thrust of this chapter will be in the consideration of the interdisciplinary determinants of life span. The consequences of change in life span, particularly the increase of life span which has occurred primarily as a result of medical technology, is another area of study in its own right. The logical order is to study determinants first.

However, a word about the consequences would be appropriate to see its integral relation to determinants. The most obvious consequence of

**Material for this chapter has been drawn in part from Rose and Bell,* Predicting Longevity—Methodology and Critique, *D. C. Heath and Co., Lexington, Mass., 1971. Many of the ideas were developed from the Normative Aging Study, sponsored by the Veterans Administration, and located at the Veterans Administration Outpatient Clinic, Boston, Mass., Benjamin Bell, M.D., Director. Another source was a dissertation completed under a Special Research Fellowship of the National Institute of Child Health and Human Development by Dr. Charles L. Rose in the Department of Sociology of Boston University.*

life span increase, or death control, is overpopulation and its attendant problems of environmental pollution and ecologic imbalance. Unless balanced by birth control, the catastrophic results will markedly decrease the life span. On a less dramatic level, increase in life span has profound social effects, such as increase in multigenerational families and shifts in economic and medical priorities for the care of greatly increased numbers of the elderly.

The study of life span should not be based merely on the determinancy of added years, but should also include the quality of the life involved in the added years. This point is embodied in the motto of the Gerontological Society: "Years to your life, and life to your years." The thought is not new: it is found in ancient Greek mythology in the story of Tithonus. Eos, the goddess of the Dawn, loved the mortal Tithonus. She petitioned Zeus to make Tithonus immortal but neglected to ask that he also retain his youth in the manner of the gods. Her wish was granted: Tithonus kept aging naturally but could not die. He was condemned to live forever, a babbling, pain-wracked old man, bedridden, and locked in a cell (Gruman 1966). What good is it then to have added years if they are years of pain and suffering? Indeed, those factors which make for a longer life also make for a good life. The quality of life in itself is a predictor of longer life. Therefore, the very predictors of life span should give us some ideas as to how life for the elderly might be improved.

The determinants of life span will be presented in an interdisciplinary framework. Genetic determinants will be shown in their relation to physical and social determinants; more generally, any one determinant will be examined in relation to the other two.

Genetic Factors

The genetic determination of life span operates at both the species and individual level. At the species level, it determines that one species lives longer than another, for example, that the elephant lives longer than man, and man lives longer than the mouse. At the individual level, it accounts for long-lived strains within a species, and it is this level that we will examine.

There is a genetically determined upper limit that represents the top of the genetically determined distribution of life span within the human species. This upper limit is within the range of 110 to 115 years (Korenchevsky 1961) and would theoretically occur under optimal environmental conditions. Variation in environment also determines variation in life span, so that for any one individual, life span is a function of genetic and nongenetic determinants. These determinants are not simply additive, but interact in complex ways. For example, the organism may be genetically programmed to branch to a given effect upon experience of a given environmental condition.

Genetic transmission of longevity has been demonstrated in a broad range of subhuman organisms (Comfort 1956). This is difficult to demonstrate in the human case because one cannot experimentally control the human environment. For example, long life of parent may genetically produce long life in offspring, but at the same time long life of parent may well produce a more favorable environment which could account for long-lived offspring. Actually, both factors are operating and one does not know what the relative importance of each is. Identical twin studies where the genetic endowment is largely controlled does offer some basis for determining the effect of each. Data regarding genetic transmission are presented below under genealogical studies, twin studies, and studies of special populations.

GENEALOGICAL STUDIES

The study of upper-class British genealogies (Beeton and Pearson 1899) showed a clear relationship between parental and offspring life span. Other genealogies showed the same thing. Alexander Graham Bell, the inventor of the telephone, became interested in the study of longevity in his later years and published a volume in 1918 entitled, *The Duration of Life and Conditions Associated with Longevity, a Study of the Hyde Genealogy.* Wilson and Doering (1926) also studied a single genealogy which showed a relationship in longevity of fathers and sons.

The genealogy of a Chinese family over five centuries (Yuan 1931) also showed the same relationship. Life expectancy tables of sons whose parents died at ages 20 to 29 showed lower expectancy than those whose parents died at ages 50 to 69; and these sons had lower expectancy than those whose parents died at 70 and above. The differences, however, were small after age 45.

Jalavisto (1951), the most recent student of genealogies, likewise found evidence of intergenerational transmission of longevity. Jalavisto investigated records of Finnish and Swedish nobility and middle class from 1500 to the beginning of the 20th century.

TWIN STUDIES

In his twin studies, Kallmann (1957) found smaller mean intrapair differences in longevity of identical twins than fraternal twins. Since the former were genetically more similar, and since the two types of twins were presumably similar with respect to parental care, these findings present a good case for the operation of the genetic factor as distinct from the factor of nurturance.

The greater concordance in longevity of monozygotic twins, however, tended to disappear in the oldest dying twin pairs (Jarvik et al 1960). In this case, the selective effect of survivorship necessarily decreased variability. A fraternal twin surviving to age 80 has a superior genetic endowment for longevity just as the identical twin has who survives to age 80. Therefore, the genetic concordance between 80-year-old dizygotic twins cannot be too different from the concordance between monozygotic twins.

SPECIAL POPULATION STUDIES

In order to characterize broader and more representative groups, Pearl (1931) collected primary data on age-at-death of parents and offspring in working-class families in Baltimore. Pearl took this step after he failed to find significant intergenerational relationships through genealogical material. Applying life table analysis, Pearl indeed found that parents of longer-living sons had greater life expectancy at all ages than parents of shorter-living sons; and, conversely, that sons of longer-living parents had corresponding higher life expectancies at all ages.

Pearl and Pearl (1934) tabulated the ages-at-death of parents and four grandparents and constructed an index called the "Total Immediate Ancestral Longevity" simply by summing the six ages. They then applied this index to a group of nonagenarians and earlier dying individuals from the Baltimore area, and indeed the index was higher for the longevous group. It was found, though, that about one-half the nonagenarians did not have two long-lived parents. This could only be explained on the basis of nongenetic factors neutralizing the effect of genetic factors, or at least that nongenetic determinants are also present (Korenchevsky 1961).

There were some defects in the use of this index. The requirement that all six ancestors be dead tended to overrepresent those with earlier dying ancestors, and the requirement that age-at-death be known tended to overrepresent those nonagenarians whose ancestors died at later ages because informants would find it easier to recall a more recent death.

Preas (1945) analyzed data from a Public Heath Service morbidity study in a rural county of upstate New York and was able to demonstrate intergenerational concordance in longevity. She appreciated the fact that this finding did not result from the genetic factor alone but from the combined effect of the genetic factor and concomitant favorable environmental conditions.

A study by Van Zonneveld and Polman (1957) using living persons 65 years of age and over found more of the octogenarians had parents who attained that age than did the younger subjects. If one could assume that the younger subjects will have a shorter life span than the older subjects, these findings favor the familial transmission of longevity. However, since age-at-death of either group was not available, the findings were on somewhat shaky ground.

Studies of deceased life insurance holders (Dublin, Lotka, and Spiegelman 1949) showed higher mortality rates for those with less longevous parents. The relationship was weaker for older groups, due to the "homogenizing" effect of survival, as noted in connection with senescent twin studies (Jarvik et al 1960).

A curious finding in other life insurance studies (eg, Dublin and Marks 1951) is that the living or dead status of parent at time of offspring's application for insurance is a better predictor of offspring's age-at-death than parents' age-at-death. The explanation offered by Cohen (1964) is that insurance companies require applicants with poor family survivorship to have a higher level of health than applicants with a more favorable family history. By selection, this would weaken the true relationship between survivorship of insuree and his parents. Another possibility of error is the tendency of the applicant not to reveal a poor family health history as he knows that this would result in higher premiums.

Cohen (1964) proposed an epidemiological study of the genetic basis for longevity, keeping open the possibility that similarity in familial longevity was due to environmental factors. Her proposal involved studying age of death and cause of death of deceased persons with a control group of living relatives. The groups were matched with respect to sex, birth year (the living were born within previous five years of deceased group to make sure living control would live as long as deceased), race, and neighborhood (defined in terms of "closest neighbor" to control for social class). All subjects of the study were white and native born and there were 550 deaths matched by 550 controls. The deceased were to be compared to controls within five cohort groups, defined as falling within 10-year class intervals of birth year.

The full analysis of this study has not appeared. This is unfortunate because its design controlled for the secular effect by dint of comparing living and dead groups matched for birth year. If the comparison groups were born at different times, the ability to survive could be ascribed to the differences in environment of these groups because they lived at different times.

Family Factors

In addition to the intergenerational transmission of longevity already discussed, there are a number of other family factors to be considered. These are: relative importance of maternal and paternal influence, the effect of parental age at birth of subject, a genetic mutation theory of maternal influence, birth order, and marital status. These factors involve both genetic and nongenetic effects.

MATERNAL VERSUS PATERNAL INFLUENCE

The literature is conflicting on this point. In a study of a German religious sect (Korenchevsky 1961), the effect of mother or aunt appeared to be more pronounced than that of father or uncle. Jalavisto's genealogical study concurred with this finding and in addition found that the maternal influence was stronger for sons than for daughters. Bell's genealogical data, however, showed an opposite finding: a higher percentage of offspring lived until age 80 when the father attained that age than when the mother did. Cohen (1964) also found a lower probability of survivorship in fathers of shorter-lived offspring than in mothers of shorter-lived offspring. Kallmann (1957), on the other hand, found there was no difference in the maternal and paternal effect in his identical twins studies. Although there was a definite relationship between parental and offspring life span, there was no difference whether it was the father or mother who lived longer. One wonders whether this particular finding was influenced by the special independent variable of twinning.

In general, the discrepancies in the findings can be understood in terms of the different times and associated different life expectancies represented in the different studies, as well as differences in sampling and methods of recording. With respect to whether a genetic or social effect is involved, one might say the following: greater maternal influence could be explained by a genetic hypothesis, but also by a social one, that is, a greater factor of nurturance may be operating when the mother lives longer than when the father does. (Nurturance is here defined as operating not only during the early years of offspring, but over a longer period which terminates with the mother's death.) The "no difference" finding could also be accounted for under a social hypothesis, even if genetically the father's influence was more important. One simply does not know whether these parental influences are primarily genetic or social.

PARENTAL AGE

The next area to be considered is the relationship between parental age at time of offspring's birth and offspring's longevity. This predictor may be considered a nongenetic one if one may assume there is no change in genetic influence with age. (However, there may be such change from accumulated mutations of germ cells.) This predictor also leaves open the possibility for social environmental influences in addition to nongenetic physical influences. The general findings, spanning both human and subhuman sources, point to the importance of parental age as a predictor, and to the greater importance of maternal over paternal age.

The older the mother was, the less long-lived was the offspring in rotifers, a microscopic water organism (Lansing 1954), and in rabbits (Sawin 1954). The effect also appeared in Jalavisto's Scandinavian genealogies. Older human mothers also had more neonatal mortality, premature births, and stillbirths, which suggests that surviving children would also have decreased vitality and longevity (Yerushalmy 1939; Heady et al 1955). Also consistent with these findings is the relationship between maternal age and mongolism (Penrose 1954) as well as malformations in the offspring (Murphy 1954).

Paternal age also has an effect on longevity of offspring but considerably less than that of the mother. Jalavisto found that the paternal effect was negligible, while Yerushalmy found a definite effect, but still less than that of the mother.

The findings both from the human and animal sources suggest a physical basis upon which is superimposed a sociopsychologic factor. In humans, older mothers may not only be giving offspring a poorer start because of deficiencies in the reproductive apparatus, but also may not be in as good a position psychologically (or even physically) for proper child rearing as a younger mother would. It should be kept in mind that the social norms dictate that children be borne and raised during younger years. On this basis, the younger parent has advantage over the older parent in bringing up a child. The fact that paternal age is less important is consistent with both the physical and social hypothesis, since the father is less involved in the reproductive and child-rearing process.

Yerushalmy found a curvilinear effect: *very* young mothers have more abnormal births (and, therefore, presumably less long-lived children), somewhat older (but still young) mothers have fewer abnormal births, while still older mothers again have more abnormal births. Both social and physical explanations may be made for the higher incidence of abnormal births in the immature mothers, on the basis that a certain degree of both social and physical maturity is necessary for optimal maternal functioning.

BIRTH ORDER

In addition to the findings on parental age are the highly related findings on the effect of order of birth, namely that older siblings tend to live longer (Beeton and Pearson 1901–1902; Yerushalmy 1938; Dublin et al 1949; Heady et al 1955). Obviously, as age of mother goes up, so does birth order of children successively born to her, so that birth order, for most cases, may simply be maternal age in another form. On the other hand, it is conceivable that even if maternal age is controlled, the mother's reproductive capabilities with her fourth or fifth child may not be as good as with her first and second. Unfortunately, this latter type of analysis has not been presented in the literature. On the basis of a social hypothesis, there would be somewhat less reason to believe that birth order would make any difference with maternal age controlled, since at a younger age a mother should be able to manage her younger children better than when she is giving birth to her younger children at a later age. (The case of the extremely young mother would be excepted.) In other words, in weighing the relative importance of a physical and social explanation, a physical explanation would be relatively more important in explaining effect of birth order than effect of maternal age.

A cultural view of the birth order hypothesis may also be set forth. In a society where the rule of primogeniture obtains, or where first born are more esteemed, the first born would certainly have the advantage. However, when there are opposing norms, such as in an ultimogeniture society, the first or early born would be disadvantaged, and whatever biological advantages exist may well be reversed.

A GENETIC MUTATION THEORY OF MATERNAL INFLUENCE

A genetic mutation theory to explain the relationship between maternal age and longevity of offspring has been proposed by Curtis (1963). This theory adds a genetic dimension to the nongenetic physical and social theories already set forth, and provides an intriguing example of the interdisciplinary approach in explanation.

The Curtis theory uses the molecular level of explanation, namely the DNA-RNA protein replicating system. DNA molecules make up the genes that are within the chromosomes that are within the nuclei of all cells. These molecules regulate the cell through intermediate RNA molecules. Since cell differentiation is achieved by repressor genes allowing expression of one set of genes and not that of another, differentiated cells have a great many nonfunctional DNA molecules. Thus, ordinarily, a great many nonessential DNA molecules can be destroyed without harming the cell. However, under conditions of cell division the cell could very well die or at least have an impaired function if DNA molecules have been destroyed, since cell division is the most difficult thing that a cell is called upon to do.

If DNA is being destroyed through mutations based on radiation or other physical or chemical mutagens, such deleterious effects are less apt to be passed on in dividing cells, since deleterious cells are thrown off because of their inability to survive the competition of normal cells. This is not so in nondividing cells, where deleterious effects are retained.

We now come to maternal age effect. It is widely held that ovocytes, which are all present at birth, do not undergo mitotic division during the postnatal period, and can, therefore, pass on accumulated deleterious mutations to offspring. In the male, however, the spermatogonia divide continually and thereby do not pass on deleterious mutations to germ cells because the defective spermatogonia never get to the stage of a viable gamete. Thus the older mother who has had more time to accumulate deleterious genes through mutation has a better chance to be genetically responsible for shorter life of offspring than would an older father.

In essence, the greater effect of maternal age can be explained either by social factors or other nongenetic factors. We do not know whether there is multiple causation, and what is the relative importance of the several causes. Our inclination would be to set up a model of multiple, interacting, multistep causes.

The Curtis theory on maternal age is essentially a composite of nongenetic (mutations causing deleterious genes) and genetic (passing on of deleterious genes to offspring) theories. Actually, this particular theory is a special aspect of a larger theory of aging, the somatic mutation theory, which is nongenetic in the sense that it occurs in somatic cells aside from any initial influence from germ cells. Accumulation of mutations that produce poorly functioning cells in tissues composed of nondividing cells (and most somatic cells are nondividing) causes senescence in the tissues which may eventually cause death of the organism. Thus the rate of mutations would account for age-at-death as related to aging. Evidence for this theory is that dividing cells over time do not show evidence of the chromosomal aberrations caused by mutations as do nondividing cells. Although the theory is essentially magnetic in the sense that no genetic transmission to offspring is involved, still it does involve change in the genetic material. The theory really shows that genetic and nongenetic mechanisms are not clearly separable, and further punctuates the relatedness among the domains of longevity determinants.

MARITAL STATUS

The married have greater life expectancy at all ages except for females aged 20 to 24. This exception is presumably related to the increment of risk associated with pregnancy and childbirth (Dublin et al 1949). The general finding may be ascribed to a preceding predominantly biologic factor and a succeeding predominantly social factor. By selection, those in poor health and of unfavorable temperament are less likely to marry either because they elect not to marry or are passed by. The least healthy in the population, then, tend to be screened out by the requirements of marriage. In addition, once married, the individual has the advantage of an environment more favorable to longevity, such as emotional support, better nutrition, and better chance for a spouse's care in time of illness.

It is possible that the selective health factor in entering marriage has become less important with the increase in the proportion of the population who enter marriage. Thus, during the period 1940 to 1960, there was a 10 percent increase in the numbers married (Spiegelman 1963), which means that a less healthy group may now be getting married that did not before unless, of course, there has been a general upgrading of the health of the population so that the increment getting married still falls within a health group. With greater supports from an improved socioeconomic system, it is possible that the effects of marginal health, otherwise discouraging to marriage, are being neutralized. Perhaps a little bit of each is operating: better health in the population and better socioeconomic support to compensate for poor health.

Buttressing the life expectancy figures, there is an excess mortality for the single for each of the leading causes of death. This higher mortality is more marked for males than females (Spiegelman 1963). One might speculate that females are more hardy to begin with (note the sex differential in longevity), so that health as a selective factor for entry into marriage plays a less important role for females than males. A particularly significant factor increasing mortality of the single is the greater incidence of deaths by violence among them. This factor particularly applies to males.

Social change may be weakening the advantage of the marital environment, because of relegation of kinship functions outside the kinship system, which facilitates adjustment outside of the marital bond. For example, single people can secure food, clothing, and shelter in quite acceptable ways outside of the marital or kinship bond by resorting to bachelor apartments, restaurants, laundries, and so forth, resources that were formerly not available. Beard (1962) has pointed out that relatively more "never married" individuals now survive to old age than do married individuals. In a critique appended to Beard's report, Milhoj suggested this finding was due to decreased marriage rates now manifesting themselves by more single people in older groups. Although Beard's finding should not be interpreted as a change from a positive to a negative relationship between married life and longevity, certainly the data should be seen as a straw in the wind with respect to a lessening of the importance of the marital environment for longevity.

In the future, then, the longevity differential to be accounted for by the marital environment will be lessened due to the convergence between marital and nonmarital environments with respect to their favorableness for longevity. Second, with higher marriage rates any biologic selective factor for marriage or remarriage will also play a less important role. This effect is probably facilitated by medical and socioeconomic advances which bring people into marriage who otherwise would not be. These trends, if they do materialize, will make less crucial the controversy as to the relative importance of the selective factor or the protective environment in explaining marital longevity differentials (Shurtleff 1956; Berkson 1962).

Physical Factors

Physical determinants of longevity will be discussed under autoimmune theory and environmental influences on metabolism.

AUTOIMMUNE THEORY

A special elaboration of the somatic mutation theory of aging is the autoimmune theory. This theory attempts to link basic aging processes with age-related disease states. The theory is relevant for life span because the aged usually succumb to age-related disease (Blumenthal and Berns 1964). Both incidence of age-related disease and accumulation of somatic mutations show the same logarithmic relation with age in accordance with the Gompertz equation.

The link between the somatic mutations and age-related disease under the autoimmune concept is as follows: a function of the DNA-RNA protein replicating system is to maintain immunogenetic homogeneity. The accumulation of somatic mutations, however, creates an immunogenetic diversification and injurious autoimmune reactions. Specifically, disturbance in the DNA-RNA produces protein with a different structural characteristic than has been genetically determined for the individual. The resulting autoantibodies cause cellular injury, disease, and death. The major age-related causes of death, such as cancer, degenerative cardiovascular disease, diabetes, and senile dementia have an autoimmune basis.

But aside from the molecular events triggered by mutations, social factors can be operating in the role of independent variable to the mutation process itself. Thus, social conditions or behavioral factors that increase exposure to mutagenic agents would operate in this way. This is one illustration of interaction among domains of influence on life span.

ENVIRONMENTAL INFLUENCES ON METABOLISM

In addition to mutagenic agents, the most common example of which is ionizing radiation, there are other physical factors involved in longevity insofar as it is related to aging. It should be noted that not all longevity is related to aging, for example, automobile accidents are related to longevity but not to aging; that is, a person meeting an untimely death in an automobile accident cannot be said to have aged rapidly. Aside from genetically determined interspecies differences in metabolic rates and therefore in longevity (higher metabolism goes with lower longevity), physical environmental effects related to metabolism also may account for intraspecies differences in longevity. These metabolism-related effects are temperature, feeding, and energy expenditure.

Temperature. In the Drosophila (fruit fly), longevity was lengthened by dropping the temperature (Loeb and Northrup 1917; Maynard-Smith 1959; Strehler 1961). Strehler has specifically suggested the possibility of drugs to reduce human body temperature by a degree or two for prolongation of life.

Feeding. Underfeeding (but not starving) of subhuman forms has definitely lengthened life and retarded aging (McCay 1952; Maurizio 1959). Probably overfeeding is life shortening because of excessive production of partly oxidized catabolites (Korenchevsky 1961).

Another example of accumulation of metabolic products is collagen accumulation, as in the skin, where it gives the tissue an aged appearance (Sobel et al 1958).

Life insurance company data show conclusively that obesity is related to increased mortality (Dublin and Marks 1951; Armstrong et al 1951; Metropolitan Life Insurance Company 1960). In these studies, obesity was specifically found related to higher mortality from cardiovascular and kidney disease and diabetes.

Obesity is also related to psychological conditions. During World War II food restriction in the Scandinavian countries, there was lower mortality from arteriosclerosis and coronary artery disease (Henschen 1951). Also, ethnically related food preferences as well as individual idiosyncracies could influence life span both in terms of caloric intake and nutrition.

Energy Expenditure. The factor of energy expenditure may be illustrated by the reduced longevity of heavy laborers such as coal miners, sawyers, and Chinese coolies (Pearl 1928). In this instance, the factor of energy expenditure cannot alone be held responsible, since the occupational groups involved are also subject to lower social class life conditions that would account for the reduced longevity, such as poor nutrition, poor sanitation, and so forth. (See material on social class.)

Heterosis, Race, and Sex

Before we launch into a discussion of social determinants per se, three other determinants that involve both biological and social factors will be presented. There are heterosis, race, and sex.

HETEROSIS

Heterosis, or outbreeding, is related to longer life. Thus, interbreeding of related species of ciliates enormously increased their length of life (Sonneborn 1960). In Drosophila, hybrids lived longer than their nonhybrid parents (Comfort 1956).

In the human case, on the other hand, assortative mating (inbreeding) which concentrates genetic predisposition to longer life will, of course, increase longevity of offspring, but by the same token if it concentrates genes deleterious to long life, it will decrease longevity of offspring. The social factor in this way determines mating patterns and resulting genetic patterns.

Under one set of social conditions, for example, homogamy (the sociologic equivalent of assortative mating) will encourage breeding of deleterious genes, such as occurs in the high fertility of Jukes-like families. Under another set of conditions (which may coexist with the first set), homogamy encourages breeding of healthier and longer-lived individuals, such as may occur as an extracurricular consequence of coeducational institutions of higher learning. Social mobility, both vertical and geographic, directly encourages heterosis. The social factor not only influences longevity indirectly through the gene pool, but also directly, so that the two processes may be hypothesized to be going on at the same time.

RACE

The racial differentials in mortality are well known. Using age-adjusted death rates (to control for differences in white–nonwhite age distributions) the nonwhite mortality rate was 58 percent higher than white mortality in 1900 and 47 percent higher in 1963. Using the life expectancy statistic, nonwhite life expectancy was 14.6 years less than among white individuals in 1900, and 7.1 years less in 1963 (Chase 1965). Also, racial differences are greatest among unskilled workers (Guralnick 1962). There is then a definite differential in favor of whites, although this differential has decreased since the turn of the century.

If we assume both genetic and social factors to be operating, we must say that the reduction in the differential is due to socioeconomic improvement among nonwhites rather than genetic improvement, since it is unlikely that genetic change would be operating during such a short period of time. If we take the position that there are not racial differentials on genetic grounds (as some do, see Dorn 1959), we would interpret the closing gap in mortality as due to reduction in socioeconomic differences between white and nonwhite. To determine whether a genetic component is present, it is necessary to examine white–nonwhite mortality with socioeconomic status controlled, or wait to see whether the mortality differential is wiped out along with the socioeconomic differential.

A basic problem in relating race to life span is the unreliability in assessing race from skin color and self-report, in view of widespread racial admixtures. This would weaken the validity of a race differential in a biologic sense, and would tend to give more weight to socioeconomic factors in explaining so-called racial mortality differentials.

The prevailing tendency among demographers is to interpret trends in racial mortality differences as being due entirely to socioeconomic differences (Linder and Grove 1947). Since there are genetically determined interracial differences, the inclusion of genetically determined life span differences among these biologic differences should not be rejected without definitive evidence.

SEX

There is a clear-cut female superiority in life span at all species levels. Kallman and Jarvik (1959) found that females outlived males in fruit flies, beetles, spiders, and rats. Landauer and Landauer (1931) found the same effect in chickens. In humans, females have a lower death rate at all ages in the United States as well as in all other industrialized countries (Spiegelman 1966). These cross-species findings suggest a genetic factor at the human level. A genetic factor is further suggested by female fetal superiority, with more male stillbirths occurring than female (Ciocco 1938; Dublin et al 1949).

The result is an excess of females over males, especially at older ages. For 1960, the sex ratio was 115 females to every 100 males for the age group 65 to 74, and 133 females for every 100 males for the age group 75 and over (Spiegelman 1963).

The biologic influence probably operates through the effect of the genetically based secondary sex characteristics, which produce differences in behavior, rate of metabolism, and body structure rather than through the direct effect of harmful sex-linked genes. The reason that deleterious recessive X-linked genes would not account for shorter male life span is that they would tend to be eliminated by selection (Clark 1964).

A ready-made control of social environment in Catholic orders made it possible to test the genetic hypothesis for female superiority in life span. Male and female Catholic teaching orders provided equal health conditions, fairly homogeneous strains and hazards, and removal from the differential sex roles of ordinary living. Yet the female religious showed a consistently higher life expectancy at age 45 (Madigan 1957), thereby providing evidence for a biologically based female superiority. The Madigan study is noteworthy as a sociologic study since it finds for a genetic rather than an environmental theory.

Social factors that would tend to reduce male life span include occupational hazards and greater incidence of deaths by violence (Bogue 1959). Further evidence in favor of the environmental factor is the higher mortality of females than of males in backward countries where social status and health treatment of females is low, including greater exposure to risks of larger number of pregnancies. However, in industrialized countries where mortality is low and females are no longer in a position of social inferiority, their longevity rises above that of males (Thomlinson 1965).

Related to the effect of lowered death rates in industrialized countries is the trend to increase in sex difference in life expectancy in favor of the female. In the United States in 1900, females had a higher life expectancy over males of 2.9 years. By 1964 this differential had risen to 6.9 years (Spiegelman 1966). This changing differential was related to the decline in tuberculosis and maternal mortality at younger female ages, and decline in disease related to high blood pressure at older female ages, all associated with social and medical advance. At the same time, male deaths increased because of car accidents, lung cancer, and coronary artery disease, also associated with male behavior and life styles (Enterline 1961).

Thus the reversal of sex differentials in mortality was due to social change, and the continual increase in the differential in favor of the female was apparently due to a continuation of this social process. One cannot help but feel that the underlying female biological superiority was overwhelmed under adverse environmental conditions which were targeted particularly to the female, and when these were lifted, the female was able to come into her own, in terms of longevity. Under this hypothesis, female longevity will rise still further over male longevity under conditions of continued or increased preferential social treatment.

On the basis of the most recent information from the United Nations Statistical Office, there are only six countries left (out of a total of 86 with population of over 100,000) which have a higher male life expectancy than female (Population Index 1968). These countries are Upper Volta,

Cambodia, India, Jordan, Pakistan, and Ceylon. These countries are also underdeveloped and have generally low life expectancy; for example, India has a male life expectancy of 41.9 years and female life expectancy of 40.5 years.

More favorable female longevity now appears to be fairly well stabilized. The resulting low sex ratio, especially at older ages, has had a number of social consequences, for example, a surplus of widows and female control of wealth. At the present time in the United States population, there is a seven-year differential life expectancy both racially and sexually, favoring the white and female, respectively. This differential, however, has been decreasing in the racial area and increasing in the sexual area. Specifically, the white superiority has been reduced, and male superiority has shifted to female superiority. In the racial case, the socioeconomic factor still favors the whites but less so, and this could account for the present race differential even if there were no genetic differences. In the sexual case, preferential treatment for the female may well be augmenting a female sexual superiority. In order to get at the relative importance of nature versus nurture in each case, we would have to assess the diachronic changes in social treatment for each case, at the same time comparing differences between the racial and sexual status differentials.

Social Factors

We now take up those determinants that are social in form although, of course, intimately linked with the substrate domains. These may be organized under social class, social change, population increase, geographic factor, and nativity.

SOCIAL CLASS

There is a complex of highly related social factors that powerfully influence longevity, namely social class. The three major components of social class are occupation, income, and education. These may be hypothesized to be interrelated as follows.

Higher education facilitates attainment of higher status jobs, and higher status jobs usually bring higher incomes. Higher status salaried positions are generally less hazardous to health. Lower status positions are more prone to occupational hazards such as fatigue, inorganic dusts (notably silica and asbestos), absorption of poisons, excessive heat, and sudden variations in temperature and dampness. For example, Whitney (1934) found the mortality rate of unskilled workers almost double that of professional workers. Higher status positions also have more liberal sick leave benefits, which make it unnecessary to stay on the job when one should be home nursing one's health. Higher education, in addition to placing individuals into "healthier" occupational roles, also sensitizes individuals to the importance of health maintenance and the availability of health-maintaining resources. Higher income, which also goes with higher education and healthier occupation, furthers implementation of health-maintaining resources such as food, clothing, housing, and medical care. Poverty and economic status are thus powerful predictors of longevity (Stevenson 1921; Altendorfer 1947).

This complex of factors creates or negates the optimum environment for the attainment of the biologic life span. The fact that the environmental optimum has not yet been reached in the United States despite its standard of living, technology, and so forth is suggested by the even lower mortality of the Scandinavian countries and the Netherlands. There is no reason to believe that the gene pools involved are any different with respect to longevity (National Center for Health Statistics 1964). On the basis of the latest available information from the United Nations Statistical Office, 22 countries have a higher male life expectancy at birth than the United States, and eight have higher female life expectancy (Population Index 1968).

In addition, the more physically and mentally competent selectively tend to occupy the higher status occupations. Thus, there is a double effect: the genetically superior with respect to longevity are better able to elbow their way into the more protected and lucrative occupational roles which, in turn, augment even further on nongenetic grounds any genetic predisposition to longevity. The genetic factor not only favors longevity in its own right but also indirectly favors longer life by inducing a more favorable environment such as is associated with higher occupational status. This is schematized in Figure 1. Please note that effects A and B are synchronic, while effect C is lagged. The testing of this hypothesis would be difficult, however, because of the lagged effect and problems in measuring presence of genetic endowment for longevity.

The contribution to the mortality rate of general life styles which accompany given educational and occupational status has been neatly demonstrated by the reports of the Registrar-General of England and Wales (1938). Since the age-at-death of spouse is recorded on the death certificate, it is possible to find out whether there is any concordance in longevity between husband and wife. It was found that the mortality of husbands was in accordance with their occupation, and the mortality of wives followed that of their husbands. This suggested a general life cycle factor related to an occupationally determined social class position which contributed to mortality, rather than merely the particular conditions of husband's occupation.

The correspondence in the English case between social class and mortality seems to be strengthened by the more rigid correspondence between occupation and social class. For example, despite tremendous reduction in infant mortality, the social class mortality relationship has persisted in England, more so than in the United States (Logan 1954). This would also appear to be related to social class mobility, so that in an "open" society there would tend to be less rigid correspondence between

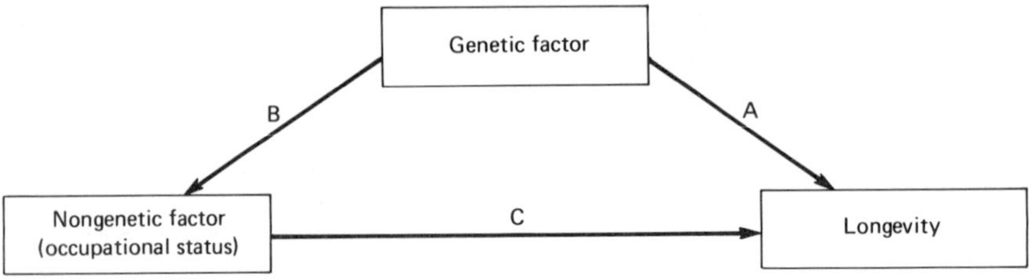

FIG. 1. Genetic factor, occupational status, and longevity.

occupation and social class. Also, with more upward mobility there is some breakdown of social class verticality and life style differentiation.

Intelligence. An early Metropolitan Life Insurance Company study (1932) showed that college graduates from eight eastern colleges had a better life expectancy than the general white male population, and honor men among the college graduates had an even better life expectancy. If we may assume the honor men to be an especially intelligent group, this suggests that intelligence is also a longevity determinant. Terman's gifted children at midlife did indeed show better longevity characteristics than would be expected at their age group (Terman and Oden 1959).

Assuming that distinguished professional and business men listed in the *Who's Who in America* are intellectually superior to the general population, the finding about their superior longevity (Metropolitan Life Insurance Company 1968) is also evidence for the relationship between intelligence and longevity. The age-specific mortality of a sample of the *Who's Who* listing was compared to the mortality of the general white population in similar occupations. For all ages studied (45 to 64) the mortality of the *Who's Who* group was more than half that of the general population. The best longevity within the *Who's Who* group was that of scientists, and the poorest was that of journalists. If *Who's Who* scientists and journalists are equally well endowed intellectually, we would infer that scientists have the most favorable vocationally related environment and the journalists the least favorable. This inference can only be made for the top scientists and top journalists, however. In any case these data suggest the interplay between environmental and genetic effects.

SOCIAL CHANGE

At any one time there is a variation in mortality by social class. Over time, there has also been a trend to less hazardous occupation, and shifting of the occupational distribution over to higher status roles (nonmanual, salaried, and technical). In short, there has been a shift from lower status to middle-class occupational roles (Spiegelman

1963). Life expectancy of United States whites doubled in the two and a half centuries up to roughly 1950, due to the additional resources and *Lebensraum* of the new world, distribution technology, industrial and agricultural technology, and control of disease by medical technology.

Longevity and concomitant technologic changes across nations have not been even. An example is the mortality difference between Sweden and the Moslem population of Algeria, which corresponds to the difference between Sweden today and Sweden 175 years ago (Dorn 1959). Despite such unevenness, the general direction of social change has involved advances in industrial and medical technology, better food supply, better income, and more widespread education. This has also had a homogenizing effect on life styles across social class so that, in effect, the social class mortality differentials have shrunk (Dublin and Vance 1947; Guralnick 1962). In turn, this has correspondingly shrunk mortality differentials in such a way that the overall mortality rates have decreased.

POPULATION INCREASE

The reduction of infant mortality and mortality from infectious disease during early adult years have enabled more survival to later years and provided a larger base for increased numbers of long-lived people. In addition, the reduction of mortality from chronic disease during later years through medical and surgical advance has added even further to a large number of longer-lived people. Survival of greater numbers of females into reproductive years has also helped to increase the population. Better living conditions also tend to increase fertility so that still another factor is operative to increase population.

The problem of overpopulation is particularly acute when medical technology is brought in before industrialization and its concomitant rise in education occurs. In a developed country, industrialization has already produced medical technology plus a higher level of education. In this case, medical technology serves to increase the population, but higher educational levels act as a brake. In the case of the developing country, however, medical technology is imported and wreaks its effect on population growth before industrialization and higher educational levels begin to have their retarding effect.

The result is two-pronged: excessive population growth and poverty. Growth is excessive because education is not present to brake it, and poverty is rampant because industrialization has not yet developed sufficiently to create needed jobs and consumer goods. Thus the crucial variable in determining whether longer life leads to overpopulation is education. Education plays a homeostatic role: it increases population by increasing longevity, and decreases population by decreasing fertility.

If overpopulation does occur, whether as a result of increased births or increased longevity at various ages, or both (the mix is different in different places, depending on age distribution, educational distribution, status of public health, and industrial development), it may eventually create deleterious effects of air and water pollution, and deleterious social effects of population density, which in the end can only reduce the life span.

Another danger to longevity levels may arise from the thwarting of natural selection which will adversely affect life expectancy during later adult years. Such can occur by maintaining through medical technology deleterious gene groups into the reproductive period (which generates further deleterious genes), and maintaining such adults beyond the reproductive period so that they develop degenerative age-related disease. This effect, if any, will be apparent after the death of those cohorts who survived the selective screening effect of infectious disease in early life. The result will depend on the etiology of age-related disease, whether genetic, environmental, or a particular interplay between them.

Thus, we are faced with the possibility of a curvilinear relationship between technology and longevity: low longevity with low technology, high longevity with high technology, and lower longevity at still higher levels of technology. With a finite limitation to *Lebensraum*, there will have to be finite limitation to the product of population times longevity. Beyond a certain level of population increase, longevity will have to decrease, and beyond a certain level of longevity, population will have to be controlled. We trust that it will be the latter.

The relationship between social change, longevity, and population size as sketched calls for the ability to predict longevity from social factors, and the examination of this relationship as social change occurs over time, in order to provide guidelines for the maintenance of balance between longevity change and population growth.

GEOGRAPHIC FACTOR

Cross-national differences are closely related to differences in standard of living (Dublin et al 1949), including adequacy of food supply and medical and public health practice. Within the United States, this shows up clearly in North-South differentials, even when controlling for race. The highest mortality rates in the country were in the mountain states which contain a large concentration of Spanish-Americans who live under extremely poor health conditions (Dublin et al 1949). The agricultural states of the Midwest, with its low population density, had the lowest mortality. Next lowest were the industrial states of the Northeast.

Later census figures showed that at younger ages New England had the lowest mortality and at older ages the agricultural midwestern area has the lowest mortality (Thomlinson 1965). The finding on New England probably reflects the excellent public health standards of that area, while for the midwestern agricultural area, other factors are probably reflected, such as favorable living standards combined with those characteristics of low density areas conducive to lower mortality. The fact that areas of the country with more benign climates but lower economic levels than New England or the Midwest have higher mortality suggests that economic characteristics are more important than climate.

The favorable finding regarding low density areas is less marked with the spread of urban life styles into rural areas. As of the 1950 census, however, white farmers still had the lowest mortality rates of all occupational groups (Guralnick 1962). Aside from the rural-urban life style variable, which is probably diminishing in importance, one should look for differences in delivery of medical services and age and sex composition (Thomlinson 1965) to explain any mortality differences. In rural areas, the dominant causes of death tend to be those that could be conquered by modern medicine while in the cities they tend to be more those that are beyond "the state of the art" of modern medicine (Thomlinson 1965). On these grounds, rural mortality should improve even further over urban mortality differential. Another factor may be faulty definitions of the hand, the increasing presence of females and younger people in the cities would tilt favorable mortality to urban areas.

The favorable mortality picture of rural areas may also be due to sick rural dwellers moving to cities in order to have access to better medical treatment; also, rural dwellers often die in urban hospitals. Such cases are credited to urban mortality, and serve to increase the urban-rural mortality differential. Another factor may be faulty definitions of the rural-urban variable which do not use criteria other than that of community size. Because of such problems, the findings cited herein must be regarded as tentative and even unreliable.

NATIVITY

Somewhat related to the geographic factor is the case of the immigrant from a foreign country. Although this is a disappearing problem because of decreasing immigration since before World War I, it does provide a dramatic illustration of the importance of the social class factor. With the immigrant, there is involved an unsatisfactory environmental factor motivating the immigration in the first place, plus the stress of adjusting to a new environment which is accompanied by the additional stress of low social status. These factors are illustrated by the life expectancy differential in 1900 between native born and foreign born. At that time, for age 20, native born expectancy was 43.2 years and foreign born expectancy was 40.7 years. By 1930 the gap had narrowed to one year (Dublin et al 1949). These figures are best explained by the secular improvement in conditions with which the immigrant is faced upon his arrival, plus the fact that later immigrants were not as impoverished as the pre-World War I group.

Another effect is upward mobility over time. This is shown by the following: in 1900, the standardized death rate of foreign born at all ages was 20 percent over that of native born, and by 1940 the death rates were equal. During this period the foreign born actually had a greater rate of improvement in their mortality than native born, the foreign born decreasing 47 percent in death rate and the native born decreasing 35 percent (Dublin et al 1949). This was due, at least in part, to the foreign born starting with a more unfavorable death rate (with more room for improvement) but the "recovery" capabilities of immigrants are still impressive. It also might be noted that the nativity differentials were less than the sex and race differentials previously discussed. Very crudely, this might be explained by the absence of any biologic factors in the nativity differential, although arguments could be made to explain the smaller nativity differential on sociologic grounds alone, particularly the difference between racial and nativity differentials.

Two Interdisciplinary Studies

It should be abundantly clear from the foregoing review that there is a complex determinancy of longevity with interactions among various domains of determinants. Two studies will be presented that llustrate the interdisciplinary approach through multivariate analysis of variables from both physical and social domains. The first study was conducted by Palmore (1969a, 1969b, 1971) at the Duke University Center for the Study of Aging and Human Development. The second study was conducted by the authors at the Veterans Administration Normative Aging Study in Boston (Rose and Bell 1971).

PALMORE STUDY

Essentially, this investigator demonstrated how the predictive power of life table expectancy terms can be improved by adding physical and social variables to the age, sex, and race predictors already built into the table.

In 1955, 268 subjects (median age 70) of a longitudinal aging study at Duke University were first examined. By 1968, 121 of these subjects had died. The remaining 147 were assigned a survival of 13 years, the lapse of time between 1955 to 1968, plus the expected number of years of additional life based on actuarial tables for North Carolina for their age, sex, and race. This procedure yielded the survival (remaining years of life) for all cases, living and dead. This was used as the criterion variable for a multiple regression and analysis. Predictor variables for the regression analysis were the life expectancy of the subjects as of 1955 taken from actuarial tables, plus five other predictors taken from the 1955 examination.

Results of the analysis showed that two of the five variables increased the variance explained by the criterion by less than 1 percent. These two were dropped, leaving the life expectancy variables plus the following three: (1) a physical functioning rating based on medical history, physical examination, audiogram, chest X-ray, electroencephalogram, electrocardiogram, and blood and urine studies; (2) a work satisfaction score; and (3) the performance score of the Wechsler Adult Intelligence Scale.

The life expectancy term alone explained 31.5 percent of the variance in the criterion. The additional three variables increased the explained variance as follows:

Actuarial expectancy	31.5%
Physical functioning	5.9%
Work satisfaction	1.9%
Intelligence	1.1%
Total variance	40.4%

When the expectancy term was not inserted into the procedure, the three other variables explained 20.2 percent of the variance. Thus the expectancy term was in part summing up the effects of the other variables because of some correlation with them.

In another analysis, Palmore removed the expectancy term from the predictor set and used it to construct a new criterion, the longevity quotient, made up of the original criterion (actual years remaining) divided by the expectancy term (actuarially expected years remaining). This was done to control for the effect of age on the original criterion: Older subjects died earlier during the period 1955 to 1968, or, if still alive as of 1968, had a lower expectancy. The longevity quotient controlled for age by showing how much more or less an individual survived than the average of his own age.

With the longevity quotient as a dependent variable, the four best predictors for males in order of importance were: work satisfaction, happiness rating, physical functioning, and smoking. For males age 70 and over, physical functioning was more important than work satisfaction and happiness. Palmore found no relationship between parental and subject's longevity, which he felt supported an environmentalist rather than a genetic basis for longevity.

ROSE AND BELL STUDY

A special longevity study was undertaken in connection with the Veterans Administration Normative Aging Study. The Veterans Administration project is a longitudinal, interdisciplinary study which will eventually yield findings on the prediction of life span. The special study was undertaken for two reasons: to develop methodology for prediction of life span both in measurement techniques and data analysis, and to identify predictors for building into the long-term design of the longitudinal study. The special study used a "one shot" technique, described below, to yield immediate findings, in contrast to the longitudinal design which, although an optimal approach methodologically, involves a protracted waiting period.

The data were obtained by interviewing next of kin of 500 recently deceased males from the Boston area. There were 69 variables selected for insertion into various univariate and multivariate procedures. By this method 15 to 25 variables were found to be significantly involved. In the regression analysis the criterion was the continuous variable age-at-death, which ranged in the sample from 50 to 90, while in the discriminant analysis the criterion was age-at-death below 70, and 70 and above, representing the dichotomization at the mean of the age-at-death distribution. The same variables plus age-at-death were also inserted into factor analyses of the full population and parallel factor analyses of the lower and upper age-at-death groups.

A preliminary hypothesis-generating study was conducted on Spanish-American War veterans (Rose 1964). These living octogenarians were evaluated with respect to social characteristics which appeared to be survivor characteristics in that they deviated from demographic norms. These variables were then tested in the study of the 500 deceased Bostonians.

In the univariate analysis by zero order correlation, the 10 best predictors in order of importance were:

1. not smoking cigarettes,
2. fewer illnesses, age 40 to 49,
3. less worried,
4. amount of smoking,
5. better health, age 40 to 49,
6. looked younger than age up to age 40,
7. fewer illnesses, age 30 to 39,
8. more off-the-job physical activity, age 40 to 49,
9. younger wife,
10. conserved energy.

A factor analysis of the full population produced two factors on which age-at-death loaded highly. The first included higher occupational levels, greater ability (intelligence and school performance), more off-job physical activity, and less drinking. The second life span related factor included more on-job physical activity, not smoking cigarettes, and less worried. Amount of cigarette smoking appeared in a third factor, which was primarily a health factor, on which age-at-death, however, did not load.

Parallel factor analyses of the earlier and later dying subpopulation each produced one life span related factor. In the earlier dying group the most prominent loadings were less on-job physical activity and longer life. In the later dying group, the most prominent loadings were optimism, sense of humor, and longer life. Thus, physical factors are more predictive of life span under age 70, and psychological factors are more predictive of later age at death.

Linear discriminant analysis placed younger wife, health ratings, and age-at-death of mother in more important predictive position than did the previous analyses. Also, physical activity variables appeared in a lesser position of importance. Results from regression analysis were similar.

An unsolved problem in this research is the secular effect. In the design used, it was necessary for subjects to be born at different times in order to have different ages at death and still die within the same year. It was necessary for deaths to occur within the same year because, for the purpose of a reliable "one shot" data collection from a survivor, it was important that the death occur one to three months before the interview. Likewise, the logistics of conducting a time-constrained research made it necessary to cluster the interviews within a circumscribed period. The next major step in the research is to carry out a "one shot" yet secular free design, as previously described, along the lines suggested by Cohen (1964).

This is important because many of the variables one would want to use are susceptible to contamination from this source. Examples are smoking and education. Since smoking has increased over time, subjects born earlier (and therefore older at death) would have been smoking less. Likewise, subjects born earlier would have a lower education. In both cases, less smoking and less education could not be assumed to be predictors of longer life, but merely characteristics of older age cohorts. A secular free design as suggested by Cohen would compare longevity characteristics of similar age cohorts and, therefore, avoid the problem.

References

Altenderfer MD: Relationship between per capita income and mortality in cities of 100,000 or more population. Public Health Reports 62:1681, 1947

Armstrong D, Dublin L, Wheatley G, et al: Obesity and its relation to health and disease. JAMA 147:1007, 1951

Beard BB: Longevity and the never married. In Tibbetts C, Donahue W (eds): Social and Psychological Aspects of Aging. New York, Columbia Univ Press, 1962, pp 36–50

Beeton M, Pearson K: Data for the problem of evolution in man, II: A first study of the inheritance of longevity and the selective death-rate in man. Proc R Soc Med 65:290–305, 1899

———: On the inheritance of the duration of life, and on the intensity of natural selection in man. Biometrics 1:50–89, 1901–1902

Bell AG: The Duration of Life and Conditions Associated with Longevity, A Study of the Hyde Genealogy. Washington, DC, Genealogical Record Office, 1918

Berkson J: Mortality and marital status: reflections on the deviation of etiology from statistics. Am J Public Health 52:1318–1326, 1962

Blumenthal HT, Burns AW: Autoimmunity and aging. In Strehler BL (ed): Advances in Gerontological Research, vol. 1. New York, Academic Press, 1964, pp 289–342

Bogue D: The Population of the United States. Glencoe, Ill, Free Press, 1959, p 197

Chase HC: White–Non-White Mortality Differentials in the United States. HEW Indicators, June 1965, pp 27–38

Ciocco A: The masculinity of stillbirths and abortions in relation to the duration of uterogestation and to the stated causes of foetal mortality. Hum Biol 10:235, 1938

Clark AM: Genetic factors associated with aging. In Strehler BL (ed): Advances in Gerontological Research. New York, Academic Press, 1964, pp 207–255

Cohen BH: Family patterns of mortality and life span. Rev Biol 39:130–181, June 1964

Comfort A: The Biology of Senescence. New York, Rinehart, 1956

Curtis HJ: Biological mechanisms underlying the aging process. Science 141:686–694, 1963

Dorn HF: Mortality. In Hauser PM, White OD (eds): The Study of Population. Chicago, Univ Chicago Press, 1959, Chap 19

Dublin LI, Lotka AJ, Spiegelman M: Length of Life. New York, Ronald Press, 1949

Dublin LI, Marks HH: Overweight shortens life. Statistical Bull, Metropolitan Life Insurance Co., 32:1, 1951

Dublin LI, Vance RJ: Occupational mortality experience of insured wage earners. Monthly Labor Rev 64:1003, 1947

Enterline PE: Causes of death responsible for recent increases in sex mortality differential in U.S. Milbank Memorial Fund Q 39:312–328, 1961

Gruman GJ: A History of Ideas about the Prolongation of Life. The Evolution of Prolongevity Hypotheses to 1800. Trans Am Philos Soc vol 56, part 9, 1966

Guralnick L: Mortality by Occupation and Industry among Men 20 to 64 Years of Age: United States, 1950. Vital Statistics—Special Reports, Sept 1962, vol 53, no. 2, pp 59–70

Heady JA, Daly C, Morris JN: Social and biological factors in infant mortality. II: Variation of mortality with mother's age and parity. Lancet 1:395, 1955

Henschen F: Pathogenesis of arteriosclerosis in the light of food restriction on Scandinavia during the war. J Gerontol 6:102, 1951

Jalavisto E: Inheritance of longevity according to Finnish and Swedish genealogies. Ann Clin Res 40:163–274, 1951

Jarvik LF, Falek A, Kallmann FJ, Lorge I: Survival trends in a senescent twin population. Am J Hum Genet 12:170–179, 1960

Kallmann FJ: Twin data on the genetics of aging. In Wolstenholme GEW, O'Connor CM (eds): Methodology of the Study of Aging. London, J. A. Churchill, 1957, pp 131–143

———, Jarvik LF: Individual differences in constitution and genetic background. In Birren JE (ed): Handbook of Aging and the Individual. Chicago, Univ Chicago Press, 1959, pp 216–263

Korenchevsky V: Physiological and Pathological Aging. New York, Hafner, 1961, pp 12, 16

Landauer W, Landauer AB: Chick mortality and sex-ratio in domestic fowl. Am Naturalist 65:492–501, 1931

Lansing AI: The influence of parental age on longevity in rotifers. J Gerontol 3:6, 1948

Linder FE, Grove RD: Vital Statistics Rates in the United States: 1900–1940. Washington, DC Govt Prtg Office, 1947, p 12

Loeb J, Northrup HH: On the influence of food and temperature upon the duration of life. J Biol Chem 32:103–121, 1917

Logan WPD: Social Class Variations in Mortality. Public Health Reports, Dec. 1954, vol 69, no 12, pp 1217–1223

Madigan FC: Are sex mortality differentials biologically caused? Milbank Memorial Fund 35:202–23, 1957

Maurizio A: Factor influencing the lifespan of bees. In Wolstenholme GE, O'Connor CM (eds): The Lifespan of Animals. Boston, Little, Brown, 1959, pp 231–246

Maynard-Smith J: The rate of aging in drosophila subobscura. In Wolstenholme GE, O'Connor CM (eds): The Lifespan of Animals. Boston, Little, Brown, 1959, p 267

McCay CM: Chemical aspects of aging and the effect of diet upon aging. In Lansing AI (ed): Cowdry's Problems of Aging. Baltimore, Williams and Wilkins, 1952, pp 139–202

Metropolitan Life Insurance Co.: College Men Long Lived. Statistical Bull 13(8), 1932

———: Longevity of Prominent Men. Statistical Bull 49(1), 1968

———: Mortality Among Overweight Men. Statistical Bull 41(2):8, 1960

Murphy DP: The birth of congenitally malformed children in relation to maternal age. Ann NY Acad Sci 57:503, 1954

National Center for Health Statistics: The Change in Mortality Trend in the United States. Vital and Health Statistics, P.H.S. Pub. No. 1000, series 3, no 1, Public Health Service, Washington, DC, 1964

Palmore EG: Physical, mental and social factors in predicting longevity. Gerontologist 9:105–108, 1969a

———: Predicting longevity—a followup controlling for age. Gerontologist 9:247–250, 1969b

———: Longevity predictors—implications for practice. Postgrad Med 50:164, 1971

Pearl R: The Rate of Living. New York, Knopf, 1928

———: Studies on human longevity, IV: the inheritance of longevity. Hum Biol 3:245–269, 1931

———, Pearl RD: The Ancestry of the Long-Lived. Baltimore, Johns Hopkins Press, 1934

Penrose LS: Mongolian idiocy and maternal age. Ann NY Acad Sci 57:494, 1954

Population Index: Complete Expectation of Life at Various Ages in Selected Countries. Vol. 34, Oct–Dec 1968. Princeton, NJ, Office of Population Research, Princeton University, pp 513–517

Preas S: Length of life of parents of offspring in a rural community. Milbank Memorial Fund Q 23:180–196, 1945

Registrar-General's Decennial Supplement: England and Wales, 1931, Part IIa. London, Occupational Mortality, 1938

Rose CL: Social factors in longevity. Gerontologist 4:27, 1964

———, Bell B: Predicting Longevity: Methodology and Critique. Lexington, Mass, Heath, 1971

Sawin PB: The influence of age of mother on pattern of reproduction. Ann NY Acad Sci 57:564–574, 1954

Shurtleff D: Mortality among the married. J Am Geriat Soc 4:654, 1956

Sobel H, Gabay S, Wright ET et al: The influence of age upon the hexosamine-collagen ratio of dermal biopsies from men. J Gerontol 13:128–131, 1958
Sonneborn TM: Enormous differences in length of life of closely related ciliates and their significance. In Strehler BL, Ebert JD, Glass HB, Shock NW (eds): The Biology of Aging. Washington, DC, Am Instit Biol Soc 1960, Pub. No. 6
Spiegelman M: The changing demographic spectrum and its implications for health. Eugen Q 10:161–174, 1963
———: Significant Mortality and Morbidity Trends in U. S. since 1900. Bryn Mawr, Penn, Am Coll of Life Underwriters, 1966, p 23
Stevenson THC: The incidence of mortality upon the rich and poor districts of Paris and London. J Roy Stat Soc 80:90, 1921
Strehler BL: Studies on the comparative physiology of aging. II: On the mechanism of temperature life-shortening in drosophila melanogaster. J Gerontol 16:2–12, 1961
Terman LM, Oden MH: The Gifted Group at Mid-Life. Palo Alto, Stanford Univ Press, 1959, p 29
Thomlinson R: Population Dynamics, Causes and Consequences of World Demographic Change. New York, Random House, 1965, pp 131–133
van Zonneveld RJ, Polman A: Hereditary factors in longevity. Acta Genet Statist Med 7:160–162, 1957
Whitney JS: Death Rates of Occupation Based on Data on the U. S. Census Bureau, 1930. New York, Natl Tuberculosis Assoc, June 1934. Cited by Dublin et al, 1934, pp 213–214
Wilson EB, Doering CR: The elder pierces. Proc Nat Acad Sci U S A 12:424–432, 1926
Yerushalmy J: Neonatal mortality by order of birth and age of parents. Am J Hyg 28:244, 1938
Yuan I-Chin: Life tables for a Southern Chinese family from 1365 to 1849. Hum Biol 3:157–179, 1931

4

THE PSYCHOLOGY OF NORMAL AGING

Andrew S. Dibner, Ph.D.

How Old Are You?

How old are you? As old as you look? As old as you act? Actually, most people, when asked that question, would reply by giving a number—their age in years. Some might think of their age in years but not want to say it, for that magic number, if it is thought to be "too high," brings up negative connotations of old age, and they would rather not be judged by an unfair standard. Psychologic research lends support to this skepticism about the importance of chronologic age because, although many changes in structure and function of the aging person have been documented, it has also been documented that there is great variability among individuals at any age, and this variability increases with age. Thus, applying a conception of age behavior based upon group results to any individual may be much in error. Some 40-year-olds are biologically older than some 80-year-olds, and any individual might "age" much more or less during one discrete time period in his life than in another.

CHRONOLOGIC AGE

This deceptively simple figure, chronologic age, has led to much misunderstanding in gerontology. Chronologic age is not an attribute of a person. It is a concept external to the person, a dimension along which he is existing, but not affecting him directly. It is almost as if, when each person is born, a clock is set ticking. The clock works independently of the person—he cannot make it slow down or go faster—and it ticks at the same rate for everyone, marking the days and years at a constant clip. Any changes occurring in the individual, however, occur at a pace unique to him, and the pace may change and vary. Only for large groups of persons might averaged results show a relationship to the clock. To try to understand any one person's condition in relation to age, therefore, necessitates the assumption, for example, that since people in general "slow down" in old age, Mr. X does too. Actually, group results are subject to error in interpretation. Take, for example, a group result of poorer performance on a timed test of finger dexterity. The averaged score for an older group may show a lowered score, but it may be that only those who are sick are slowing down, thus lowering the group average. There may be no change at all in speed for many. Such an error of interpretation has been pointed out by Schaie (1970) and others shedding doubt on previous studies of intellectual decline in old age. (See later section on intelligence.)

Thus, using chronologic age as an indicator for an individual, and using group data to provide "proof" of changes with age can be highly misleading. Why then do we use chronologic age? Mainly because it is so quantifiable and so easily obtained compared to other, perhaps more meaningful indicators such as biologic age or social or psychologic age. At this point there are few who could agree on practical definitions of the last named concepts, whereas chronologic age is comfortably accepted by all who have not given serious thought to its shortcomings.

CROSS-SECTIONAL VERSUS LONGITUDINAL STUDIES

The method of psychologic study most used in relation to aging has been the cross-sectional method. Typically, the characteristics or performance of younger and older groups of subjects are compared and differences are attributed to the difference in age. We have learned how unreasonable this very reasonable approach can be. Are the subjects in the various age groups comparable? How can they possibly be? The good investigator would try to match subjects on all pertinent variables, not just the ones being subjected to scrutiny. But how can one match on education, for example, when the cultural norm on education has shown such shifts from generation to generation? It is obvious that if one sought only college graduate 80-year-olds to compare with college graduate 25-year-olds, you would have a group of old people that is superselected compared to the more common sample of young adults.

The same error is made in health matching. We would want the age groups to be comparable on health if we are focusing on age differences, not health differences. But any group of 80-year-olds has already demonstrated that its members are superior physical specimens because they are still alive. A sample of young adult would certainly include many who would not live to the age of 80.

Does the longitudinal study overcome the shortcomings of the cross-sectional method? In the longitudinal study, the same individuals are repeatedly examined at different time periods to look for changes in persons rather than differences between different persons who are of different ages. Even in the longitudinal study approach there is the possibility of error in understanding. The "changes" we see at different time periods may actually be due to "environmental effects" (Schaie 1970) rather than changes in the individual. Tests given the same person at different times may have different meanings to him because of practice effects or differences in testing circumstances.

Longitudinal studies more closely approach the measurement of age changes rather than age differences, but such studies are so difficult to pursue that they are not often attempted. They take many years to complete, requiring long-term commitments from experimenters and funding agencies. Also the subject samples undergo losses through death and removal or loss of motivation, introducing progressive errors in repeated testings.

BIOLOGIC, SOCIAL, AND PSYCHOLOGIC AGE

The concept "biologic aging" generally considers physical changes in the organism which have been found in general to be associated with aging. These changes may be in cell structures, organ systems, or their functioning. "Social age" refers to socially ascribed roles that a person fills, roles that then dictate his expected social behavior. The role of grandmother, retired person, old man—these are examples of socially ascribed roles for the aged.

Psychologic age refers to age-correlated changes in the person's behavior as a unique individual in perceiving, in feeling, thinking, and acting. In this chapter we will consider results of behavioral studies of age differences and age changes, then consider the relationship of psychologic aging to biologic and social factors.*

PSYCHOLOGIC CHANGES WITH AGE

We see each person existing as part of a psychologic life space (Lewin 1954). Each individual with his capabilities, potentials, and limitations is always behaving within a context—surrounded by stimuli in his social and physical environment at the same time he is stimulated by an inner environment containing his past experiences, his goals and motivations, his values. To understand a person's behavior, we must know his present physical state, the way he senses, perceives, and organizes stimulation, his present environmental context, and the influences of his inner state. One can readily understand the complexity and variation in human behavior when it is conceptualized in this manner, for obviously each of these aspects of psychologic life space act in dynamic interaction with each other.

**The serious student is referred to these excellent texts and handbooks which give more detailed summaries of research findings: Birren 1959; Bromley 1974; Riley and Foner 1968; Eisdorfer and Lawton, 1973.*

CHANGES IN SENSATION

Vision. Visual and auditory efficiency have been found to decline in old age. Many factors seem to be responsible. In the eye, pupil size and reactivity often are reduced, leading to reduction in light reaching the retina. Also, the eye reacts slowly to dark adaptation, creating poor vision especially in low illumination. Older people may have difficulty seeing well at night. Visual acuity under most conditions is drastically reduced in old age especially after the age of 65 to 70 (Fig. 1).

Not only are detection thresholds lowered but discrimination thresholds are lowered even more. The *detection threshold* is the minimum amount of energy to which a person is responsive. For example, the minimal intensity of light that he can perceive against a background is said to be a detection threshold. The *discrimination threshold* is the minimal change in any stimulus that is noticeable to the observer. The change must be proportionate to the original intensity of the stimulus in order to be noticed. That is, if a stimulus is weak, more subtle changes can be observed. The more intense the stimulus, the greater it must change for the change to be noticed. This constant relationship of stimulus intensity to change is called the Weber ratio.

Significantly, the Weber ratio is found to increase with age, requiring still greater magnitudes of change for changes to be perceived. Probably related to this effect is the fact that the aged need greater contrast between figure and background than do younger people. In general, they need greater intensity of light to see as well as younger subjects.

Color vision is not as well understood for the aged as other aspects of vision, but there is some evidence that as a result of structural changes in the eye, blues, greens, and violets are harder for the older person to

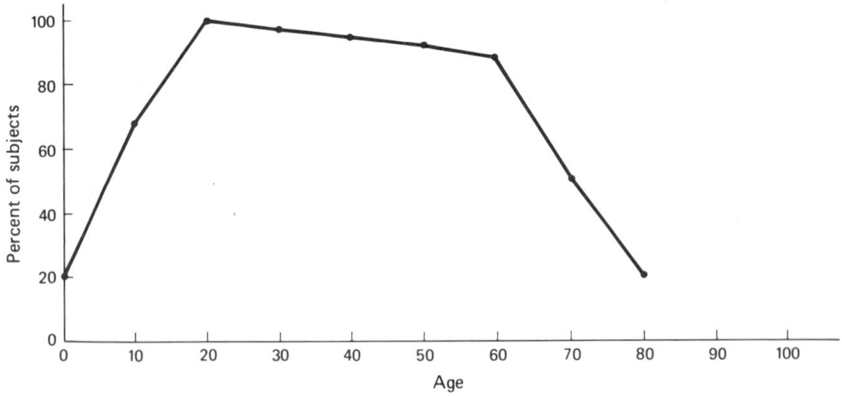

FIG. 1. Changes in visual acuity with age. Percent of subjects having normal 5/5 acuity at different ages. (Adapted from Weiss: In Birren (ed): Handbook of Aging and the Individual: Psychological and Biological Aspects, 1959, p 510, Courtesy of the University of Chicago Press.)

distinguish. There seems to be little change with age in ability to see stimuli at the periphery of the visual field except under low illumination.

One other visual phenomenon is important to mention, and that is the Critical Flicker Fusion (CFF) phenomenon. This is the perception of steady light that occurs when a light is flashed at fast enough frequency. There is a decline in CFF in old age, meaning that the older person is slower to perceive separate stimuli. Although decrease in retinal size is partly responsible, retinal changes and central nervous system changes also play a part. This evidence of a timing change in visual perception is mirrored in timing changes in other perceptual, performance, and cognitive functions in the aged.

Hearing. Hearing deficiencies are common in older persons. These changes are so common and so subtle in their onset through the adult years that many individuals have hearing loss of which they are unaware. The main changes in hearing appear in the upper frequencies with decline beginning at age 10 for sound at 17,000 cycles/second. In general, the older the adult the lower is his ceiling for perception of high frequency sounds (maximum of 12,000 cycles at age 65). Also, the intensity must be greater if sounds of any frequency are to be perceived (Fig. 2).

The changes in hearing illustrated in Figure 2 are for pure tones, and

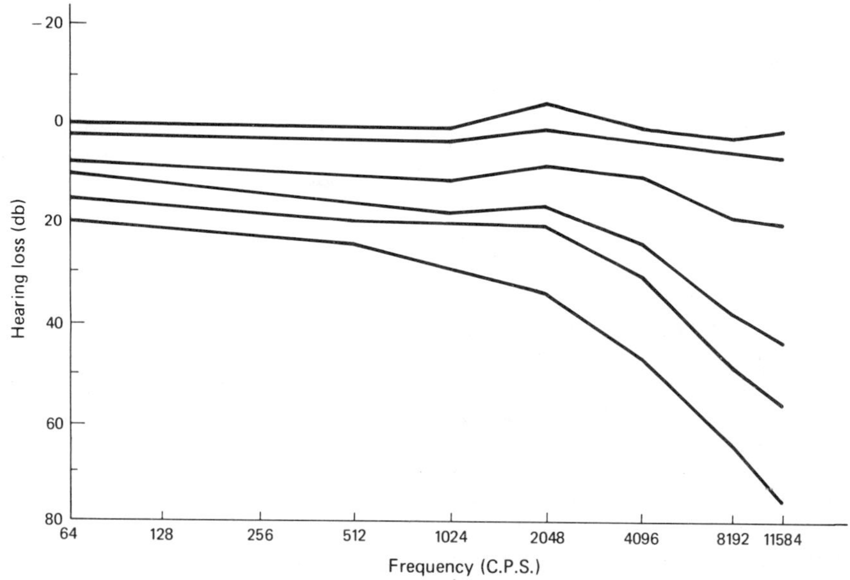

***FIG.* 2.** Hearing loss at various frequencies with age. a) 11–15 yrs, b) 21–25 yrs, c) 41–45 yrs, d) 51–55 yrs, e) 61–65 yrs, f) 70–82 yrs. (Adapted from Weiss: In Birren (ed): Handbook of Aging and the Individual: Psychological and Biological Aspects, 1959, p 521. Courtesy of the University of Chicago Press.)

reflect hearing by both bone and air conduction. Even more striking are changes in discrimination of speech. In speech, not only are perception of tones involved but also timing discriminations. There is a slowing in perception of auditory timing just as there is in CFF.

Taste and Smell. There are few research studies on these senses. They are difficult to measure. Still, results show decline in sensitivity to salt and sugar taste, with anatomic studies showing a slight decline in the number of taste buds in the mouth between ages 20 to 70, with a strong drop after 70. With age a more marked change occurs in the sense of smell although the person is often unaware of a loss in the sense of smell.

Other Senses. Clinical findings with the aged (more than research studies) report greatly diminished body sensations. For example, an older person may feel no pain when they contract such diseases as pneumonia or peritonitis. The tactile senses are generally diminished, especially in the sensitivity of the hands and feet. The thresholds for touch perception are raised, and there is less tolerance for hot and cold environments. The older person's body is said to be less capable of maintaining relatively steady states under changing temperatures.

CHANGES IN PERCEPTION

These sensory changes refer to straightforward reactions of the organism to physical or temporal changes in the environment. However, in perception, as compared to sensation, the organism is not merely a passive reactor to physical input, but is an active organizer. Perception is a more phenomenologic process where stimuli are not sensed as a chaos of independent events, but are rather given meaning. Examples of elemental perceptual processes are the Gestalt "laws" of proximity. Patterns of stimuli are perceived as patterns (eg, pairs) when they are grouped in a certain way rather than perceived as trios or other combinations; or in laws of "closure" where incomplete figures are seen as whole ones because the organism seeks closure and meaning.

In understanding aging, changes in perception are of the greatest significance because they influence actual behavior more directly than changes in sensation. Structural and sensory changes can be adapted to or substituted for. A person may turn up the volume on a TV set, but what could he do to change the way his central nervous system organizes the sounds coming from the set?

Comalli (1970) summarized life-span changes in visual perception, demonstrating many changes in advanced age that show the perceptual performance of children and the aged to be similar, compared to that of young adults. Similarity in performance does not mean similarity in cause for these perceptions nor does it necessarily mean that older persons have "regressed," but it does give valuable information on the modes of organizing stimuli that old people utilize and may then explain much of their global behavior.

Do you think that the two horizontal lines of the Muller-Lyer figure (Fig. 3) are equal? The illusion makes the line on the right seem longer. On the Titchener circles (Fig. 4), do the inner circles appear to be the same size? In this illusion, larger outer circles make the inner circle appear to be smaller by contrast.

Age changes in perception of the two visual illusions are presented in Figures 5 and 6. Figure 5 indicates that as children develop they become less susceptible to the Muller-Lyer illusion. After the age of 40, there is an increase in illusion that continues with advancing age. Figure 6 shows an opposite trend. Young children are not as subject to the Titchener circles illusion, developing more susceptibility as they grow older. Past the age of 40 there is a decline in the illusion perceived.

Psychologists are far from agreeing on the meanings and interpretation of these illusions. Some interpret the Muller-Lyer illusion as the result of environmental and cultural conditioning to perceive depth in certain geometric perspectives. Comalli considers the Muller-Lyer task to be an assimilation illusion where the observer must "disembed" the horizontal line from its context in order to achieve accurate perception. He interprets the Titchener circles task as a contrast illusion where dif-

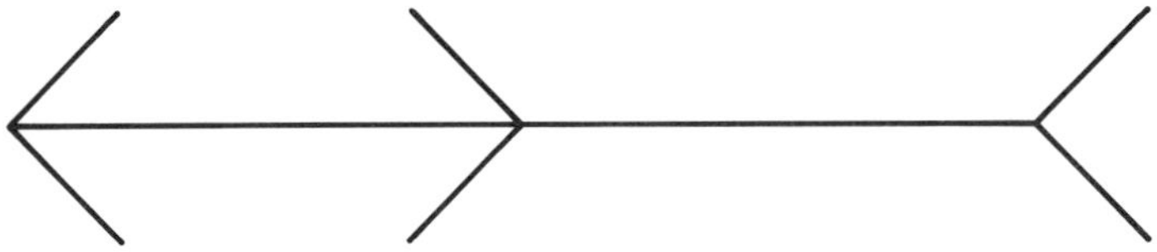

FIG. 3. Muller-Lyer illusion.

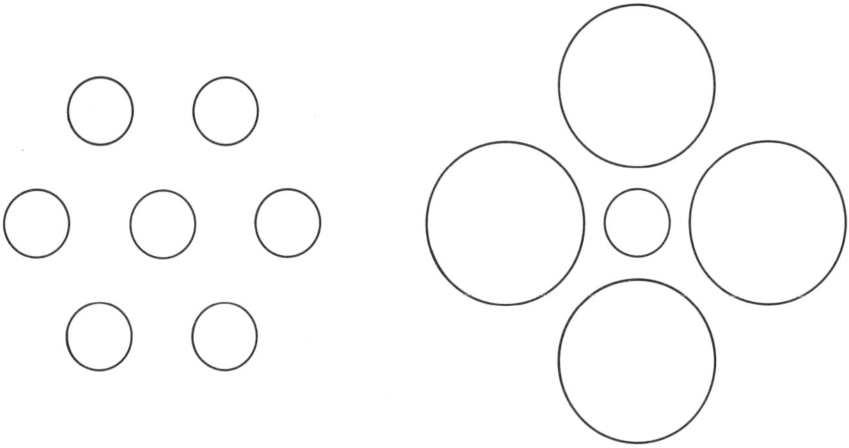

FIG. 4. Titchener circles illusion.

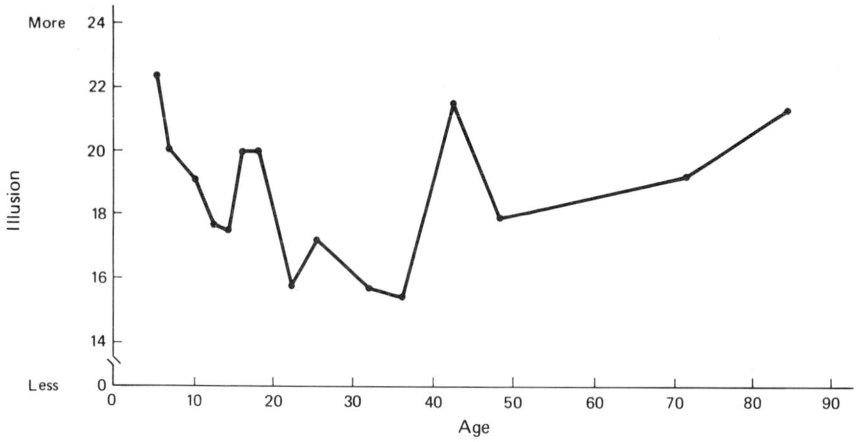

FIG. 5. Age changes to Muller-Lyer illusion. (Adapted from Comalli: In Goulet and Baltes (eds): Life Span Development Psychology, 1970, p 212. Courtesy of Academic Press, Inc.)

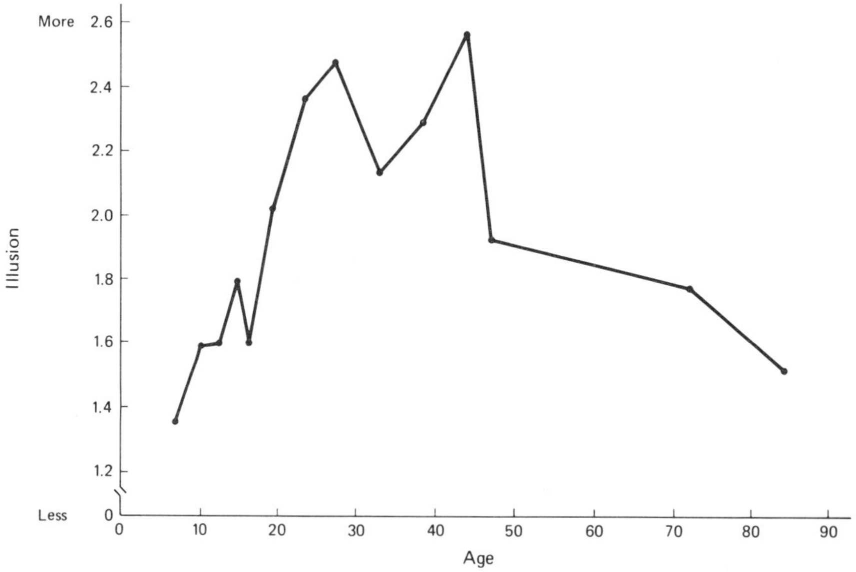

FIG. 6. Age changes to Titchener circles illusion. (Adapted from Comalli: In Goulet and Baltes (eds): Life Span Development Psychology, 1970, p 213. Courtesy of Academic Press, Inc.)

ferentiation of the inner circles from their context (outer ring of circles) leads to more illusion.

Other perceptual phenomena show similar life-span trends indicating greater differentiating ability in adults and less in children and the aged. Children and older people show greater "field dependence." They tend to see a rod as vertical when it is lined up with its frame, even though the frame is tilted. They are more influenced by field conditions in making judgments.

Not only do older persons seem to have increasing difficulty in disembedding stimuli from context, but there is also much evidence that timing is a critical factor. Older people need more time to perceive complex or incomplete figures. Speed in form discrimination progressively improves from early childhood to the mid-twenties, then begins to rapidly decline (Comalli 1970).

In studies of perceptual speed, there is always the problem of distinguishing factors of recognition from factors such as cautiousness in responding. A slow response may be due to either cause. When shown ambiguous figures, older persons are more cautious in interpretation, and once having decided on an interpretation are more hesitant to change their minds even though the figure is altered by the experimenter to look like something else. When first shown a card with a picture of a cat, older subjects proceed to interpret following cards with ambiguous lines upon them as cat figures. This has been interpreted to mean that older persons are more influenced by "set." Because of having first seen a cat, the aged viewer is influenced by his preconception that the fellowing cards will show a similar figure. A younger subject has more flexibility to reinterpret each card.

SENSATION, PERCEPTION, AND BEHAVIOR

We can see the aging person facing changes that require unique methods of adjustment. Because of structural changes in his sensory equipment, he is receiving less information and poorer information from his environment. It is poorer in intensity and in quality. There are other changes occurring in his ability to organize information, his ability to handle fast pacing, and his ability to differentiate and disassemble parts from contexts. There is also the stimulus from his expectations or preconceptions resulting in less flexibility once his mind is "made up."

There is a host of compensations people make to accommodate to such changes. We use means of amplifying intensity of signals and we increase the time we take to make discriminations and decisions. In communicating to the older person, we may be careful to establish a good set or an appropriate expectation. We may try to establish a context for the focused stimulus that is congenial, not disruptive or confusing. We may try to avoid rapid changes in tasks or instructions.

PSYCHOMOTOR PERFORMANCE

A fascinating problem in the study of aging is to try to distinguish changes in capacity from changes in approach, which are defenses against or attempts to compensate for changes in capacity. Are older people's nervous systems slower, or is the slowness the result of a cautious reaction in the face of difficulty in perceiving the essentials to the problem in the first place? Is cautiousness in the aged a basic change or is it an adaptive measure in the face of other basic changes? Understanding the difference is crucial, for if such changes are really adaptive mechanisms, they are reversible or modifiable if other compensations are developed for the deficiencies.

Changes in the physical structure of the individual as well as adaptive measures influence psychomotor performance. We have already discussed changes in sensory and perceptual ability. Studies of the neuromuscular system show gradual loss in maximum muscular strength after the 20s. There is even more marked effect upon continuous exertion. The older person takes in less oxygen, gives off less carbon dioxide, his pulse rate does not go up as much on exertion—in effect, his body is just not as prepared to work that hard.

Simple reaction time (the time between a signal and the beginning of a subject's response to that signal) is found not to be highly affected by age but the reaction times of the aged are highly affected by central processes such as memory and decision making. When tasks involve chaining of reaction sequences or overlapping of planning future movements with execution of preceding movements, the older person's performance suffers. Performance with age may be relatively unaffected on a task involving pressing one of four buttons when it lights up, but the difference appears with the instruction to press the button that lit up two or three times before the present one.

Bromley (1966) points out that it is "maximum" performance that suffers most, and since most life tasks make demands that are well below maximum standards, the older person may maintain passable performance. The age differences appear dramatically in the laboratory where younger persons show a large difference between optimal preferred performance and optimal performance whereas for the aged there is little difference. In facing complex tasks, older persons may use such compensatory techniques as working more slowly, more carefully, or dividing the task into smaller units to be handled sequentially.

COGNITIVE BEHAVIOR

Intelligence. The most commonly used tool to study adult intelligence has been the Wechsler-Bellevue Scales. The tests are administered individually and consist of 11 subjects that call for different types of thinking. There have been highly consistent findings which show that a decline in ability comes with age in certain cognitive areas. Older persons do as well as younger individuals on the subtests measuring verbal abilities and stored information. However, performances on subtests measuring psychomotor performance, speed, and abstract thinking show a decline. Tests that do not show a change, or hold up with age, are said to "Hold." The tests are Vocabulary, Information, Comprehension, and Arithmetic. Examples of "Don't Hold" tests are Digit Symbol Substitution, Picture Arrangement, and Block Design.

Wechsler (1958), upon standardizing the test, found the relative decline in the subtests so consistent from ages 18 on that a ratio of Don't Hold Tests to Hold Tests could be used as a standard of decline by which to assess an individual's change in relation to his aging peers. Wechsler called this the Deterioration Quotient.

Figure 7 illustrates Deterioration Quotients determined from Wechsler's reported norms and results obtained by Dibner (1961) on 23 men who were aged 73 to 79 and another 27 healthy veterans of the Spanish-American War aged 80 to 89. Do people with high intelligence decline with age as rapidly as those with average intelligence? The same rate of decline occurred among the veterans who had above-average intelligence as in Wechsler's subjects, an average group.

Several other studies have attempted to understand the relationship between initial level of intelligence and subsequent changes with age. Results, unfortunately are contradictory. Some have found greater increases in verbal areas among the brighter subjects. The result of practice, perhaps. Some have found only greater variability among all subjects as they get older.

Memory. One of the best known intellectual changes in age is the decrease in memory ability, especially "short-term" memory. Careful research has been illuminating the complexity of memory tasks especially when the total context of the situation is considered. One important factor is the meaning of the material to the subject. Older persons take more time to learn words or symbols in the typical memory study. However, should the learned material be nonsense equations ($E \times Z = G$), the older person does even worse. Is this difficulty in coding, classifying, or integrating nonsense material? Or is it not in the interest of the older person to bother with meaningless material? Other studies have

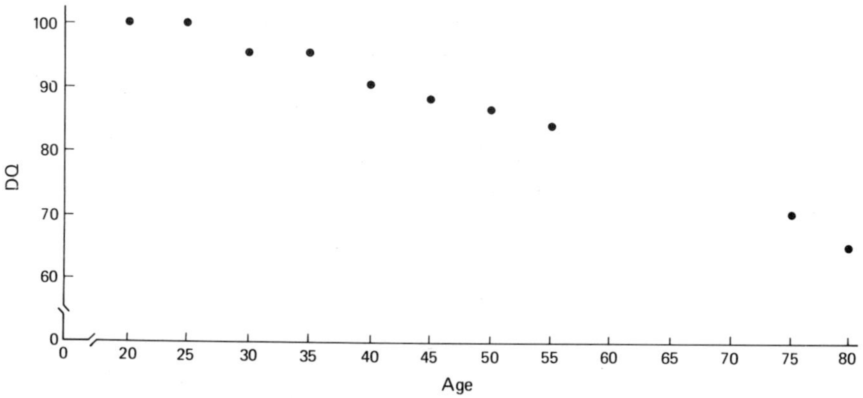

FIG. 7. Average deterioration quotients on Wechsler Bellevue Test with age. (Adapted from Dibner and Cummins: J Consult Psychol 25:2, 1961.)

shown that if the older person can see meaning in the task, his score improves.

This point (context of recall) is similar to the point previously made about the importance of set to the aged. Set gives meaning to the unexpected and the older person seems to have more need for this meaning.

Findings of change with age of incidental learning is consistent with the theory that older persons are more concerned with meaning. Incidental learning is learning of material other than that which is focused upon during the learning situation. Older people cannot recall incidental material as well as do younger persons and it may be that they are paying attention more exclusively to the central, meaningful aspects of the task, neglecting irrelevancies.

The common finding that immediate memory falls off more rapidly than the ability to remember items learned long before may possibly be due to the opportunity for more frequent rehearsal of the earlier learned material. Also the aged in good health may have relatively little loss in old memories whereas old people suffering from psychopathology, such as senile psychoses, frequently have severe old memory loss.

Botwinick (1967, p 197) reminds us of the tremendous variability in memory function in the aged:

> While the literature shows decline in memory ability with advancing age, it also shows that some subjects, regardless of how old they may be, never show measureable memory impairment. It may be more correct to think about the memory decline as describing more and more people as they get older, rather than as descriptive of every aging person.

Problem Solving. Many research studies (mostly cross-sectional) have shown decline in problem-solving ability with age in both verbal and nonverbal situations. Older people show poorer performance on such tasks as describing similarities, completing analogies, constructing sentences from odd words, logical reasoning, tasks of analysis and synthesis, and tasks of inventiveness. For a while, psychologists were attributing aged performance to rigidity and loss of abstractive ability. However, newer theories propose that the reasons the older person has more difficulty in problem solving are due to difficulty in organizing complex material, in short-term memory, in making fine discriminations among stimuli and in withholding responses even though he may think they are wrong. In problem-solving tasks in the laboratory, the aged take more time and hesitate when pressed. However, even if given more time, there seems to be a decrement in problem-solving ability.

The issue of problem solving has been approached quite differently by Lehman (1953) who reported meticulous studies of the creative and productive achievements of men in many fields. Amazingly similar results appeared showing that these men made their most creative contributions earlier than the age of 40. The more stringent the criterion of greatness of contribution, the lower was the average age. For example, in chemistry, the greatest number of creative contributions were made in the age range 30 to 34. Only 3 percent were produced by men over 60 years of age. However, those contributions judged to be of most significance were made by those aged 25 to 29. Similar results were found for artists, musicians, chess champions, and writers. Lehman (1953) cites multiple causes for these results, including the better education of younger people, physical decline, motivational changes (including resting on one's laurels), and increase in family and administrative responsibilities.

Learning. Since learning ability can never be directly observed, but is evidenced by improvement of performance on some task, other factors that affect performance are always involved. Most important of these factors in relation to the aged are speed of response, health, and motivational states (Botwinick 1967). Although lowered speed in older persons has been implicated in many studies showing poorer learning, Botwinick concludes that they do not rule out learning changes but rather that both factors interact in their effects on performance. Ill health, either physical or mental, has been demonstrated to show effects on learning.

Studies of the effects of motivation on learning have recently stressed the role of general drive level, or state of psychophysiologic arousal. But arousal state is hard to measure. Different physiologic measures of arousal state show contradictory changes in relation to age in humans. For example, "data on the amount of free fatty acids, adrenalin, and possibly of Electroencephalogram (EEG) suggested that elderly subjects are more aroused by . . . experimental situations than younger subjects. On the other hand, data of Galvanic Skin Response (GSR) and peripheral vasoconstriction, support the hypothesis that elderly subjects are less aroused than are the young." (Botwinick 1967, p 192.) The fact is that arousal as a psychologic concept involves much more than the physiologic state of the subject, but also his interest in the task, comfort or tension in the surroundings, familiarity with the experimental procedures, anticipation of future involvement in the studies, and so forth. Studies of learning have in general avoided consideration of these factors.

Learning performance declines with age in conditioning, new verbal learning, and incidental learning. Is rigidity in holding onto old ways inhibiting new learning, or is there also a deficiency in learning ability? This question is still unresolved.

PERSONALITY

Personality is probably the most difficult psychologic concept to define and measure. There are many popular conceptions as well as numerous clinical reports and research studies concerned with changes in personality that come with age. To attempt to make sense of all the material is a formidable task, but some areas of clarity may be perceived. It is clear, for example, that there is no such thing as a "personality" of the aged or even several personality profiles. Unfortunately, the excellent report by Reichard et al (1962) has been taken by many to be a contribution of this sort. By means of factor-analysis on extensive ratings of interview material, the authors were able to discriminate three positive and two negative profiles of adjustment of old men to retirement. They describe a *mature* man who is nonneurotic, self-accepting, and who actively enjoys activities and personal relationships appropriate to his age status; a *rocking chair* man who gains great pleasure from the passivity that may be indulged in during retirement; and an *armored* man who maintains rigid defenses against the anxiety generated by the aged status and keeps active in an attempt to avoid feelings of passivity and helplessness. The poorly adjusted types they describe as the *angry* man who is bitter about having failed to be the success he hoped when young. He blames others because he cannot accept his aged status. The *self-hater* is disappointed with his early life but blames himself with resulting feelings of worthlessness and depression.

These may be seen as possible adjustive reactions of men to retirement and old age. However as the authors themselves report,

> With the exception of the mature group, many of whom had reported difficulties in personal adjustment when younger, these personality types were relatively stable throughout life. Poor adjustment to aging among the angry men and the self-haters seemed to stem from lifelong personality problems. Similarly, the histories of the armored and rocking chair groups suggest that their personalities changed little throughout their lives. (Reichard et al 1962, p 171.)

Although some personality characteristics may change through aging, it is clear that personality is more continuous than discontinuous throughout a person's life span. At any point in time, a person is more like he has always been than he is like peers of his age group. A mature, nonneurotic younger person is likely to be a well-adjusted older person. The neurotic aged were most likely neurotic through much of their lives.

Forces acting to effect change in personality in old age are numerous and varied. There are, of course, biologic changes ranging from lowered energy through lowered basal metabolism, to changed appearance through wrinkled skin and flabby abdominal muscles. There are the losses that accumulate—losses of friends through death and moving, losses of children through their establishing independence, loss of income and habitual activities through retirement, loss of some pleasures through diminished senses. There are role changes that may be unwanted for many—the role of old person, grandmother, or widow. There may be more free time than the person has ever had to deal with in his adult life.

Add to these forces the effects of the kinds of psychologic changes we discussed earlier in this chapter—slower responses, poorer learning, especially of complex material, more field-dependent perceptions, and all the rest. After reviewing some of the research findings of how groups of young and older individuals have been found to differ in personality characteristics we will attempt to tie these measured changes to the forces mentioned.

Introversion. One of the better documented personality changes is increased introversion in the aged. This term is sometimes used in contrast to social extroversion. Here it is meant in a broader sense to refer to an inner-directedness, preoccupation with the self, one's body, one's thoughts, one's emotional states rather than concern with stimulation from the outer world from physical surroundings, events, or social stimuli. On personality tests, introversion has been shown to increase with age, possibly from the 40s on. Older persons show more concern with their bodily states and physiologic functioning on interviews and symptom checklists. Neugarten calls this process "interiority" and finds it beginning in middle age. "In both sexes, older people move toward more egocentric, self-preoccupied positions and attend increasingly to the control and satisfaction of personal needs. . . . There is a movement of energy away from an outer-world to an inner-world orientation." (Neugarten 1968, p 140.)

Neugarten's studies showed a shift from active to passive modes of mastery of the environment. She analyzed stories told by middle-aged and older subjects to the projective pictures of the Thematic Apperception Test, (Neugarten and associates 1964). Stories were rated in terms of introduction of conflict and complexity, and type and intensity of affect ascribed to the characters. The middle-aged saw the world as rewarding of aggressive striving on their part and felt up to it whereas 60 year olds saw the world as threatening and complex and beyond changing through their active efforts. They preferred adaptation through accommodation and conformity.

The shift toward an inner orientation in the aged is evidenced not only in the feelings and thoughts reported by aging subjects but also in his observable interactions with the environment. The "theory" of disengagement (Cumming and Henry 1961) expects social relationships to be lessened in quantity and quality in normal aging.

Looking at the psychologic rather than the social process, "disengagement" is also noted on the decreased expression of emotionality in the aged. For example, Lakin and Eisdorfer (1960) scored older and younger subjects' responses to a task of reporting their feelings when looking at stick figures which were in different postures representing emotional states. They found older people reporting fewer affects and they were more passive. They interpreted this to mean a decrease in reactivity potential, although they also considered the older person to be less interested in the task and possibly evidencing a lessened sensitivity to the affect of the "other," represented by the stick figure. This is another instance of how unready we are at this stage of knowledge and theory building to be able to distinguish those causal factors which reflect basic changes in aging individuals from others which illustrate environmental effects. Are older people less capable of emotional reactivity, or is it that they are not as stimulated to react given a standard stimulus? It reminds one of the learning studies mentioned earlier where incidental learning was found to be lower in the aged, but we cannot yet tell whether it is reflecting inefficiency in learning ability or lack of attention to those aspects of the environment that the older person finds of less concern.

Conservatism. Consistent with findings of increased introversion and lessened emotional reactivity are observations of conservatism in the aging. Conservatism means, here, a general attitude of preservation of the *status quo* rather than seeking change. This is evidenced in behavioral rigidity, unyieldingness, greater consistency in social and political attitudes. Older persons are less tolerant of ambiguities, and tend to impose structure in uncertain conditions, even though it may mean endorsing mutually conflicting statements. Their tendency to preserve previously established sets and unwillingness to shift in their approach to problems has already been mentioned.

Conservatism also extends to restraint in making judgments or taking risks. More than younger persons, they are apt to be serious and deliberate rather than carefree (Riley and Foner 1968). This increased cautiousness has been measured in a variety of circumstances, and has often been as a means employed by the older person to be more sure before committing himself, as if he were aware at some level of less efficiency in his information-gathering or integration processes. It would be like the cautiousness appearing in any driver when he enters a pocket of fog on the highway.

Although researchers find greater "restraint" on the part of older persons, there is also a kind of freedom from social restraint. This may be evidenced in outspokenness which seems to violate usual social standards. For example, an older woman may wear clothes that seem inappropriate although she has previously not been the kind of person who defied custom. Or an old person will make an outspokenly critical or derogatory remark in circumstances where restraint would be expected. This discrepancy has not been researched. It may reflect, however, an increasing introversion of the aged, a growing "distance" or insensitivity to surroundings and more rigid reliance on inner standards rather than outer guides for one's behavior.

Values and Interests. That the personality retains considerable consistency throughout life is attested to by longitudinal studies of interests and values. In any individual, interests are related to social class, occupational identification, or personal adjustment rather than to age group or sex. But some personal goals do change in adult life and differently for men and women.

Using his Vocational Interest Blank, E. K. Strong (1931) compared the interests of over 2,000 men of ages 20 to 60. Such a study is highly subject to the errors of the cross-sectional method using comparisons of groups reared in different cultural milieux. However, his findings are still worth considering because the VIB has come to be respected as one of the most reliable and productive personality tests in research.

The test is composed of over 400 items wherein the subject reports his degree of liking for a great variety of occupations, amusements, activities, characteristics of people, reading materials, and so forth. Changes in interests were found to occur over the adult age span but they were gradual and they were not as great, even comparing extreme ages, as differences between occupational groups of the men. Characteristic interests that did show age differences were less interest in activities involving physical skill and daring, less interest in trying the new or unusual, less interest in social activities as compared to solitary ones, and sharpening of likes and dislikes of peoples' personal characteristics. In general, however, Strong concludes that those interests which are liked at an early age are liked even more when the person grows older. Dislikes are similarly reinforced.

Activity, Disengagement, and Life Satisfaction. Since there are trends toward more passivity and less interest in physical activities, men may be said to become more feminine in their interests and orientations with age while women become more able to express aggressiveness and egocentricity. The changes in social expectations for women as they age do not change as greatly as the changes expected of men. If older women have the opportunity to continue social-emotional activities which may have characterized their earlier lives, their life satisfaction will remain high. It is not surprising that it is women, primarily, who participate in the adult-education classes, group functions, or Golden Age Clubs whereas men are not as well represented. For men, such activities often associated with retirement may not be as highly valued. To them, activity meant productive work which, after retirement, is neither expected nor usually available. In recent studies of life satisfaction related to activity in the aged, the expected correlation appeared in the case of women, but not for men (Zibbell 1970; Seymour 1971).

For the past 10 years or so, there has been controversy in social gerontology as to whether activity or disengagement represents the more desirable mode of adjustment in old age. The many findings of life satisfaction related to continued activity (Maddox 1963, 1965; Havighurst, Neugarten, and Tobin 1964) are pitted against the concepts of the disengagement theory (Cumming and Henry 1961). The essence of Cumming and Henry's theory is that there is a mutual withdrawal of contact, engagement, and expectations between the older person and society. Disengagement is seen not only as a normal process but also as a desirable one which leads to high morale and preparation for the ultimate in disengagement—death.

The activity theory fits the prevailing American ethic of activity, work, and productivity as human ideals, while disengagement can be seen as an appropriate adjustment mode for many aging persons although the process does not fit the society's ideals.

There has been a series of studies to elucidate the many possible adjustments to aging that can yield satisfaction to different persons. These studies take into consideration such factors as differences between men and women of different ages, different backgrounds, and different previous life styles. Maddox (1970) feels the most meaningful method of examining life satisfaction in the aged is by the case method, examining the life style of individuals in a longitudinal design. He found persistence in life styles with 79 percent of his sample displaying high satisfaction and high activity level. Only 14 percent showed the disengagement pattern, that is, high satisfaction with low activity level. He finds his data arguing that the disengagement pattern is not simply a function of age. That some persons may have had this as a lifelong pattern while others may have come to the pattern after a lifestyle of high satisfaction associated with high activity level. Maddox (1965) found that when high morale accompanied low activity it was generally among his oldest subjects, and it was affected by several other factors. Such persons were in relatively good health, felt personally adequate, and had a sense of usefulness despite their low activity level.

A Theory of Psychologic Aging

Have we been convinced that there are psychologic changes with age? Even the most critical research methodologist would have to agree that some people change with age although different people change at different rates and probably for different reasons. For some there are only slight if even discernible psychologic changes. The clearest reasons for changes in adults seem to be dramatic, nonuniversal biologic causes such as illness or traumatic physical losses. The next most convincing reasons include the influence of life events, such as widowhood, retirement, or changes dictated by societal role expectations. The behavioral changes that seem to be the most subtle and least universal are those that could be seen as programmed genetically or biologically.

Can one meaningfully speak of psychologic *development* in old age? As the child developmentalist, Flavell (1970), points out preadult changes (he is referring to cognitive changes) although influenced by environmental factors, show undeniable and inevitable influences of biologic-maturational (programmed) factors.

> Cognitive change is inevitable—guaranteed to occur—in neurologically-intact, growing children the world over. . . . There are truly *big* changes, both quantitatively and qualitatively. Furthermore, the evidence suggests that at least the major landmarks in the child's cognitive evolution emerge in a fixed order. There is, in other words, considerable intrinsic directionality and inter-individual uniformity in the developmental progression. And finally the changes that occur are

> largely irreversible; that is, the cognitive structures and operations that eventually emerge are essentially permanent, essentially unextinguishable. (Flavell 1970, p 248.)

Thus, Flavell challenges the concept of development in old age since there is little evidence of changes being inevitable, of great magnitude or uniform across aging persons. He concedes, however, that observed changes may be irreversible and even uniform in direction although they do not show progression in specifiable stages.

Flavell joins other theorists who lean toward the view that genetically determined programming of the developing adult probably ceases to be of critical importance in maturity past the age of highest reproductive potential. The changes occuring in the adult in maturity are, therefore, primarily due to experience and interaction with the environment. This conception accounts for the tremendous interindividual rates and kinds of changes since individual experiences are so different. It also gives adequate attention and weight to the influence of social variables on human behavior in old age. Since there are sociocultural uniformities of a kind facing most older people as described, for example, by Erikson's conception of developmental tasks (1959), one may expect certain uniformities in adaptive response to these demands.

Uniformities in adaptive and changed behavior have been variously described as a general change toward reduction, slowing down, inhibition, conservation, withdrawal, or disengagement. Although many theories of personality or human development have been applied to these changes in later adulthood (Kastenbaum 1965; Reigel 1959), as yet none have been completely successful in explaining and predicting.

The uniformities of psychologic change have a quality of direction and control of behavior that may reflect motivational change. If we see the aging adult as an organism slowly undergoing changes in his physical constitution and if we see behavior as a function of the organism adapting his resources to conditions of his environment, then we can conceive of changes in behavior with age as a response of the less energetic, physically inefficient although more experienced organism coping with a world continuing with its demands and stimulus characteristics.

Early theories of motivation considered man as primarily driven by principles of drive-reduction or satisfaction of needs (internal states). However, this conception could not account for much human activity which went beyond need satisfaction. People often seek situations that are stimulating rather than just satisfying. And, environments help create need states rather than merely satisfying them.

Recent research on brain stimulation in animals suggests that organisms have brain centers that promote either excitatory or inhibitory behaviors, which may mean that under certain circumstances individuals may seek arousal and stimulation and at other times avoid such stimulation.

Some motivation theorists contend that individuals seek optimal levels of arousal at which they are "comfortable" and presumably most effective (Fiske and Maddi 1961).

We present the thesis, then, that psychologic changes in old age are evidences of a basic change in the organism from a primarily arousal-seeking to a less arousal-seeking state. The basic motivation of the older person is preference for simplicity rather than complexity which characterizes the young organism (Dibner 1971).

The young organism, in a state of high energy and adequate resources, adapts to the environment through seeking complexity, stimulation, and novelty, and by this means maintains high levels of arousal and becomes more highly differentiated. However, in states of illness or fatigue, even the young organism will evidence preference for simplicity. Preference for simplicity is functionally of importance in the case of waning energy and lessened resources.

Preference for simplicity as a motivational state affects the person's perceptions, cognitions, and his actions upon the environment. It is characterized by an attitude of conservation and self-protection, a preference for simplicity, redundancy, and security.

Table 1 lists terms that characterize this motivational state in contrast to preference for complexity. Some words describe characteristics of stimuli that are preferred, for instance the old versus the new or the unchanging versus the changeable. Some characterize preferred operations of the actor such as conservative versus nonconservative or disengaged versus engaged.

TABLE 1. Terms Characterizing Preference for Simplicity Versus Complexity

Simplicity	Complexity	Conservative	Nonconservative
Invariant	Variant	Interiority	Exteriority
Redundant	Unique	Global	Differentiated
Old	New	Leveled	Sharpened
Symmetrical	Asymmetrical	Reminiscing	Nonreminiscing
Order	Disorder	Unchanging	Changeable
Predictable	Unpredictable	Categorical	Noncategorical
Unsurprising	Surprising	Past-oriented	Future-oriented
Structured	Ambiguous	Disengaged	Engaged
Congruent	Incongruent	Consistent	Inconsistent

In the past few years there has been much interest in establishing the parameters of sensation seeking, complexity seeking, arousal seeking, but mostly in children and young adults. If we consider the entire life span, there is experimental evidence for preference for moderately increased complexity and increased arousal in children through young adulthood, but only indirect evidence of lowered sensation seeking in older persons. It is common experience, however, that sick or fatigued individuals of any age seek less stimulation.

Why might the older person adopt a preference for simplicity? Primarily because he can conserve energy by avoiding arousal. Many organ systems decline in efficiency in aging adults, certainly those concerned with energy, such as basal metabolism rate, respiratory function, and cardiac output. Even if there is no age deficit when the body is at rest, functional capacities tend to be less effective in older persons when faced with and recovering from challenges from the internal and external environment (Riley and Foner 1968). The older person may feel as if he has less energy, and he knows he has less reserve.

Another reason for preference for simplicity in the aged may be that because of decreased sensory acuity and slower speed of integration of information, the arousing collative properties of stimuli might be at times more potent for the old than for the young, and potentially more arousing. To illustrate: Berlyne (1963) designated *indistinctness* as a collative property that induces subjective uncertainty. If a person with failing hearing perceives a conversation indistinctly, he might be made to feel more uncertain and be more aroused and feel uncomfortable. The person with failing hearing may avoid conversation because it is too disturbing.

A third reason for preference for simplicity is the subjective uncertainty already preexisting in the older person because of his awareness of changes in his sensory processes, integrative skills, and motor skills. If he has become aware, for example, of changes in his memory ability, he may be predisposed to feel uncertain if faced with new or complex, arousing situations and might prefer to avoid them.

Behavior reflecting the motivational state of preference for simplicity may take many forms. The person might avoid certain conditions as described in the example of poor hearing. He might not like to meet new people or hear new ideas. He might avoid complicated situations. Normal aged have been found to be more restrained, more cautious, with narrowed interests.

A second mode of preferring simplicity is by occupying oneself with repeating old, familiar behavior. Examples are rituals, habitual behaviors, or reminiscing where one concerns oneself with the safer past rather than the complex present or uncertain future. Tests of various behaviors find older people to be more rigid, persisting in earlier learned approached to new problems and not accepting new approaches.

A third form of preference for simplicity involves imposition of structure on a too unstructured stimulus. This may take the form of categoric thinking or adhering rigidly to rules to avoid the bothersome middle ground. In attitude studies, old persons give more extreme responses, avoiding neutral ones and are more dogmatic when forced to take a stand.

Thus the concept of preference for simplicity seems to bring into meaningful relationship many findings in perception, cognition, and personal-social behavior which we have presented. Cumming and Henry's (1961) disengagement behavior and Neugarten's (1964) interiority behavior both stress simplification of the individual's life through diminished involvement in his social environment. Many reported cognitive changes in old age are consistent also with a theory of preference for simplicity. Slower speed of response, the best documented of performance changes in the aged may be mostly a behavioral manifestation of control in the face of uncertainty rather than a reflection of neurologic changes. Old subjects learn better when they can pace their learning. They are more cautious in new learning situations. They commit omission errors rather than performance errors, reflecting a need to be certain before acting. The decline in incidental learning in the aged, also may result from conservation of attention since there is limited energy.

The life-span data on visual perception discussed earlier are also compatible with this theory. It challenges Comalli's (1970) conclusion that perceptual field dependence and poor differentiating ability of the aged are evidences of regression because their perceptions are like that of the child.

We are suggesting that even if the older person is capable of differentiating, he may not do so, prefering the more global perception because it requires less expenditure of energy. If young children and old people were both tested under conditions of high incentive, we suspect that the old but not young children would give a more differentiated performance on the illusions and other perceptual tasks.

This motivational theory must now be tested through experiments that isolate the relevant variables and permit their unbiased examination. Some studies have already been done. Isotti (1967) examined the importance of interest to learning in the aged. Lewis (1970) tested the hypothesis that reminiscence in the aged, as a focus on the past, may be an anxiety-reducing social device. Zibbell (1970) and Seymour (1971) examined factors in activities of the aged which demonstrated that only those activities that were close to the central concerns of the aged are related to life satisfaction. Biddle (1971) sought to make old people less cautious through use of beer and group discussion. This study indicated that cautiousness is a modifiable, motivational state of the aged.

The theory of preference for simplicity will provide incentive for closer examination of motivational factors in many psychologic behaviors, speed of response, functional loss of hearing and vision, cautiousness, rigidity, and disengagement. If this general theory is true it may explain, on a motivational basis, many behavioral changes in old age which have been explained previously as resulting from organic deficiencies with irreversible loss of ability.

The theory has practical and theoretic implications. It presents a view of the aged not as structurally different, as permanently or progressively incapable, but as differently motivated. This implies reversibility or changeability. Psychologic age becomes a matter of how one approaches problems, how one interacts with the presenting environment, rather than a state or a status. The preference for simplicity is not a type of adjustment held only by the chronologically old. It is independent of age, yet correlated with it. If we could measure psychologic aging through the concepts of motivation, we might understand better the behavior of some younger persons which varies from the norm or expected.

If we do not take age differences in behavior to be the result of irreversible structural changes, but adaptation to lessened resources, we are challenged to pay more attention to factors that cause energy decline—such as improper diet or unusual temperatures. We would also be more alert to factors influencing self-concept, especially self-esteem, since anxiety about the self often leads to ego-constriction.

We would pay more attention to motivating (collative) factors in new situations for the aged. Is the new situation stimulating enough? Is it too stimulating? This would be an important consideration in relocations (eg, change in residence), and any situations involving new learning. We must raise incentives for old people to learn, whereas the young would be more aroused by the novelty and challenge alone.

Understanding changed behavior as changes in coping also leads us to a greater respect for the coping mechanisms. We may want to promote them rather than discourage them.

The progress made by scientists in understanding aging, although by no means complete, has far outstripped society's attitude toward the aged. We know now that older people are not a different kind of person but are like persons of any age, coming to terms with their psychologic world in the most effective manner they can devise.

References

Berlyne DE: Motivational problems raised by exploratory and epistemic behavior. In Koch S (ed): Psychology, A Study of a Science, vol 5. New York, McGraw-Hill, 1963

Biddle J: Modification of cautiousness in old age. Unpublished Ph.D. diss, Boston Univ, 1971

Botwinick J: Cognitive Processes in Maturity and Old Age. New York, Springer, 1967

Bromley DB: The Psychology of Human Ageing, 2nd Ed. Middlesex, England, Penguin Books, 1974

Comalli PE Jr: Life span changes in visual perception. In Goulet LR, Baltes PB (eds): Life Span Developmental Psychology. New York, Academic Press, 1970, pp 211–26

Cumming E, Henry WE: Growing Old. New York, Basic Books, 1961

Dibner AS, Cummins JF: Intellectual functioning in a group of normal octogenarians. J Consult Psychol 25:2, 1961

Dibner AS: Psychological Aging as Preference for Simplicity. Paper presented at 24th Annual Meeting of the Gerontological Society, Houston, Texas, October 1971

Eisdorfer C, Lawton MP (eds): Psychology of Adult Development and Aging. Washington, DC, American Psychological Association, 1973

Erikson, EH: Identity and the life cycle: selected papers. Psychol Issues 1:50–100, 1959

Fiske DW, Maddi SR (eds): Functions of Varied Experience. Homewood, Ill, Dorsey Press, 1961
Flavell JH: Cognitive changes in adulthood. In Goulet LR, Baltes PB (eds): Life Span Developmental Psychology. New York, Academic Press, 1970, pp 248–57
Havighurst R, Neugarten B, Tobin S: Disengagement, personality, and life satisfaction in the later years. In Hansen PF (ed): Age with a Future. Philadelphia, Davis, 1964
Isotti E: The relation of ego-constriction and interest to recall in the aged. Unpublished Ph.D. diss, Boston Univ, 1966
Kastenbaum R: Theories of human aging: the search for a conceptual framework. J Social Issues 21,4:13–36, 1965
Lakin M, Eisdorfer C: Affective expression among the aged. J Per Assess 24:403–408, 1960
Lehman HC: Age and Achievement. Princeton, NJ, Princeton Univ Press, 1953
Lewin K: Behavior and development as a function of the total situation. In Carmichael L (ed): Manual of Child Psychology, 2nd ed. New York, Wiley, 1954, pp 918–970
Lewis C: Reminiscence and self concept in old age. Unpublished Ph.D. diss, Boston Univ, 1970
Maddox GL: Activity and morale: a longitudinal study of selected elderly subjects. Social Forces 42:195–204, 1963
———: Fact and artifact: evidence bearing on disengagement theory. Hum Dev 8:117–130, 1965
———: Persistence of life style among the elderly. In Palmore E (ed): Normal Aging. Durham, NC, Duke Univ Press, 1970, pp 329–331
Neugarten BL, Berkowitz H, Gutman D et al: Personality in Middle and Late Life. New York, Atherton Press, 1964
Neugarten BL (ed): Middle Age and Aging. Chicago, Univ Chicago Press, 1968
Reichard S, Livson F, Peterson PG: Aging and Personality: A Study of Eighty-seven Older Men. New York, Wiley, 1962
Riegel KF: Personality theory and aging. In Birren JE (ed): Handbook of Aging and the Individual: Psychological and Biological Aspects. Chicago, Univ Chicago Press, 1959
Riley MW, Foner A, et al: Aging and Society, Vol 1: An Inventory of Research Findings. New York, Russell Sage Foundation, 1968
Schaie KW: A reinterpretation of age related changes in cognitive structure and functioning. In Goulet LR, Baltes PB (eds): Life Span Developmental Psychology. New York, Academic Press, 1970
Seymour G: Activity Level, the Sense of Personal Autonomy, and Life Satisfaction in Old Age. Unpublished Ph.D. diss, Boston Univ, 1971
Strong EK: Change of Interests with Age. Stanford, Calif, Stanford Univ Press, 1931
Wechsler D: The Measurement of Adult Intelligence, 3rd ed. Baltimore, Williams and Wilkins, 1958
Weiss AD: Sensory Functions. In Birren JE (ed): Handbook of Aging and the Individual: Psychological and Biological Aspects. Chicago, Univ Chicago Press, 1959, pp 510, 521
Zibbell R: Activity Level, Future Time Perspective and Life Satisfaction in Old Age. Unpublished Ph.D. diss, Boston Univ, 1970

5

SOCIOLOGIC PERSPECTIVES ON AGING

Dorrian Apple Sweetser, Ph.D.

The past is father to the present, and nowhere is this more evident than in gerontology. The influence of the past on the present is evident in the lives of individuals, but—and here is a major theme of the chapter—there is a temporal aspect in society as well, so that there is change from one generation to the next in the relation of age categories of people and social institutions, and in the personal characteristics of age categories of people and social institutions, and in the personal characteristics of age categories. As a result of these dual influences, the processes and events of aging are in some ways repetitive from one generation to the next, while in other ways they differ.

Distinguishing age-related characteristics that are likely to persist from those that will change is both an essential and a difficult task in gerontologic research. Why the task of identifying change over generations, called temporal change in this chapter, is essential, and how it can be done, is the first topic. Next are sections on demography, the family, and the distributive process. Each of these summarizes what is known with some certainty about growing old in American society today, and each assesses what is known about temporal change in the phenomena discussed. The chapter concludes with prospects for improved well-being of older people.

Aging and Temporal Change

There are many gerontologic topics in which a key question is the extent to which the aged of today are dependable guides to what the aged of tomorrow can be or will be. For example, if some aged today exhibit disengagement (Cumming and Henry 1961), is this a potential inherent in the psychosocial processes of aging or a transient phenomenon dependent on changeable social conditions? If the aged today are politically conservative in certain matters, will they be so tomorrow? If there is a market for one kind of retirement home today, will the market continue? These are not questions of interest only to researchers. The implementation of any kind of planned social change takes some considerable time, often a generation or more, and there are few things more wasteful and more productive of recrimination than a social policy whose customers have left it behind.

Any research has to begin with conceptual or theoretical analysis, and studies of change in aging are no exception. This statement is not a prescription but an element in the activities of research. To study change in aging is to have decided that such change might be present, and this is a theoretical decision. Further, to study change in aging requires decisions about what information is needed, and these are also theoretical decisions. The collection and analysis of information tests the results of this first step against the recalcitrance of facts.

Youth and age can be compared in a cross-sectional study in which a sample representing different generations or, more exactly, different age cohorts is studied at a single period in time. Where temporal change is in question, a cross-sectional study suffers from the limitation that observed differences between age categories may be due to persisting characteristics of aging or to temporal influences that will change or to both, and there is no way to distinguish the two. What is required in addition is longitudinal information about age categories over at least one generation.

If the subject matter permits it, such information can be obtained during a cross-sectional study by asking the aged about the period of their youth. People can answer some questions about their past with reasonable accuracy. An example is an occupational history. Other variables (eg, attitudes) cannot be studied by depending on people's memories of long-ago facts.

If a retrospective inquiry is not appropriate, the alternative is a longitudinal study, in which either the same people are followed over a period of time, or else the population is resampled periodically and changes over a generation are traced through the successive samples. A study in which the same people are restudied is not without its own difficulties, including loss of subjects and the vicissitudes of staffing and financing the project for the necessary period. A longitudinal study using periodic resampling faces the same difficulties, except for the loss of subjects.

Sometimes longitudinal studies based on resampling can be carried out by means of data collected by others, for other purposes. Census data and data archives containing, for example, surveys of public opinion are important sources for this kind of longitudinal research. A common difficulty with using such available data is that they frequently do not contain some crucial piece of information, so that the researcher has to alter his problem to fit the available data or collect his own information after all.

Thus the research design of a gerontologic study is crucial in the plausibility of any of its conclusions about change in aging. *An Inventory of Research,* by Riley and Foner (1968), which is volume 1 of the landmark three-volume *Aging and Society,* has the merit of not only synthesizing research findings but also of reviewing the design and methods of the investigations. It is, therefore, the best place to begin further study of many of the topics of this chapter, and is cited frequently, both for its ideas and for the summaries of research that it contains.

Demographic Changes

Demography is the study of the composition of populations and of factors influencing their composition. Demographic phenomena basic to gerontology are the age structure of the society, the average length of life including the life expectancy of persons in later life, and temporal changes in these matters.

The age and sex composition of a population result from two biosocial variables, these being mortality rates and fertility rates, and from a social variable, migration rates. "Biosocial" means that the rate is generated by physiologic events that are influenced by social conditions. Mortality and fertility are influenced by the level of medical knowledge and by the extent of its application, plus such other social influences as nutrition in the case of mortality, or the desire for children in the case of fertility. Migration is a consequence of the attractiveness of an area to residents of another, in combination with conditions that impede or encourage moving.

In a broad, comparative perspective, the United States today exhibits an age structure with relatively large numbers of persons of mature years, and will doubtless continue to do so. The age composition of its population in the foreseeable future will be little affected by immigration. The age structure, is determined not only by the mortality rate but by the fertility rate as well. Although it is true that individuals in the United States live longer on the average than they did in the past, the age structure is a matter of proportions of the whole who are in various age categories. Therefore, the proportion of older people depends not only on the number of aged but principally on the number who have been born at subsequent periods, and these numbers reflect the fertility rate.

Immigration, when the numbers are substantial, decreases the proportion of aged in the population by increasing the number of young adults. Since most young immigrants are men, the sex ratio within age categories is also affected.

As a consequence of the heavy migration to this country at the turn of the century, ratio of males to females among the aged is somewhat higher than it would otherwise be. Other consequences of this period of heavy immigration are that many of the foreign born in this country are old, and that the level of education of older people is lower than it would otherwise have been (Riley and Foner 1968, p 113).

Turning to the average length of life, or life expectancy, the change in this demographic feature of our population is well known. Life expectancy has increased considerably since the founding of the country, in continuation of a temporal trend observable in Europe over previous centuries. The average length of life in Massachusetts and New Hampshire before 1789 was 35.5 years, as compared with 70 years in 1966 (Petersen 1969, p 246). Most of the decline in mortality rates has occurred in the age-specific rates of the earlier years, where infectious diseases and childbearing now cause far fewer deaths than formerly. Indeed, there is very little further decrease possible in the mortality rates of age categories below 40, because these rates are already so low (Petersen 1969, p 245). Decline in the mortality rates of later age periods, where the chronic diseases take their toll, seems dependent on the development of new methods of treating heart disease and cancer.

Although life expectancy has increased, and can increase still further, this increase has an upper limit, called the life span, which is not now susceptible to alteration. The life span is generally considered to equal the biblical three score years and ten.

For various reasons, including physical hardiness, women are likely to outlive men by several years (Petersen 1969, p 204). The influence of this demographic phenomenon on the family will be discussed in a later section of the chapter.

Besides the general life expectancy of a population, and the difference between the sexes, there is a further difference by race and by age. The points to be made are based on demographic information such as that shown in Table 1, which is taken from Riley and Foner (1968, p 28) and which gives the expectation of additional years of life for men and women, by race, at ages 45 and 65 in the United States in 1900 to 1902 and in 1964.

Several points can be made about the information shown in this table. First, it shows the increase in life expectancy in later life to which reference has previously been made; it is unlikely that this temporal trend can continue without major advances in medical knowledge. The increase is evident in every sex, race, and age category when life expectancy in 1900 to 1902 is compared with life expectancy in 1964. Second, the table also shows the previously mentioned difference by sex in life expectancy. With one exception, the eight comparisons of men and women within racial categories show greater female expectation of life.

A third point to be made about the table is the consistently shorter life expectancy of nonwhites as compared to whites. Six of the eight com-

TABLE 1. Expectation of Additional Years of Life

	1900–1902		1964	
	Age 45	Age 65	Age 45	Age 65
White males	24.2	11.5	27.4	13.0
White females	25.5	12.2	32.9	16.3
Nonwhite males	23.6	12.1	24.7	12.8
Nonwhite females	22.6	12.4	28.7	15.6

parisons of whites and nonwhites within sex categories show this disadvantage.

The persisting difference by race is almost certainly a consequence of differences in socioeconomic status, both in adult life and in childhood. Higher socioeconomic status, by definition, means higher income and this in turn allows greater access to health care and implies the avoidance of certain hazards. It seems likely that the causal force runs mostly from socioeconomic status to longevity by way of better health, although there is doubtless some influence the other way, from better health to higher socioeconomic status. A relation between occupational status and longevity has been observed in other contexts (Riley and Foner 1968, p 34).

The disadvantage of nonwhites in expectation of life means that improvement in this regard is less dependent for nonwhites than for whites on major advances in medical knowledge. In fact, in recent years the life expectancy of nonwhites has been increasing faster than that of whites (Riley and Foner 1968, p 33).

A final point to be made about this table concerns life cycle change in expectation of life. In a sense, aging confers an immunity to death. That is, the total life expectancy of a person who has attained age 65 is greater than the total life expectancy of a person of the same race and sex who is aged 45. It can be noted in all of the eight comparisons in the table that the total life expectancy for those aged 65 is more than the total life expectancy of those aged 45 reduced by 20 years. Presumably this kind of age-related change in life expectancy is a stable phenomenon that will persist in the foreseeable future.

Changes in Family Composition

One of the themes of gerontology is happiness in old age, and family and kin relations in later life are therefore particularly important topics. During middle age, most people are married and have children and living siblings. Among people 65 and over in the United States today, over half have a spouse, about three-quarters have at least one living child, well over half have grandchildren, and over three-fourths have living siblings. Because women outlive men, wives are usually younger than their husbands, and men 55 and over are more likely to remarry than are women, marital status differs greatly by sex in later life; most older men are married, while a little over half of older women are widowed (Riley and Foner 1968, pp 158–160).

Four temporal trends are important for their effects on family composition in later life. First, people spend more time in the married state than formerly. This is due to a decline in age at first marriage, an increase in the proportion ever married, and the increase in average length of life (Carter and Glick 1970, pp 387–389). Second, from the 1880s to the early 1950s there was a clear trend upward in the proportion of childless ever married women, from under one-tenth to one-fifth. Since then, the trend appears to be moving in the other direction, but it is not possible to say at this time whether the trend has truly been reversed (Petersen 1969, p 508). Although the long-run decline in mortality rates has increased the probability that children will survive, it cannot be concluded that older people today are more likely than their predecessors to have living children, since the decline in mortality is offset to an unknown extent by decline in fertility. Third, because of the increase in average length of life, older people are more likely than in the past to have parents surviving, and if they had siblings, to have siblings surviving (Riley and Foner 1968, p 163). But it is not certain whether there is an increase in the proportion of older people with siblings alive, because there has been a long-run decline in the size of families. The fourth temporal trend is the longer duration of the so-called stage of the empty nest—the period between the marriage of the last child and the death of one of the spouses (Carter and Glick 1970, pp 146–147). This trend results from the earlier age of marriage, smaller family size, and longer life.

In regard to household composition, most older people live with their spouse or with children or other relatives; slightly under a third share a household with a child (Riley and Foner 1968, pp 167–169). The principal life-cycle changes in household composition are the departure of the children and the death of the spouse.

Over the past several decades, there has been a decline in the proportion of older people who share a household with children or other relatives. However, this cannot be taken to be a sign of change in family sentiments, since other age categories have shown a similar tendency to establish separate households (Beresford and Rivlin 1964, 1966). It rather appears to be a consequence of greater affluence.

One of the misconceptions about the American family is the notion that household sharing with relatives other than spouse and children used to be far more common than now. In fact, the available evidence indicates no trend of this kind. In the past, as now, the common way for individuals to live was as members of nuclear families. Beresford and Rivlin compared data from the Massachusetts state census of 1885 with 1960 census data. The figures given below are from their 1964 paper (p

14). In 1885, 93.7 percent of men who were living in their own household or in the household of relatives were either the head of the household or a son of the head. The comparable figure in 1960 was 95.6 percent. Similarly, in 1885, 90.6 percent of females who were living in their own household or with relatives were either head, wife of the head, or daughter. The comparable figure for 1960 was 93.3 percent. In other words, in 1885 as in 1960, the great majority of men and women living in some kind of family household were either parent or child.

A similar picture was obtained from a comparison of Rhode Island census data for 1875 with 1960 data. Single family households were the rule at both periods. In 1960, 85 percent of households contained only the nuclear family, and 82 percent were of this kind in 1875 (Pryor 1967, p 10).

The remaining topic to be discussed is interaction between older people and close kin who are not sharing a household. This is a relatively new subject for study, and nothing is known about temporal change. There are, however, two causal influences on frequency of interaction that will be noted. One of these causal hypotheses is well established by a considerable body of evidence taken from a number of different societies; the other is only just beginning to be studied. The former is the matrilaterality hypothesis. The latter concerns the effects of population migration on the distance between parents and their grown children and thereby on the frequency with which parents and children interact.

In later life, frequent interaction with kin appears to be the rule rather than the exception. A survey of persons aged 65 and over in the United States, Denmark, and England showed that about three-fourths of older people had a child living within a half-hour journey (Shanas 1968, p 193). In each of these societies, over three-fourths of the sample had seen a child within the previous week, and this statement is made excluding those older people who were sharing a household with a child (Shanas 1968, p 197).

The "matrilaterality hypothesis" explains a consistent feature of kin ties in the United States and in similar industrial societies. This feature is a modest but consistent tendency for women to be more active than men in ties with relatives. Evidence indicates that this is a consequence of the separation of men's work from ties with kin which is characteristic of the United States and other industrial societies. In such societies, breadwinning takes place outside of the family, while the chief female responsibilities are carried out in the household. Relatives are thus useful to women in a way that is not true of men, and the reasoning is that this difference is sufficient to bring about the moderate predominance of women in activities and communication with relatives which has consistently been noted. Available evidence on the United States and other societies, and the formulation and initial testing of the explanation of matrilaterality, is to be found in Sweetser (1966). The hypothesis has been further tested in studies conducted for this purpose in Finland and

Norway (Sweetser 1968, 1970, 1973). A review of recent tests of the matrilaterality hypothesis by other investigators will be found in Sweetser (1973).

Finally, the effects of population migration on the kin ties of older people deserves further study. The frequency of interaction of kin declines markedly as the distance between them increases, but the implications of this self-evident fact in combination with population migration has received little attention. Bultena (1969) made explicit the connection between population migration and parent-child interaction when he reported that, in a Wisconsin sample, urban aged saw more of their children than rural aged, because in rural areas young people were more likely to migrate than were young people in cities.

Two points about migration are important. One is that migrants tend to be young adults. The other is that migration exhibits patterns; in other words, despite the individual nature of decisions about whether or not to move out of one's local area, enough people come to the same decision so that one can speak, for example, of migration to cities, or migration to some geographic region. Indeed, migration information is an important part of the data that demographers study. These two points about migration mean that there are identifiable areas in any country from which many young people move away, and other areas from which few move away. In the former type of area, the probability is greater that a parent will have no children living nearby. In the latter type of area, parents are more likely to have some of their children nearby. The effects of migration on kin ties has been intensively investigated in an urban Norwegian sample (Sweetser 1973), in continuation and expansion of an earlier study made in Helsinki (Sweetser 1970).

The Distributive Process

One of the main concerns of gerontology is social inequality as it relates to aging; that is, the question of how older people compare with younger adults in capacities and opportunities. One aspect of this topic is how older people stand in relation to the distributive process, and it is with this sociologic process that this section is chiefly concerned.

The distributive process is a convenient label for the answer to the question, "Who gets what and why?" (Lenski 1966, p 3). The "what" is transferrable resources that are in limited supply; money and power are the resources considered here. Resources are held by persons by virtue of the social roles these persons occupy. Another way to state this is to say that resources are attached to social roles. They are produced in, or held and exercised by, persons in roles. In discussing the distribution of money and power in later life, therefore, the key roles involved will be specified. Not surprisingly, occupational roles are often central.

In addition to money and power, the distribution of health and happiness in later life will also be reviewed. These four possessions are a reasonable catalog of aspects of well-being in later life. Health and happiness are not resources in the same sense as money and power, but they are related in important ways to the possession of resources.

CHANGES IN INCOME

Changes in income in later life, together with temporal change in this regard, will be described. Sex, occupation, and citizenship are the key roles in the distribution of income in later life.

Income appears to increase up to the decade of the 60s and then to begin a sharp decline. The decline is substantial, something on the order of 50 percent for those who have retired (Riley and Foner 1968, p 454).

The most important influence on income change in later life is unemployment (Riley and Foner 1968, p 73). It is harder for older men to find a new job than it is for younger men, although older men if employed are less likely than younger men to lose their job (Riley and Foner 1968, pp. 46–48). The percent of men in the labor force (either employed or looking for work) begins to decline among men in their fifties and shows a steeper rate of decline thereafter (Riley and Foner 1968, p 42).

Retirement from the labor force has a number of causes (Riley and Foner 1968, pp 56–67). Mandatory retirement is important; one-fifth of a large sample of retired men gave this reason. The availability of benefits induces retirement, as does poor health. The difficulty that older men face in finding a new job has been mentioned. Reasons for this difficulty include the greater pension costs to employers and the probable lower education of an older applicant for a job compared to a younger applicant.

Continued employment of men in later life, whether part time or full time, is strongly related to two interdependent factors: status of the occupation, and education of the individual. This correlation of socioeconomic status with continued employment is manifest in the fact that the higher the average earnings of older men in the previous decade, the greater the percent who are employed (Riley and Foner 1968, p 451).

Education is strongly related to being in the labor force at all ages (Riley and Foner 1968, pp 48–49). At present, there is considerable disparity between age categories in years of education, in part because of the numbers of foreign born among the aged, in part because of the temporal trend toward longer schooling for more people. This disparity is indeed considerable; today, one-fifth of older people are functional illiterates, meaning that they have less than five years of schooling (Riley and Foner 1968, p 112).

Higher status occupations exhibit relatively high rates of employment for men in later life, and there are several possible contributing factors (Riley and Foner 1968, pp 50, 213, 450–451). The occupations in question are professional and technical workers, managers and proprietors, and farmers and farm managers. Part of the explanation may be that these occupations are more likely to permit continued employment, full or part time. There is also some evidence that men in higher status occupations have better health and, in addition, work in these occupations may be more of a pleasure than it is in lower status occupations.

The effect on income of not working is not compensated by benefits. Much retirement income is fixed, and its purchasing power is eroded by inflation, and even when postretirement income is increased to maintain its purchasing power, the temporal trend upward in the standard of living due to economic growth generates of itself discrepancy between generations (Riley and Foner 1968, pp 74, 83–85). However, the temporal trend toward greater benefits for older people means that a smaller proportion of older people are destitute in some stark sense (Riley and Foner 1968, pp. 79–80). Financial aid from children is negligible, except possibly for sharing a household with an aged and infirm parent (Riley and Foner 1968, pp 129, 181, 553). Retirement benefits commonly apply to widows as well as to the male breadwinner. Married women who have worked are subject to a disadvantage under Social Security rules in comparison with wives who have not worked; both may be entitled to widow's benefits, but the wife who has worked enough to be entitled to retirement benefits in her own right cannot receive both these and widow's benefits.

In this century, there has been a temporal trend downward in the percent of men 65 and over who are in the labor force, both in this country and in other industrial societies. Such a trend has not been observed for women, but it may be present and concealed by the increase in the proportion of women who enter the labor force (Riley and Foner 1968, pp 42–45).

This trend toward earlier retirement is not completely understood. It is not clearly associated with any of the changes in the occupational and industrial structure, and there is no evidence that it is due to a decline over time in the health of older men (Riley and Foner 1968, pp 51–58). Together with the trend toward longer life expectancy, the effect is a trend in the direction of more years of life in retirement for men (Riley and Foner 1968, pp 422–424).

There is no reason to expect major change in age-related disparity in income, although, as previously stated, the proportion of old people who are destitute should decrease. This trend illustrates why citizenship was named as a key role in the distribution of income in later life. Citizenship was once a restricted privilege, an important source of inequality, but there is a temporal trend in industrial societies toward an equalitarian definition, which includes the idea of rights to various kinds of services and financial support (Lenski 1966, pp 428–430). Governmental programs that provide income and payment for health care are examples.

Decrease in age-related disparity in education can be expected, in part because of the death of the foreign born, in part because it is not practical for the upward trend in average years of education from one generation to the next to continue indefinitely. But this change will not of itself reduce age-related disparity in income. It is true that having more education leads to getting a higher status job (see, eg, Blau and Duncan

1967, pp 165–177), and that, as previously noted, socioeconomic status in middle life is related to income in old age. But these correlations pertain to how individuals get distributed in the occupational structure. Age-related disparity in income, on the other hand, results principally from events due to aging, such as retirement, and to economic growth, which in the language of this chapter is temporal change.

CHANGES IN POWER

Power is defined here as command over the actions of others, and control of resources. The incumbency of roles with managerial or political power illustrates the first kind of power; being rich ilustrates the second. Power is not quantifiable in the convenient way that purchasing power can be quantified. It is therefore not possible to parallel the discussion of income by reviewing the distribution of "average power" over age categories. However, very powerful positions can be identified, and the distribution of these over age (and sex) categories will be reviewed. Similarly, the distribution of very high incomes over age categories will be discussed.

Up to the point of retirement, aging tends to confer on men greater access to powerful occupational and political positions. This appears to be due in part to the advantages of experience plus growth in income and in part to customs conferring access to advancement on the basis of age, such as seniority rules, and the belief that a superior should not be younger than a subordinate.

Extremely powerful positions, in politics and in organizations, are often held by older men. Where there is no mandatory retirement, tenancy of these positions commonly continues after the man has grown old. Everyone is familiar with the advanced age of Congressional leaders and members of the Supreme Court, for example (Riley and Foner 1968, pp 475–478; Lenski 1966, pp 406–407).

Age is no barrier to the possession of great wealth, since such wealth does not result from earnings and consequently is not subject to the age-related impediments to employment in later life. Working is no way to get rich; indeed, the time thus consumed is a hindrance to the acquisition or management of a fortune. Many of the wealthy are old people (Riley and Foner 1968, pp 76, 89–92; Lenski 1966, p 406).

Information is lacking as to whether extreme power and extreme wealth are more or less concentrated in older hands today than in the past. The phenomenon is, however, probably characteristic of industrial societies in general in recent history (Lenski 1966, p 407).

CHANGE IN HEALTH

The occurrence of certain chronic diseases, impairments, and disabilities increases with age, although this increase begins well before old age. It is not known whether the extent of decline in health from middle age to old age is different now from what it was in the past (Riley and Foner 1968, pp 204–205, 212).

In old age, disability is inversely related to income, but this is true of all ages, and the direction of causation is not certain. The death rate has usually been observed to rise among adults as occupational status drops, which suggests, as previously noted, that socioeconomic status is the cause and bad health the effect (Riley and Foner 1968, pp 34–35, 213).

How people evaluate their own health is a phenomenon important in its own right for numerous reasons, quite apart from how a physician might assess their condition (DiCicco and Apple 1958; Apple 1960). Although older people rate their health as generally good or excellent less often than do younger people, about 40 percent consider themselves in good health; after allowing for actual health status, a better self-rating of health is associated with higher socioeconomic status (Riley and Foner 1968, pp 294–295).

CHANGE IN HAPPINESS

Happiness, self-rated, declines with age, but this decline begins before old age. On the other hand, the reported amount of worrying generally declines with age. Overall, and apart from the effects of specific problems, there seems to be no general tendency for elderly people to be less content than are adults in young and middle age (Riley and Foner 1968, pp 341–344).

Among men, retirement is associated with lower morale, independent of health and of socioeconomic status, which are also related to morale. However, over half of retired persons were found to have a positive view of retirement. Worrying about finances has been found to decline with age (Riley and Foner 1968, pp 348–358, 453).

Among older people, socioeconomic status is related to satisfaction, and this relation is independent of health. Among the elderly, as among other age categories, education is positively related to happiness (Riley and Foner 1968, p 348).

Prospects

Possibly the worst difficulties of older people in American society today have to do with income and health. What can be forecast in these areas? First, it is likely that the trend toward expansion of citizens' rights to include more adequate retirement and health benefits for older people will continue, because trends of this kind have generally been observed to persist in industrial societies. Although there should be a further decline in the proportion of old people who are poor in an absolute sense, a degree of relative poverty in later life is likely to continue, if for no other reason than economic growth, which confers an advantage on younger generations.

Economic well-being in later life is partly a consequence of socioeconomic status in middle life, and this status will doubtlessly continue for some time to be related to race. These influences, together with increasing life expectancy for nonwhites, mean that in the future a larger proportion of older people will be nonwhite and relatively poor.

Better health for older people depends on how health care is financed, on improvements in medical knowledge, and on more emphasis on health maintenance and rehabilitation. There are grounds for optimism regarding at least the first two of these factors.

Older people of future generations will be better educated than those of the present generation. This will not, for the reasons previously discussed, have much effect by itself on income inequality between age categories. But it should have a beneficial effect of another kind.

It will be recalled that a substantial minority of elderly people are functional illiterates. There is a quality which can be called sophistication, and which is manifest by the ability to manage one's every day affairs so as to avoid being victimized, to take advantage of rights and opportunities, and to make reasonable judgments about events in the world at large. Some minimum amount of formal education seems necessary for the development of this quality. Whatever this minimum may be, it is certainly above the level that defines functional illiteracy. Better educated old people, therefore, means more sophisticated old people.

Sophistication, as defined, is no guarantee of happiness, but the lack of it is certainly an obstactle to happiness. Better educated old people can therefore be expected to be less vulnerable to some of the causes of unhappiness in old age.

References

Apple (see Sweetser)

Beresford JC, Rivlin AM: The multigeneration family. Paper prepared for the Univ Michigan Conf on Aging, Ann Arbor, Michigan, June 29-July 1, 1964

———: Privacy, poverty, and old age. Demography 3:247–58, 1966

Blau PM, Duncan OD: The American Occupational Structure. New York, Wiley, 1967

Bultena GL: Rural-urban differences in the familial interaction of the aged. Rural Sociol 34:5–15, 1969

Carter H, Glick C: Marriage and Divorce: A Social and Economic Study. Cambridge, Mass, Harvard Univ Press, 1970

Cumming E, Henry, WE: Growing Old. New York, Basic Books, 1961

DiCicco L, Apple D: Health needs and opinions of older adults. Public Health Reports 73:479–87, 1958

Lenski GE: Power and Privilege: A Theory of Social Stratification. New York, McGraw-Hill, 1966

Petersen W: Population, 2nd ed. New York, Macmillan, 1969

Pryor ET Jr: Rhode Island family structure: 1875 and 1960. Paper presented at the 1967 annual meeting of the Population Ass of America

Riley MW, Foner A: Aging and Society, Vol. 1: An Inventory of Research Findings. New York, Russell Sage Foundation, 1968
Shanas E, Townsend P, Wedderburn D, et al: Old People in Three Industrial Societies. New York, Atherton Press, 1968
Sweetser DA: How laymen define illness. J Health Hum Behav 1:219–25, 1960
———: The effect of industrialization on intergenerational solidarity. Rural Sociol 31:156–70, 1966
———: Intergenerational ties in Finnish urban families. Am Sociol Rev 33:236–46, 1968
———: The structure of sibling relationships. Am J Sociol 76:47–58, 1970
———: Urban Norwegians: Kinship Networks, and Sibling Mobility. Oslo, Institute of Applied Social Research, 1973

6
ECONOMICS OF AGING

Blanche Fitzpatrick, Ph.D.

I am an old woman
When Germany had awoken
Pension rates were cut. My children
Gave me the pennies they could spare. But
I could hardly buy anything now. So at first
Less often I went to the shops where I'd gone daily.
But one day I thought hard, and then
Daily once more I went to the baker's, the greengrocer's
As an old customer
With care I picked my provisions
Took no more than I used to, but no less either
Put rolls beside the loaf and leeks beside the cabbage and only
When they added up did I sigh
With my stiff fingers dug into my little purse
And shaking my head confessed that I didn't have enough
To pay for those things, and shaking my head I
Left the shop, observed by all the customers
I said to myself:
If all of us who have nothing
No longer turned up where food is laid out
They might think we don't need anything

But if we come and can't buy anything
They'll know how it is.

From "The Shopper," by Bertolt Brecht*

As the findings of Congressional hearings or academic studies appear in the daily press, there is an occasional flurry of concern with respect to the economic plight of older Americans. Understandably, public sympathies become hardened to accounts of distressful situations and only spectacular emergencies of fire or flood call forth an outpouring of funds, or appeals for governmental action. Yet, if the average citizen had a clear

*"Gedichte," Band 5, © Copyright Suhrkamp Verlag, Frankfurt, a. Main, 1964.

vision of the deprivation and often utter destitution awaiting after age 65, there might be more pressure on Congress to make adequate provision for the economic security of the aged.

The question as to whether aged citizens should be given any share in the economic product in their retirement years, or how large that share should be, cannot be answered by economic theory. Economics is not normative, although economists may be. Economic forces will dictate a division of the total product of economic activity among the productive factors in proportion to the respective contributions of land, labor, and capital. Nonfactor income must be drawn from the shares of productive factors, and awarded by social decisions. Ideally, this decision with respect to the aged nonproducer should be made by society members fully aware of their own progress toward retirement and the hazards thereof.

To assist in the social decision, economic analysis can point out the effects of alternative decisions with respect to taxing, spending, and employment policies of the public sector, and the effects of discriminatory programs in the private sector, on the economic welfare of the aged, and of the whole society.

This chapter is intended to present data on the economic status of the aged in the 1970s, to provide information not only for those in social service professions dealing with the aged but also to sharpen the consciousness of workers approaching retirement as to the adequacy of financial provisions. The economic situation of the aged will be analyzed under four headings:

The economic status of the aged.
Causes of poverty among the aged.
Economic effects of present policies affecting income of aged.
Summary; suggested remedies for financial distress of the aged.

In the following discussion, "aged" will be used to refer to those 65 and over, unless otherwise indicated. Aging is a continuous process, as pointed out in earlier chapters, and proceeds at different rates among different individuals. Some of the handicaps borne by persons 65 and over, in the areas of employment and income, may also affect persons 10 or 20 years younger. Indeed, as President Johnson indicated when signing the Older Americans Act of 1965, discrimination in employment may begin at 40 or 45, and the economic plight of persons retiring at age 62 may in fact be worse than that of 65-year-old retirees, because of reduced Social Security benefits. Nevertheless, since most detailed data is available after the 65-year cutoff point, attention herein will be focused on those of that age or above.

The Economic Status of the Aged

In the 1968 Survey of the Aged, over half the aged were poor, or near-poor, in terms of a very restrictive living standard established by the Social Security Administration.

Advertisements for retirement homes in sunny climes, with smiling oldsters enjoying leisure activities, may lead one to believe that the years after 65 will be "golden years." How accurate is that impression? The most recent comprehensive study indicating the numbers of aged and their financial status was made in 1968 by the Bureau of the Census for processing by the Social Security Administration. The American population 65 and over at the end of 1967 consisted of an estimated 19.3 million persons, 8.1 million men and 11.2 million women. There were 15.8 million aged units consisting of almost 6 million married couples (with at least one partner 65 or older) and almost 10 million nonmarried persons (Tables 1 and 2).

The median annual income reported in this study was $3373 for married couples and $1306 for nonmarried persons, 65 and over. The

TABLE 1. Estimated 1967 U.S. Population Persons Aged 65 and Older by Sex and Marital Status*

Marital Status	Men	Women
Total number (in thousands)	8,108	11,186
Percent	100	100
Married, spouse present	72	34
Nonmarried	28	66
Widowed	18	54
Other	10	12

**From Bixby: Social Sec Bull 33(4):6, 1970.*

TABLE 2. Income Size: Percentage Distribution of Aged Units by Money Income Class, 1967*

Total Money Income	All Units	Married Couples	Nonmarried Persons		
			Total	Men	Women
Number (in thousands):					
Total	15,779	5,989	9,789	2,356	7,434
Reporting on income	12,186	4,417	7,770	1,954	5,816
Percent of units	100	100	100	100	100
Less than $1,000	21	3	31	20	36
1,000–1,499	19	6	26	23	27
1,500–1,999	14	11	16	18	15
2,000–2,499	10	12	10	15	8
2,500–2,999	7	11	5	7	4
3,000–3,499	6	10	3	4	3
3,500–3,999	4	9	2	3	1
4,000–4,999	6	11	3	4	2
5,000–7,499	7	15	2	3	2
7,500–9,999	3	7	1	2	1
10,000–14,999	2	3	1	1	1
15,000 or more	1	2	1	1	1
Median income	$1,828	$3,373	$1,306	$1,692	$1,227

**From Bixby: Social Sec Bull 33(4):8, Table 1, 1970.*

median defines the mid-point in a distribution, with half the group above and half below that point. In order to evaluate the adequacy of this "average" income, it is necessary to compare the figures above with the dollar amount required for an adequate living standard for couples and single aged persons.

Definitions of an adequate living standard differ between government agencies. The Social Security Agency has established an income threshold based on the minimum food requirements identified by the Department of Agriculture, with all other expenditures for two-person families estimated at about three times the food expenditure. On this basis, income standards for "poor" and "near-poor" classifications are shown in Table 3.

With respect to the above dollar amounts in the "poor" and "near-poor" categories, it might be possible for someone trained in home economics to buy a nutritionally adequate diet within the food component of the budget, and for a resourceful and energetic shopper to buy in economical quantities, and at sale prices, other necessary items. Whether such a consumption pattern is possible for the aged is open to serious question. Even at this minimal standard of adequacy, 44 percent of the aged units in 1967 were classified as poor and another 11 percent as near-poor.

When compared to the less stringent and more realistic living standard developed by the U.S. Bureau of Labor Statistics, the shortfall of the typical income of the aged is even more pronounced. As indicated above, with a moderate level of living defined at $3930 for a retired couple and $2170 for the nonmarried, only about one-third of the aged couples were at or above this income level, and the nonmarried fared even worse (Bixby 1970, p 9).

The "moderate level of living," as may be inferred from the dollar amount specified, does not provide the aged couple with luxuries. The 1969 report of the Special Committee on Aging of the U.S. Senate commented ". . . the Bureau of Labor Statistics moderate budget for a retired couple is little more than a rigid austerity budget, but even this level of living is far out of reach for most elderly Americans today." (U.S. Senate

TABLE 3. Poverty Thresholds for Aged*

Defined by:	Aged Income Standard	Thresholds, 1967	
		Couples	Nonmarried
SSA	Poor	$2,020	$1,600
SSA	Near poor	2,690	1,900
BLS	Moderate	3,930	2,170

**From Bixby: Social Sec Bull 33(4):8, 1970. For later adjustments to poverty threshold, see Social Sec Bull 34(7):11, 1971, fn 1; 35(8):4, 1972, fn 4.*

1969.) As an example of the representative items and quantities, the BLS budget, which assumes "an average inventory" of the usual possessions, permits a new suit for the husband every three to four years, one new street dress and one new house dress for the wife each year. Purchase of a used car is provided for every six to eight years, and operating expenses are calculated for a car of average age seven years. For nonowners of cars, the annual allowance for public transportation is 107 fares, or about one joint expedition per week for the elderly couple (U.S. Department of Labor 1966, app. A, pp 21–31).

Medicare and Medicaid have eased much of the financial anxiety associated with chronic or prolonged illness in old age. Nevertheless, out of an average medical care bill of about $800, the average aged person in 1970 paid $226 directly (Cooper and McGee 1971). Thus the aged individual's higher expenditure for medical care, more than double that for younger persons, further restricts discretionary purchases from his limited income.

It might be contended that the aged person has less desire as well as less need for personal communication items. Sociologists and psychologists can better define the "needs" of the aged in contemporary society. Yet the argument that 50 years ago the average older American was able to survive without telephone, TV, or automobile is not sufficient to define these items as luxuries today, even in economic terms. In a changing economic structure, there may be a necessity for an automobile to reach outlying supermarkets; with changing institutions for the delivery of medical care, a telephone may replace the vanished family physician, a TV set provides the recreation once available at now boarded-up local theatres.

Thus it seems fair to say that, by either definition, the majority of aged units in 1967 were living in poverty or near-poverty. Even though there appears to be some underreporting of income and assets in the 1968 Social Security study by persons at the upper end of the distribution, as compared to Internal Revenue Service data for the same period, the Social Security analysts estimate that the median would be unlikely to change significantly.

Viewed historically, poverty among the aged is not an unusual phenomenon, as the biblical account of the widow Naomi testifies. Whether in hunting, pastoral, agricultural, or industrial communities, a person who is not himself a producer, nor related to a producer, depends on the good will of the community, and even more, on the productive capacity of that community, for subsistence. The 1968 Social ScSccurity Administration study indicates that relatively few aged can be classed as current producers judging by the percentage of units reporting income derived from earnings (although other sources of income listed may relate to past productive activity). The distribution of income by source, in Table 4 and Figure 1, provides the basis for analysis in the next section of the causes of poverty among the aged.

TABLE 4. Income Sources: Percent of Aged Units with Money Income from Specified Sources, 1967*

Source of Money Income	All Units	Married Couples	Nonmarried Persons		
			Total	Men	Women
Total number† (in thousands)	15,779	5,989	9,789	2,356	7,434
Percent of units with:					
Earnings	27	46	15	19	14
Wages and salaries	21	36	12	14	12
Self-employment	6	12	3	5	2
Retirement benefits	89	90	89	91	88
OASDHI	86	87	85	86	84
Other public pensions	10	11	9	11	8
Railroad retirement	4	5	3	5	3
Government employee	6	7	5	6	5
Private group pensions	12	19	7	13	5
Veterans' benefits	10	12	9	11	8
Unemployment insurance	1	2	1	1	1
Public assistance	12	6	15	14	16
Income from assets	50	60	44	44	45
Private individual annuities	2	2	2	1	2
Personal contributions‡	3	2	4	2	5

**From Bixby: Social Sec Bull 33(4):10, Table 2, 1970.*
†Substantially all respondents reported whether or not they had income (although not necessarily its amount) from each source except assets, on which 84 percent reported.
‡Contributions by relatives or friends not in household.

Causes of Poverty among the Aged

LACK OF INCOME FROM EMPLOYMENT

Only about one-fourth of the aged units reported earnings as a source of income in 1967. Although poor health is a factor in withdrawal from the labor force, restrictive public and private policies prevent some able aged individuals from working.

The fundamental reasons for elderly poverty lies in their lack of work force attachment. Participation in the labor force is overwhelmingly the chief source of income for younger persons and provides the best assurance of sharing in rising national output. Only 27 percent of all aged units reported earnings as a source of income in 1967 (Table 4). Almost half the married couples reported labor force participation during the year (typically, but not always, the husband only) but only one-sixth of the nonmarried persons reported such labor force participation. Among nonmarried persons over 65, three-fifths are 73 years of age and older (Bixby 1970, p 8).

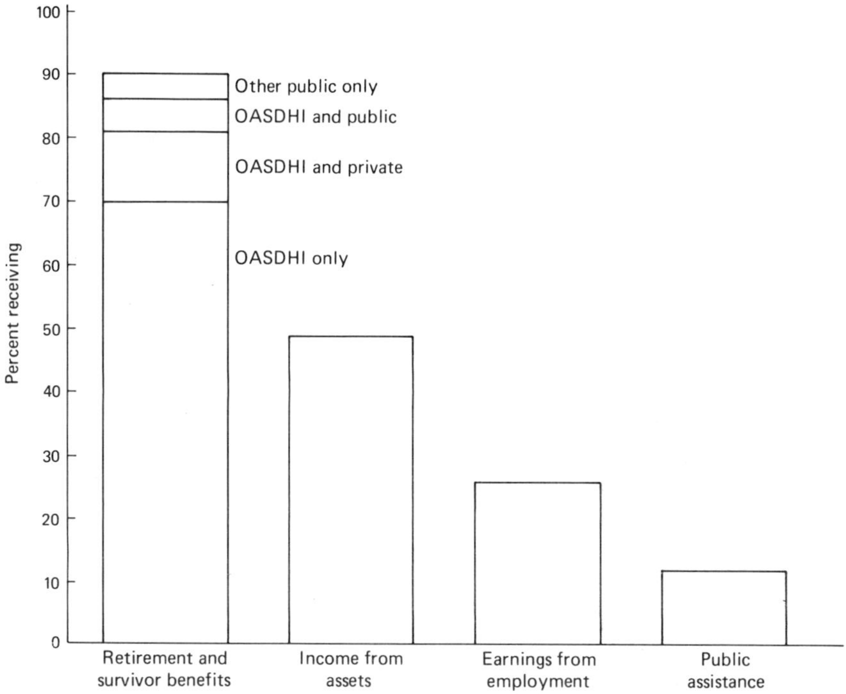

FIG. 1. Main sources of money income for aged units, 1967. (From Social Sec Bull 33(4):10, Chart 2, 1970.)

As compared to 1900 when approximately two-thirds of men 65 and over were in the labor force, by 1969 only one-fourth were so reported (U.S. Bureau of Census 1970). Aged women, while reporting low participation in both periods, increased their participation slightly from about 8 percent in 1900 to 9 percent in 1969, reflecting changing customs and greater opportunity for less physically taxing work. A variety of reasons underlie the sharp decline in male labor force participation. Employment in 1971 as compared to 1900 is concentrated much more in services than in goods production, and requires fewer workers who are unskilled, more who are better educated and technically trained. Among aged Americans, only half completed elementary school, their working life beginning before the advent of high technology industries, when strength, not skill, was the prime requisite.

Because of the sequence of technologic development, older workers today are typically found to predominate in declining industries like textiles and railroads, while younger workers predominate in expanding industries, such as electronics and computer services. Thus the older worker who loses his job when the mill closes may possess only an obsolete skill related to a production process in an industry that is disappearing.

The older worker, though often protected by seniority provisions when trade slows down, will tend to be unemployed longer than younger workers when all workers are laid off in a shutdown. Finding new employment may be impossible, not only because of lack of specialized skills but also because of employer reluctance to assume the higher pension costs attaching to older employees. The difficulty of reemployment for the aging worker not only leads to lower labor force participation rates for those 65 and over but also to early claims for reduced Social Security benefits at 62, which intensifies the problem of low retirement income.

Declining health may also be a factor in early retirement. It is hard for a psychologist, and impossible for an economist, to separate the motives that lead to retirement before the "normal" age of 65. But when workers file for benefits at age 62, claiming ill health as the reason, after being unemployed or out of the labor force for periods ranging from six months to over three years, as was the case with almost half the 62-year-old beneficiaries in the 1969 Survey of Newly Entitled Beneficiaries (SNEB), it is at least as possible that continuing reemployment difficulties may have worsened physical problems, as that causation ran in the opposite direction. With workers who retired at age 65, in the same study, only 21 percent reported ill health as the main reason for leaving their last job (Reno 1971, pp 8, 13).

Voluntary withdrawal from the labor force is the more likely, the higher the expected retirement income. For a fortunate few, the opportunity to combine relatively high Social Security benefits with private pensions may induce voluntary retirement. Thus three-quarters of those with combined Social Security and private pension income of $5000 or more reported that they wished to retire (Reno 1971, pp 10, 11). However, *with a median annual retirement income of only $1,770* anticipated from private pensions and Social Security benefits combined, it is not surprising that, overall, 70 percent of those retiring should have done so because of poor health, compulsory retirement, loss of their jobs, or poor returns on their own businesses, as reported in the same study. Over half the 65-year-old retirees reported compulsory retirement as the main reason for leaving the last job. Whatever the causal sequence in the case of workers aged 62 to 64, of whom over half reported health as the main reason for leaving, it may be stretching a point to classify as voluntary the early withdrawal from the labor force of an older worker who has been unemployed six months or more, who chooses to accept below-poverty line Social Security benefits while possessing no other pension income (Reno 1971, pp 8, 13). It may merely represent the rational decision that something is better than nothing.

To sum up, why do not older workers remain in the labor force when such attachment is the best guarantee of adequate income? Very often they do not because they cannot. They cannot continue in employment because the firm or plant and/or union requires retirement at a stipulated age; or the plant shuts down, or the firm merges with another, or introduces automatic machinery, and the unemployed older worker is unable to find a market for outmoded skills; or poor health may cause the employer to require "retirement" or the worker may "voluntarily" retire for the same reason. When the anticipated income is below poverty levels, nonparticipation in the labor force may reasonably be taken to reflect impediments rather than choice.

INADEQUATE INCOME FROM RETIREMENT BENEFITS

Social Security benefits in the 1968 study were inadequate of themselves to maintain even a poverty-level living standard, for two-thirds of the married couples, and almost all nonmarried individuals. Private pensions were received by only 12 percent of the aged units studied, and these were usually persons receiving higher Social Security benefits as well; this was true also of the 10 percent receiving other public pensions.

Although earnings from employment contribute to substantially higher incomes for aged units with an employed member, only 27 percent of all aged units reported such earnings. By contrast 89 percent of all units in the 1968 survey reported income from pensions of one form or another, which provided 37 percent of aggregate aged income (Tables 5 and 6). Pension income as shown in Table 3 may be classified as: *OASDHI* benefits under the Social Security Act of 1935, payable at age 65 to persons meeting work-experience requirements, and at age 62 at a reduced rate. *Other public pensions* are payable to federal or state workers, and rail-

TABLE 5. Income Shares: Percentage Distribution of Money Income by Source for Aged Units, 1967*

Source of Money Income	All Units	Married Couples	Nonmarried Persons		
			Total	Men	Women
Number (in thousands):					
Total	15,779	5,989	9,789	2,356	7,434
Reporting on income	12,177	4,474	7,779	1,954	5,816
Percent of income	100	100	100	100	100
Earnings	29	39	15	17	14
Retirement benefits	46	42	51	56	48
OASDHI	34	30	40	40	39
Other public pensions	7	6	8	10	7
Private group pensions	5	6	3	6	2
Veterans' benefits	3	3	4	5	4
Public assistance	4	2	7	5	8
Income from assets	15	13	18	14	19
Personal contributions†	1	‡	1	‡	2
Other sources	3	2	4	2	4

**From Bixby: Social Sec Bull 33(4):11, Table 3, 1970.*
†Contributions by relatives or friends not in househould.
‡0.5 percent or less.

TABLE 6. Income Shares: Percentage Distribution of Money Income by Source for Aged Units, 1967. Adjusted by Data from IRS, Administrative Records, and 1968 DECA*

Source of Money Income	Percent of Money Income	
	100%	
Earnings	30	
Retirement benefits	37	
OASDHI		26
Other		11
Veterans' benefits and public assistance	6	
Income from assets	25	
Other	2	

From Bixby: Social Sec Bull 33(4):14, 1970.

road employees meeting age and service requirements; *private group pensions* are payable to employees meeting age and service requirements under employer or union unilateral or collectively bargained provisions. (Annuities, or other forms of individually provided retirement income, will be considered under asset income.)

Since pension income is received by so large a fraction of the aged population, the fact that so many are nevertheless classified as "poor" indicates that pension levels cannot usually, of themselves, provide adequate retirement income.

Of the public pensions, "Social Security" (OASDHI) is clearly the most extensive in coverage. In 1967, 86 percent of all aged units reported OASDHI pensions compared to only 10 percent receiving "private group pensions." Originally, when the 1935 Social Security Act was passed, coverage was limited, with exclusions of governmental, agricultural, domestic, casual, and nonprofit employees, and the self-employed. In succeeding years, coverage was gradually broadened so that in the 1970's over 90 percent of the population 65 and over are eligible for Social Security benefits, although some elect to continue working, and postpone or reduce benefits.

Although Social Security benefits are thus available to most of the aged, the level of benefits is low, especially in comparison with previous earnings levels. The computation of benefits was designed to give low-income workers relative to high-income workers a greater fraction of preretirement earnings. Thus, a 65-year-old nonmarried worker, meeting requirements for quarters of coverage, with a record of average *annual* earnings as little as $200 yearly, or less than $20/month, could be awarded the current minimum *monthly* benefit ($85 in 1973). However, a 65-year-old worker with preretirement earnings equal to the average wage in manufacturing would receive OASDHI benefits amounting to less than one-third his preretirement earnings, or less than one-half such earnings, if married (Horlick 1970, p 6).

The 1968 study clearly indicates the inadequacy of Social Security benefits alone to provide for the needs of the aged. In 1967, the median benefit payment was $1,090, with almost two-thirds of the beneficiaries receiving less than $1,250 in OASDHI payments. Less than one-third of the married couples received as much as $2,000, which is below the extremely low poverty line cited as established by Social Security for couples (Kolodrubetz 1970, p 6).

It might be argued that the Social Security benefit is meant only as a basic income, to be supplemented by income from other public or private employment-related pensions and by private annuities and savings. Private annuities and other forms of savings will be discussed in a subsequent section. The extent of coverage and adequacy of public and private employment-related pensions will be considered in following paragraphs. Before moving on from the question of adequacy of supplements to Social Security benefits, a general point might be made. The 1968 study showed that one-third of the nonmarried Social Security beneficiaries *received less than $150 for the year in income* other than Social Security benefits, while almost one-fifth of the married beneficiaries had *less than $300 in additional income* (Bixby 1970, p 24). Over 60 percent of aged units received no other periodic retirement benefits (Kolodrubetz 1970, p 3).

It is obvious that only a small fraction of the aged population will be eligible for other public pensions, as former employees of governmental units at all levels. In the 1968 study, only 10 percent of all aged units were so entitled (Table 4). As might be expected, since about two-thirds of the aged units receiving such pensions were also on the OASDHI rolls, such beneficiaries enjoyed more favorable economic circumstances than recipients of OASDHI only, with median pension income of $3,060 for married couples as compared to a $1,480 median for OASDHI beneficiary couples with no other pensions.

Again, with respect to private group pensions, the percentage of recipient aged units was low, 12 percent in the 1968 study (Table 4). The median pension income of such private pension recipients who also received OASDHI benefits was about $3,000, double the amount received by the recipients of OASDHI only (Kolodrubetz 1970, p 11). In the case of private group pensions, the popular press has noted that coverage is becoming more widespread and may have created the impression that a majority of retired workers in the future will have adequate pension income through a combination of OASDHI and group pension coverage. Private group pension programs, either granted unilaterally by the employer or obtained through collective bargaining, have indeed become more widepsread in recent years. By 1970, 30 million persons, most of whom were also covered under Social Security, were covered by private group pensions with reserves of over $100 billion (U.S. Senate Special Committee on Aging 1970, p 1426). But the growth of such pension plans seems to be slowing, as most of the large firms or industries, particularly those unionized, have now been reached. The most optimistic projections for extension of private pension coverage envision that by 1980 only between 30 percent and 40 percent of all aged persons will have income from this source, and these recipients will be concentrated, as now, at the upper end of the Social Security benefit distribution.

The basic drawback to reliance on supplemental pensions under private group plans is that not all of the 30 million "covered" at present under private plans will ultimately collect, and many employees of smaller firms do not have the option of being covered by such a pension. A long-time student of private pension programs, Professor Merton Bernstein, Professor of Law at Ohio State University, once described the current chance of collection under private group pension program: "If every year an employee were given what represented his retirement earnings for that year and was sent to a racetrack and told that he had to bet on a 10 to 1 shot or a horse with longer odds and that would be the way he would provide for his retirement from the private sector, we would consider that an irresponsible arrangement. If, in addition to that, the U.S. Government gave a tax subsidy to this arrangement, we would be aghast. And yet that is what we are doing with the private pension system. We are having each worker, who is fortunate enough to begin with, to be under a private-pension plan, bet against heavy odds that he will reach eligibility (U.S. Senate Hearings 1970, p 1426).

Until the passage of the Employee Retirement Income Security Act in 1974, the majority of plans required 10 to 15 years service before "vesting," that is before the employee acquired the right to take the contribution with him when his employment is terminated. With a mobile work force, that condition might not be met, and a worker might be "covered" by several plans in successive employment and yet not acquire eligibility for collecting a pension under any of them. Even when a worker chose to remain with one firm, company failures, mergers, or plant closings might prevent the worker from collecting a pension, as in the Studebaker case. The funding arrangements set up by the company as a source of future pensions likewise might be inadequately safeguarded. These characteristics of private pension plans induced the comment by Assistant Secretary of Labor for Labor-Management Services, Thomas R. Donahue:

> In all too many cases the pension promise shrinks to this: "If you remain in good health and stay with the same company until you are 65 years old, and if the company is still in business, and if your department has not been abolished, and if you haven't been laid off for too long a time, and if there is enough money in the fund, and if that money has been prudently managed, you will get a pension." (U.S. Senate Hearings 1970, p 1541.)

It is not necessary to assume double dealing by the employer to recognize that the collection of benefits by only a small fraction of those originally covered by private pension plans necessarily follows from the insurance principle. This was brought out in hearings on private pension plans before the U.S. Joint Economic Committee in 1966, in the following interchange between Senator Javits of New York and Henry T. Ivers,

Chairman of the Board of Trustees of the Western Conference of Teamsters Pension Trust (U.S. Senate Hearings 1970, p 1540):

> Senator Javits: But your estimate is that one-sixth of the total for whom there are contributions will get benefits. Will that one-sixth get the contributions which were paid in for the other five-sixths as well as the contributions paid in for them?
>
> Mr. Ivers: That is the only way the plan could be supported. Your death and attrition rates are what support the plan. . . .

Thus, reliance on private pension programs as a universal supplement to inadequate Social Security benefits has been reliance on a very slim reed.

The Employee Retirement Income Security Act, signed into law September 2, 1974, has improved the prospects for future pensions for those currently employed, but provides no retroactive recourse for pension contributions previously lost. The new law requires that private pension plans meet new strict standards governing plan administration by "fiduciaries," so that funds will not be dissipated through unsound management. The prospects for vesting, under three alternative formulas, are greatly increased, since vesting would typically occur after five years of employment under the plan. Moreover, the creation of a federally chartered insurance corporation (Pension Benefit Guaranty Corporation) will guarantee that participants will receive their vested benefits (subject to certain limitations), even in the event of plant closings or other unforeseen circumstances.

Yet of the 93 million persons in the labor force in October 1974, only 30 million are enrolled in private pension plans; 23 million will be covered by the insurance provisions. There is every reason to believe that the new stricter requirements for plan administration will deter the initiation of new plans, because of the higher costs to employers. Vesting provisions are effective for new plans on enactment, but not until December 31, 1975 for existing plans, and in some cases may not be put into effect until 1980 (US Dept of Labor October 1974).

A further question, that of the equitability of the favorable tax treatment accorded private pension plans, will be considered in Section III, with respect to economic effects. At present, to quote again from the 1968 SSA Survey of the Aged, 12 percent of all aged units reported income from private pensions. Median 1967 private pension income was $900 for all units, lower than the OASDHI median, but with a much wider range (Kolodrubetz 1970, p 7). Social Security analysis indicated that persons with private pensions were likely to have higher OASDHI benefits than those without private pensions.

> This difference is not surprising since private pension coverage historically has been concentrated in industries and occupations covered by OASDHI since its beginning, and characterized by average and above

> average earnings. Furthermore private pensions normally accrue to those persons who spend most of their worklife in one job and thus have few interruptions in employment that could affect the average monthly earnings used to compute OASDHI benefits (Kolodrubetz 1970, p10.)

Thus, private group pensions are typically received by those in the higher range of Social Security benefits, and the aged person receiving the minimum Social Security benefit is not likely to receive additional income from this source (Kolodrubetz 1970, p 9). "Forty-one percent of the married couples with PIA's of $140 or more had private pensions compared with only 5 percent for those with PIA's under $100" (Kolodrubetz 1970, p 10).* A further weakness of reliance on private pensions is that few of these pension programs provide survivor benefits.

INADEQUATE INCOME FROM ASSETS

The unskilled worker with a lifetime attachment to low-income jobs, frequently subject to periodic unemployment, cannot accumulate enough assets to provide a supplemental income for his retirement years. The problems of inflation, rising productivity of the work force, and indeterminate life expectancy make individual provision a highly unsatisfactory method of insuring adequate income after age 65. In the 1968 Survey of the Aged, although about three-fourths of the married couples, and also about two-fifths of the nonmarried aged reported equity in their homes, assets in this form cannot readily be converted into income supplements because of the difficulty of finding suitable alternative quarters. With respect to financial assets (money in bank, U.S. bonds, stocks) "half the married couples who reported on such assets had amounts less than $2,000; two-thirds of the nonmarried persons had less than $1,500." As Social Security analysts comment: "Clearly, a majority of the elderly could not have counted on much income from such savings" (Murray 1972).

As reported in previous sections, only about one-fourth of the aged units receive income from employment; although OASDHI benefits are almost universally received, median benefit levels are low; other public or private pensions are received by a very small minority of aged units, and these are generally the couples or individuals with relatively high Social Security benefits. The possibility of individual saving during the working years remains to be explored as a means of providing an adequate level of living in retirement years.

With respect to asset accumulation, the 1968 Social Security survey indicates that income from assets amounted to only 15 percent of income of the aged (Table 5); however, comparison with mandatory income reporting of persons 65 and over to the IRS indicates that 25 percent of all

**The PIA is the "primary insurance amount" that would be paid a worker at age 65, based on past average earnings.*

income of aged units derives from this source. (See Source Distribution, Adjusted, Table 6.) Underreporting in SSA data appears to reflect incomplete information provided by members of upper income groups. IRS data, for a somewhat different concept of income—"adjusted gross income," including net capital gains and excluding public and private transfer payments— indicates that taxpayers 65 and over with adjusted annual gross income of $10,000 or more (representing 5 percent of aged units) received 56 percent of the income from assets, as well as 49 percent of the income from employment, received by the aged (Bixby 1970, p 9).

> Half the married couples and nonmarried persons aged 65 and over reported some income from assets in 1967. . . . Many of those reporting income from assets, however, had only small amounts, and the proportion of aggregate income from this source was smaller than that from benefits and earnings. . . . The median reported value of equity in the home was $12,000 for married couples and $10,000 for nonmarried men and women. For 45 to 50 percent of the aged units the value was between $5,000 and $15,000, and for 10 to 15 percent it was $25,000 or more. (Murray 1972.)

With respect to asset holdings, then, despite the above-noted underreporting in the 1968 asset data, it may fairly be assumed that most of the aged lack substantial holdings of cash or other readily convertible financial assets. It may be asked why the aged poor have made so little provision for their inevitable old age. It is recognized that savings have been made, even by low-income receivers during the working years in the form of home ownership. About three-fourths of the aged couples own their homes, with 80 percent mortgage free. Assets in this form, however, cannot readily be converted into income supplements in old age because of the difficulty of finding suitable alternative quarters at modest results, although rising property tax rates sometimes do force such conversion.

Property tax reductions for the elderly exist but vary between communities even within a single state, and, as noted below, may increase the burden on young, relatively poor homeowners for the benefit of comparatively well-off aged. In some rural communities, the high proportion of aged in the total population may make tax relief impossible or, if granted, may place an intolerable burden on the few remaining young families, and thus intensify outmigration.

The lack of private savings other than in the form of owned homes may be explained by the relation of income and expenditures over the working lifetime. The Task Force Working Paper "Economics of Aging: Toward a Full Share in Abundance" compares the possibility of savings for occupational groups from 1961–1962 data on incomes and expenditures as follows:

> Annual incomes exceed expenditures of the self-employed and professional workers families for most of the age cohorts, leaving sources of savings at practically all stages of work-life. Semi-skilled workers

> whose expenditures are below income for families in the middle and later years, also have a small margin for saving. For clerical and skilled workers, expenditures are barely balanced by income over the worklife, with the years of slight deficits roughly matched by years of small savings. *In the case of unskilled workers, no balance of income with expenditure is achieved except by the 55–64 age group.* (Special Committee on Aging, 1969; emphasis added.)

Even for those of the labor force able to save because of a recurring surplus of income over expenditures, the rise in national output (and per capita real earnings) over time progressively raises the consumption levels appropriate to a "moderate" living standard at retirement beyond the amount planned for in the earlier years of working life; as retirement progresses, income of retirees continues to be reduced as a proportion of average income received by those currently in the labor force. As rising prices outrun returns from modest asset holdings in the retirement years, the foregoing of consumption in earlier periods of working life may well seem in retrospect to have been ill-advised. The Task Force concludes: "If past performance is a guide, private savings cannot be expected to contribute significantly to raising the level of income in old age." (Special Committee on Aging 1969.)

The low median income, $3,373 for married couples and $1,306 for nonmarried persons 65 and over, indicates that the three major sources of income for aged, retirement pensions, earnings, and assets, provided inadequate income in 1967. Therefore, these three sources, which were envisioned as providing retirement income as a matter of right, and thus an assurance of dignity for elderly persons, required supplementation by Old Age Assistance, one of the categoric aid programs set up under the Social Security Act of 1935, requiring a means test. Although far outstripped by the 16 million aged receiving OASDHI benefits as a matter of right, the Old Age Assistance program in that year provided about 2 million persons with average monthly benefits of about $70 (Social Security Bulletin 1971, p 46). Twelve percent of all aged units reported receipt of OAA in 1967 (Table 4). Although OAA recipients have declined by about 25 percent since 1950, the low OASDHI benefits received by low-income workers, and especially the low benefits by persons receiving actuarially reduced benefits at retirement ages before 65 required that OAA continue to provide for about 2 million elderly in 1972.

To recapitulate: the aged in America in the 1970s are poor because the great majority are not attached to the labor force. Some do not work for reasons of health; some cannot work because institutional arrangements with union or management set an arbitrary retirement age; some cannot work because their firms shut down, or merge, or substitute machinery for labor; some do not work because part-time work is not available, or not available in their community; and some with adequate financial resources choose leisure rather than work.

The aged in America in the 1970s are poor because the average OAS-

DHI benefit is low for persons with a lifetime of attachment to low-wage sectors of industry, marked frequently by intermittent spells of unemployment. Periodic recessions, plant moves, and shutdowns diminish the credits toward an adequate retirement benefit that it is possible to earn in a working life.

Few OASDHI units receive income from private group pensions. Although the 1974 pension security act, as noted previously, has shortened the vesting period, tightened regulations for fiduciary responsiblitiy, and provided insurance against fund bankruptcy, these provisions at best enhance the prospects of pensions only for the one-third of the labor force now covered by such plans. There is little indication that other employers will become more willing to incur the financial constraints on funds required by the new federal legislation. Thus, the majority of aged units in the coming decades will not receive any income from this source.

The narrow margin between income and expenditures over a working life for all but the professional and upper-income groups militate against the private provision of sufficient income-bearing assets for the retirement period. In addition, rising national output, as well as continuing inflation progressively discriminates against the retired person in favor of those still in the labor force. Home ownership, the form of asset-holding common among aged units, does not serve the immediate needs of the aged for current consumption.

Old Age Assistance, based on need rather than right, remained the necessary supplement of inadequate incomes for about 12 percent of aged units in 1967. Additional numbers of needy aged may have been reluctant to submit to a "means" test, or unaware of possible public assistance. Because of the problem of reaching such aged, as well as to minimize administrative costs, Public Law 92–603 in 1972 "federalized" old age assistance. By the end of 1974, over three and one-half million aged, blind, and disabled had been transferred from state public assistance rolls to federal "supplementary security income."

However desirable the planned improvements with respect to minimizing variations between states, and the providing of a benefit floor for residents of poorer states, the goal of the revised law is to assure (after July 1974) a minimum of $146 a month for an individual, and $219 for a couple. Additional state supplemental payments can still be made, through state-federal agreements (Joint Publication Committee on Finance 1972). Yet in those states that either are unwilling or unable financially to so supplement, the annual "supplementary security income" (SSI) of $1,752 for an aged individual, or $2,628 for an aged couple, must be compared to the most recent BLS "moderate" budget for a retired couple. The "moderate" budget in autumn 1973 was $5,414 for a couple, and $2,978 (estimated at 55 percent of the amount for an aged couple) for the aged individual. Even though living costs vary among the cities included in the study, a substantial gap remains between the "supplemental security income" minimum and living costs of the elderly, allowing for "maintenance of health, normal participation in community life," . . . and "conventional social and physiological needs." When the 12 percent increase in the Consumer Price Index between October 1973 and 1974 is also taken into account, the inadequacy becomes even more apparent. (Sherwood 1974, pp 57–61.)

Economic Effects of Present Policies on Income of Aged

Since the U.S. individual and collective provision of economic security for the aged appears inadequate, should increased resources be devoted to that end? As a final step, it would be well to examine the current public and private policy to determine in what respects the present employment, transfer payment, and taxation arrangements may be inefficient or inequitable. That is, before any greater amount of resources are committed, to what extent could the income for the elderly be increased by a change of policy without increasing the burden on the younger productive group? The economic effects, involving efficiency as well as equitability of existing policies and programs, will be discussed below in reference to the areas from which 90 percent of aggregate aged income is drawn: (a) employment, (b) pension, and (c) asset holdings.

ECONOMIC EFFECTS OF EMPLOYMENT

In any society, with but a few exceptions, it is the working members who must provide subsistence for the nonproductive group, regardless of individual or group saving in the past. With this in mind, it is obvious that in a full-employment economy, policies that prevent or inhibit able aged citizens from working constitute a double burden on the younger group.

This is so because the younger working group must cut back their own consumption to permit a transfer of goods and services to the older group, while the lack of participation by the aged in the productive process means that the total product to be shared is smaller than it might be.

Since half those aged 65 and older are 72 or more, and because ill health is a factor in retirement in over 40 percent of cases, not every aged person can continue year-round or full-time labor force participation after age 65. Of those who would continue, not all have the skills required by modern technology. But to the extent that some who would participate are prevented from doing so by government policies and private institutuional arrangements, national output is correspondingly reduced. Among the policies that inhibit employment of the aged are the following.

1. Restrictive national economic policies which slow down economic growth adversely affect job changes for the aged. A primary requisite for the creation of job opportunities for the aged worker is the creation of job oppor-

tunities for all. The earnings-test limitation on earnings of Social Security beneficiaries was originally imposed largely to preserve scarce job opportunities for younger men with dependent families. When jobs are available for all seekers, the elderly worker may indeed add to current output in full- or part-time work schedules without depriving younger workers of employment. In contrast, the restrictive economic policies of the 1950's and late 1960's which checked the growth of the economy and of employment served both to decrease job opportunities of elderly workers and to decrease the total output amount from which the aged could be supported.

2. The same argument may be applied with respect to the earnings-test limitation. In 1974, the aged Social Security beneficiary could earn up to $2,400 without forfeiting Social Security benefits; beyond that amount he lost $.50 for every $1.00 he earned. This may have deterred some aged from labor force participation on a full-time basis. Under full employment conditions, this inefficient utilization of labor resources cuts back potential national product. The policy is also inequitable in its effect on aged persons of widely differing income. The person receiving the minimum Social Security monthly benefit is visited with the same penalty for attempting to raise his income through employment as is the aged person with a maximum Social Security benefit coupled perhaps with private pension and asset income enjoying favorable tax treatment. Thus, as a percent of his small income, the low-income Social Security beneficiary is paying a much higher tax on his earnings above $2,100.
3. In the area of private institutional arrangements, there are also inhibitions to the employment of the aged. The great growth of pension plans has reflected employer interest not only in the welfare of aging employees but also in eliminating from the work force the less-skilled, possibly more illness-prone older workers (although Department of Labor studies have indicated that some older workers may, in fact, be more productive than the average younger worker). The existence of a cutoff date makes retirement more automatic and thus less difficult for the employer to implement. Younger union members may likewise understandably wish to see promotion paths open up. The net effect of private pension arrangements on continuing employment for the aged worker is negative.

The worker dismissed from the highly productive sector of the economy where pension plans are most heavily concentrated will, if he insists on continuing to work, be forced to turn to the marginal sectors of the economy where productivity and pay are apt to be lower. This is so because the highly productive sectors with existing pension plans must pay higher contributions into the pension fund for older as compared to younger workers. The influx of pensioners into low-wage sectors must then further depress wages for all workers in these areas. If full employment conditions do not prevail, job opportunities for some younger workers may also be diminished, since the older worker seeking only "supplementary" income, and mindful of the 50 percent tax rate on earnings above $2,400, may work for less.*

4. The imposition of the Social Security tax (5.85 percent in 1974) on only the first $13,200 of a worker's earnings, paid by both employer and employee, constitutes a disincentive to employers to increase the labor force in periods of expansion. In high-wage industries, the employer is induced to utilize existing labor force more intensively, rather than to increase employment, and therefore tax payments.
5. With respect to equitability, the Social Security system may be described as regressive. A tax system is characterized as regressive if a person with low income pays a higher fraction of that income in taxes than does a person with higher income. The local sales tax is usually regressive. In contrast, a tax system is progressive if persons with lower incomes pay a smaller fraction of that income in taxes than do persons with higher income.

   The federal income tax is generally progressive even though loopholes weaken the apparent progressivity of the tax schedules. Since the Social Security tax (1974) applies only to the first $13,200 of earnings, a person earning just that amount will pay $772 in annual taxes, 5.85 percent of his annual income. However, another worker earning double that amount, or $26,400, will also pay $772 in taxes, or 2.9 percent of his income. As the wage income rises even higher, the tax as a percent of income shrinks into insignificance. Thus the low- and moderate-income worker must contribute most heavily in proportion to his income, not only toward his own retirement, but toward the support of those even poorer. These include those with patterns of irregular employment, who receive a higher percentage replacement as retirement income, and also those becoming disabled, or families becoming dependent before the breadwinner reaches 65. The regressivity of the tax is evident also in the fact that even those low-paid workers with dependents who are exempt from federal income tax payments, must nonetheless pay a Social Security tax on the first dollar of earnings.

   Furthermore, among industrialized nations the United States has been unique in that its retirement income program drew no funds from general revenues (except for small special allotments to persons 72 and over without other

**In January 1975, earnings on which Social Security taxes are paid have risen to $14,100; beneficiary maximum earned income not subject to reduction rises to $2,520.*

retirement income).* This intensifies the regressive nature of the Social Security tax burden, since property income, accruing mainly to upper income receivers, is not taxed for OASDHI purposes.

6. Under former Old Age Assistance regulations, recipients were discouraged from improving their financial status by high marginal tax rates on earnings. This was partially corrected by the 1972 amendments, which provided an initial $20 income disregard, plus an additional disregard of $65 of earned income, plus one-half of any remaining earnings (Joint Publication Committee on Finance 1972, pp 25–26).

ECONOMIC EFFECTS OF PRIVATE PENSIONS

In recognition of the fact that Social Security benefits taken alone are not sufficient to provide an adequate retirement income, the provision of supplemental retirement income through private pensions has been encouraged by tax policies of the federal government. With a given level of federal spending, any taxes not paid by individual A must be paid by individual B. Thus the equitability of such tax policies comes into question.

1. Persons covered by private pension plans are typically higher paid workers employed in larger firms in the more profitable sectors of the economy. If the pension contribution by the employer is viewed as deferred wages, then it is to the benefit of the worker to receive part of his recompense in later years when, because of tax policies that are favorable to income received by the elderly, his tax liability would be less. It is, of course, of even greater benefit to higher paid executives. Government tax subsidies of such private plans, by means of revenue foregone on employer contributions to the pension fund, as well as on fund earnings must be compensated for by higher current tax payments by other individuals, the majority of whom will not be beneficiaries of a private pension plan, and thus will not receive the subsequent advantages. The effect of this favorable tax treatment of private pensions is to shift more of the tax burden to the generally lower-paid workers who are outside pension programs. To emphasize what was noted above as to the minor role of general revenues in furnishing income for the needy aged, the cost to the Treasury of private pensions' favorable tax treatment substantially exceeds treasury contributions to Social Security.

**In January 1974, over 3% million adult recipients of public assistance under programs for aged, blind, and disabled, began to receive "supplementary security income" financed from general revenues.*

2. To foster economic growth; that is, a growing national output, it is desirable that workers respond to changes in technology and consumer demand by job changes. The growth of private pensions is generally conceded to be a factor in worker reluctance to shift to other jobs and industries. The lack of universal private pension coverage throughout industry may decrease the willingness of workers to respond to market changes. Thus plant cutbacks in declining areas and sectors leave some workers still clinging to the chance of any remaining jobs that will contribute toward retirement benefits with consequent adverse effects on the dynamic growth of the economy.
3. With respect to workers over age 50, the employer reluctance to hire older workers for (assumed) declining productivity is increased because of the increased chance of pension payout. Since the contributions an employer must make to such a fund are decreased by forfeitures, the younger worker who may not remain to collect a pension represents cost savings to the potential employer. The 1974 pension security act cited previously may modify these employer attitudes, since workers starting a job five years before the plan normal retirement age may be excluded.
4. Again, the new law specifies eligibility beginning at age 25, which may lead to preferential hiring of younger workers to achieve lower contribution rates for the employer. However, because mobility leads to forfeiture of employer contributions, the shift of tax burdens noted in item 1 above will work to the disadvantage of other mobile elements of the work force, such as women, unskilled, or blacks.
5. With further respect to equitability, the receipt of private pension income, however large, does not adversely affect the amount of Social Security benefits. Thus the recipients of private pensions in addition to Social Security income have an advantage over the aged worker who supplements his Social Security benefits by current employment. In the latter case, annual earnings over $2,400 require a reduction of Social Security payments by $0.50 for every $1.00 earned.
6. The steady growth of private pension savings (as contrasted to the counter cyclical pattern of private savings) may create excessive restraint on consumption in economic recessions, if employer obligations remain unchanged, thus adversely affecting national output and economic growth.
7. Moreover, despite the reporting provisions of the Welfare and Pensions Disclosure Act, the long-run soundness of private pension funds depends on investment decisions made by fallible trustees in a volatile market, or on the fortunes of one firm or industry. The pensions promised in a private program may not be payable when the pensioners

put in their claims, as for example in the coal industry. Thus, reliance on private pensions for major contributions to retirement income may be illusory. The lack of interest or understanding by workers who are future fund beneficiaries leaves pension fund trustees, even assuming honest motives, with considerable latitude in choice of fund managers or investments. Thus the $200 billion in assets in pension funds is recognized as a source of economic power which may, for good or ill, affect the economic viability of small firms as compared to large.

ECONOMIC EFFECTS OF ASSET ACCUMULATION

The possibility is slight that a low-income, blue-collar worker can save enough over a working lifetime to provide an effective supplement to the Social Security benefits associated with low-income work experience. For a worker becoming 65 in 1970, the 45-year span stretching back from 1970 includes the depressed thirties, the high unemployment levels in the immediate aftermath of World War II, the recessions of 1949, 1954, 1958, 1961, and 1969, when as an older worker, he would have been most susceptible to prolonged unemployment. *Average* hourly earnings of production workers in manufacturing in 1925 were $0.55; in 1930, $0.55; in 1940, $0.66; in 1950, $1.46; in 1960, $2.29. At what sustainable rate could the average worker, raising a family, have saved in that working life (U.S. Bureau of Census 1965)?

However, there are a few individuals with incomes high enough in younger years to permit them to forego some current consumption in order to enjoy higher income after retirement. These individuals will, in the retirement period, receive favorable tax treatment under federal income tax provisions with 1970 regulations now permitting a couple with both partners 65 or over to receive $3,500 in income without tax liability. The aged persons with no income from privately accumulated assets, of course, receive no benefit from such tax concessions. The tax shift in this case leads to increased taxes being paid by the younger worker, even of low income, for the benefit of the possibly well-off retiree.

Income tax credits for the aged, then, represent a burden to the younger productive worker, but not necessarily a benefit to the low-income aged. In commenting on the IRS compilation of tax data for taxpayers 65 and over, the Bixby article states: "It is striking that only about two-fifths of all aged units had incomes that required them to file a Federal income return for 1967 and that about three-fifths of these returns were taxable. In other words, only 3.9 million aged units, or one-fourth of the 15.8 million units in the population had taxable incomes in 1967." (Bixby 1970, p 9.) Local property tax exemptions may be of more general benefit to the aged poor because of the widespread home ownership; nonetheless, here, too, unless income distinctions are made, the young, relatively poor, property owner may be forced to assume the tax burden of the wealthier aged.

Treatment of asset income also serves to exacerbate the inequality of income of the aged. In contrast to income from earnings, income from assets does not diminish Social Security benefits. Thus, while an aged worker receiving over $2,100 in earnings annually will have his Social Security benefits reduced, an individual with identical asset income will receive the full Social Security payment.

Summary

The preceding pages indicate all too sketchily the financial distress of the aged citizen in the 1970s. In summary, first, the aged are poor, because the majority do not have sufficient earnings, or have no earnings at all, from productive employment. Some may not be physically able to work, but some of those able and willing to work are barred from continuing by company retirement policy; or are forced into marginal employment at low pay; or above a certain level of earnings, must sacrifice at a 50 percent rate their Social Security benefits (although equivalent income from assets or private pensions bears no such penalty). Current recipients of Old Age Assistance may be subject to 100 percent tax on earnings, although this situation is being corrected. In effect, while work is the major route to enjoyment of an adequate income, we often prevent the able aged from pursuing that route.

Second, the aged are poor because the OASDHI benefit for persons with a lifetime of attachment to low-wage sectors of industry, marked by frequent spells of unemployment, is below the poverty line, and such beneficiaries are least likely to have additional sources of income other than Social Security. Furthermore, although it is in the national interest, and tends to expand national output, that some firms and industry within the economy should shut down or merge, and others appear and expand as consumer demand and technology change, for the individual the resultant unemployment, or lower wage employment history means lower credits toward public retirement benefits.

Third, the aged are poor because not all are covered by private pensions to supplement retirement benefits under the public system, and only a fraction of those ever working under such private pension plans will ultimately collect. Unless new requirements as to vesting and portability are introduced, as well as safeguards on fund management, the majority of aged units in the coming decades will not receive any income from this source. Likewise, few will receive other public pensions.

Fourth, the old are poor because the narrow margin between income and expenditure over a working life for all but the professional and skilled upper income groups militate against private provision of sufficient income-bearing assets for the retirement period, even if there were not complete uncertainty as to how long that retirement will be. In addition, rising national output, as well as rising prices progressively discriminate against retired persons in favor of those still in the labor force. Although the 1972 Social Security law amendments provided for "indexing" (when the Consumer Prize Index rises 3 percent, there will be an automatic cost of living adjustment), that first adjustment will not occur until June 1975. This adjustment will reflect the percentage difference between the average index level of the 2nd quarter of 1974 and the 1st quarter of 1975. Prices in October 1974 were already 12 percent higher than in October 1973. The 1974 successive 7 percent (March) and 4 percent (June) increases have not kept pace with double-digit inflation; the lag of possible 12 to 15 months between a deterioration in purchasing power and the subsequent correction works a hardship on retirees living on fixed incomes. With respect to rising productivity of the labor force, there is as yet no automatic adjustment incorporated to prevent a widening gap between the standard of living of the employed and the retired.

Fifth, public and private policies purporting to aid the poverty-stricken aged often provide more assistance to the aged at upper income levels than to the poor. Among such policies are favorable tax treatment of asset income of the aged as compared to earnings income in establishing eligibility for Social Security payments; favorable tax treatment of private pensions going mainly to upper income groups, but very little federal subsidy of public pensions from general revenues; the regressiveness of the maximum $10,800 base, which requires the low-paid worker to pay a higher percent of his income into the OASDHI fund than that paid by the higher income worker; and finally income tax exemptions for persons 65 and over which are of little use to low-income aged.

Finally, economic policies that tend to slow a growth in national output penalize young and old alike. The creation of a full employment economy would make the greatest contribution to the general welfare of all members of society.

SOME SUGGESTED REMEDIES

It should be noted that although much of the data are necessarily drawn from the 1968 Survey of the Aged, as the latest source of detailed data, there should be not delusion as to any substantial improvement in the economic status of the aged since that time. Certain improvements have been made: across-the-board percentage increases in benefit levels were made in 1971 and 1972 to "catch up" with rising living costs. The 1972 amendments of Public Law 92-603 improve eligibility for certain classes of aged (ie, widows) and establish a higher and uniform national income floor for indigent aged. Yet we must compare the annual amounts assured under this legislation (as of 1974, $2,340 for an aged couple, and $1,560 for an aged individual) with the BLS "intermediate" budget for the aged, autumn 1971 ($4,776 for the couple, $2,627 for an individual). We should at the same time bear in mind what was so clearly brought out by both 1963 and 1968 surveys of the aged, that Social Security benefits are often the major or sole source of income.

The base on which Social Security was built in the 1930's conceived of reliance by the aged on *three* sources of income—from continued part-time employment, from assets or private pensions, and from Social Security benefits. If indeed such a conception had any great validity even in the 1930s, in the 1970s it is simply fiction.

What, then, should be the present public and private programs to improve the economic status of the aged? First, maintenance of a strong and growing economy is fundamental to any improvement in the income position of the aged. Since 1962, more than half the men awarded initial retirement benefits each year have received reduced benefits, so that by the end of 1969, one-third of retired male beneficiaries were receiving reduced benefits (Reno 1971, p 1). Fiscal and monetary policies designed to foster a growing national output were effective in the mid-sixties to sustain a high level of employment. Although full employment policies are more difficult to implement in a peacetime economy, the post-World War II experience of Western Europe indicates that such a course is possible, given government commitment to the priority of employment policy. Only a prosperous and productive nation can support its aged population.

A second requisite is commitment by the general public to the provision of an adequate level of living for the aged. This should not mean the imposition of a higher payroll tax, which in the 1970s has passed 10 percent for employer and employee combined contributions, and is scheduled to go higher (Brittain 1971). While it seems desirable to increase the base salary to which the tax applies, it might be more equitable to lower the rate of payroll tax deductions, or at least to halt further increases. As noted earlier, the payroll tax is regressive. Also, the young worker, to provide for his family, must often borrow funds at many times the interest rate he is earning on the "forced saving" of the Social Security program. Given public acceptance of the need to provide support for aging workers, general revenue, drawn from all income sources in the economy, should be used to provide a decent minimum level of living for all the aged who cannot work. This would require faster adjustment of benefits in response to annual rises in prices, as well as in recognition of the rising real income of the productive labor force.

In a 1962 study of old people in three industrial societies (Britain, Denmark, and the United States), it was found that there is a greater disparity among incomes of the aged in the United States than in either of the other countries, intensified because of the almost universal reliance on Social Security benefits which are wage-related and based on an earning period that is too long, given continuing inflation (Shanas et al 1968). It is feasible for the United States to devise a program similar to the proposed Family Assistance Program whereby a simple income-reporting form could be used to insure a decent minimum income for all aged, with no sacrifice of personal dignity and privacy.

Third, the provision of income sufficient to maintain an adequate level of living for the elderly would obviate favorable tax treatment for those 65 and over. Housing allowances would permit the aged to remain in familiar surroundings, while relieving the local community of losses through tax exemptions which may discriminate in favor of the upper income aged.

Fourth, with a full employment economy, resistance by both employers and younger employees to the employment of older workers would presumably diminish. Promotional public campaigns to induce major firms to take a quota of older workers would assist the placement of the elderly who may be able to work only part-time. A "pool" of such elderly workers could make some contribution to total output, increase the income of such workers, and permit them to enjoy the social and psychologic benefits of employment with congenial fellow workers.

Other and better public measures to improve the living standard of the elderly will be forthcoming if the voting public recognize the economic distress of the current aged population as a portent of their own future. Old age is sometimes listed in texts, together with unemployment, disability, and the like, as one of the hazards of an industrial society, against which provision must be made. Unlike these hazards, however, there is no satisfactory alternative to aging. This being the case, it must become apparent to those treading on the heels of the current aged that adequate income must be provided to make the final years of life a fitting sequel to a productive lifetime.

Some infirmities of old age cannot be corrected and must be endured. It is otherwise with respect to financial deprivation, which can be corrected by a prosperous nation with the will to do so. Improving the economic status of the aged is not a cure-all for physical pain, bereavement, loneliness, or "disengagement"—yet a little money for an occasional treat might lessen these burdens of old age. As the 1970 Senate hearings pointed out, many aged Americans must give up even modest pleasures for lack of funds.

> "I don't" is a most accurate description of the older adult living in retirement. I don't entertain. I don't go out with friends. I don't eat in restaurants. I don't go to movies. I don't buy new clothes. I don't ride subways and buses. I don't buy cake. I don't eat a lot. I don't take care of my health like I should. I don't, I don't, I don't. (U.S. Senate, Economics of Aging, 1970.)

Because the older American gives up so many of these ordinary, everyday activities, he may become quite literally invisible, even to the middle-aged workers who will soon tread the same path. The July 1974 median monthly benefit was only $193 for a retired individual, and $284 for a couple.* With inflation persisting, the Brecht poem goes to the heart of the matter:

> *But if we come and can't buy anything*
> *They'll know how it is.*

**Source: Social Security Bulletin 37(11):49 (Table M-13), 1974*

References

Bixby LE: Income of people aged 65 and older: overview from 1968 survey of the aged, Social Sec Bull 33(4):8, 1970. For later adjustments to poverty threshold, see Social Sec Bull 34(7):11, Footnote 1, 1971; 35(8):4, Footnote 4

Brecht B: The shopper. Boston Univ J 19:32, Fall 1971 (Translated by Michael Hamburger)

Brittain JA: The incidence of Social Security payroll taxes. Am Econ Rev 61:110–125, 1971

Cooper BS, McGee MF: Medical care outlays for three age groups. Social Sec Bull 34(5):3, 1971

Horlick M: Earnings replacement rate of old age benefits: an international comparison. Social Sec Bull 33(3):6, 1970. See also Henle P: Recent trends in retirement benefits relative to earnings. Monthly Labor Rev June 1972, pp 12–20

Joint Publication Committee on Finance, US Senate, and Committee on Ways and Means, US House of Representatives: Summary of Social Security amendments of 1972: P L 92–603 (H.R.I.), Nov. 17, 1972

Kolodrubetz W: Private and public retirement pensions: findings from the 1968 survey of the aged. Social Sec Bull 33(9):6, 1970

Murray J: Homeownership and financial assets: findings from the 1968 survey of the aged. Social Sec Bull 35(8):pp 3–5, 1972

Reno V: Why men stop working at or before age 65. Social Sec Bull 34(6):8, Table 4; p 13, Table 13, 1971

Shanas E et al: Old People in Three Industrial Societies. London, New York, Atherton Press, 1968

Sherwood M: Retired couple's budget updated to Autumn 1973. Monthly Labor Rev, October 1974, pp 57–61

Social Security Bulletin: Sample of 9,128 retired persons, surveyed by Census for Social Security Administration in 1968, covering 1967 income. 33(4,8,9), 1970

Social Security Bulletin: Data drawn from on-going sample (monthly) of all workers awarded benefits for first time. 34(6): 3, 1971

Social Security Bulletin, Table M-24, 34(6):46, 1971

Special Committee on Aging, U.S. Senate, 91st Congress, 1st session: Economics of aging: toward a full share in abundance. Part 1, April 29–30, 1969, p 217. In Kreps JM, Pursell DE: Lifetime earnings and income in old age. U.S. Joint Economic Committee Compendium, Part II, pp 261–264, 1967

US Bur Census: Historical Statistics of the US, Washington, DC, 1965. Series D26-634, p 92; and Continuation to 1962, p 15

US Bur Census: Statistical Abstract of the US, Washington, DC, 1970. Table No. 317, p 214; Historical Statistics of the United States, Washington, DC, 1960, Table D13-25, p 71

US Dept Labor, Bur Labor Statistics: Retired couple's budget. Bull 1570-4, App A, pp 21–31, 1966

US DUS Dept. Labor, Labor-Management Services Administration. News about the Employee Retirement Income Security Act of 1974, October 1974, pp 1–32

US Senate Hearings, Special Committee on Aging, 91st Congress, 2nd Session, Part 10a: Pension aspects of the economics of aging, Washington, DC, 1970, p 1426

US Senate, Special Committee on Aging, 91st Congress, 2nd session: Developments in Aging, 1969. May 15, 1970, p 9

US Senate, Special Committee on Aging, 91st Congress, 2nd session, 1970:

Economics of aging: toward a full share in abundance. Washington, DC, Govt Ptg Office, 1970, p 34. In Schiller: The Economics of Poverty and Discrimination, Englewood Cliffs, NJ, Prentice-Hall, 1973, p 69

Bibliography

PUBLIC DOCUMENTS

US Dept HEW: Social Security Admin, Div Retirement and Survivor Studies, Office of Research and Statistics. Preliminary findings from the survey of newly entitled beneficiaries, Report No. 2, March 71, p 1

US Dept Labor, Bureau of Labor Statistics: Three budgets for an urban retired couple, Spring 1969. Washington, DC, January 1970

US Dept Labor: Manpower report of the president. Washington, DC: Govt Ptg Office

US Senate, Special Committee on Aging, 91st Congress, 2nd session: Pension aspects of the economics of aging: present and future roles of private pensions. Washington, DC, Govt Ptg Office, January 1970

BOOKS

Brown J: An American Philosophy of Social Security. Princeton, NJ, Princeton Univ Press, 1972

Carlson V: Economic Security in the United States. New York, McGraw-Hill, 1962

Friedman M: Capitalism and Freedom. Chicago, Univ Chicago Press, 1962

Green C: Negative Taxes and the Poverty Problem. Washington, DC, Brookings Institution, 1967

Pechman JA, Taussig M: Social Security: Perspectives for Reform. Washington, DC, Brookings Institution, 1968

Schiller BR: The Economics of Poverty and Discrimination. Englewood Cliffs, NJ, Prentice-Hall, 1973

Thurow LC: Poverty and Discrimination. Washington, DC, Brookings Institution, 1969

Turnbull J, Williams C, Cheit E: Economic and Social Security, 3rd ed. New York, Ronald Press, 1967

ARTICLES AND PERIODICALS

Lauriat P: Benefit levels and socio-economic characteristics: findings from the 1968 survey of the aged. Social Sec Bull 33(8):3–20, 1970

Orshansky M: Counting the poor: another look at the poverty profile. Social Sec Bull 28(1), 1965

Social Security Bulletin: Assets of people 65 and older. 27(11):5–7, 1964

US Dept Labor, Bur of Labor Statistics: Retired couples, autumn 1971. Monthly Labor Rev (7):35–36, 1972

7

SOCIAL WELFARE AND THE AGING

Louis Lowy, Ph.D.

This chapter provides an overview of social welfare as it relates to aging and the aged in the United States. It begins with various conceptualizations of social welfare and looks at aging as a biologic, psychologic, and sociologic process, and the aged as a heterogeneous subpopulation with particular human needs manifested and expressed in a variety of ways and influenced by a changing aging process. Needs that are unsatisfied, however, create problems, and a country's social policy attempts either to cope with them or to anticipate them through provisions of laws, benefits, programs, and services.

An analytic schema is presented to indicate the types of interrelated human needs and problems that have led to the present provisions for the aged in the United States (see pages 148–150). Housing needs are singled out for two reasons: (1) to illustrate the approach of the schema in some detail and (2) to emphasize the importance of meeting such problems because of their close interdependence with income, health, and social needs and the implications for our future social policy. An example from the South End of Boston highlights these factors.

A discussion of the organization, delivery, and planning of services leads to a brief review of the availability and training of personnel for providing such programs and services and eventually to a listing of some major "frontier" issues that constitute the social welfare agenda for the aged of tomorrow.

Conceptualization of Social Welfare

Currently there are at least four conceptualizations of social welfare; it can be viewed as a philosophy, a goal, an institution, and a field.

As a philosophy, social welfare is concerned with such questions as: "What is the ultimate purpose of man?" and "How shall man's relationships to his fellow men be governed to insure the well-being of everyone?" This goes back to the writings of the Old and New Testaments and social welfare as a philosophy, therefore, is rooted in the concepts of the Judeo-Christian ethics of "our brother's keeper" and "neighborly love." Tensions between the Hebraic ideal of social justice and the Christian ideal of charitable love have permeated the social ideology of Western man and have been reflected in the practical affairs of state throughout our history (Frankel 1965). Different and changing views of the nature of man and his relationship to society have determined the ways in which the poor and the sick, the infirm and the old were treated. Egalitarian slogans notwithstanding, since the end of the 18th century, those who could not fit into the dominant culture or social structure were regarded as inferior, as deviants, or as charges of society who were to be further excluded from its mainstream. This was done ostensibly for mutual protection, and financial assistance was to be provided so that they could be adjusted and socialized into the dominant culture, preferably with some expression of sympathy on the part of the general public. Changes in these viewpoints have been slow in coming. A more recently adopted philosophic ideal espouses the doctrine of the indivisibility of social justice and charity which now has become a main tenet of social welfare as a philosophy in the Western world.

When a society views social welfare as a goal, it seeks to achieve an equilibrium between meeting the needs of individuals and those of society. That is, a society attempts to promote the general well-being of its population and, at the same time, tries to safeguard its own survival. It attempts to insure optimal functioning of people and its social institutions for the benefit of all individuals, families, groups, and communities. In order to achieve this, societies exact laws, benefits, programs, and services. "Social policies are rooted in traditions, beliefs and cultural patterns; they therefore reflect the weltanschauung of a society at a given historical stage" (Monk 1971, p 97). Programs under governmental and nongovernmental auspices, developed in American and other societies and designed to provide social welfare services, have led to the creation of social welfare as an institution. Wilensky and Lebeaux (1966, pp 140-147) in *Industrial Society and Social Welfare* have developed five distinguishing characteristics for delineating social welfare as an institution in America. They are: (1) formal organization, (2) social sponsorship and accountability, (3) absence of profit motive as dominant program purpose, (4) an integrative rather than segmented view of human needs, and (5) direct concern with human consumption needs. In this sense, social welfare ranks with the family, religion, education, health, and so on as a social institution.

It has been found useful to differentiate between the "residual" and "institutional" views of social welfare. According to Wilensky and Lebeaux (1966, pp 138, 139), the residual view holds

> that social welfare institutions should come into play only when the

> normal structures of supply of the family and the market break down. The "institutional" concept, in contrast, sees welfare services as normal first-line functions of a modern society. . . . The residual formulation is based on the premise that there are two natural channels through which an individual's needs are properly met: the family and the market economy. These are the preferred structures of supply. However, sometimes these institutions do not function adequately. Family life is disrupted, (economic) depressions do occur. Or, sometimes individuals cannot make use of normal channels because of old age or illness (or personal problems). In such cases, another mechanism is brought into play; the social welfare structure.

It is conceived as "residual" since it is attending primarily to emergency functions and is expected to be withdrawn when the regular social structure is working properly again. Because of this temporary, substitute characteristic, social welfare thus conceived often carries a stigma of dole or charity. The institutional view, on the other hand, implies legitimate function of modern industrial society in helping individuals achieve self-fulfillment. It recognizes the complexity and vicissitudes of modern life, the inability of individuals to provide fully for themselves or to meet all their needs in family and work settings.

The reality of American social welfare has veered between these two views. Residualism, a heritage of the Elizabethan Poor Laws of 17th-century England has persisted since colonial times despite inroads of institutional approaches, particularly with the passage of the Social Security Act of 1935. Medicaid, with its reliance on the means test, illustrates well the residual notion of social welfare; Medicare, based on prepaid insurance against risks of illness in old age, demonstrates a reluctant movement toward an institutional approach to illness—if not health insurance.

Recently, a developmental view of social welfare has emerged, particularly in parts of the third world of developing nations. This view assigns to social welfare a function to enhance the developmental potential of a community or a society and makes social welfare part of an overall economic and social development effort. It enhances society's capacity to solve its own problems by reducing citizens' apathy, by imparting organizational and substantive skills, and by creating institutional structures that permit and promote citizen-participation for self-help purposes.

Many social programs emanating from the "War on Poverty" in the United States have been based on this principle and today the developmental view of social welfare has begun to permeate those schools of thought which view both the residual and the institutional conceptions as static rather than as dynamic. Within an "order" or "equilibrium" perspective, social problems have been defined as deviating from a value orientation which a dominant group postulates as valid. Behavior that departs from such norms has been labeled "pathologic," and an extension of social control through adjustment programs has been the prevailing solution. In the "conflict perspective," the other polar, ideal type, social problems have been equated with unrealized standards of aspirations of a subgroup or subpopulation, such as the blacks or the aged. "Deviant" behavior here is seen as functional to achieve a necessary transformation of the social system and rupture of social control mechanisms and achievement of group identity through heightened self-awareness are the indicated solutions to these type of problems (Horton 1966, pp 701–713). The "conflict perspective" is more closely allied to the developmental view of social welfare, although both perspectives are ideal types "which are not consistently found in the inconsistent ideologies of actual social research and political practice" (Horton 1966, p 704).

The way in which a social problem is defined and who the authors of that definition are have a significant bearing upon the solutions proposed and their eventual implementation. For this reason, social welfare as an institution demands an analytic understanding of its underlying assumptions about man in society.

Social welfare is also referred to as a field. As such, it encompasses "the full range of organized activities of voluntary and governmental agencies that seek to prevent, alleviate or contribute to the solution of recognized social problems, or to improve the well-being of individuals, groups, or communities. Such activities use a wide variety of professional personnel such as physicians, nurses, lawyers, educators, engineers, ministers, social workers and paraprofessional counterparts of each" (Encyclopedia of Social Work 1971, p 1446). Here the emphasis is on organized activities of agencies as they relate to the solution of problems or to the enhancement of the well-being of people.

Regardless of which conceptualization is used, it is generally agreed that social welfare has become a major goal of developed and developing societies, based on philosophic value assumptions about the good and welfare of people in interaction with one another and with their social structures. In order to attain this goal, various laws and programs are created which result in organized activities and services that are available to people. These, in turn, influence the quality and standard of life of the population and also affect the fabric of the social structure.

Social Welfare and the Aging

Many groups in a population have been considered "deviant" or "aspiring," "in need of attention" or "pathologic," "exceptional" or "unfortunate," "maladjusted" or "deprived." Throughout history, the aged have been viewed as such in many parts of the world. The Bible, accounts in Greek and Roman history, medieval records, and modern-day writings are all available to us to assess the predominant cultural attitudes toward the elderly, the consequences of such attitudes for them and for their offspring, the treatment accorded to them by societies, and the dilemma that the conflict of generations has created right up to the present. It has been said that a civilization can be judged by how it treats its older members. There is little doubt that our present-day achievement- and change-oriented society has created greater tensions between the values and experiences of the old and the values of the young, between those born before World War I and those after World War II. The acceleration of change in geometric proportion has created a new time and space perspective that has increased the gap between young and old and is likely to create even wider divergencies of views, standards, knowledge, and skills in the future. Given a social welfare philosophy that subscribes to the interdependence of man and society, the present and future goals of social welfare must encompass an inclusive view of all age groups and must provide, as a matter of right, programs and services specific to the needs and tasks of each age group. Within this context, then, let us examine what the aged are like in order to better understand their needs for today and their aspirations for tomorrow.

What Is Aging?

Aging is a developmental process with its own developmental patterns. We can speak of biologic, psychologic, sociologic, and behavioral changes and adjustment to old age. Changes in the physical organism are commonly regarded as a natural process of progressive changes in body structure and function. In addition to these internal changes, others occur in the circumstances or in the position of the individual as a member of the family, community, and society. They include retirement from work, reduced income, reduced or completed parental roles, separation from friends and associates, loss of husband or wife or friend, and a very considerable increase of uncommitted time. Concomitant with these are changed societal expectations expressed toward older people.

The responses of older people to these changes can be roughly grouped into two categories. First is the individual's inner attitude and reactions to his self-concept as he ages, whether based on acceptance or denial of the facts; the second category includes factors that are expressed in external behavior; he may look upon the added years as opportunity to expand its horizons and perspectives of life or he may reject new opportunities, narrow his range of interests, and gradually withdraw into himself.

There are different stages in the later life cycle and there are different groupings of aged. It would be a serious mistake to lump all aged together as if they were a homogeneous cohort. We have to recognize that each individual has his own personality structure which has evolved early in his life and which he takes with him when he reaches the threshold of old age. Each person is a product also of his social environment, the kind of responses he has given to societal tasks, the kind of social roles that he has assumed in his lifetime. All these have helped to define and shape his attitudes, his personality, his character, his life orientation.

A person's position in the social structure influences his personality. An individual is a product of group influences such as a family, work associations, social groupings of peers and colleagues, and of social class, religious, racial, and ethnic norms. Within a broad framework of a generalized aged category, we have to be conscious of individual responses of various age levels of older people. Roughly speaking, gerontologic research has divided aging into three stages: middle age, later maturity, and old age. Middle age would extend chronologically from 45 or 50 to about age 65. Later maturity would begin around 65 and would stretch approximately to 75. Old age would begin at 75. These chronologic checkpoints, however, can only serve as approximations, because individuals do not follow a linear development. Some people are most active at 75, others think of themselves as old at age 50. We must look at the total consideration of biologic, psychologic, and social processes rather than at chronologic age per se. Kastenbaum, Derbin, Sabatini, and Artt (1972) introduced three concepts about age: personal age (how old the person seems to himself), interpersonal age (how old he seems to others), and consensual age (degree of agreement between personal and interpersonal ages).

Keeping in mind that individuals adjust differently to various stages of aging, we might employ this oversimplified scheme to establish three groupings of individuals in terms of their adjustment to aging. Such a categorization is useful for purposes of approaching the needs of people on a differential basis. (1) Individuals who are making a satisfactory adjustment to aging. Those who have the energy and vitality to face the basic environmental demands and tasks of aging and develop satisfactory solutions to them ("autonomous"). (2) Individuals who have some serious physical difficulty, reality concerns, and personal anxieties which prevent them from making the best adaptation to the pressures and problems caused by aging. They may be described as people who are hampered in their ability to continue in their social functions. (3) Individuals who are quite isolated and withdrawn. Many are seriously handicapped physically and/or emotionally. These people often have strongly impaired egos and cannot meet any of the developmental tasks ("anomic"). In addition to these differentiations, it is also advisable to examine the sexual, and racial, ethnic, and socioeconomic backgrounds of each (Lowy 1961, pp 3–5).

In summary, the following assumptions about aging and the aged as a subpopulation are made in this chapter.

1. Aging is viewed developmentally, occurring as a process throughout the life cycle, and culminating in biologic death as an end of human development.
2. Different aspects of the aging process affect people differently at various times in their lives; in turn, people respond differently to biologic, organic, psychologic, and sociologic changes.
3. Dominant value orientations in a society shape

significantly the societal attitudes toward aging and thereby influence conditions that allow social structures to determine the position of older people.
4. This social position of older persons in turn has impact upon (a) behavorial expectations for the aged as a group, (b) the roles they are expected or allowed to assume and to perform, (c) the needs that are to be satisfied, and (d) the problems that occur as a result of the gap between needs that are met and those that remain unfulfilled.
5. There is an identifiable, heterogeneous cohort of aged people in a population. This cohort can be differentiated according to their responses to biologic, psychologic, and sociologic changes during their continuing development. Consequently, we can speak of well aged and not so well aged; of younger, middle, or older aged; of autonomous, adjusted, or anomic aged; of integrated passive-dependent, and unintegrated aged; or of poor and middle-income aged; of Jewish aged, black aged, Puerto Rican aged, and so on. The heterogeneity is colossal.
6. Aged people in a locality (either rural, urban, or suburban) are found in different types of living arrangements: either (a) living independently alone, with spouse, relatives, or friends in the community, or (b) in congregate facilities such as homes for the aged, nursing homes, hospitals, and so on.
7. All people, by virtue of being human, are interdependent and have a right to achieve maximum self-fulfillment. A system of services to meet their own needs, as well as to harness their abilities and energies toward fulfilling the needs of others is a sine qua non to achieve the goals of human fulfillment and of societal requirements of a just social order (Lowy 1970).

Who Are the Aged?

In order to provide a better understanding of the social consequences of old age and some of the implications for social welfare efforts, it is desirable to examine some statistics regarding the aging population in the United States.

On Numbers—During the past 70 years, the total population of the United States grew to almost three times its size in 1900. The older population has grown to almost seven times its 1900 size—and it is still growing. Between 1960 and 1969, older Americans increased in number throughout the nation by approximately 18 percent, as compared with a 13 percent growth in the total population, according to the Census Bureau estimates. Greatest percentage growth (a third or more) occurred in Arizona, Nevada, Florida, Hawaii, and New Mexico. Florida had the highest proportion of older people in 1969, 13.3 percent of its total population, while New York had the largest actual number of older people, almost 2 million.

On Age—Most older Americans are under 75; half are under 73; a third are under 70. Almost 1.3 million are 85 or over.

On Health—81 percent get along well on their own. While only 14 percent have no chronic conditions, diseases, or impairments of any kind. The vast majority that do have such conditions still manage by themselves. Older individuals are subject to more disability, see physicians more often, and have more and longer hospital stays. In 1969, per capita health care costs for older Americans came to $692: $335 went for hospital care; $107 for physician services; $28 for other professional services; $80 for drugs; $111 for nursing home care; and $31 for miscellaneous items. Of the total amount spent for health care, $499 of the bill was taken care of by public sources, but the elderly still had to pay $193 from their own limited incomes.

On Aggregate Income—Some $60 billion a year. More than half comes from retirement and welfare programs (52 percent), less than a third from employment (29 percent), and about a fifth from investments and contributions.

On Personal Income—Older persons have less than half the income of their younger counterparts. In 1969, half of the families headed by older persons had incomes of less than $4,803; the median income for older persons living alone or with nonrelatives was $1,855. Almost 5 million or over a quarter of the elderly live below the official poverty line; every fifth person in the United States is aged 65 or over. Many of these aged poor became poor on reaching old age.

On Expenditures—Older Americans spend proportionately more of their incomes on food, shelter, and medical care. They do not necessarily need other things so much less; they simply cannot afford them—and often, cannot find appropriate needed items, such as clothing, in the marketplace.

On Life Expectancy—At birth—70 years; 67 for men but 7 years longer or 74 for women. At age 65—15 years; 13 years for men but 16 years for women.

On Sex—Most older individuals are women—over 11 million as compared to over 8 million men. For the total 65 and over population, there are about 135 women per 100 men; the ratio increases from 120 women per 100 men at ages 65 through 69 to 165 women per 100 men at 85 or over.

On Marital Status—Most older men are married; most older women are widows. There are almost four times as many widows as widowers. Of the married older men more than 40 percent have wives under 65. An estimated 16,000 older women and 35,000 older men marry in the course of a year. Both bride and groom are 65 or over in approximately 14,000 marriages; the remaining 2,000 older brides and almost 22,000 older grooms take partners under 65.

On Education—Almost half never completed elementary school. Close to 3 million older people are 'functionally illiterate', having had no schooling or less than 5 years. Over 6 percent are college graduates.

On Living Arrangements—Seven out of every 10 older persons live in families; about a quarter live alone or with nonrelatives. Only one in

20 lives in an institution. Most older men (about two-thirds) live in families that include the spouse but only a third of the older women live in families that include their spouse. Three times as many older women live alone or with nonrelatives as do older men.

On Mobility—In the year ending March 1970, 8.6 percent (1.7 million) of all older people moved from one house to another: 6 percent moved to another house in the same county, 1.6 percent moved to a different county in the same state, and only 1 percent moved across the state line.

On Voting—In the 1970 elections, 57 percent of the older population actually voted; they accounted for 17 percent of all the votes cast (Brotman 1971).

On Race—Nonwhites (of whom the bulk are black) constitute 11.4 percent of the total population but only 7.7 percent of those over 65. However, differences of mortality rates have been diminishing (Kent 1971).

On Geographic Distribution—About two-thirds of the elderly are urban residents. More of the elderly are concentrated in central cities (rather than suburbs), in rural areas, and in smaller cities and towns (Encyclopedia of Social Work 1971, pp 52, 53).

Needs of the Aged

An organizing principle in the field of social welfare and the aged is the concept of "human needs" which are specifically related to the conditions of aging—biologic, psychologic, and sociologic. "Human needs" as outgrowths of human drives, are influenced and conditioned by cultural imperatives and by the processes of aging; for example, food needs or sexual needs change with age. In addition to meeting human needs, every society must meet certain functional prerequisites in order to operate as a viable social system. Since functional requirements for a society and concerns to meet the needs of its population are in a state of quasi-stationary equilibrium, discrepancies exist between these two areas. This is evident in the organization of services and programs to the aging population in the United States and in several other countries around the world (Lowy 1970).

Leo Simmons, a noted anthropologist, in his study of various cultures in diverse historical settings has looked for the persistent, recurring interest of aging persons. He summed up his findings by citing five major interests or needs: (1) to live as long as possible; (2) to get more rest, to get relief from humdrum tasks; (3) to remain an active participant in group affairs; (4) to safeguard or strengthen any perogatives acquired; (5) to withdraw from life when necessity requires it, as honorably and comfortably as possible (Social Work Education for Better Services for the Aged 1958, p 10).

Erikson reminds us that people do not only have "needs" that demand gratification, they also have "tasks" that they must fulfill during their stage of development in their life cycle (Erikson 1950). Havighurst (1953, p 2), speaks of developmental tasks which in the case of adults are related to ten social roles of adulthood: worker, mate, parent, homemaker, son/daughter, citizen, friend, organization member, religious affiliate, and user of leisure time. Obviously, there are changes when an adult becomes old and these social roles undergo modification. Peck (1956) has elaborated upon Erikson's stage of development with respect to old age and has identified three types of "crises" that have to be negotiated: (1) Ego Differentiation versus Work Role Preoccupation; (2) Body Transcendence versus Body Preoccupation; (3) Ego Transcendence versus Ego Preoccupation. Instead of finding personal fulfillment or status in the working world, the person now must learn to find satisfaction in being himself and in reviewing life and its meaning; instead of relying on physical dexterities and prowess, the older adult must adapt to changing and often waning, bodily functions; instead of remaining fixed to the issues and concerns of the "here and now" of life, the older man and woman must prepare for the world "beyond," must accept the finiteness of living, and cope with the inevitable fact of death.

Lowy (1963) suggests the following tasks for older persons in our society: (1) a redefinition of social identities with development of new social goals in an associational context, (2) the linkage of past and present to the future with regard to family, peers, associations, services, and community, (3) redefinition of the indivudal's value system, (4) adjustment to physical and mental changes, (5) development of new self-image transcending the societal expectations of behavior of older people, and (6) development of a sense of integrity, as defined by Erikson, which leads to a profound concern for system, order, and meaning of human existence.

Social Policy and the Aged

A society concerned with the well-being of its older population must take heed of these needs, tasks, and crises and devise arrangements that respond to them and thereby assure its older people their optimum development. It does so by designing a social policy that is formulated toward this end.

We have witnessed a marked increase in interest in aging in the United States since the 1935 passage of the Social Security Act. In 1961, the first White House Conference on Aging was convened which led to a series of recommendations in a variety of areas of concern to older people. In 1965, two historic laws were passed: the Older Americans Act which created a central agency for the aged in the federal government, and the Administration on Aging (AOA) and the Social Security Amendments, which provided a national system of health insurance for the elderly (Medicare). Many other pieces of legislation, though not always aimed specifically at older people, either have some specific sections (eg, the National Housing Acts) or include entitlements that can be mobilized in their interests. In

1971 the White House Conference was designed to develop a national policy on aging.

Another significant development was the creation of the United States Senate Subcommittee on Aging in 1959 followed by the establishment of the Senate Special Committee on Aging. Its hearings and printed reports constitute one of the best compilations of current thoughts, opinions, and concerns about various aspects in the field of aging in the United States.

Professional interest in the aged led to the formation of organizations such as the American Geriatrics Society (1942) and the Gerontological Society (1945). Older people themselves have organized into the American Association of Retired Persons (1958), the National Retired Teachers Association (1947), the National Council of Senior Citizens (1958) and the National Caucus of the Black Aged (1969) among other such associations. The National Council on Aging (1960) is a central, national resource that works with and through other organizations to develop interest for the conditions of older people and resources to meet their needs.

"In spite of the many surveys, books and conferences on aging, the greatest accomplishment to date has been the output of words." Thus spoke Representative Fogerty when he called for a White House Conference on Aging in 1961.

Frank Church, Chairman of the Special Committee on Aging, United States Senate in 1971 said: "Representative Fogerty when he made the comments excerpted above, perhaps had more reason for impatience than do present members of Congress. Today, after all, we have made considerable progress since the 1961 White House Conference on Aging. . . . Nevertheless, as this Nation approaches another White House Conference on Aging (in 1971), we must ask ourselves the question suggested by the late Mr. Fogerty's comment: 'Will conferees merely contribute to the output of words, or will they shape a genuine strategy for action or clear cut goals during the next decade?' " (U.S. Senate Special Committee on Aging 1971, Preface, p ix) This second conference was designed to develop policies, recommendations for further research, and action in the field of aging. Three years later it can be safely stated that these expectations have hardly been realized. In all likelihood such expectations were unrealistic to begin with and therefore could not have been fulfilled (Lowy 1974).

Presently, our social policies toward the aging have moved toward selective assumption of societal responsibility and away from reliance upon exclusive kin or filial responsibliity, toward acceptance of rightful entitlement of benefits rather than dependency upon charitable supports that are stigmatized, and toward more institutional services geared to meet individual requirements rather than residual, undifferentiated services (Monk 1971, p 102). Despite this progress, the gap between need and action is wide, knowledge has been utilized inadequately, the elderly are still given low priority in allocation of funds and resources. Negative attitudes and stereotypes persist among the public as well as professionals and no coherent, comprehensive social policy toward the aged has as yet been formulated in the United States, despite an attempt to do so during the 1971 White House Conference (Post White House Conference on Aging Reports 1973).

The social welfare system in the United States has gradually evolved into a series of laws, benefits, programs, and services for older people, which presumably respond to some of their needs and assist in coping with some of their developmental tasks such as have been outlined.

Based on the "human needs" concept and related to the societal task demands, Eli Cohen and Walter Beattie Jr. have developed a typology of services. Cohen, for example, classified services on the basis of (a) financial assistance, (b) medical orientation, (c) enhancement of social contact and social participation, and (d) problem solving and social support (Cohen 1965, p 52). Beattie relates specific levels of services for the aging to specific conditions of older people. He differentiates: (a) basic services, (b) adjustment and integration services, (c) supportive services, (d) congregate and shelter care services, and (e) protective services (Beattie 1965, pp 14–16). This author has developed the following system of categorization:

> (1) Services to the aged living in the community and to those living in congregate facilities, (2) services which are age-integrated versus those which are age-segregated, that is, services which are offered to older persons as part of an overall system of services to the total population versus services offered exclusively to older people, (3) categorical versus comprehensive services. In the former, the service will be given to meet a specific need or to alleviate a specific problem, for example, to provide a medical service or to offer a recreational program. In the latter, services are provided across-the-board, meeting a variety of needs jointly, for example, an approach which attempts to cope with health, social, legal, and recreational needs together. The categorical type of service can also be called 'uni-service' approach and the comprehensive type can be classified as a 'multi-service' approach. (4) Social utilities and social interventive programs and services: Services provided as a social utility are benefits which are automatically available to all older persons. They are provisions to maintain the family, group, and community life considered vital and include public facilities (such as parks, libraries, beaches) to be used as one pleases, and developmental provisions available automatically to support needs and requirements of individuals in a given social status of circumstance. Income security, housing arrangements, physical, and mental health services are included here. The user of a social utility comes as a claimant who determines whether or not he needs the service. Services that are interventive in nature are individualized attempts to improve social interaction where it is problematical, or to relieve stress, change behavior that may be deemed deviant, reduce disabilities or other impairments—physical, economic, social, cultural. The user of such services is either a client or a patient. Several of these types of services have also been referred to as 'supplementary' or 'special'. They are required by older people who have particular problems at a particular

> time or which are necessitated by personal or social conditions (or both) which are more permanent or lasting and which frequently lead to institutionalization in a congregate care facility. Within such facilities different types of ancillary, supplementary or special 'interventive' services are being developed geared to the differential needs or problems of older people. A person who is more 'autonomous' and self-sufficient obviously requires a different mode of care than a person who is 'anomic' and highly dependent upon physical support. In fact, we have seen examples of a continuum of services for older people in several European countries. Such a continuum provides services to an aged person in his home, in a day center, in outpatient clinics, and in a congregate care facility according to the needs of the person at a particular time. Return to his home with appropriate back-up services after discharge from a nursing home or rehabilitation center-hospital becomes much more feasible if such a continuum of services exists. (5) Services that exist under governmental and nongovernmental, sectarian and non-sectarian auspices. Recently in the United States, many tax-supported institutions have subcontracted with voluntary agencies and in turn, receive governmental grants. Differing relationships to constituencies and governing bodies can be traced to these developments. Whether services are designed in or for a neighborhood, a locality, a region, or a state has further implications for design and delivery of such services (Lowy 1970, pp 23–24).

Social welfare functions in relation to meeting needs and solving problems of older people can be divided into three parts: (1) the curative function, which provides for the solution of problems that have occurred as a result of malfunctioning within the individual or because of external factors; this can also be termed a therapeutic, adjustmental function; (2) the preventive function, which attempts to meet needs before they turn into problems; here human needs have to be identified well in advance; (3) the promotional function, which concerns itself with advancing the social standard for all older people by reducing many risk conditions that beset old age specifically and thereby can lead to the achievement of the highest level of physical and social functioning of which persons are capable. This is most in accord with the developmental view of social welfare.

In the immediate past, social welfare has been mostly concerned with alleviating existing problems and with helping in the adjustment of people to cope with conditions in their environment. Recently, there has been increasing recognition that efforts have to be expanded to insure that known risk conditions should be reduced as far as possible. The goal has been to get people to accept inevitable developmental phenomena of aging as normal tasks of living in later years and to minimize traumatic effects upon this adjustmental process. In other words, people have to learn to consider "aging" as normal as "adolescence," recognizing that it has many biologic, physiologic, psychologic, and social concomitants. Our youth- and work-oriented society, while ignoring, if not rejecting, the aged, has created problems that call for new approaches to the adjustmental problems of aging. This is why demands for creating a network of social services are increasingly made to minimize the vicissitudes of old age and to help the aged come to grips with some of the problems that are none of their making and are therefore victimized as a result.

A Schema of Needs, Problems, and Provisions

The schema shown on pages 148–150 was developed by this author to suggest the interface of the needs of people with biologic, psychologic, and sociologic processes of aging.* At the same time these interfaces reveal problems of the aged if these needs with which individuals and society must contend are met insufficiently. They point to the types of social provisions or benefits in the forms of policies, laws, programs, and services that can or should emerge to satisfy these needs or to cope with existing or incipient problems.

FOOD NEEDS

Diet in the older years changes for various biologic and psychologic reasons; there may be dietary adjustment due to loss of teeth, decreased perception, or diminished taste or smell, loneliness, anxiety, or stress may be expressed in terms of appetite loss. There are also cultural and social meanings of food and eating habits. If any of these needs are disregarded, problems in the nutrition of people are likely to occur that demand provisions in the form of programs (eg, meals-on-wheels) or services (eg, counseling). Future policies have to deal with creating a network of meals-on-wheels programs and with designing special food programs for the elderly.

Since human beings of any age show an inextricable cross-linkage of needs, the "human needs" column must also be read vertically. For example, food needs are correlated with income needs or, to put it another way: The amount of income available has an influence on the type of food one can buy, the kind of nutrition the body will get, and the frequency of meal intake one can afford. As Elaine Brody (1971, p 56) states: "Illness would be significantly reduced, for example, by the elimination of poverty, through welfare services and by preventive care such as nutritional services. Similarly, the high incidence of depression could be alleviated by the creation of meaningful social roles. In dealing with problems of aging, it is essential to keep those interrelationships in mind."

This schema is offered as an analytic device to locate needs, problems, benefits, programs, and services and to present to the reader a view of the

**Credit for the original idea is given to the Projects Division of the Gerontological Society, Social Welfare Committee, which developed a basis framework to assist in the identification and organization of the content in the fourth volume of their series, "Working with Older People–Guides to Practice." 1970.*

ANALYTIC SCHEMA OF NEEDS, PROBLEMS, PROVISIONS

	Human Needs	Specific Factors Associated with Aging			Problems of Aged	Laws		
		Biologic	Psychologic	Social		Fed.	State	Local
Primary Needs	**Biologic/Physiologic** Food—Nutrition—Eating							
	Sex							
	Clothing							
	Housing							
	Economic Income							
	Health Physical							
	Mental							
	Care and Safety							
Secondary Needs	**Psychologic** Love—Response—Security Usefulness—New Experiences							
	Sense of Identity and Status							
	Social Interactional Role and Interpersonal Relationships in: Family							
	Peer Groups							
	Nonpeer Groups							
	Interactions with Organizations							
	Social Institutions							
	Activity Occupation (work)							
	Mobility							
	Leisure Recreative							
	Cultural Information—Knowledge							
	Aesthetic							
	Play							
	Political Legal Status & Protection							
	Participation & Involvement in Affairs of Community & State							
	Spiritual (religious) Meaning of Existence							
	Relating to Unknown (including death)							

Provisions									
Programs					Services				
Government			Nongovernment		Government			Nongovernment	
Fed.	State	Local	Nonsectarian	Sectarian	Fed.	State	Local	Nonsectarian	Sectarian

	Human Needs	Future	
		Policies Needed	Laws, Programs, and Services Needed
Primary Needs	**Biologic/Physiologic** Food—Nutrition—Eating		
	Sex		
	Clothing		
	Housing		
	Economic Income		
	Health Physical		
	Mental		
	Care and Safety		
Secondary Needs	**Psychologic** Love—Response—Security Usefulness—New Experiences		
	Sense of Identity and Status		
	Social Interactional Role and Interpersonal Relationships in: Family		
	Peer Groups		
	Nonpeer Groups		
	Interactions with Organizations		
	Social Institutions		
	Activity Occupation (work)		
	Mobility		
	Leisure Recreative		
	Cultural Information—Knowledge		
	Aesthetic		
	Play		
	Political Legal Status & Protection		
	Participation & Involvement in Affairs of Community & State		
	Spiritual (religious) Meaning of Existence		
	Relating to Unknown (including death)		

phenomenon of aging within a human needs context. Any analysis of the social welfare system as it affects older people must be concerned with an identification of specific need-areas. The following outline is suggested for this purpose: (a) nature of need or problem; (b) current policy toward need on problem; (c) types of laws, programs, and services to meet the need or to cope with the problem; (d) future policies and provisions.

It would be impossible in this chapter to describe and analyze all the need-areas by our elderly population and all existing social welfare programs for the aging. However, this author would like to single out "housing needs" since they illustrate the horizontal and vertical interrelationships mentioned both in the "need" and "need-meeting areas." Housing needs also happen to be of major concern, since "man lives in a world of physical objects as well as in a defined territory under specified climatic conditions. . . . Physical space, open space, and the aesthetics of a territory, within a community, a neighborhood or residential environment—independent or congregate—may support or negate functional capacity" (Beattie 1970, p 191).

HOUSING NEEDS AND THE ELDERLY: AN ILLUSTRATION

Nature of Needs and Problems. Adequate housing facilities are necessary for everyone; however, the basic needs in housing for older people are somewhat different from the needs of a growing younger family. With smaller incomes and poorer health, older people require less room in their homes. Smaller size and efficient arrangements are important considerations which have to include proximity to and availability of public transportation and access to shopping facilities, recreation, church, and cultural centers so that the older person can remain active in the community. There are two major elements that combine to make housing for older persons an important issue: one of these elements is social, the other physical. A striking change in American families in the turn of the century has been the shift from a lower extended multigeneration unit to one that generally includes only parents and their children, the nuclear family. The change has been accompanied by reciprocal alteration in the relationship between older persons and their adult children. The physical nature of many modern American homes and apartments is that they are often not appropriate dwelling units for older persons. Adequate housing also means housing units for older persons that they can afford, and housing that meets the special physical needs of the aged and is designed to avoid isolation from the rest. Since older people are not a homogeneous group, they need a variety of housing types from which to choose depending on their health, life experience, income expectations, and personality.

> Logic and the consensus of opinion both support the premise that far too many older Americans live in substandard or unacceptable housing. While it is known that household costs—shelter, utilities, and repair-

> —constitute the most expensive item for the aged (about 34 percent of the Bureau of Labor Statistics retired couple's budget), it is not known with anything like precision how many live in inadequate housing. Virtually all the studies available today are projections from the 1960 Census which revealed that 30 percent of all households headed by persons aged 65 occupied housing that was dilapidated, deteriorating, or lacking some facilities. This figure represents about 2.8 million substandard units.
>
> The 1970 Census abandoned the collection of data regarding "substandard housing" because it was thought that the term was too subjective; accordingly, the new Census will not provide a precise up-date of the 1960 statistics. Regrettably there are few other broad range studies which have considered the housing needs of the elderly. The most notable of these surveys is the report in 1968 of the President's Committee on Urban Problems. The report, entitled "A Decent Home," sets out in detail the housing needs of the poor. Some extrapolation of statistics is possible, based on the rationale that the elderly represent 20 percent of 5 million out of the nation's 24 million poor.
>
> The Committee noted, "There is an immediate and critical social need for millions of decent dwellings to shelter the nation's low income families."
>
> In answering the question of how many units were needed, the Committee called for 6 to 8 million federally assisted units for the poor to be built in 10 years or a building rate of 600,000 per year.
>
> Since the elderly constitute 20 percent of the poor their need can be projected as between 1.2 and 1.6 million units or a minimum building rate of 120,000 units a year. By contrast only 41,000 units could be identified as approved or committed for the elderly poor last year.
>
> Another method of anticipating present housing needs is by projecting the 1960 Census statistics. Recent evidence indicates that 14.2 million units were built in the 1960's, which was 6 percent less than the amount built in the 1950's. With total housing building rate in decline by 6 percent and since the number of elderly has increased from 16.5 million in 1960 to 20 million in 1970, it is logical that the elderly continued to need at least the same level of housing as in 1960 when 30 percent lived in substandard (2.8 million) units.
>
> If 30 percent of the elderly continue to live in substandard housing then 6 million today need decent housing. Assuming that there are two seniors per dwelling (which is unrealistic since a majority of those over 65 are single or widowed) a minimum of 3 million units would be needed which compares favorably with the 2.8 million units needed in 1960. In all probability, however, the housing needs of the aged have risen since 1960, largely because government programs accounted for only 336,000 units in the last years (U.S. Senate Special Committee on Aging 1970, Chap. III).

We can differentiate at least four types of living arrangements: (1) people living at home, either in their own household, with relatives, with others, or under a boarding house of foster arrangement; (2) housing units specially constructed for the elderly, either as a part of the general housing development or as a segregated housing facility under public or private auspices; (3) institutional or congregate group care arrangements, which would include homes for the aged, nursing homes, hospitals, and so on, and (4) retirement centers. It has been estimated that 69 percent of the elderly live in their own apartments or homes, 25 percent in other people's homes, 21 percent live with relatives, 4 percent with other people, and 4 to 5 percent in institutions. One out of four older persons lives alone. Living alone is not without difficulties. This is true where there is a couple living together or a surviving spouse. For older couples, who have raised families and through them have resolved many of their differences, it may come as a shock to realize how irritating these differences can become when only two people are involved. Living with one's children may have satisfactions but it also has its problems if the arrangement is an involuntary one. Generations do not easily adjust to one another, especially when over a span of years their roles are now reversed. When the third generation arrives, many of the difficulties in the child-rearing process may be reactivated; it is not easy for a parent who has reared one generation to refrain from imposing lessons upon the next generation. Many older people who live in their own homes often find it quite difficult to maintain them.

Many of the aged living alone live in rooming houses, usually in one of the blighted sections of the city and/or usually shunted off from contact with others. Their sense of isolation and aloneness is aggravated by the problem of living alone in rooming houses that are sometimes maintained by absentee landlords. It has been recognized that for older people to live alone successfully and in dignity, it is essential to have a battery of health and social services available which are easily accessible to them. Some of these include home health care and assistance, friendly visiting, homemaker and chore services, home-delivered meals, sometimes called meals-on-wheels service, transport, information services so that the older person is enabled to function, if physically and mentally possible, in his own home.

Unfortunately, these services are not found in all parts of the country and very few of these services are well coordinated even in those communities that have them. They are a great help in making life easier and more comfortable for those whose physical conditions make it difficult or impossible to care completely for themselves. Older people living alone need a battery of professional services such as visiting nurses, social workers, medical aides, and others.

Current Policy. Already the 1961 White House Conference recommended more housing of every type so that the elderly would have a wide range of choices and easy mobility from one type of housing to another and proper planning of units from the point of view of design and placement within the community mainstream. The 1971 conference was even more insistent when it stated that a national policy on housing for the elderly must have a high priority and must embrace not only shelter but services of quality that extend the span of independent living in and outside of institutions as a right. Although present Housing and Urban

Development (HUD) programs have shown some progress toward implementing these recommendations, the record, according to the United States Senate Special Committee of 1971, is far from impressive. What is particularly lacking is a definitive public policy which advances goals that are based on the following research evidence with regard to housing for older people: "(1) Older people prefer independent living and economic supports are required to permit options, (2) governmental and voluntary programs are needed to provide suitable housing and to facilitate relocation, (3) housing for older persons should be supportive in its provisions of services and in architectural design to meet their physical and social deficits and needs, (4) services systems and transportation should be designed so as to make health and welfare services accessible" (Encyclopedia of Social Work 1971, p 63).

Types of Laws, Programs and Services. The Housing Acts of 1949, 1954, 1968, 1970 and the Demonstration Cities and the Metropolitan Development Act of 1966 (Model Cities) have been the basic laws upon which programs for elderly housing were developed. The United States Department of Housing and Urban Development now administers 21 programs dealing directly or indirectly with the housing needs of the elderly. Such programs include low-rent public housing, rent supplements, mortgage insurance, and long-term loan programs. In addition, state and local housing programs and neighborhood housing development programs in many states and communities have been in operation to attempt to cope with the housing problems of the elderly. Many communities have begun to take advantage of these programs and have developed special housing projects with a battery of medical, recreational, educational, and social services attached to the housing projects themselves. It was recognized that one of the most important features in housing for the elderly is to have available a series of services easily accessible to the residents.

In several communities across the country, provisions have been made to arrange for a network of health, social, and recreational services in order to maintain older people in their own homes as long as possible and to avoid institutionalization in congregate care facilities unless absolutely necessary. As of 1972, the Department of Elder Affairs in Massachusetts, in accordance with its policy to find alternatives to unnecessary institutionalization, provides services directly to the elderly population through home care and nutrition services. Home care is offered through a series of locally based non-profit organizations called "Home Care Corporations." Under the supervision of the Department, they plan, develop, and implement homemaking and chore services, transportation, information and referral, health maintenance, and legal and nutritional services. Presently, seven out of a projected fifteen for 1973-1974 are operational (Commonwealth of Massachusetts 1974).

Before illustrating in greater detail such an arrangement in the Boston area, we will review briefly a number of social services that have been developed as a response to the social (in distinction to biologic/health and economic) needs, because such services form an integral part of a well-developed housing program for the elderly.

SOCIAL NEEDS AND SOCIAL SERVICES

Meeting intrapersonal and interpersonal relationship needs are as significant for older people as meeting their primary biologic, health, and income needs. As has been pointed out, older people have to fulfill new developmental tasks and make adjustments to new demands at a time when some of their resources internally and externally are shrinking, when their losses frequently exceed their gains. It is small wonder, therefore, that the usual problems that affect people in their younger years show their aggravating effects in their older years and that many require help in coping with their family relationships, with loss of peers, loss of jobs, loss of income, and with their shrinking social world (Rose and Peterson 1965). To assume that older people have different emotional needs from younger people is evident by the fact that they are older. To assume that because they are older they do not have similar needs for emotional sustenance and gratification as young people do is a fallacy.

In a study done by the United Charities of Chicago (1966) as part of their casework services for the aged, the agency has provided some evidence of the problem areas for which their aged clients have sought service from them during the last few years. The following problems have been identified in order of priority. (1) Problems in individual adjustment and family relationships. It was found that there were relatively fewer marital problems, evidenced by the fact that few of their clients were still married. However, many of the problems concerned the relationships between aged parents and their adult children that could be labeled as "intergenerational conflict" and "filial crisis" and problems of isolation and loneliness. (2) Problems of physical illness and medical planning. They were numerically most significant; there was a link between physical illness and emotional breakdown; also, physical illness in one of the partners when they were still married created heightened anxiety. (3) Acute breakdown and inability to manage their own affairs. These were problems whereby many of the people living alone could no longer fulfill their regular responsibilities and needed assistance, home care and, at times, protective services. (4) Economic problems, such as financial deprivation as well as problems with budgeting and shopping. (5) Living and housing problems. Older people found it difficult to adjust to their home and living situation or to an institutional setting.

Family casework and counseling, group work, information and referral, protective services, consumer information, meals-on-wheels, friendly visiting, and homemaker services are probably the major types of social services that have been developed to cope with such problems.

Family Casework and Counseling. This service is offered by public and voluntary social agencies. The Public Welfare Association has been developing special training programs to sensitize staff workers to the needs of the aged. Since public assistance agencies are usually the ones that have the greatest frequency of contact with older people through the Old Age Assistance Program they are in greatest need of becoming sensitized to the needs of the elderly and to provide to them counseling services. Social casework is one of the major methods used in counseling. Only in a minority of cases, however, are such services available as a part of the general community service via family service agencies, public welfare departments (usually only for people qualifying for public assistance), mental health clinics, Red Cross chapters, centers for the aged, and others. In a few large cities, special departments have been organized for the aged, specifically in a few family service and public welfare agencies, notably in New York, Chicago, Boston, Detroit, and Los Angeles. The Family Service Association of America has been active in developing such special departments among its member agencies. The network of counseling resources is widespread but very thinly drawn and as yet has reached relatively few older persons. The emphasis is still upon the initiative of the older person who comes to these counseling agencies to request service, although attempts to bring counseling services to the older person in his own home through contact with a social agency or by a treatment team, for example Home Medical Care, have increased in the last few years. Counseling has been in heavy demand wherever programs have been organized.

The Public Welfare Amendments of 1962 and 1967 put greater emphasis on rehabilitation than on financial handouts in public assistance programs. It was anticipated that when these would be implemented by state departments of public welfare, better qualified staff would be able to engage in counseling programs for their aged clients. However, the facts have not borne out this hope, since funding and training of personnel have been inadequate to do the job.

The amendments to the Social Security Act of 1972 have led to a separation of income payments from social services in public welfare programs and have created a new Supplemental Social Security Income category combining the former Old Age Assistance, Aid to the Permanently and Totally Disabled, and Aid to the Blind categories into a new title and guaranteeing a minimum income floor for the elderly across the nation. While laudable as a step in the right direction as far as income is concerned, the emphasis of an income strategy and the "benign neglect" of a service strategy have created an imbalance as regards services by setting up a false dichotomy: it is *not* a question of either income *or* services, but a goal of income *and* services that ought to guide social policy toward the elderly.

Consequences resulting from these new programs have not yet been assessed systematically and await the results of empirical studies that will provide data to this effect.

Group Work. The service and treatment form is used to an increasing extent today. Originally performed as a spontaneous recreational activity in centers for the elderly or in golden age clubs, it is recognized now that group work demands specially trained personnel with special skills. More and more recreation centers, golden age clubs, day care centers, family agencies, public welfare departments, hospitals, homes for the aged, and so on, are beginning to develop specialized group work services when older people find it difficult to cope with their peer and social relationships. Groups are formed with the help of a social group worker and the group experience of the members is utilized for resocialization purposes. Group workers are attuned to individual needs and work with individuals in the group and also outside the group and, if necessary, make referrals to other community agencies, such as mental health clinics, where more specialized individual treatment is available.

Information and Referral Services. These are designed to offer information to individuals and to agencies in order to reduce wasteful wear and shopping around by persons who are uninformed about services, incapacitated, handicapped, or sick and to assemble important data by which to evaluate community needs, gaps in services, and resources. Over 100 special information and referral service agencies have been especially organized in large communities by community welfare councils, by their affiliated social agencies, and by councils on the aged. The nationwide OHSDI program, however, does not provide a service that deals with the complicated problems people may have in using community services. Public welfare departments can provide information to public assistance clients if staff is available. Many older people find it very difficult to utilize information and referral services and the majority of the aged are not even aware of their existence. In some other instances, it has been found (eg, in Worcester, Massachusetts) when some of the older people utilized the information and referral services, they really were in need of highly skilled treatment services which were not available right then and there.

Protective Services. These offer assistance to older people who may need help in managing their money or have fears of daily living but do not yet need the elaborate legal protection of a court-appointed guardian. These services are needed in every community because many older people cannot take care of themselves and are often exploited by commercial enterprises. Protective services can be defined as a constellation of social services that assist older people who manifest a degree of incapacity or limited mental, emotional, or physical function which may result in harm or hazard to themselves or others by helping individuals to continue to remain at a level of competence and function that will enable them to manage their own affairs. These services are sporadically available under the auspices of voluntary as well as public agencies. In addition to protective services, older people need competent assistance in understanding the lawful means for making their needs known and having them met. As a result, the Legal Research and Services for the Elderly Project sponsored by the National Council of Senior Citizens through the United States Office of Economic Opportunity was initiated in 1968, which has spearheaded many legal aid services, a program of lay advocates, and has also promoted among the aged a new awareness of their legal rights.

Consumer Information. Older people have less disposable income than younger age groups; yet they are often the targets of advertisement and promotions of fraud and quackery schemes. A number of federal agencies are working together now to pool some informational efforts into a more concerted program of consumer information for older people. Relatively little of this has filtered down to the community level as yet.

Meals-on-Wheels. This term is given to a variety of portable meal services by which warm meals are made available to older people in their own homes, usually once a day. The service is sometimes combined with shopping aid and homemakers' service. This combination makes it possible to help all those who like to prepare their own meals and those who need to have them prepared. Several communities have developed such programs and have taken advantage of federal funding under OEO. Under Title VII of the Older Americans Act (1973) as amended, special federal funding for nutrition programs have been made available. As a result, a series of meals programs have arisen in many communities throughout the country. The potential that this service holds, however, has hardly been tapped as yet.

Friendly Visiting. Through this service, volunteers or paid personnel not only help in marketing and shopping but also provide a contact with the outside world, so that the older person living alone has somebody with whom to talk and listen. These people are establishing a visiting relationship similar to casework services in the past when the watchword was "Not alms, but a friend." The friendly visitor has to be a person who is understanding of the older person and his needs when he feels lonely or isolated. He has to be a good listener and to be available on a regular basis.

Homemakers' Service. This usually consists of sending a "trained" woman in to private homes to help with cooking, shopping, cleaning, perhaps to help the older person dress and get about the house, and to be a friend who can provide a link with the outside world. The homemaker may be needed for only a few hours, several times a week, or she may come more regularly. It is a flexible service. In only 40 states and only in approximately 200 communities are homemakers' services for the elderly presently operating. Even where the service exists, the number of homemakers actually available is small and there is no uniformity of standards as to qualification, supervision, availability, and continuity. Homemaker service programs can offer a front line defense to older people seeking to remain in their own homes after illnesses, disability, or when frailty threatens their capacity for independence.

The prospect of expanding these services through voluntary and public agencies appears somewhat encouraging. Starting in 1963, 75 percent of the cost of such programs could be provided by federal funds in local public assistance programs. In 1970 the Social and Rehabilitation Services of the Department of Health, Education and Welfare issued regulations which provide that public assistance plans must provide for homemaker services by April 1, 1974 to be reimbursed at 75 percent by the federal government. It should be remembered, however, that this regulation only applies to those 2 million older people who receive old age assistance and presently does not cover the rest of the aging population.

In summary, we can say that all these social services (plus others such as transportation) are essential for our aging population and the fuller development of these types of services as well as their availability to all older people are the most important challenges. If we can make available such services in order to help our aged cope with difficult situations, the chances of maintaining them in their own homes or returning them to their own homes after they had been institutionalized because of acute or chronic illness are improved. This was clearly spelled out in the 28 recommendations adopted by the Section on Facilities, Programs and Services of the 1971 White House Conference, which regarded the maintenance of the older person's "independence, their self-worth, their dignity and their continuous contribution to our society" as an overriding purpose (1971 White House Conference on Aging, Recommended for Action, "Facilities, Programs and Services," p 1).

At this point it seems opportune to illustrate the operation of a coordinated health and community service program in a housing project for the elderly.

Health and Community Services in the Castle Square Housing Development in the South End of Boston

In 1966, the United South End Settlements in Boston, Massachusetts initiated a meeting of a number of community, social, and health agencies with the Boston Housing Authority to explore ways of planning a delivery system of supportive human services to be located within a new combined private and public housing development in the South End of Boston. This system would serve the elderly in both the public and private sectors. The initial contacts were made prior to and during the stage of physical planning and construction of the housing units. The Boston Housing Authority worked cooperatively with a number of social agencies, accepting suggestions related to architectural design, special features such as emergency alarm bells, facilities, and space necessary to house the services. The physical arrangements of this combination of public and private housing with high-rise buildings of seven floors and garden-type dwelling units for families and individuals consists of two seven-story buildings known as "Eva Whiting White Homes" which are the properties of the Boston Housing Authority. These buildings are joined by a landscaped terrace on the second floor level and they overlook a central ground level plaza.

Because of the relatively small size of the elderly population and the type of facilities, several community agencies found it feasible to develop a "model" of providing comprehensive services. As a result, the Castle Square services project for the elderly came into existence in order to demonstrate the value of comprehensive community and health services within housing developments which would provide greater accessibility to services for the residents when needed. The resulting proposal of a system of delivery of services was designed for the elderly residents with the following major objectives in mind: to provide coordinated, comprehensive, and continuous supportive service; to show that these services do help to prevent deterioration and prolong independence of the aging; and to develop a model of a service delivery system that can be adapted and included in the initial planning and design of public and private housing for the elderly in Boston or anywhere else in the country. One indication that at least part of the objectives are being achieved is the fact that in the two and a half years of the project's operation, just two tenants have left permanently from the public housing sector to move into nursing homes, two to chronic and mental hospitals, and one couple was evicted. Deaths account for all other residents' departures from the Castle Square public housing project. Since public funding was not forthcoming, the participating health and community agencies agreed to reassign personnel or employ new staff for the demonstration project, thus absorbing the cost of this outreach service in their respective agency budgets.

Initially a limited number of services was available when the housing units opened for occupancy in April 1968. The United South End Settlements provided staff to coordinate the project and develop group work and community programs, as well as a recreation program. The Family Service Association of Greater Boston, Department of Services for Older People, provided a full-time social worker on site in addition to a part-time social work assistant, and graduate students from the Boston University School of Social Work. The Visiting Nurses Association of Boston assigned one of its nurses on a part-time basis as an initial step in developing the health component. The nurse assigned had served this area of Boston for more than 20 years and had known or cared for many of the residents during that length of time. During the first two years of its operation, the major gap in the project services was a fully developed medical component.

In the spring of 1970, a new chief of Home Medical Services of University Hospital (Boston University School of Medicine) offered a health screening program for all residents in public housing and for those elderly in private housing participating in other phases of the project program. Approximately 50 percent responded with findings that resulted in further preventive or corrective treatment or continued follow-up observation. Since then, a clinic has been set up and is in operation on a one-day-a-week basis, available to all elderly residents in either housing sector. The visiting nurse, the social worker, and the physician work as a team in prevention and treatment of health problems of elderly persons. Presently, attempts are under way to secure consultant dental and psychiatric services to round out the health unit. Arrangements have been made with a local pharmacist to pick up and deliver medical prescriptions.

The social services component is another significant part of the program. Of the 125 elderly residents in the public housing unit, the social worker maintains approximately 50 percent of residents as an active case load, and 10 percent of the 100 residents in the private housing sector. In line with the objectives of the total program, social service assistance includes any supportive service that the resident needs in order to function better to maintain himself or to help him through a crisis. Services may be casework counseling, a provision of homemakers, working with a newly discovered diabetic toward acceptance of the illness, shopping for groceries for a temporarily ill client. However, the major thrust of social service has proved to be crisis intervention and most situations contain a health problem either physical or mental, or both. The visiting nurse provides health care to patients in the project who are a part of her regular case load. She also screens the patients who are to see the doctor and assists him during clinic hours. The social worker, physician, and the nurse work closely together and there is continual referring and conferring among them.

The "Companions Unlimited Program" of the Women's Education and Industrial Union accepts referrals of residents in need of a "friend" and also provides transportation to pick up and deliver surplus food items to residents twice monthly.

A resident council which meets monthly deals with issues of direct concern to the residents such as safety and security, housing comforts, adaptation and integration with the surrounding community, lack of supervision of small children in the area, and problems that arise largely because of living in close proximity with one another.

A community room is open daily under the supervision of an elderly resident affiliated with the Massachusetts Commonwealth Service Corps, and is paid a nominal salary by this agency. There, a variety of activities are offered such as health information programs, nutritional demonstrations, crafts, music, movies, socials, and programs for special occasions that include dinner and parties. These activities are carried on with group leaders, holiday dinners are prepared and served entirely by residents, and continuous attempts are being made to strengthen existing leadership and to develop new leaders.

The role of the coordinator of the project is vital in linking the various services and in monitoring the delivery. She arranges for conferences and meetings between project and community resources and also serves as staff and liaison person to the policy board.

The policy board, composed of board members and executives of the participaitng agencies, meets regularly to review the project, develop guidelines and evaluate its operation. Although initial attempts to involve representation from the residents on the board had not been successful (they thought it placed them in an authoritative role that estranged them from their peers), they have now agreed to participate in groups of two or three on a rotating basis. So far, this has worked out well and their presumed fear has been proven groundless. New leadership is being groomed and the residents themselves assume increasing responsibility for the direction of the project (Allen 1970; Aging 1971, pp 10–11).

The program is now in its sixth year of operation and has been evaluated by the Research Department of the United Community Services of Metropolitan Boston (1972). This evaluation component had been built into the design of the project since its inception. The report concluded that "the original objectives have been met and that a comprehensive coordinated health, social, and community service delivery system is workable and can contribute to maintaining older people in their homes. When such services are provided, they are heavily used by the residents and, for the most part, residents hold positive attitudes toward the service delivery system. This model of a service delivery system can be established through the combined efforts of existing public and voluntary agencies." Such programs, however, cannot be implemented on any significant scale without additional funding from public sources. This type of program has proved successful in early identification of problems of the elderly and, therefore, has strong potential as a program in prevention (A Coordinated Service Delivery System for the Elderly in Public Housing 1972). Presently, a study of life satisfaction of the residents is being undertaken. Data are expected to be available shortly.

FUTURE POLICIES AND PROVISIONS

In anticipation of the 1971 White House Conference on Aging a series of goal statements had been prepared which were subject to review and discussion by the 3000 delegates. These goal statements covered those aspects that had been considered of highest priority by agencies, organizations, and the aged themselves. They included nine need-areas: income, employment and retirement, nutrition, health, housing, transportation, retirement roles and activities, education, spiritual well being, and also such need-meeting areas as: planning and evaluation, facilities, programs and services, training, research and demonstration, government and nongovernmental organizations.

The goal statement regarding housing needs reads as follows:

> In the ideal community, older people would have a number of choices of where to live and how much to spend. There would be low-cost housing built with features for the convenience and comfort of older people, including areas for recreation and services. There would be moderately priced housing for those with slightly higher incomes. There would be congregate housing for the frail elderly where group meals were served.
>
> Older people, if they chose, could live in retirement developments where they would have the companionship of people their own age or they could continue to live in the community with neighbors of all ages.
>
> Elderly homeowners would be able to obtain low interest loans to

keep their houses in good repair and some method would be provided for them to meet their real estate taxes.

Today a few communities in the United States provide some of these choices but the availability of housing for older people is haphazard. Some areas have almost too much of certain types while in others there is no specially designed housing at all for the elderly.

A number of federally financed housing programs, providing the special features older people need, have been in operation for 10 years or more. Under the low-rent public housing program, for example, 187,000 units for the elderly have been completed but in many communities there is not even a local housing authority to develop such housing.

For middle-income older people, about 33,000 units accommodating 45,000 persons have been completed under the Federal direct-loan program and 10,000 more units will soon be ready. Another 2,300 have been built with rural housing loans.

For the more well to do elderly, more than 40,000 units have been completed under the mortgage insurance program.

But compare the total number of units constructed under all these programs with the fact that 8 million—40 percent—of the present total of 20 million older people are poor or near poor and most of them inadequately housed. Obviously there have not been enough units built for them.

And the statement with respect to programs and services says:

'If we are ever to have a better world for older people, we must have the resources—the facilities, programs, and services—to meet their needs.'

The incomes of a large proportion of older people is so low they cannot totally support the services they need. Should such services be subsidized out of public funds? If they are, will this then make it harder to ensure that all older people receive adequate incomes?

Many of the services required by the elderly—for example, medical care and nursing, are also required by persons of all ages. But often when older people must compete with other age groups for a service, they fail to receive their fair share. Should, therefore, specialized programs for older people, even then, get their share of community services?

Traditionally, members of a family have assumed personal care responsibilities for the disabled or feeble older people of that family. With the increased mobility of modern life and the physical separation in living arrangements of generations, the ability of families to provide this care has been sharply reduced.

In addition, there is the great increase in the number of people reaching old age. A couple—who may themselves be retired—can look after one aged parent. It is nearly impossible to care for four.

If care is to be provided in their own homes and communities for older people, priorities must be changed to emphasize a network of home help, home maintenance, and personal care services. In addition, special consumer counseling and legal services should be developed to safeguard older people and their property.

> At present, planning and coordination of these home services is fragmented among a number of independent organizations, some private and some public. Should these functions be transferred to newly created public agencies provided with administrative authority and adequate finances?
>
> In any system no matter how financed or whether all people or only older people are served, information and referral should be available (Second Reader 1971).

The 1971 White House Conference Housing Section actually approved 25 recommendations addressed to such policy questions as allocating a fixed proportion of all government funds to housing and related services for the elderly with a minimum production of 120,000 units per year, developing diversified types of living arrangements which should be available to meet changing needs, assuring financial aid programs for homeowners and renters, providing supportive services to help older people remain in their own homes, formulating guidelines for architectural standards, and so forth.

Specifically, the recommendations were as follows.

Recommendation I. A fixed proportion of all government funds—federal, state, and local—allocated to housing and related services, shall be earmarked for housing for the elderly, with a minimum production of 120,000 units per year.

Recommendation II. Eligibility for the benefits of publicly assisted low and moderate income housing and related services shall be based on economic, social, and health needs. Recipients having incomes above an established minimum level shall pay for the benefits on a sliding scale related to their income.

Recommendation III. The federal government shall ensure that state, regional, and local governments and private, nonprofit groups produce suitable housing for the elderly on the basis of documented need. The federal government shall encourage production through the uniform application and use of appropriate incentives.

Recommendation IV. A variety of living arrangements shall be made available to meet changing needs of the elderly. Such arrangements shall include residentially oriented settings for those who need different levels of assistance in daily living. The range shall include (1) long-term care facilities for the sick; (2) facilities with limited medical, food, and homemaker services; (3) congregate housing with food and personal services; and (4) housing for independent living with recreational and activity programs.

Recommendation V. Supportive services are essential in the total community and in congregate housing. Emphasis shall be given to providing more congregate housing for the elderly, which shall include the services needed by residents and provide outreach services to the elderly living in adjacent neighborhoods when needed to help older people remain in their own homes.

Recommendation VI. The state or federal government shall provide mechanisms to make possible local property tax relief for the elderly homeowner and renter.

Recommendation VII. Every effort shall be made to eliminate red tape and procedural delay in the production of housing for the elderly.

Recommendation VIII. Particular attention shall be given to the needs of all minority groups and the hard-core poor elderly. At least 25 percent of the elderly housing shall be for the hard-core poor elderly, those with incomes at the poverty level or less per year.

Recommendation IX. All federal agencies dealing with housing for the elderly shall be required to establish multidisciplinary teams to formulate guidelines for architectural standards based on the needs of the elderly. The multidisciplinary teams shall also have authority to review and approve innovative proposals.

Recommendation X. Minority nonprofit groups shall be encouraged and assisted in developing housing for the elderly.

Recommendation XI. When housing units for the elderly are eliminated for any reason, adequate replacement units must be available and relocation programs provided before such persons are displaced.

Recommendation XII. Congress should revise the definition of a family in the National Housing Act to include single persons 55 and over.

Recommendation XIII. The federal government shall encourage the preservation of neighborhoods of special character through rehabilitation, and selective replacement of substandard dwellings with new dwellings, with full provision for the elderly of the area to remain in their familiar environment.

Recommendation XIV. Housing funds now impounded by the Administration should be released and the highly effective Section 202 of the Housing Act with its special guidelines related to space, design, construction, and particularly favorable financing restored.

New Section 202 projects should be established by recirculating monies now being sent to the United States Treasury from mortgage payments and Section 202 conversions to Section 236 or like programs. Such conversions of current Section 202's should be encouraged by establishing incentives.

The Senior Housing Loan Section 202 administrative component of Department of Housing and Urban Development should have management audit responsibility for all Section 202 projects and all Section 236 elderly projects.

Recommendation XV. The Rent Supplement Program shall be increased in dollars and eligibility.

Recommendation XVI. Financial incentives shall be available to families providing housing and related care in their own homes, or in appropriate accommodations for their elderly relatives.

Recommendation XVII. The federal government shall provide financial incentives to state and local governments to encourage property tax exemption of voluntary, nonprofit-sponsored elderly housing projects.

Recommendation XVIII. The inability of the elderly to financially maintain their homes because of high maintenance costs and increasing taxes resulted in the recommendation that interest-free, nonamortized loans be made available, the amount of the loan to be related to income, with repayment either upon the death of the borrower or the transfer of the property. As an additional element of national policy, it is proposed that ways or mechanisms be researched to enable older homeowners to voluntarily utilize the equities in their homes, to increase their discretionary income while remaining in their own homes.

Recommendation XIX. Congressional action shall be taken to establish within the Department of Housing and Urban Development an Office of Assistant Secretary of Housing for elderly. This office shall have statutory authority and adequate funding to provide overall direction toward the implementation of a national policy and the production of housing for the elderly.

Recommendation XX. Executive action shall be taken to create an Executive Office on aging within the Office of the President.

Recommendation XXI. Congressional action shall be taken to create a Special Committee on Aging in the House of Representatives.

Recommendation XXII. The Congress shall enact legislation to safeguard the elderly property owner or purchaser from unscrupulous real estate developers and/or promoters.

Recommendation XXIII. The Congress shall enact legislation providing special funds for adequate housing and supportive programs to meet the unique needs of rural elderly Americans including those on Indian Reservations.

Recommendation XXIV. Standards for physical and environmental security should be developed and applied as an integral and basic element of all housing projects serving the elderly.

Recommendation XXV. Competent service to the elderly in housing requires sound research widely disseminated and utilized, covering many aspects of their living arrangements.

Such research shall be undertaken to cover the health, physical, psychologic, and social aspects of environment in urban and rural areas; to delineate the needs of elderly over 80 years of age; to determine the needs of transient elderly; to establish the importance of selecting appropriate locations; and to provide safe and adequate construction. Particular attention is directed to the consequences to vulnerable older people of improper sales methods and inadequate housing arrangements.

There also shall be undertaken a well-conceived and well-financed program of training for professional and semiprofessional staff to develop efficient and competent management in developments for the elderly (1971 White House Conference on Aging, Recommended for Action, Section Recommendations on Housing).

ORGANIZATION, DELIVERY, AND PLANNING OF SERVICES

At the eighth International Gerontological Conference in 1969, this author addressed himself to organization, delivery, and planning of services. He stated:

> It is becoming increasingly rare that only one type of services is needed at any one time; in fact, everywhere a series of different types of services are needed concurrently. An older person who has been discharged from a hospital is likely to require a home-nursing service, a homemaker service, meals-on-wheels, and, in all probability, a friendly visitor to alleviate feelings of fear, apprehensiveness, and estrangement from others in his immediate surroundings.
>
> Continuity, comprehensiveness, and coordination, the three 'C's' are criteria in the development and evaluation of a network of services answering to the needs of a "whole person" and through a holistic approach only will we be able to counteract the prevailing practice of fragmentation.
>
> Several types of multi-service approaches have been tried out in many communities in the United States. Multi-service centers offering a series of health, legal, information-referral, counselling, recreational, and educational services under one roof or, at least closely linked in geographic proximity, have sprung up in various parts of this country and have had some degree of success as perceived by the aged consumers and as evaluated by various research organizations (Lowy 1970, p 29).

He continued in his paper:

> Three analytic concepts can serve as guidelines for the organization and planning of services: (1) availability, (2) accessibility, (3) acceptability.
>
> (1) Social utilities (financial services, medical care, housing facilities) and social interventive services (counselling, homemaking, group treatment) must be available when people need them as claimants, as clients or as patients, possibly 24 hours a day, seven days a week. They must be in existence and organized in a comprehensive, coordinated way on a continuous basis, so that older people can utilize them when they are required;
>
> (2) Such services must be accessible where the aged need them, in geographic proximity to their place of residence, whether in the community or in congregate care facilities. In addition, accessibility demands that services which are provided not be hampered by elaborate control procedures, especially at the point of entry. These procedures discourage people from using these services, especially when they fall into the category of social intervention, for example, retirement counselling;
>
> (3) Availability and accessibility do not guarantee that existing services are utilized. Experiences with medicare and hearings conducted by the United States Senate (1966) confirm the reluctance of older people in particular to avail themselves of services. Lack of information is only one of the reasons given. Other reasons point to lack of acceptability of such services on the part of the aged persons. Apart from our social insurance programs, most services have not achieved the status of social utilities. As a consequence, these services have not lost their stigma. Pride and a sense of dignity prevent many people—young and old—from applying for public assistance or from requesting a homemaker service. Related to the problem of stigmatization are the

problems of red tape; they experience difficulties in negotiating an impersonal 'system' which is predicated on the assumption that people have to reach out to the dispensers of service rather than have them reach out to the people" (Lowy 1970, p 33).

Delivery of Services. The phrase "delivery of services" tends to imply a unilateral transfer of a commodity from a producer to a consumer. Not only does this suggest a one-way process, but it artificially isolates one phase of what is actually a dynamic and continuous process.

Three major dimensions are suggested to construct models for service delivery:

1. Mode of delivery: technologic/human;
2. Orientation of delivery: outreach to persons only upon demand by persons;
3. Timing of delivery: regular (routinized) or nonregular (nonroutine). Technological modes, for example, refer to the use of mail-delivered checks to provide income payments in contrast to the use of personnel to provide postretirement counseling. An outreach orientation does not wait until an older person asks for help but acts on the basis of presumptive need. This is closely related to a regularized system of delivery which institutionalizes the rendering of services, for example, regular medical check-ups every three months for aged people in senior citizens housing.

What mechanisms are available to make services accessible and acceptable? This is a vital, but complicated question. In many instances we need a fundamental reshaping of organizational structures. The system model of organization is most useful here since it formulates the kind of questions which can provide impetus for constructive changes. How can the organization be structured to increase the likelihood that it achieves its goals? How can maximum use of existing resources be utilized to serve the "consumer" most efficiently and effectively? A beginning can be made in one part of the system, for example, an agency may redeploy its staff and make it mobile and thereby affect other units of service as well. It can begin to institute an active outreach program, based on the experience of Medicare Alert and the subsequently reported project FIND (U.S. Senate 1971). It can initiate a meeting of older people in the community to get them engaged in developing a service of self-help and to act as advisors to its own operation. It can involve users of the service in policymaking and in service delivery. The reciprocal utilizations of producer, dispenser, and consumer of service holds promise to arrive at a more equitable and beneficient service delivery approach.

Planning of Services. Since it is unlikely and unrealistic to expect that we will be able to develop a comprehensive, coordinated, and continuous service delivery system which meets all the criteria mentioned, it is obvious that priorities have to be established. Unfortunately we do not have the kinds of social planning mechanisms in this country that allow for judicious decision making in setting priorities. But we will not be able to develop model services unless we pay attention to the development of such machinery. Our national scene has not been encouraging in this respect. The Federal Administration on Aging has not been invested with either the mandate or the resources to move in this direction.* In addition, local communities have to get the process going and the older population must be actively engaged in this venture. Councils on aging on the local, county, and state levels must be vested with authority by governmental bodies and charged with a planning function. This planning function requires commitment of financial, technologic, and human resources to do the job, which means enunciating clear goals, harnessing of support behind these goals, and a stated willingness to be held accountable for achieving these goals. Widespread involvement of the potential and actual consumers of services, that is, the older people, conjointly with the younger segment of our population in this process is imperative.

Planning must be based on data made available through computers and through expert witnesses of older people as well as of professional and subprofessionals; it must project the needs of the older population of tomorrow, rather than be tempted to base its plans on a static conception of today. "Model cities" offer opportunities to test out such models. Those who will assume central functions in planning will need to be skilled in collecting data and projecting services into the immediate and long-range future, and also in performing at least three different roles when appropriate: enabler, broker, and advocate. Decision-making bodies will have to agree on goals and sort out priorities. Mediating activities will be required to reconcile differing viewpoints of different segments of the population (old and young) and some positions will have to be advanced and advocated which are likely to be in conflict with those of others. None of these three roles is unilateral; all are essential in a planning stance.†

Personnel and Training. Ultimately the delivery of services to meet the needs of the aged rests on the availability of trained personnel, both in quality and quantity. If we have learned one thing about reducing social problems, we have learned that they cannot be tackled alone; they are interrelated and the attack on only one part of the problem will leave out other parts. For this reason, community planning has to include a variety of disciplines, professions, and organizations. This requires an involvement of a variety of personnel and coordination of personnel on the governmental as well as the voluntary agency level. It also requires the appropriate use of volunteers—young and old—in the staffing of services. Social welfare manpower comes from a variety of professions such as

**For the Administration on Aging to carry out the intent of Congress the Administration on Aging must have power and influence." (From the testimony by Elias Cohen, Chairman of the Public Policy Committee of the Gerontological Society before Joint Hearings of the Special Committee on Aging, U.S. Senate, March 25, 1971.)*

†Adapted from the aforementioned paper by this author.

social work, education, nursing, recreation, the ministry, and so on. All these professions and their paraprofessional counterparts have a stake in administering social welfare programs or in providing services to the aged. Therefore, we need in all professions people who are willing and able to work in the social welfare arena with and for the elderly, who are sensitized to their needs and problems and who at the same time, can develop links with other professionals so that they can jointly participate in providing broad social welfare programs.

> There is a serious shortage of personnel trained to serve the elderly in the United States. As the number of older persons has increased and facilities to meet their needs have expanded, this shortage has become a major problem which can only be met by the development of high quality, short- and long-range training programs designed to produce a significant quantity of competent professional and ancillary personnel in the field of aging. It is estimated that about 1/3 of a million persons in professional and technical occupations serve only or primarily older people. At least 80 percent of them have had no special preparation to help them understand the people they serve (Second Reader 1971).

Educational experts have recommended establishing multidisciplinary centers, institutes, and courses in universities throughout the country to provide training to personnel employed in service programs or to act as focal points to attract qualified recruits. The Massachusetts Task Force Report on Training (1971) states:

> Capable technicians are needed desperately to provide the elderly with health care, social services, qualified administrators and managers of housing projects, senior centers, social agencies, nursing homes, and human service technicians. In each case the government—federal, state, and local—must spearhead and, many times, supervise the creation of viable training programs and supply the funding necessary to put them into action. In addition, colleges and universities across the country must direct relevant departments (medical schools, dental schools, schools of nursing, schools of social work, and so forth) to expand present offerings and initiate new programs in the field of gerontology.
>
> Besides training young people to work with and for the elderly, senior citizens also should have the opportunity to receive training which can mean a job to supplement a meager income or a volunteer duty to fill the long empty days. Private industries should be encouraged to provide training for older employees and consider hiring them, at least on a part-time basis, whenever possible. The elderly can be particularly helpful as teachers' aides in public schools around the country. Besides relieving full time teachers of nonprofessional duties, senior citizens can offer instruction in areas of interest to them and rebuild firm contacts with the younger generation.
>
> At the same time, public school students should be motivated to participate in programs which serve the elderly and also to explore various career opportunities in the area of aging. Furthermore, colleges

and universities should endeavor to broaden their undergraduate course offerings to include material which related to the process and problems of growing old (1971 White House Conference on Aging).

The 1971 White House Conference on Aging recommended that a "fully developed training policy must focus on both the immediate needs of the present aged population and the future needs of the aging, through innovation of far-reaching policies and programs. To accomplish the training of needed personnel, the present levels of funding in all government agencies concerned with aging must be substantially increased immediately in order to increase the supply of all types of manpower: technicians, paraprofessionals, professionals, planners, researchers, teachers, and volunteers. Training must be conducted in appropriate settings both within and outside of educational institutions (1971 White House Conference on Aging, Recommended for Action, Section Recommendations on Training). Further recommendations concentrated on development of multidisciplinary research and teaching centers of excellence in gerontology, on increased federal and state financial support for all levels of training, inclusion of subject matter on aging into preservice and inservice curricula of all types of educational institutions.

FRONTIERS OF SOCIAL WELFARE AND THE AGING

There are many issues that constitute the agenda of today and tomorrow. The following list constitutes a number of those concerns that have been identified by older people themselves, by professionals working in the field of gerontology, and by political leaders who have been concerned with the problems of our aging population:

1. Assurance of an *adequate* income for every older person through a federally administered system of income security which is protected against inflation, devaluation of the dollar and pension loss.*
2. Reduction or abatement of federal, state, and local taxes for older persons and also a reduction of rates of public utilities such as transportation, telephone, gas, electricity, and so forth.
3. Reorganization and reordering of the health delivery system with stress on early detection: treatment, rehabilitation, prevention, group practice, and home assistance; development of an all-inclusive prepaid national health insurance system to remove financial worries and to assure cost control.
4. Provision of increased public social services divorced from financial needs.
5. Development of additional social and community services

**Passage of the Pension Reform Act in 1974 and tieing Social Security payments to the cost of living index in 1973 have gone part-way towards this goal.*

(as proposed by the Senior Citizens' Community Planning and Service Act of 1963) which would include many additional social services for older people and for research and demonstration projects leading to newer or improved programs to aid them.

6. Increase in senior citizens' housing projects in urban and rural areas and eligibility of single persons for moderate income and rental housing which is now only available to couples. In addition, automatic inclusion of a battery of social services in all public housing projects designed for the elderly.
7. Inclusion in the national service corps opportunity for older people who are able and willing and in a position to provide services for people with problems in all age groups.
8. Expansion of the Manpower Development and Training Act and Area Development Act in order to launch a series of experimental and demonstration projects to help older workers and those in the middle years make the best possible use of training opportunities in communities and to prepare for second careers.
9. Provision of a pool for part-time employment opportunities for older people and preretirement counseling services sponsored under industry, management, and labor.
10. Increase in the federal contribution for the building of nursing homes and provision of more uniform standards for nursing home care with enforcement possibilities. Removal of institutional stigma from institutions for the aged who are chronically ill.
11. Development of increased geriatric treatment facilities for the mentally ill and halfway houses for those who are released from hospitals and mental health institutions.
12. Provisions of increased home health and medical care services for the mentally ill as well as for the physically ill in their own homes or homes of relatives.
13. Provision of an increased program of foster and boarding care for the elderly.
14. Development of day care centers, recreation centers and outreach programs for those who cannot take advantage of existing recreational facilities.
15. Increase in educational opportunities under adult education auspices.
16. Development of a more uniform program of social services particularly homemaker, protective, consumer information, legal assistance, friendly visitor, meals-on-wheels, and multiservice centers.
17. Creation of nutritional programs coupled with social and recreational services to improve the nutrition of older people and to assist in alleviating incipient personal problems.
18. Provision of improved transportation facilities to counteract physical isolation and to advance the mobility of older persons.
19. Development of short-range and long-range plans by all

professions and organizations (governmental and nongovernmental, including older people themselves), on planning bodies to design plans for the well-being of the elderly in all walks of life, taking into account that the aged are *not* a homogenous group. Creation of opportunities for choice!

20. Expansion of research projects and facilities and provision for the utilization of research findings as soon as possible in planning and development of social welfare programs and services.
21. Development of new and improvement of existing educational and training programs for professionals, paraprofessionals, nonprofessionals, and volunteers working with the elderly.
22. Development of a system whereby the existence of projects can be readily communicated to the public and where the results of successful demonstration projects can be made part of programs and services as quickly as possible.

AND WHAT OF TOMORROW?

The politicalization of older people that re-emerged in the late 1960s when it was recognized that "senior power" has the potential for affecting essential changes through collective action will continue. The first major attempt in the 1930s which culminated with the Townsend Movement had lost its momentum in the 1940s for a variety of reasons.

However, the elderly of today and tomorrow are less likely to accept with resignation and gratitude a reduced status and a reduced standard of living, lack of opportunities, and a sense of powerlessness than did their forebears. Over 20 million voters will participate in the political and legislative processes and senior citizens' organizations, self-help groups, and social action movements are emerging to counteract the neglect of the aged by the dominant power groups in American society. If anything, the appearance of older adult organizations with the intent to produce social action on behalf of the elderly toward improving their status and social and economic conditions may have heralded a new dawn in the life of older people. Binstock thinks that, at most, only some roles in the political system may be exchanged, and aging interest groups may merely achieve incremental gains rather than power for the elderly as a whole (Binstock 1974).

The changing nature of the older population will contribute toward this trend. "In the future, more older people will be native born, better educated, will have better access to improved health care and also will have had a higher standard of living. It is, therefore, likely that they will have higher expectations in terms of health care, living facilities, and the amenities of life. During their young and middle years, they will have been more aware of the prospects of retirement. They will be more sophisticated about availing themselves of organized programs of assistance, about educational and recreational activities, and about their group potential in social action" (Brody 1971, p 70). They will also have reached a milestone period in world history as they have been exposed to rapid postindustrial social and economic changes. Therefore, any social policy with regard to the aged has to anticipate what the future needs of our present younger population will be like.

Perhaps the most important item on the agenda of tomorrow is a serious commitment to research on aging as a lifelong process and on social policy questions that affect the young *and* the old. The Gerontological Society has stated some of the most basic and crude research issues as follows: Who are the elderly? What needs do they have? What kind of services are best suited to meet their needs? How can they be delivered and by what kind of people? Do such services, when provided, affect positive changes among the elderly? Social welfare research is essential in order to base plans on a more rational footing and to provide services that are commensurate with the needs and tasks of older people. But no social welfare approach can be designed that negates the total human life span and isolates the young from the old and the old from the young.

Aristotle observed that "youth has a long time before it and a short past behind: on the first day of one's life one has nothing at all to remember and can only look forward". By contrast, the elderly live by memory rather than by hope; for what is left to them of life is little as compared with the long past; and hope is of the future, memory of the past. The old must be taught to hope and live for a future even while little is left them; the young must be taught to look to the past of which they know almost nothing. The old must look forward in imagination to what youth can see; youth must look back to discover what the old have already seen. In this way a significant present comes into being for both young and old as the spacious now is extended before and after to become a temporal matrix in which meaningful existence can flourish.

> The old, with their wisdom and earthbound experience, are necessary correctives to the soaring fantasy, untested idealism, and despair of youth. But the intensity, idealism, and despair of youth are equally needed correctives to the pragmatism, cynicism, and pallor of age. It is important, desperately important, that we accept our youth for their idealism and that they accept us for our experience. Together we are effective partners. Separate, we are murderous gangs—one intent on filicide, the other on parricide. To avoid the murder of our children, we must recognize the identity of their intended victims. Initially, their parents; eventually themselves (Silber 1971).

References

A coordinated service delivery system for the elderly in public housing (Castle Square, Boston): Research Dept. UCS, Boston, February 1972

Aging. Model services system developed in Boston housing for the elderly: U.S. Dept. HEW, Administration on Aging, June 1971, No. 200

Allen F: Health and community services in the Castle Square housing development in the South End of Boston. Report to Policy Board (mimeographed), 1970

Beattie W Jr: Matching services to individual needs of the aging. In Selected Readings in Aging. Curriculum Project in Applied Gerontology. Washington, D.C., Gerontological Society, 1965

———: The design of a supportive environment for the life span. Gerontologist 10 (3):190–193, 1970

Binstock R: Aging and the future of American politics. In The Annals. Philadelphia, American Academy of Political and Social Science, 1974, pp 199–212

Brody E: Aging. In Encyclopedia of Social Work, Vol. 16. New York, National Association of Social Workers, 1971

Brotman HB: Every tenth American. In Developments in Aging. Washington, D.C., U.S. Senate, February 1971

Commonwealth of Massachusetts: Budget in English, FY 1975, Jan. 1974

Encyclopedia of Social Work. New York, National Association of Social Workers, 1971

Erikson E: Childhood and Society. 2nd ed. New York, Norton, 1963

Frankel C: Some Paradoxes in the Ideal of Welfare. El. Wisner Lecture, New Orleans, Tulane Univ, 1965

Havighurst R: Human Development and Education. New York, Green, 1953

Horton J: Order and conflict theories of social problems. J Sociol, 0:701–713, 1966

Kastenbaum RJ, Derbin V, Sabatini P, Artt S: The ages of me. Toward personal and interpersonal definitions of functional aging. In Kastenbaum RJ (ed): Aging and Human Development. Vol. 3, No 2. Westport, Conn, Greenwood Periodicals, 1972, 197–212

Kent DP: The elderly in minority groups in variant patterns. Gerontologist 11 (1): 26–29, 1971

Lowy L: The needs of older adults. Report to Action for Boston Community Development, Boston, Mass, 1961

———: Meeting the needs of older people on a differential basis. In Social Group Work with Older People. New York, National Association of Social Workers, 1963

———: Models for the organization of services to the aged. In Kastenbaum RJ (ed): Aging and Human Development, Vol. 1, no. 1. Westport, Conn, Greenwood Periodicals, 1970

———: The 1971 White House Conference: 2 Years After. In Kastenbaum RJ (ed): Aging and Human Development, Vol. 5, no. 5, Westport, Conn, Greenwood Periodicals, 1974

Monk A: Social policies for the aged. Social Work XVI(3), July 1971

"Older Americans Act of 1965" amended in 1973 to "Comprehensive Services Amendments to Older Americans Act of 1965."

Peck R: Psychological developments in the second half of life. In Anderson JE (ed): Psychological Aspects of Aging. Washington, D.C., American Psychol Association, 1956

Post White House Conference on Aging Reports, 1973: Committee on Labor and Public Welfare and Special Committee on Aging. U.S. Senate, Sept. 1973

Public Welfare Amendments of 1962 and 1967. Cited in Social Security Act, Titles I and IV of 1962 and 1967: U.S. Dept. HEW, Social Security Administration, Washington, D.C.

Report of Task Force on Training: Massachusetts Governor's Special Planning Commission on Elderly Affairs and 1971 White House Conference on Aging, Boston, November 1971

Rose AM, Peterson WA: Older People and the Social World. Philadelphia, Davis, 1965
Second Reader: 1971 White House Conference on Aging, Administration on Aging, U.S. Dept. HEW, Social and Rehabilitation Service, Washington, D.C., 1971
Silber JR: The pollution of time. Bostonia, Boston Univ Alumni Mag, Boston, 1971
Social Security Amendments, 1972: U.S. Dept. HEW, Social Security Administration, Washington, D.C.
Social Work Education for Better Services to the Aged, Vols 1,2. New York, Council on Social Work Education, 1958
United Charities of Chicago: Study of Services to Older People. Chicago, 1966
U.S. Senate Special Committee on Aging: Developments in Aging, 1970. Washington, D.C., February 1971
1961 White House Conference on Aging: The Nation and Its Older People. U.S. Dept. HEW
1971 White House Conference on Aging: A report to the delegates from the conference
———: Delegate workbooks on: education; employment and retirement; physical and mental health; housing; income; nutrition; retirement roles and activities; spiritual well-being; transportation; facilities, programs and services; government and non-government organizations; planning; research and demonstration; and training
———: Recommended for action (booklets on same needs and need-meeting areas as delegate workbooks)
———: Facts and figures on older Americans (an overview, 1971—national)
———: A profile of Massachusetts' elderly, November 1971
———: Massachusetts, Governor's Special Commission on Elderly Affairs and the 1971 White House Conference on Aging. Reports on: education; employment; health; housing; income; nutrition; recreation; social services; transportation; legal rights and services; state government planning in aging; and training
Wilensky HL, Lebeaux CN: Industrial Society and Social Welfare, 2nd ed. New York, The Free Press, 1966

Suggested Further Readings (Selective)

PERIODICALS

Aging. U.S. Dept. HEW, Social and Rehabilitation Service, Administration on Aging. Washington, D.C., U.S. Govt Ptg Office
Geriatrics Minneapolis: Lancet Publications
Industrial Gerontology. National Council on the Aging, Washington, D.C.
J Amer Geriatr Soc. New York
J Gerontol. Gerontological Society, Washington, D.C.
Gerontologist. Gerontological Society, Washington, D.C.

BOOKS

Atchley R: The Social Forces in Later Life. Belmont, Calif., Wadsworth, 1972
Beauvoir S de. Coming of Age. New York, Putnam, 1972
Butler RN, Lewis MI: Aging and Mental Health. St. Louis, Mosby, 1973
Cumming E, Henr WE: Growing Old. New York, Basic Books, 1961

Kastenbaum RJ (ed): New Thoughts on Old Age. New York, Springer, 1964
Kent D, Kastenbaum RJ, Sherwood S (eds): Research Planning and Action for the Elderly. New York, Behavioral Publications, 1972
Kleemeier R: Aging and Leisure. New York, Oxford Univ Press, 1961
Lowy L: Training Manual for Human Service Technicians. Part II, Curriculum. Boston, Boston University Press, 1968
Lowenthal M: Lives in Distress. New York, Basic Books, 1964
Neugarten B (ed): Personality in Middle and Late Life. New York, Atherton Press, 1964
Palmore E (ed): Normal Aging. Reports from the Duke Longitudinal Study, 1955–1969. Durham, NC, Duke Univ Press, 1970
Riley MW, Foner A: Aging and society. In An Inventory of Research Findings, Vol. 1. New York, Russell Sage Foundation, 1968.
Riley M, Riley JW Jr, Johnson E: Aging and society. In Aging and the Professions, Vol. 2. New York, Russell Sage Foundation, 1969
Rose CL, Bell B: Predicting Longevity. Lexington, Mass, Heath Lexington Books, 1971
Rosow I: Social Integration of the Aged. New York, Free Press, 1967
Shanas E, Townsend P, Wedderburn D et al: Old People in Three Industrial Societies. New York, Atherton Press, 1968
Simpson IH, McKinney JC (eds): Social Aspects of Aging. Durham, NC, Duke Univ Press, 1966
Tibbits C: Handbook of Social Gerontology. Chicago, Univ Chicago Press, 1960
Townsend P: Family Life of Old People. London, Routledge and Kegan Paul, 1957
Vickery FE: Creative Programming for Older Adults, A Leadership Training Guide. New York, Association Press, 1972
Wasser E: Creative Approaches in Casework with the Aging. New York, Family Service Association of America, 1966

REPORTS

Brotman HB: Facts and Figures on Older Americans. U.S. Dept. HEW, Social and Rehabilitation Service, Administration on Aging, 1971
Eisele FR (ed): The Annals. Political Consequences of Aging. American Academy of Political and Social Science, 1974
Havighurst et al: Research and Development Goals in Social Gerontology. Washington, D.C., Gerontological Society, Winter 1969
Lowy L, Mogey J (eds): Theory and Practice in Social Work with the Aging. Boston Univ Council on Gerontology, Conference Paper Series No. 1, October 1966
Training Manual for Human Service Technicians Working with Older Persons: Vol. 1, Trainers; Vol. 2, Trainees. United Community Services of Greater Boston, Mass., January 1968. Available through Boston University Bookstores, Boston, Mass.
U.S. Dept. HEW: The Nation and Its Older People, April 1961
U.S. Senate Special Committee on Aging: Reports on variety of subjects, issues, and problems of the aged population. Prepared by the Special Committee and available through U.S. Govt Ptg Office, Washington, D.C.
Working with Older People: Guides to Practice. Vol. 1, The Practitioner and the Elderly; Vol. 2, Biological, Psychological, and Sociological Aspects of Aging; Vol. 3, The Aging Person—Needs and Services, May 1972; Vol. 4, Clinical Aspects of Aging. Prepared by the Gerontological Society for U.S. Public Health Service. Available from Govt Ptg Office, Washington, D.C., July 1971

Study-Guide Questions and Situations

1. How do present-day attitudes of our society toward the aged and aging affect our social welfare policies in regard to the aged?
2. Which basic human needs are more difficult to be satisfied by older persons in our society today, and indicate briefly the reasons for this difficulty.
3. Discuss briefly *one* social problem-area faced by many of our aged population, those in the 65–70-year-old group and those in the 70–80-year-old group.
   Indicate: (a) Nature of the problem,
   (b) Scope and extent of the problem,
   (c) Existing social welfare services to meet the problem,
   (d) Gaps in services,
   (e) Future policies to be recommended.
4. (a) What functions do social welfare practitioners perform to help older people with solutions of their problems?
   (b) What are some of the prerequisites for developing effective collaborative efforts among practitioners of various human service professions to cope with problems of our aged population?
5. Describe your concept of a multiservice approach toward meeting needs of older people.
   How do you think your own profession should function in the final organization of the community, using the multiservice approach to aid the aging population today and tommorrow?
6. You are to assist in the planning of a housing project for the elderly in your community. What types of services should be available within this project?
   (a) Discuss this in terms of the needs of the aged and the desirability and feasibility of implementing these services.
   (b) What advance research would be necessary to determine the selection of services?
7. Describe how the existing social welfare system could be reorganized in order to provide coordinated, continuous, and comprehensive health care as a multiservice social utility for all individuals. How would this proposed service be readily available and oriented to these services?
8. How does each of the three approaches to the social welfare system—residual, institutional, and developmental—reflect the attitude of the society toward the aged? What potential does the developmental system have for increased sensitivity to the needs of the older population?
9. In a hypothetical situation, a community has been funded to set up a multiservice center for the elderly. You are consulted to make suggestions for determining priorities and for blueprinting its operation. What suggestions would you make? What ideas have led you to these suggestions?

8

ADULT EDUCATION AND ANDRAGOGY: NEW OPPORTUNITIES FOR THE AGING

Eugene E. DuBois, Ph.D.

Adult education is as old as man. In America, the promise of a new land established a social climate conducive to learning. The acculturation and assimilation process that evolved required a variety of learning situations and new experiences. The minority groups, racial, religious, and political, that immigrated to America tended to create a natural climate for learning; new customs, a new language, and a democratic form of both government and living, each of which required new learnings.

The Protestant Ethic of values and knowledge which permeated the early colonies and their institutions laid a firm foundation for the arts, and eventually the sciences. The apprenticeship system, popular in the old world, was basic to the American educational system. Primarily meant for the poor, the apprentice was indentured to a master for a specified period of time where he learned a trade, and thus the consequences of a debtors' prison or a dependency upon society for sustenance hopefully was avoided. These were the factors that helped to place major emphasis upon education in colonial America.

The first permanent institution of learning at the university level was Harvard College, established in 1636, almost exclusively as a training school for an educated clergy and civil servants. Most authorities agree that the level of instruction offered by Harvard would be considered equal to that provided by a modern secondary school today.

The public school system of today also may be attributed to Massachusetts and its law of 1642. This law directed town governments to insure that parents provide schooling for their children, with appropriate fines and penalties as the result of attempts at avoidance. This law was extended in 1647 to include the following:

1. That every town having fifty householders should at once appoint a teacher of reading and writing, and provide for his wages in such manner as the town might determine; and
2. That every town having one hundred householders must provide a grammar school to fit youths for the University, under a penalty of 5 pounds for failure to do so (Cubberly 1920, p 365).

Eventually, the educational enterprise expanded throughout the colonies. Private vocational schools, conducted by individual teachers at first, and in a variety of fields, evolved. Latin grammar schools modeled after the classical schools of Europe began to appear. Indeed, many of these schools are still in existence in New England.

The New England clergymen were in many respects the adult educators of their day. Preaching education to the poor as well as the lettered and the pious, the preacher brought the biblical message to his congregation. Perhaps not always seen as *education*, it nonetheless was the early beginnings of a religiously educated adult laity.

The Junto, a discussion group founded by Benjamin Franklin in 1727, is often cited as one of the earliest, and oldest, adult education ventures in the New World. Eventually, other institutions took their place along side the Junto and other agencies. The adult education cadre was joined by the adult evening high school. As the mechanization of mills and foundries emerged, instructional programs in industry along with voluntary groups and special programs established for adult participants became increasingly popular. Included in this latter group were the Cooperative Extension programs, often cited as the most fully developed adult education programs, university evening colleges, and U.M.C.A. course offerings as well as a host of other voluntary organizations.

Defined Body of Knowledge

The first serious program to direct its attention to the specific needs of adults was organized by Columbia University in 1917. Designed to prepare teachers for Americanization courses, this program was the first step in what eventually became a rapidly growing area of specialization. In 1930, Columbia University established its program in adult education and awarded its first doctoral degrees in 1935 to Wilbur C. Hallenbeck and William H. Stacy. The succeeding year, Ohio State University inaugurated its program, with the University of Chicago, New York University, and the University of Michigan following by 1938.

Today, most major universities offer graduate programs for the preparation of teachers and administrators of adult education programs. Each program tends to place a different emphasis through either its course offerings or its research direction. For example, Boston University is primarily concerned with group process, institutional change, and adult education in community junior colleges and other institutions of higher education. The University of Michigan program specializes in community development, while Indiana University emphasizes religious and library adult education.

For many years, adult education has been viewed as a stepchild of the total educational enterprise, a marginal field of specialty. However, this is no longer the case. Adult education is now on the threshold of new opportunities for greater service.

The increase of leisure time, the rapidly changing culture, longer life span, and new technology all point to the need for lifelong learning. These factors, together with what has been discovered regarding the differences between adult learning and youth learning, has brought about a new technology or innovative learning designs for adults that will have broad implications for adult educators in the next decade and into the future.

The latest research (Okes 1969) estimates that there were 13,150,000 persons or 11.0 percent of the eligible population engaged in adult education for that year. If all of the predictions hold true, and if the history of adult education participation on a volunteer basis continues, this population should increase in geometric proportion. The fact that adult education permeates almost every institution gives additional credence to the fact that learning activities, whether they are preservice, inservice, cultural, academic or continuing education, will undoubtedly affect everyone.

AGING: IMPLICATIONS FOR ADULT EDUCATORS

The population of the United States is increasing at a phenomenal pace. Included within this growing population are the millions of adults reaching 65 years of age, the standard retirement age. The latest figures provided by the United States government indicate that over 19 million Americans were over age 65 in 1968 and that a projected figure of 25 million persons will reach this age and over by mid-1985. Figure 1 and Table 1 provide an interesting distribution of this population, indicating that the greatest concentration may be found in Florida (13.3) and Maine (11.9) and in the middle western states.

The growth of the older population in the United States has spiraled as indicated in Figure 2, with an equally dramatic life expectancy rate and projections.

Naturally, with age, as other contributors to this book have illustrated, the older adult is often plagued with disease, physical inabilities, and other abnormalities incidental to old age. As a nation, these problems have received increased attention by both governmental and private

TABLE 1. ***Estimated Population Aged 65 and Over, By State, 1968 and 1985****

	Mid-1968 Number	Mid-1968 Percent†	Rank‡	Mid-1985 Projection		Mid-1968 Number	Mid-1968 Percent†	Rank‡	Mid-1985 Projection
Alabama	309,000	8.8	33	398,000	Nebraska	179,000	12.3	3	178,000
Alaska	6,000	2.2	51	11,000	Nevada	27,000	6.1	49	50,000
Arizona	138,000	8.3	39	248,000	New Hamphire	78,000	11.1	10	92,000
Arkansas	228,000	11.4	7	253,000	New Jersey	664,000	9.4	25	942,000
California	4,692,000	8.8	34	2,651,000	New Mexico	67,000	6.7	48	103,000
Colorado	180,000	8.7	35	242,000	New York	1,914,000	10.5	18	2,397,000
Connecticut	276,000	9.3	26	383,000	North Carolina	389,000	7.6	43	550,000
Delaware	41,000	7.7	41	62,000	North Dakota	65,000	10.5	19	69,000
District of Columbia	60,000	8.6	36	92,000	Ohio	967,000	9.1	32	1,255,000
Florida	824,000	13.3	1	1,381,000	Oklahoma	283,000	11.1	11	321,000
Georgia	347,000	7.6	42	486,000	Oregon	214,000	10.7	16	263,000
Hawaii	41,000	5.3	50	60,000	Pennsylvania	1,233,000	10.5	20	1,565,000
Idaho	65,000	9.2	29	81,000	Rhode Island	98,000	10.8	15	119,000
Illinois	1,066,000	9.7	22	1,309,000	South Carolina	182,000	6.8	47	266,000
Indiana	478,000	9.4	24	588,000	South Dakota	79,000	11.9	5	81,000
Iowa	346,000	12.5	2	350,000	Tennessee	366,000	9.3	27	470,000
Kansas	260,000	11.3	9	279,000	Texas	926,000	8.4	38	1,233,000
Kentucky	329,000	10.2	21	378,000	Utah	72,000	7.0	46	102,000
Louisiana	289,000	7.8	40	396,000	Vermont	48,000	11.1	12	54,000
Maine	116,000	11.9	4	130,000	Virginia	346,000	7.5	44	510,000
Maryland	276,000	7.4	45	439,000	Washington	308,000	9.3	28	398,000
Massachusetts	619,000	11.4	8	720,000	West Virginia	192,000	10.6	17	218,000
Michigan	734,000	8.5	37	941,000	Wisconsin	457,000	10.9	14	530,000
Minnesota	400,000	10.9	13	434,000	Wyoming	30,000	9.2	30	38,000
Mississippi	214,000	9.1	31	249,000					
Missouri	543,000	11.8	6	590,000					
Montana	67,000	9.6	23	82,000	Totals	19,134	9.6	—	25,006,000

(From U.S. Office of Health, Education and Welfare: May 1970, p 13.)

† *Proportion of state's population aged 65 and over.*

‡ *States are ranked in order of decreasing percentage.*

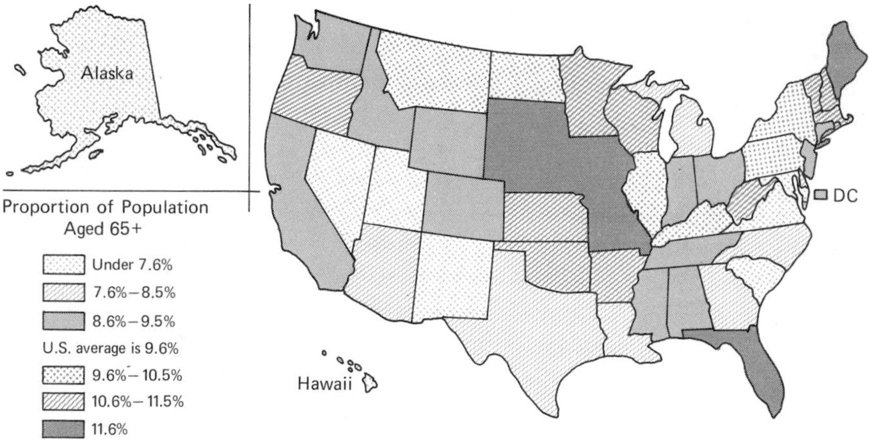

FIG. 1. Relative concentrations of older people by state, 1968. (From U.S. Office of Health, Education and Welfare: May 1970, p 13.)

agencies. Figures 1 and 2 illustrate the extent to which the aging population has been aided in more recent years. The fact that life expectancy is increasing and that medical science and social welfare agencies are attempting to meet the physical and social needs of an ever-increasing sector of the United States population places grave and significant responsibilities upon the adult educator as he seeks means by which the continuing educational needs of adults may be met.

DEVELOPMENTAL TASKS

Adults learn differently than the young. The factors mentioned earlier relative to the physical conditions and numbers within the adult population have significant implications for program planning and instruction.

Research regarding the adult population has been minimal. The earliest significant study was that of Thorndike in 1928. This study concerned university students and their wives; the sample was rather selective and not typical of the adult population. Thorndike's work was a cross-sectional study comparing young people with adults, attempting to determine how fast adults learned rather than how much they learned. In general, it was determined that adults require more time to learn than younger people, but that their ability to learn, in general, had no direct relationship to age.

Numerous other studies have been conducted with the adult population shedding light on this most significant area of education. Robert Havighurst of the University of Chicago has developed a theory of developmental tasks which has helped adult education researchers to un-

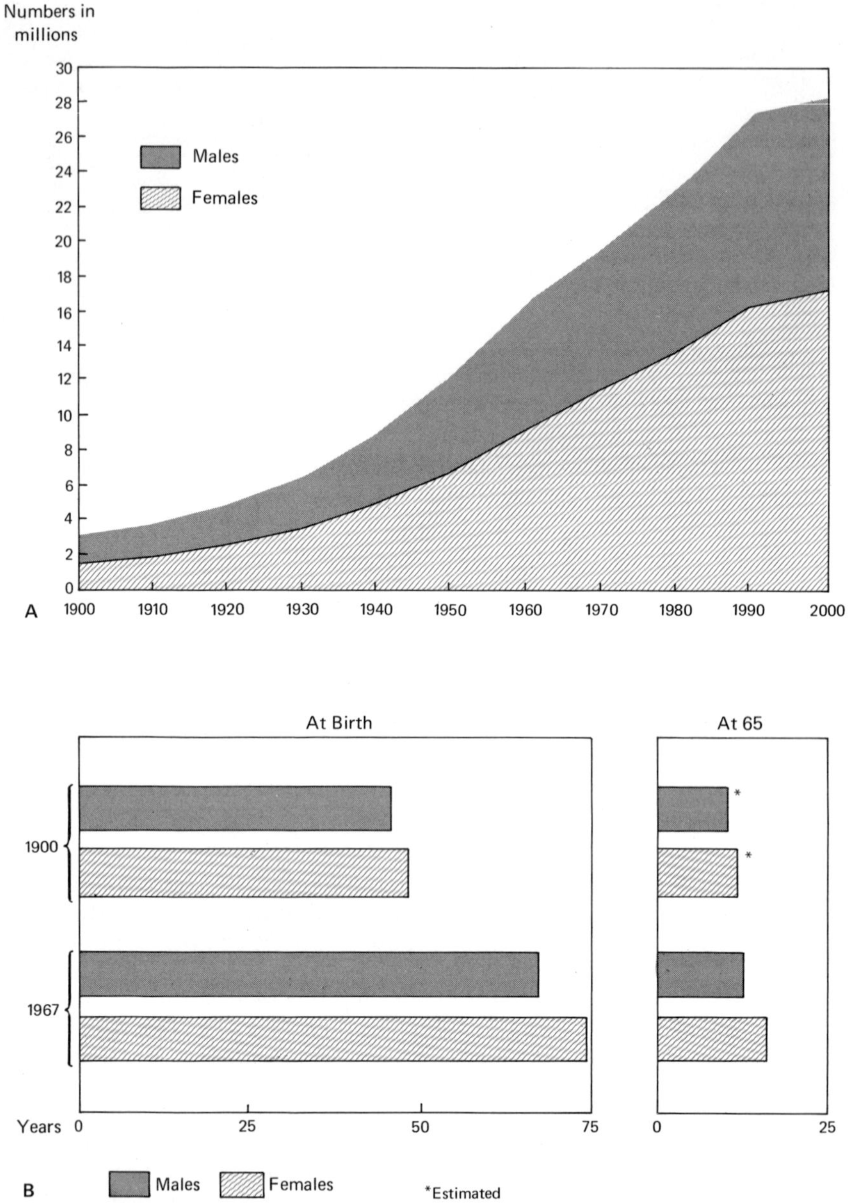

FIG. 2. **A.** Growth of the older population. **B.** Life expectancy. (From U.S. Office of Health, Education and Welfare: May 1970, p. 12.)

derstand the maturation process of man, and to relate these findings to program planning and the design of learning experiences for adults. According to Havighurst, a *developmental task* may be defined as follows.

> The tasks the individual must learn—the developmental tasks of life—are those things that constitute healthy and satisfactory growth in our society. They are the things a person must learn if he is to be judged and to judge himself to be a reasonable happy and successful person. A developmental task is a task which arises at or about a certain period in the life of the individual, successful achievement of which leads to his happiness and to success with later tasks, *while failure leads to unhappiness in the individual, disapproval by the society, and difficulty with later tasks* (Havighurst 1952, p 2).

If the task is not learned, according to Professor Havighurst, this failure will serve as a blockage to the learning of the next series of tasks. Havighurst has identified a series of tasks throughout the life span. The three stages of adulthood provide a perspective, and its accompanying concept of a *teachable moment* is believed by many adult educators to have implications for the design of learning experiences for adults.

Early Adulthood (Ages 18–30)
1. Selecting a mate
2. Learning to live with a marriage partner
3. Starting a family
4. Rearing children
5. Managing a home
6. Getting started in an occupation
7. Taking on civic responsibility
8. Finding a congenial social group

Middle Age (Ages 30–55)
1. Achieving adult civic and social responsibility
2. Establishing and maintaining an economic standard of living
3. Assisting teen-age children to become responsible and happy adults
4. Developing adult leisure-time activities
5. Relating oneself to one's spouse as a person
6. Accepting and adjusting to the physiologic changes of middle age
7. Adjusting to aging parents

Later Maturity (Age 55–over)
1. Adjusting to decreasing physical strength and health
2. Adjustment to retirement and reduced income
3. Adjusting to death of spouse
4. Establishing an explicit affiliation with one's age group
5. Meeting social and civic obligations

The Teachable Moment. There are two reasons why the concept of developmental tasks is useful to educators. First, it helps in discovering and stating the purposes of education in the schools. Education may be conceived as the effort of the society, through the school, to help the individual achieve certain of his developmental tasks.

The second use of the concept is in the timing of educational efforts. When the body is ripe, and the society requires, and the self is ready to achieve a certain task, the teachable moment has come. Efforts at teaching which would have been largely wasted if they had come earlier, give gratifying results when they come at the *teachable moment*, when the task should be learned. For example, the best times to teach reading, the care of children, and adjustment to retirement from one's job can be discovered by studying human development, and finding out when conditions are most favorable for learning these tasks (Havighurst 1952, p 5).

The fact that adult educators have accepted the developmental tasks concept is well documented. The literature supports this fact and, as we shall see later, the current evolving technology of andragogy utilizes this concept as one of its supporting and rather basic constructs.

The major criticism that has arisen out of the Havighurst theory is that some people do in fact omit certain steps which would seem to make these simple and clear-cut stages dysfunctional. For example, many people never marry and find satisfactory career and social experiences throughout their lives.

A second criticism is the tendency for these tasks to relate to the white middle class. David Smith suggests this in the following:

> . . . the stages in development are not stages in anything but an outline of the middle-class American values. This value system has nothing to do with many Negro Americans. Many young people, as well, would reject this value system outright; others would hold it suspect. These young people intend to achieve autonomy in some other way (Smith 1966, p 182).

It is rather obvious that the mere acceptance of developmental tasks by adult educators has helped to lay a theoretical foundation for this evolving field of social practice; however, its usefulness for groups other than middle-class whites may be a limiting factor. It will be the future adult educators and future theoreticians in adult education to whom the testing of the developmental tasks concept must fall as the body of content becomes more organized.

The Organization of Learning Experiences

We know from research, experimentation, and observation that adults learn differently than youths. There are a variety of reasons for this. The most significant is perhaps that adults are older and thus their experience requires a different approach which takes into account their maturation, eventual use of the learning, and personal needs.

Basic to adult education theory is the fact that man lives in a dynamic society, a changing society. A child born two or three generations ago, especially those products of an agrarian culture, experienced very little change during their lifetime, and in general, his mental and physical environment did not vary much from that of his father. Also, the life span a generation or two ago was considerably shorter. Thus, all of the knowledge necessary to provide the individual with the necessary tools for vocational and social living were learned during the earliest years of educational life.

Today this is no longer true. The rate of technologic and scientific discoveries moves at a phenomenal pace. The space age, and electronic and medical advances all have made contributions to our culture on a scale not thought possible a generation ago.

The life expectancy during the 20th century has also lengthened to such an extent that one of the major problems facing man, not only in the United States but also throughout the world, is overpopulation and whether and how this may be controlled.

These factors give rise to the need for continuous or lifelong learning in order to meet the challenges of a changing society. Thus, learning independently or self-directed learning becomes significantly more important to the adult, for whether he returns to the classroom for formal learning experiences or whether he studies independently, the unique needs and characteristics of the adult as a learner warrant special designs for learning experience.

PRINCIPLES FOR ADULT LEARNING

Professor Jack R. Gibb has developed for the adult educator six basic principles to be considered in designing learning experiences for adults (Gibb 1960, pp 54-64).

1. Learning must be problem centered;
2. Learning must be experienced centered;
3. Experience must be meaningful to the learner;
4. The learner must be free to look at the experience;
5. The goals must be set and the search organized by the learner;
6. The learner must have feedback about progress toward goals.

Each of these six principles for adult learning has one element in common, participatory involvement. Adult educators, researchers, and curriculum planners for decades have advocated that true learning as opposed to indoctrination or merely *teaching* requires active participation on the part of the learner. Indeed, much of the progressive education advocated by John Dewey, and elaborated on by such writers as Earl Kelley (1951), and others, have supported this thesis.

Active involvement in the learning experience as well as participation in the development of the learning design transforms the student from a passive consumer of new data to an active participant, and places responsibility upon the student and the teacher. Learning designs involving adults in a variety of teaching-learning settings have found participatory learning most successful (DuBois 1971, pp 14–16, 38). Experimentation and observation by students, researchers, and curriculum planners have thus made significant contributions to what we have learned regarding the teaching-learning process.

A NEW TECHNOLOGY

In recent years, adult educators have attempted to define their field and determine in what way adults learn best, and what factors differentiate the adult learner from that of the youth, and what implications, if any, do these factors have for adult education. Irving Lorge determined that adults engage in adult education for a variety of reasons. These incentives for adult learning may be grouped into four general categories (Lorge 1947, p 25).

People want to gain:

1. Health,
2. Time,
3. Money,
4. Popularity,
5. Improved appearance,
6. Security in old age,
7. Praise from others,
8. Comfort,
9. Leisure,
10. Pride of accomplishment,
11. Advancement: business, social,
12. Increased enjoyment,
13. Self-confidence,
14. Personal prestige.

They want to be:

1. Good parents,
2. Social, hospitable,
3. Up to date,
4. Creative,
5. Proud of their possessions,
6. Influential over others,
7. Gregarious,
8. Efficient,
9. "First" in things,
10. Recognized as authorities.

They want to:

1. Express their personalities,
2. Resist domination by others,
3. Satisfy their curiosity,
4. Emulate the admirable,
5. Appreciate beauty,
6. Acquire or collect things,
7. Win other's affection,
8. Improve themselves generally.

They want to save:

1. Time,
2. Money,
3. Work,
4. Discomfort,
5. Worry,
6. Doubts,
7. Risks,
8. Personal embarrassment.

Thus, there are a variety of incentives that cause adults to seek more education. However, the fact that they are adults and each has a different need, a different approach, or learning design must be remembered. This new design incorporates the fact that adults do learn differently than youths and that their developmental tasks and particular needs at the time *must* be considered by the teacher if he is going to provide a significant learning experience for the adult.

ANDRAGOGY VERSUS PEDAGOGY

Andragogy is simply defined as "the art and science of helping adults to learn," in contrast to *pedagogy,* which means "the art and science of teaching children" (Knowles 1970). Andragogy is derived from the Greek *andr* (man) as the parallel to the Greek *paed* (child) from which pedagogy is derived. It can readily be seen that the phrase *pedagogy of adult learning* is most inappropriate grammatically. On the other hand, if adults do in fact learn differently than children, then a new technology or educational design is most appropriate. Andragogy is an attempt to incorporate these differences in learning needs.

The word andragogy as applied to learning for adult dates back to the 19th century. Ger van Enckevort, a Dutch scholar, states:

> It sounds new but the name is older than a lot of people think. Before the German education theorists Diesterweg (in 1835) and Natrop (in 1894) introduced the better known term "social pedagogy" (Sozialpadogogik) the term "andragogy" (Andragogik) was proposed by a German teacher in a grammar school, Alexander Kapp, in 1833. The two words are sometimes used to denote the same field, but with a different accent. Social pedagogy stresses that educational activities outside schools are justified in cases of failed chances or for deprivileged people; andragogy says that education for adults can be as normal as education of children. Kapp used the word in a description of the educational theory of the Greek philosopher Plato. Education starts with 'Propadeutik' (propaedeutics), before birth; then there is education of children, pedagogy; pedagogy finds its fulfillment and necessary perfection in the education of adults, andragogy (van Enckevort 1970).

Andragogy is based upon four assumptions that can be made regarding the adult learner:

1. *Self-concept.* The adult is generally an independent person. He provides for his own sustenance, he is self-directed, and does not require other persons to make decisions for him.
2. *Experience.* The adult enters the learning experience with a variety of other experiences. He may have attended any number of formal or informal educational institutions, he may have read widely, he may have traveled. The fact that he is older than a child implies that he has had more experiences upon which to draw.
3. *Readiness to learn.* The adult has a variety of social roles

and developmental tasks and these, in part, determine the student's readiness to learn. The concept of a teachable moment has considerable implications here.

4. *Time perspective and orientation to learning.* The adult usually plans to utilize his new learnings immediately. Thus, his learning tends to be problem centered, whereas the youth's perspective is one of postponed application for later in life, and he tends to be more subject centered.

Table 2, designed by Professor Malcolm S. Knowles, illustrates how the process elements of pedagogy and andragogy may be compared in relation to the basic assumptions that we make about adults as learners.

GROUP PROCESS AND PROGRAM PLANNING

Program planning for adults requires a considerable amount of time, for working with adults, in groups, each with different needs, necessitates a design which, to the casual observer, has stoppages, false starts, and often complicated procedures. However, when group process or group self-directed learning is employed as part of the participatory learning design, the resources and experiences of the teacher and the student become available.

Earl Kelley discusses this point.

> The critics say that there is a great deal of confusion in the group process. This is true. There is confusion wherever real learning, with genuine contriving, goes on. This is true even when people are working by themselves, and it is multiplied when it involves a number of people. The only time there is no confusion is when one person establishes the goal for all, and enforces the action toward it. Democratic procedures require the involvement and consultation of many people, and this results in confusion, or what may appear to be confusion to the superficial observer. The more people involved, the more contriving, the more confusion, and the more learning. In education, beware the machine which runs too smoothly (Kelley 1951, p 44).

The use of groups and learning-teaching teams in adult education thus affords several distinct advantages.

1. The adult finds the course content more interesting. His peers developed the materials and the course is student centered.
2. Dull, boring lectures are minimized in favor of participatory learning.
3. A variety of learning designs evolve.
4. Adults often feel more comfortable working with their peers in groups.
5. The experience of the adult is utilized for the benefit of the entire class and thus enriches the learning experience.

TABLE 2. ***A Comparison of Assumptions and Processes of Pedagogy and Andragogy***

	Assumptions			Process Elements	
	Pedagogy	Andragogy		Pedagogy	Andragogy
Self-concept	Dependency	Increasing self-directiveness	Climate	Authority oriented Formal Competitive	Mutuality Respectful Collaborative Informal
Experience	Of little worth	Learners are a rich resource for learning	Planning	By teacher	Mechanism for mutual planning
Readiness	Biologic development Social pressure	Developmental tasks of social roles	Diagnosis of needs	By teacher	Mutual self-diagnosis
Time perspective	Postponed application	Immediacy of application	Formulation of objectives	By teacher	Mutual negotiation
Orientation to learning	Subject centered	Problem centered	Design	Logic of the subject matter — Content units	Sequenced in terms of readiness — Problem units
			Activities	Transmittal techniques	Experiential techniques (inquiry)
			Evaluation	By teacher	Mutual rediagnosis of needs — Mutual measurement of program

The understanding and utilization of group process has thus enhanced the educational experiences for adults. Working and learning together for group and individual goals adds an additional dimension to the learning experience. By working together, gathering data through independent research, and utilizing the teacher as a resource rather than as a didactic giver of information, the adult is free to use his experience, maintain his self-concept, arrive at his teachable moment, and use his new learning for himself and those with whom he is learning.

The program planning process in the design of adult education programs is equally as important as the individual experience. Professor Malcolm S. Knowles has developed seven guidelines for this process (Knowles 1967, pp 278-79).

The Program Planning Process

1. The creation of a structure for mutual planning. Ideally, such a structure would involve all those who are going to be affected by an educational activity in planning it —including participants, teachers, institutional representatives, and the community.
2. The establishment of a climate conducive to adult learning. In addition to providing the conditions described above under "self-concept," such a climate should exude support for acknowledging deficiencies and unfreezing set ways of doing things.
3. The self-diagnosis of needs for learning. This self-diagnosis must involve all parties concerned—individual participants, teacher, institution, and community—and the product is a set of mutual needs.
4. The formulation of objectives. To be truly operational, the objectives must be stated in terms that describe the behaviors that will be produced if the mutually determined needs are to be satisfied.
5. The development of a general design. This is the artistic, architectural aspect of program planning, in which the building blocks of the various types of activities—large meetings, small groups, project teams, reading, and so forth—are arranged into an esthetic composition. An esthetic educational experience, like any art form, will have such characteristics as pleasing composition, motion (sequence, with each activity building on the past activity), continuity, rhythm, color, and unity.
6. The selection and execution of techniques and materials. In keeping with the characteristics of adults as learners, the techniques that adult educational program planners tend to emphasize are those that involve the learners actively in the process and that minimize the need for one-way transmittal. The teacher's role is that of facilitator, not transmitter, of learning—and resource person.
7. The planning of evaluation. As in the case of diagnosis of needs, the kind of evaluation that is most congruent with

the adults' concept of self-direction is, of course, self-evaluation. The skillful adult educator is one who can provide the climate and the tools and procedures to enable adult learners to make responsible, objective assessments of their own progress toward their goals.

Summary

Adult education is currently on the threshold of greatness. In the past, adult education has been marginal, often thought of as a vocational at best. However, new theories of learning, longer life span, and a rapidly changing culture all have contributed to the expansion of adult education.

Adults do learn differently from youths, and the design of learning experiences must take into account these differences. Andragogy, as discussed here, is just one step in the direction toward a theory for adult learning. Research, experimentation, and experience will no doubt modify and enhance this theory. However, the need for continuous learning throughout the life span is a reality and the lock-step, traditional school is detrimental to the stimulation and zest that education and learning should impart.

The opportunities that adult education programs provide for the aging population are on the increase through a variety of agencies. Never before in the history of man has learning played such an integral part in all phases of life. Adult education as a body of knowledge, and the leisure, economic, and social needs of a technocratic society have all assisted in the development of new educational opportunities for the aging.

References

Cubberley P: The History of Education. Boston, Houghton Mifflin, 1920

DuBois E: An experiment with the learning-teaching team: group self-directed learning in undergraduate education. Adult Leadership 20:14–16, 1971

Gibb JR: Learning theory in adult education. In Knowles MS (ed): Handbook of Adult Education. Chicago, Adult Education Assoc of the U.S.A., 1960

Havighurst R: Developmental Tasks and Education. New York, David McKay, 1952

Kelley E: The Workshop Way of Learning. New York, Harper and Brothers, 1951

Knowles MS: The Modern Practice of Adult Education. Andragogy vs. Pedagogy. New York, Association Press, 1970

———: Program planning for adult learners. Adult Leadership, February 1967

Lorge I: Effective methods in adult education. Report of the Southern Workshop for Agricultural Specialists. Raleigh, NC State College, June 1947

Okes E: Participation in Adult Education: Initial Report 1969. Washington, D.C., U.S. Dept HEW, 1971

Smith D: Developmental tasks and adult education. Continuous Learning, July-August 1966
Thorndike EL: Adult Learning. New York, Macmillan, 1928
U.S. Office of Health, Education and Welfare: Older Americans Speak to the Nation, May 1970
van Enckevort G: Andragogy: a new science. Unpublished paper delivered to the I.C.U.A.E., Montreal, Canada, 1970

9

NUTRITION AND AGING

Beula B. Marble
M. Isabel Patterson

This chapter takes cognizance of the significance of nutrition in human life and of factors that impinge upon maintenance of good nutriture. The presentation is purposefully practical and pertinent to the well-being of older people.

Nutrients, in a bald biologic sense, are the very ingredients of life. They determine the possibility and the quality of human life from inception onward. Man can achieve his potential only when all materials for all of life's intricate biochemical processes are available throughout his life span. Good nutrition affords not only physical well-being, with resistance to infections and diseases that beset man, but there is also increasing evidence of a positive relationship between good diet and man's psychologic and emotional performance, even in old age. Good nutrition contributes to maintaining independence, one of the most cherished goals of the older person.

Along with knowledge of biologic needs has come appreciation of the significance of man's habits and attitudes toward food and their effect on his actual food intake. His eating customs need to be treated with respect. A person who has lived for 60, 70, or 80 years has a way of eating that has served well for him for a long time. His choice of food may be quite different from his neighbor's. Eating patterns in the United States have great variety—influenced by ethnic, cultural, and economic factors—and food is available in great variety to sustain differing ways of achieving good nutrition. Man reaches old age still requiring basic nutrients, still receiving them, in more or less adequate amounts from the food he eats. The influences of eating practices are continuous and cumulative.

The joy of cooking and of eating have been appreciated for centuries but nutrition has become a science largely in the 20th century. Knowledge of nutrients required and their food sources is available. Knowledge of how they function in the human body and of their complicated interrelationships, their teamwork, is expanding constantly. The latter adds validity to the concept of "balanced diet," meaning adequate but not excessive intake of essential nutrients from food consumed at sufficiently frequent intervals for effective utilization. Likewise there is validity in the common advice to eat and enjoy a wide variety of foods.

There may be few, if any, nutrition problems for the older person who is well and enjoys eating, whose finances are adequate, and who has companionship at mealtimes. Unfortunately, there are elderly people who are not well, who show the scars of poor nutrition.

A visit to a hospital clinic or nursing home, a walk through the deprived areas of a city, or a visit to an isolated elderly person living alone in the country or city suggest, sometimes dramatically, that better nutrition could improve the well-being of a large number of older people. For those who have neglected themselves or who have lost their sense of direction, special attention and understanding are needed to improve eating habits. Changing food habits is not easy, but it is possible. "If circumstances arise which make it expedient for the old person to adopt new eating habits, he has the capacity to accept the new ideas and to learn and follow suitable patterns of reaction. Indeed, older people derive the same exhilaration from learning and adopting new modes of behavior as do young people . . . they continue quite capable of learning throughout the major portion of the life span" (Donahue 1951).

Nutrient Needs

The nutritional needs of the older person are similar to those of the middle age adult. It should be noted, however, that there are wide *individual* variations in nitrogen and other nutrient requirements (Wohl and Goodhart 1968). In general, older people need about the same amount of protein, minerals, and vitamins as adults of all ages. Total calories may need to be reduced as a person grows older as a result of actual lowering of metabolic requirements and also decreased activity.

The Food and Nutrition Board of The National Academy of Science (1968) has formulated Recommended Dietary Allowances which serve as a universal guide in the United States to nutrient needs. For practical purposes, the Dietary Allowances expressed in nutrients need to be interpreted in terms of foods and meals. It is generally agreed that a wide variety of foods will supply the recommended nutrients. One common food guide, the Four Food Groups or the Basic Four suggests that the daily food intake include:

1. Milk—1 pint;
2. Meat, fish, poultry, eggs, legumes—2 servings;
3. Bread and cereals, whole grain or enriched—4 servings;
4. Fruits and vegetables—4 servings,
   (a) including citrus fruit or another rich source of vitamin C, and
   (b) a dark green or deep yellow vegetable rich in vitamin A.

Milk may be taken as a beverage, eaten with cereal, or used in cooking. Cheese, or one of the fermented milks such as buttermilk or yogurt, may be used to provide the nutrients in which milk is rich, namely protein, calcium, and riboflavin.

In the meat, fish, and poultry group, people may choose from a wide variety of foods; beef, lamb, pork, chicken, turkey, duck, fresh or salt water fish, and shellfish, fresh, canned, or frozen. An egg or a serving of legumes is equivalent to one-third of the average serving of meat. Legumes should be served with milk or other animal protein in the same meal in order to obtain their full protein value. This group of foods provides protein, iron, and some of the B vitamins.

The bread-cereal group also allows for many choices: wheat, oats, rye, rice, corn, and others. This group provides some of the B vitamins and iron as well as small amounts of protein. Whole grain, enriched and fortified breads and cereals should be used.

The vegetable-fruit group affords many choices. These may be fresh, frozen, canned, or dried. This group provides vitamins C and A as well as minerals and other vitamins. A reliable food table such as Handbook #72 will indicate those that are richest in a particular nutrient (U.S. Dept. of Agriculture 1971).

In addition to food groups mentioned above, other foods or larger servings from the four food groups may be eaten to maintain a desirable weight. Iodized salt, enriched or fortified bread and cereals, milk with vitamin D, and margarine with added vitamin A should be used to insure an adequate intake of these nutrients.

The "Basic Four" is a tool useful both for quick analysis of the adequacy of a person's food intake and for planning an adequate diet. It is adaptable to various cultural and ethnic eating patterns.

Since most people think of foods as meals, a suggested meal guide may be helpful to promote good nutrition. To be meaningful, a meal guide needs to be based on an individual's living habits. Some people like a light breakfast, a heavy midday meal, and a light evening meal; others prefer a heavy breakfast, a light midday meal, and a substantial evening meal. Others may prefer five or six smaller meals to three larger meals. Any meal plan can be checked against the food groups to see if all recommended foods are included. Examples of meals for a day which include all the recommended foods follow:

	I	II
Morning:	orange juice	grapefruit
	poached egg	oatmeal with milk
	whole wheat toast with butter	blueberry muffin
	coffee au lait	tea
Midday:	tuna fish salad sandwich	baked chicken
	cherry cobbler	mashed potato
	milk	broccoli
		sliced tomato
		lemon milk sherbet
Evening:	pot roast	cream of celery soup
	carrots, onions, and potato	egg salad sandwich
	tossed salad	fruit cup and cookies
	baked custard	tea
Bedtime:	apple juice	milk
		crackers

The size of servings can be adjusted to suit the individual. Small servings with an opportunity for additional helpings is recommended rather than a heaped-up plate which may be discouraging to the older person whose appetite is limited.

Chronic Illness and Dietary Modifications

For the older person with a chronic disease, a modified diet may be part of his medical care. Modified diets are based on the "normal diet" which is changed only to meet the medical prescription. Good nutritional care for a person on a modified or therapeutic diet means that his food plan is based as much as possible on his regular eating pattern. Although chronic illness occurs in all age groups, older people are more frequently its victims. It is estimated that of the 18 million Americans over 65 years, 12 million have at least one chronic condition, such as high blood pressure, arthritis, diabetes, heart disease, or mental disorders (President's Council on Aging 1963).

Diabetes is an example of a condition that has its greatest incidence in people over 40 years of age and for which medical authorities are in good agreement that a diet modified in carbohydrates is an essential part of treatment. Today, even though the diet for diabetes is a liberal one, sweet foods are restricted. Since a large proportion of people with diabetes were overweight prior to discovery of diabetes, restriction in calories as well as concentrated sweet foods means adapting to new patterns of eating. For the older person, as well as for all of us, giving up favorite foods is not easy; he may feel he is being deprived at a time when other losses are often occurring. Help in adjusting diet to follow his usual food habits as much as possible will aid in gaining his cooperation. A positive approach which shows him he can include many of his favorite foods, even though restricted in sugar content, will encourage him to make the needed changes. Following a diet is a matter of continuing education; a person with diabetes needs to have his diet reevaluated at regular periodic visits to his physician.

For an overweight person with a chronic condition such as heart disease or arthritis, a reduction of calorie intake is a vital part of rehabilitation. Again this implies taking away something at a time when other joys of life seem to be diminishing. Even though adding something such as a pill or a supplement may be more appealing than cutting down on food, unfortunately food intake must be decreased or activity increased in order to lose weight; often a combination of the two gives the best results. Because cutting down on food is difficult, charlatans and quacks seek their prey among the elderly overweight by offering them expensive supplements which they wrongly or maliciously claim will reduce unwanted pounds (Bruch 1970).

Another dietary modification used rather frequently for some forms of heart disease is a diet restricted in sodium. For persons in the habit of using salt generously, decreasing or omitting salt may diminish the pleasure of eating at least temporarily. Many adjust to the more subtle natural taste of food. People on sodium restricted diets need careful instruction because sodium occurs naturally in many foods, and depending on the degree of restriction, such common foods as meat and milk may have to be eaten in limited amounts if the dietary prescription is to be carried out successfully. Misunderstandings are frequent with this type of diet. The uninitiated in the field of dietetics do not realize that salt or other sodium compounds added to foods such as corned meats, bacon, potato chips, and crackers make them taboo. Assistance in preparing tasty foods with herbs, lemon, and spices will help to restore an interest in food to the person required to limit his accustomed seasoning with salt.

There are other chronic diseases requiring dietary modifications; suffice it to say, these are usually not easy for the patient. Understanding and support from professional and personal associates are needed if the modifications are to be followed and the patient benefited. The ability of the older person to adjust to dietary modifications should not be underestimated on the basis of age alone. Neither should the advantage of a modified diet be denied on the ground he is too old to change. If an older person can be helped to live more effectively through a changed dietary regimen, he should be given help to do so. If he appears to have fewer years to live, these years should be considered precious and no effort spared to assist him in adjusting his diet to improve his well-being.

Drugs and Diet

Modification of diet may be necessary to compensate for the effect of drugs. Drugs may interact with foods, decrease absorption of nutrients, and affect intake by depressing appetite, causing nausea and stomach irritation.

For example, adjustments to increase potassium in the diet may need to be made to compensate for the effect of diuretics which bring about a renal loss of potassium. An increase in the intake of vitamin B_6 may be needed for a person taking isoniazid, and attention paid to a person's intake of folic acid and other B vitamins if he is receiving sulfonamides. A person taking tranylcypromine should be warned of the effects of cheese, herring, or red wine and cautioned to omit these and other foods which are rich in pressor amines, since the drug deactivates the enzyme monoamine oxidase and allows the pressor amines to gain access to the circulation and cause headache, diarrhea, high blood pressure, or even death. Drugs may alter serum electrolytes, the functioning of vitamins, protein synthesis, and the metabolism of fat and carbohydrate. Christakis and Miridjanian (1968) have published a concise account of interrelationships between drugs and nutrients, a new and expanding field of investigation. Close cooperation is essential between physicians, nutritionists, patients themselves, and others involved in the nutritional care of persons who are taking certain medications.

Dealing with Common Physical Changes

Nutritional needs must be considered in the light of physical changes that come with growing old. Years may bring increasing handicaps that interfere with eating. Fatigue comes more quickly and with it a lack of energy to eat or to prepare food. Easy methods of food preparation and the use of ready-to-eat foods can be a boon to the older person with diminished strength. However, since he neither grew up nor lived as an active adult in the days when the markets were abounding in ready-to-eat foods, he may need a little encouragement to try the "new-fangled" products which recent scientific advances have produced to minimize food preparation. Frozen prepared dinners offer a variety of foods and require little effort to prepare. Canned or frozen soups or stews need only to be heated. Frozen or canned fruit and vegetables require limited effort to get ready and diminish the task of disposing of peelings and refuse. Granted the quality may not be as good as homemade or freshly prepared nevertheless modern technology has produced acceptable products that provide variety. Some ready-to-eat foods may not be appropriate for those on certain restricted diets as they frequently contain considerable amounts of either salt or sugar.

A lack of teeth, sore gums, or poorly fitting dentures are sometimes a drawback to eating. A new set of teeth or a visit to the dentist may provide a solution to a better diet. When oral conditions make eating difficult, softer foods may encourage improved eating patterns. Meat cut off a chop, potato removed from the skin, apples made into sauce or oranges squeezed as juice are examples of making foods easier to eat. Pureed foods should be used only as a last resource. They are usually unattractive in appearance and may make an older person feel he is being treated like an infant.

Lessened mobility may make preparation of a meal difficult. Suggestions about better kitchen planning or placing of equipment may be welcomed by the person for whom just getting in and out of a chair is a major effort (Klinger et al. 1970). Shopping may need to be done by telephone or with help from a neighbor or a community agency. Cooking involves a fire hazard for those who are not too quick afoot and care needs to be used in lighting a flame and in handling pots and pans with hot foods. Impaired balance may also interfere with an older person's having the courage and strength to prepare a meal.

Impairment of eyesight or hearing have their effects on eating; such things as bones in fish may prove a hazard to the person who does not see well. Being ostracized from the conversation at the table because of not hearing also diminishes appetite.

Failing memory may be a real detriment to good eating. An older person with arteriosclerosis may not be able to recall what he ate at his last meal or whether he ate at all. Such a person may need someone to prepare meals for him and to encourage him to eat.

Tastebuds decrease with age; this along with other factors may result in poor appetite. However, attractive, good-tasting meals encourage a jaded appetite. Salt in moderate quantities should not be restricted unless medically contraindicated. At times, a compromise may need to be worked out if a person refuses to eat unsalted food. Zestier seasoning with spices and herbs may be the answer.

When physiologic factors diminish food intake, nutrition counseling can help to insure that the older person gets "the most" in what he does eat. Soups with meat, chicken, and milk are preferable to clear soups; vegetables with cream and/or butter can increase calories and satiety, cooked cereals or concentrated dry cereals provide better nutrition for the effort involved in eating than puffed ones. For the person with lessened food intake, nutritional care can contribute to well-being. Nutritional care means considering the person first with all his qualities—strengths, disabilities, fancies, and foibles, as well as the food he needs.

Feelings about Food

"Food intake and eating habits represent one of the most complex facets of human behavior. When one attempts to influence food habits, one is not dealing just with physical nourishment or an intellectual matter. It has been said that feeding activity ranks with sexual behavior as a demonstration of that peculiar and delicate interaction of biological, psychological and cultural influences so often found in the study of human wants" (Young 1960).

Early feeding experiences affect feelings about food throughout life. Many people in their 70s were brought up in the days when children were seen and not heard, when plates must be cleaned regardless of the child or his feelings. For such people, attitudes toward eating and especially toward being told what they should eat now that they have reached an honorable age may well be negative. Only an understanding counselor will be able to overcome such an attitude and gain cooperation. Many people resent being told what to eat as an infringement of cherished independence. Some react best to a direct definite approach; however, participation in planning how changes may be made usually will bring better results than dogmatically telling an independent older person what he must do. A careful analysis of what a person is now eating should be made before any changes are suggested; then only as few changes as necessary should be instituted. The proof is in the pudding—improved well-being, decreased shortness of breath, better locomotion, less fatigue, will convince an older person that improved eating is worth the effort.

Loneliness is one of the hardest burdens of aging. Eating alone may intensify feelings of loneliness when formerly there was always someone present with whom to eat, or for whom to prepare food. Some may overeat, but often incentive to eat is diminished and interest in eating is at a low ebb when lonely. Real effort and ingenuity are needed to overcome and deal with the void of loneliness at mealtimes. Taking the first difficult step to join a club or community group, inviting a friend to share a meal, or doing volunteer work, and through serving others forgetting oneself may reestablish or improve appetite better than forcing oneself to eat. Some people find a favorite television or radio program or a good book helps to make solitary meals more enjoyable. Also emotions may bring about metabolic changes. Swanson (1964) reports that an alert, energetic woman, 75 years of age, was leading a busy life although she lived alone. She ate well, but metabolic studies showed her to be in severe negative nitrogen balance. She was observed two years later; a marked change in nitrogen metabolism had taken place and she was now retaining nitrogen. Her grandson had come to live with her. Someone to cook for and to share meals with had played a role in maintaining nutrition for this woman. Emotional stress, grief, loneliness, fear, and anxiety have been found to affect metabolism of some nutrients—protein, calcium, and cholesterol at all ages. The effects of stress on the metabolism of all nutrients has not been explored.

Crisis situations may precipitate an older person into poor eating patterns. Bereavement, retirement, illness, or a change in living may affect appetite and bring about bizarre eating, over- or underindulgence in food. Time and patience are needed both by the person and the counselor to prove that the rewards in well-being due to dietary change are worth the effort. Helping an older person to help himself is often a long, slow, and somewhat difficult process. Feelings and emotions must be considered.

Social and Cultural Factors

Where, how, and with whom older people live affect their eating habits. It is believed, although not scientifically proven, that a positive relationship exists between companionship and the digestive process. Data for people over 65 in the United States show that the majority of the elderly live in families (90 percent of the men and 63 percent of the women) (Howell and Loeb 1969). However, after 74 a larger proportion of widows live alone. It is also reported that higher income elderly are more likely to live alone and separate from children and other relatives. Adjustments either to living alone or to living with adult children will need to be made in regard to food and meals. The practitioner who is counseling an elderly person about his diet will need to give careful consideration to where the person lives and with whom he lives.

Today's society is youth centered. Old age does not mean a venerable and respected state as it does in some cultures. Therefore, some older people strive constantly and understandably to appear younger than their years. Quacks and faddists try to cash in on this desire by offering for sale expensive elixirs or herbs, weird concoctions, organic foods and devices to preserve youth and strength. Money better spent for regular food may be used for useless remedies purported to maintain youth and efficiency.

Foods take on cultural values. Milk may be thought of as a food for the young only—a baby food; meat, a masculine food; salads, feminine foods; turkey, holiday food.

Foods assume ethnic values too. Sour cream and baked potatoes, oatmeal, porridge, chicken soup, homemade bread, bacon and eggs, rice and beans, fondues, and pasta are associated with particular ethnic or nationality groups. For the elderly and the ill, who often revert back in their thoughts to earlier, happier times in life's pathway than the present, ethnic foods may have special meaning. To encourage a jaded appetite, the serving of culturally linked foods may act as the spark to improved eating. A lethargic elderly Italian patient was sent home from the hospital following a lengthy stay after the determination was made that no more could be done to improve his condition. After several weeks of eating home-prepared Italian dishes, usually not prescribed for an invalid, the man improved beyond all expectations. Cultural food habits are ingrained deeply; they should be considered carefully and appreciated when planning meals or counseling an older person.

Economics and Food

Many retired and older people have little money to spend for food; in addition, many feel insecure about money matters when their capacity to earn is lessened or nonexistent. Worry about having enough to "see them through" influences them to hold onto, sometimes to hoard, more than is really necessary. A desire to save something to leave to one's heirs is a stronger motivation for some people than to feed themselves adequately. Many older people do not have sufficient income to eat an adequate diet. In 1967, one third of unrelated older men had under $1,000 and one half of unrelated women had under $1,000 in income (Howell and Loeb 1969).

Both a real or an imagined lack of money for food needs careful consideration in giving dietary advice to older people. For older people with limited facilities for food preparation and storage or limited knowledge about cooking, adherence to good eating practice is often compromised by the money available for food. An older person may need to use public programs in order to eat adequately. Food stamps or commodity foods will help to stretch limited food money. Accepting these programs is not easy, nor are people participating in these programs always treated with respect and dignity.

People need help to plan, to shop, to prepare, and to store foods most economically.

Planning helps an older person to look ahead. If meal plans are sketched out, a shopping list can be prepared. Such a list deters impulse buying and helps to be sure that the foods needed for a good meal are on hand. Planned meals are usually better balanced than hit or miss meals put together at the last moment. Shopping may provide inexpensive recreation if a person meets friends at the market; it may also give him a good excuse for some exercise. The older person who is able to go shopping can stretch his limited money through careful planning of his shopping list, through noting good buys, and through picking out personally only good quality foods.

Storing foods carefully help to stretch food money. Leftovers wrapped in plastic wrap do not dry out so quickly. Even a small freezing compartment can be put to good use in freezing meats. For example, an extra pork chop or a half-pound package of ground meat can be safely stored in the freezer. Most fruits and vegetables keep better in a refrigerator. Frozen vegetables should be kept frozen until cooked; stored only in a freezing unit. Sometimes the larger package or plastic bag of loose vegetables offers a considerable saving. It is easy to remove a small portion from the loose pack of frozen peas, beans, or other vegetables.

A tested cookbook is an investment to save money. Several good cookbooks are listed in the bibliography (Heseltine and Dow 1967; Senior Citizens, Inc.; MacDonald 1967). Some are available without charge (U.S. Dept. of Agriculture 1968).

With limited money, good eating requires ingenuity and careful planning, shopping, food preparation, and food storage. In the realm of food budgeting, a nutrition counselor can make many contributions to the older person with limited funds.

Community Programs

Most older people prefer to live in their homes whenever possible. Among the basic essentials to independent living is the availability of daily meals. Living at home usually means greater happiness and economy than living in an institution. Recently group dining services in housing projects, churches, schools, senior day centers, and so forth have developed. They serve one or more meals a day and provide an opportunity for socialization. There are other programs that help to maintain older people in their own homes, each of which has a nutrition component.

Home Care

Under the auspices of hospitals and medical centers, home care programs have developed in areas close to teaching hospitals. These are for the sick or disabled who through routine home visits from a medical team are able to remain in their homes rather than in the hospital. Close communication is maintained between the home and the hospital. Nutrition consultation is frequently included in these programs and where it is not, it needs to be developed. The right food must be available at home if the patient is to receive the care he needs and be able to progress to the maximum. If a modified diet is prescribed, the person preparing the meals may need help with carrying out the prescription. Consultation with a dietitian or nutritionist or an aide working under the supervision of a nutritionist enhances the effectiveness of home care programs.

Homemaker Services

Through the services of a homemaker who helps with the running of a household for a certain number of hours a day, an elderly person may often stay in his own home when it would otherwise be necessary for him to go to an institution. Homemakers may take over while the breadwinner goes to work or when an elderly couple or individual is unable to maintain the running of a household completely. The homemaker prepares meals and does light housekeeping. Homemakers usually have a period of organized training which includes sessions on planning and preparing adequate meals and learning about foods for use on modified diets. The services of a nutritionist or a dietitian are a valuable adjunct to the training programs for homemakers and also as a resource to the homemaker when she meets problems in her work.

Portable Meals

Some communities have programs for serving meals to people in their homes. Such meals are prepared at a central place and then delivered to homes. These meals are generally prepared under the supervision of a dietitian and transported to homes by volunteers. Those who deliver the meals make a bonus contribution by providing a social contact for the person confined to his home. For elderly people living in communities where portable meals are available, the service offers an option of living at home among familiar surroundings rather than in an institution. At times, portable meals may be needed on a temporary basis while a person is recovering from a disability; they tide him over until he is able to resume responsibility for preparing his own food. Unfortunately, portable meals or "meals-on-wheels" programs are available in a somewhat sporadic fashion.

The programs briefly described above indicate trends toward aiding the elderly to maintain independence in their own homes. The provision of adequate food is vital in these programs.

Domiciliary Care of the Elderly

Nursing homes and homes for the aged will be discussed together despite the fact that they serve somewhat different purposes. People in nursing homes require more medical and nursing care than those in homes for the aged. The number of these homes has increased greatly in recent years. The food in such places needs careful supervision since the people are largely a captive audience wholly dependent on the management for the food they receive. To a large extent, both types of homes are run as businesses by which those in charge earn their living. Many managers do all in their power to serve good food and to cater to the individual needs and likes of their guests; others leave much to be desired.

Nutrition and Well-Being

Good nutrition affects the total well-being of the older person. It can never be considered apart from the individual, his feelings, his economic status, his culture, and his state of health. It makes its greatest impact when a pattern of good eating has been continued throughout a life span. The influences of eating practices are continuous and cumulative.

Good nutrition plays a significant role in recovery from illness and in the maintenance of well-being when chronic conditions require a modified diet. With the changes and crises that aging brings, older people need wise support and sympathetic understanding to follow recommended dietary practices.

The provision of adequate nutritional care is an important aspect of community programs which help to maintain older people in their homes; it is also a vital concern for the elderly population living in nursing homes or homes for the aged.

No program concerned with gerontology is complete without the inclusion of attention to nutrition and all of its ramifications.

References

Bruch H: The allure of food cults and nutrition quackery. J Am Diet Assoc 57:316, 1970

Christakis G, Miridjanian A: Diets, drugs, and their interrelationships. J Am Diet Assoc 52:21, 1968

Donahue WT: Psychologic aspects of feeding the aged. J Am Diet Assoc 27:463, 1951

Heseltine M, Dow EM: The Basic Cook Book, 5th ed. Boston, Houghton Mifflin, 1967

Howell SC, Loeb MB: Nutrition and Aging, A Monograph for Practitioners. Gerontologist 9:1–122, 1969

Klinger JL, Frieden FH, Sullivan RA: Mealtime Manual for the Aged and Handicapped. New York, Essandess Special Editions, Simon and Schuster, 1970

MacDonald P: A Cook Book for Leisure. Garden City, NY, Doubleday, 1967

National Academy of Sciences, National Research Council, Washington, D.C.: Recommended dietary allowances—a report of the food and nutrition board, 1968

President's Council on Aging: The older american. Washington, D.C., 1963

Senior Citizens Cook Alone and Like It. Ithaca, N.Y., Senior Citizens, Inc

Swanson P: Adequacy in old age, Part 1. Role of nutrition. J Home Economics 56:651, 1964

U.S. Dept. of Agriculture, Consumer and Food Economics Res Div, Agricultural Res Serv, Washington, D.C.: Nutritive value of foods, Home and Garden Bulletin No. 72, 1971

U.S. Dept. of Agriculture, Human Nutrition Res Div and Consumer and Food Economics Res Div, Agricultural Res Serv, Washington, D.C.: Family fare, home management and recipes, Home and Garden Bulletin No. 1, 1968

Wohl MG, Goodhart RG: Modern Nutrition in Health and Disease, 4th ed. Philadelphia, Lea and Febiger, 1968

Young CM: Interviewing the patient. Am J Clin Nutr 8:523, 1960

10

MEDICAL CARE OF THE ELDERLY

Benedict J. Duffy, Jr., M.D.

Elderly people are basically quite healthy or they would not have survived to become elderly. The average life expectancy (1968) in the United States from birth is 66.6 years for males and 74.1 years for females. The further life expectancy for an individual who has attained the age of 65 is 13 years for a male and 16 years for a female. The persistence of this improved survival capacity of women into later years would suggest that increased male mortality was not due to wars, genetic viability, or even hormonal influences. Changes in female roles in American society may clarify this sex difference in mortality but presently it is a persistent and completely unexplained evidence of female biologic superiority. Whether medical research can extend life expectancy to any significant degree, considered both as scientifically improbable and demographically calamitous by many professionals, there is already an expanding population of elderly Americans, some of whom need considerable medical care which they may receive in variable fashion and with great difficulty particularly if they are poor.

This chapter will be concerned with the following questions:

1. What are the medical care needs of the elderly?
2. How might these medical care needs best be met?
3. What prospects are there for the development of better medical care programs for the elderly?

Need of the Elderly for Medical Care

The most important fact about the health status of older people in the United States is that most of the elderly get along rather well. The National Center for Health Statistics survey (1965) of general hospitals, nursing and convalescent homes, and homes for the aged indicate that only 3 percent of the total population of American citizens over the age of 65 are institutionalized. In other words, the overwhelming majority (97 percent) of elderly Americans are not in hospitals, nursing homes, or other institutions but are living at home or otherwise in the community. This does not mean that they are all well but there is good reason on the basis of such findings to establish programs to maintain independent living capacity of the elderly and postpone or prevent institutionalization (Fig. 1).

The medical care needs of the elderly in terms of disability periods, hospital admissions, and physician office visits are determined from hospital and institutional reports, National Health survey data, and individual studies of health needs of the aged at home. The only study that measured the health status of an entire aged population at home and in varied care facilities was carried out in Rochester, New York (Berg et al 1970). Health status of the aged was determined by a systematic survey and health evaluation of a sample of a large metropolitan population of those over age 65. The health assessments were done by physicians and public health nurses. The appropriateness of the home or institutional location of those elderly needing medical care was also evaluated (Fig. 2).

The important findings of the Rochester study relate to age, socioeconomic level, and appropriateness of the medical care setting. With regard to age, 92 percent of the 65 to 69 age group were able to live independently or without special supervision. The percent of those living independently declined sharply after 75 years of age and by 90 only 20 percent were judged to have this capability.

There was little variation in physical care need at various economic levels, although there was some increased need for physical medical care in the lowest socioeconomic bracket compared to the more affluent elderly. The mental and emotional needs of the elderly were much more sharply related to socioeconomic status. The prevalence of mental impairment was 10 to 15 percent in the upper socioeconomic group and 55 percent at the lower end of the socioeconomic scale. The relationships of education and household (family) composition were evaluated and did not explain the increased incidence of mental health needs by the poor elderly in the survey.

When appropriateness of medical care setting was studied it was found that over 40 percent of the elderly needing care were inappropriately placed. The misplacement involved all aspects of treatment but concerned the institutionalized primarily with "most inappropriately placed patients receiving too high a level of care." The greatest misplacement was in the State Hospital where it was judged that 94 percent of the aged patients could have had their needs met "in nursing homes or homes for the aged, except for the reluctance of these institutions to accept patients who need supervision because of mental impairment." The experience was general throughout the study that individuals were institutionalized for other than medical care requirements.

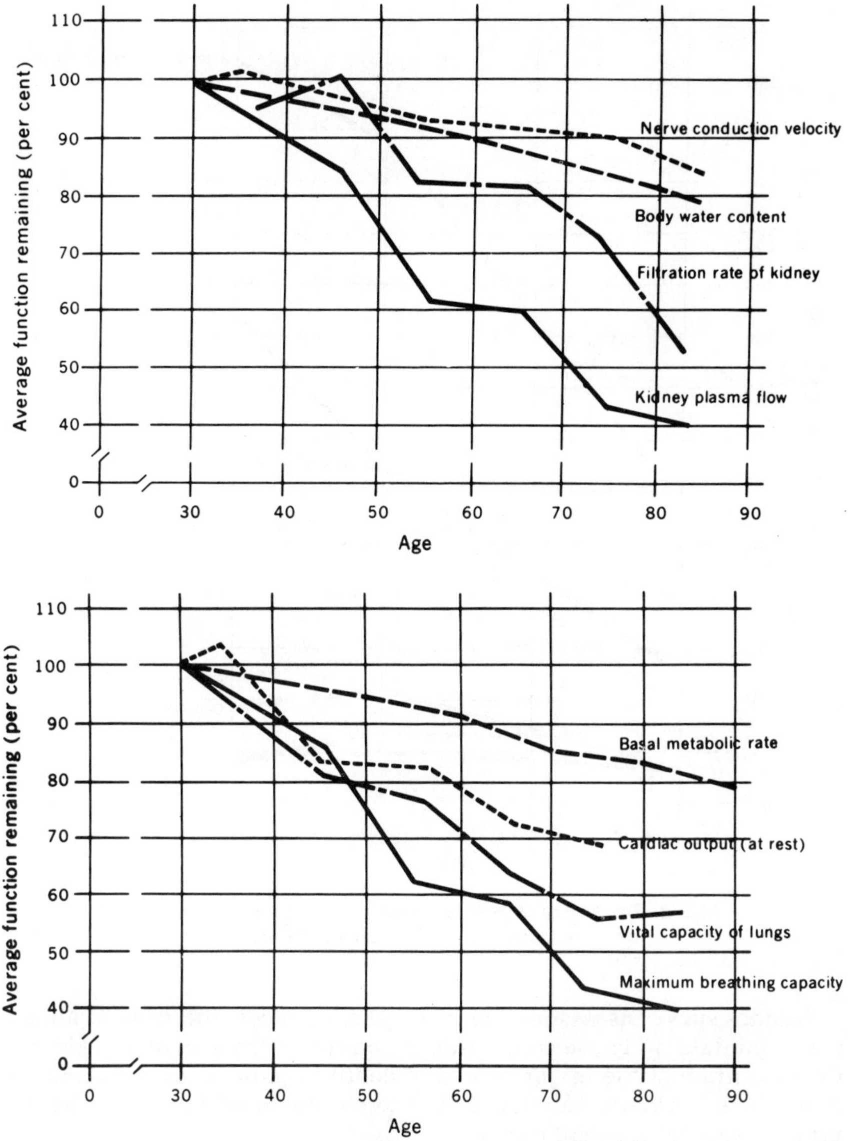

FIG. 1. Estimates of the decline of physiologic functioning after age 30. Percentage changes with age. The average value for each function at age 30 is taken as 100 percent. (Adapted from Shock: Sci Am 206:110, 1962)

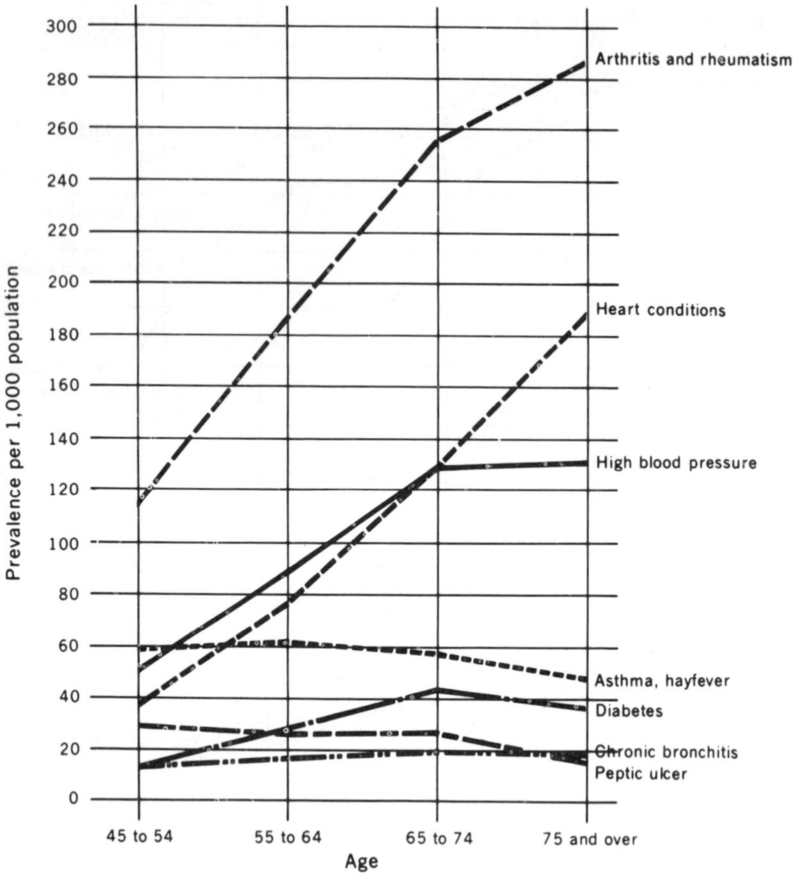

FIG. 2. Prevalence of selected chronic illnesses among persons 45 and over, United States, 1957–1959. (Adapted from U.S. National Health Survey: Health Statistics, Series C, 4:31, 35, 1960)

Besides survey assessment of medical care needs, there are available actuarial data on causes of mortality and morbidity among the elderly. Consideration of the major causes of death in patients over 65 and the limitations of elderly individuals due to chronic conditions can suggest priority areas of medical care need.

It should be emphasized that disease classifications are far from exact and reflect fashions in medical education. For example, it is known that chronic lung diseases (bronchitis, emphysema) are major medical care problems in those elderly with previous lung disease and long smoking histories. The lack of reporting in both the mortality and morbidity statistics until recently was due to a lack of attention in American medical schools (compared to British schools) and the confusion with heart disease (Tables 1,2).

TABLE 1. Causes of Death for Persons 65 and Over, U.S., 1965

Cause	Rate/100,000 population
Disease of the heart	2,823.9
Cancer	901.4
Stroke	901.0
Influenza and pneumonia	213.7
Arteriosclerosis	198.9
All accidents	155.0
Diabetes	122.9
Other diseases of the circulatory system	97.4
Other bronchopneumonia diseases	47.3
Other hypertensive diseases	47.3

Source. National Center for Health Statistics, The Facts of Life and Death, Washington: U.S. Govt Printing Office, 1965, PHS Publication 600, Revised 1967.

TABLE 2. Noninstitutionalized Persons 65 and Over Limited in Activity due to Chronic Conditions, U.S., July 1963–1965

Condition	Percent limited as a result
Heart conditions	22%
Arthritis and rheumatism	21%
Orthopedic impairments	11%
Visual impairments	9%
High blood pressure	8%
Mental and nervous condition	6%
Genitourinary conditions; paralysis	4% each
Diabetes; asthma and hay fever; hernia; hearing impairments	3% each
Varicose veins; chronic sinusitis and bronchitis	2% each
Cancers; peptic ulcer	1% each
Hemorrhoids; tuberculosis	less than 1% each

Source. National Center for Health Statistics, Chronic Conditions and Activity Limitation, United States, July 1963-June 1965. Washington: U.S. Govt Printing Office, Publication Series 1051, February 1969.

The treatment of heart disease, including hypertension, affords very real opportunity for prolongation of useful living. There is also very real patient improvement possible in the treatment of arthritis and such metabolic diseases as diabetes. The problems that limit the sensory capacity of the elderly such as hearing and vision, and walking impairment due to foot problems also offer good opportunities for beneficial rehabilitative services.

The problems of accompanying disease and complications of treatment of some elderly people can be seen from a study (Furey 1961) of some 267 consecutive hip fracture patients who were admitted to a chronic disease hospital for convalescence following surgery. The following diseases were of importance in the management of this group of patients:

Disease	Incidence
Arteriosclerotic heart disease	124
Cerebral arteriosclerosis	88
Cataracts	45
Diabetes mellitus	22
Chronic alcoholism	18
Arthritis of knees	17
Pulmonary emphysema	17
Hemiplegia (side of hip fracture)	15
Hypertensive cardiovascular disease	15
Generalized arteriosclerosis	13
Parkinsonism	13
Malignancy	12
Obesity	11
Congestive heart failure	10
Miscellaneous	100

An elderly patient with such interlocking illness and disability requires competent and comprehensive medical management including emotional support and maintenance or home care. Attention to detail can result in greatly improved medical care of the elderly ill or disabled. The maxim that the secret of patient care is "caring for the patient" is particularly appropriate in the medical care of the elderly.

In addition to patient illness and disability surveys there is supporting evidence from Medicare records to indicate that the individual 65 to 69 years of age has between two and three times the requirements for both hospital care and physician services as does an individual of 40 to 59 years of age and an even more disproportionate need for services as compared to younger adults and children. Medicare is also estimated (1972) to cover only 43 percent of the medical care costs of the elderly.

Types of Medical Services

PRIVATE PHYSICIAN OFFICES

The overwhelming majority of Americans, some 75 percent (Bodenheimer 1970), utilize the offices and services of private physicians for medical care. The largest number do not have a private physician but use self-referral according to what their self-diagnosis suggests as the problem and who is available. The standard technique to find a physician in many communities is to go to a hospital emergency room. Although there is a current movement to develop family practice, the evidence from all medical care studies to date indicate that there will have to be other alternatives for private medical care.

NEIGHBORHOOD HEALTH CENTERS

There are 70 comprehensive medical care centers which have been developed by the Office of Economic Opportunity and HEW mostly for urban populations in areas without physician services. The elderly comprise a significant number of the patients seen in such centers but problems in transportation and certification similar to those that limited the use of hospital clinics limit the use of the neighborhood health center by the elderly. Although the growth rate of neighborhood health centers is well below that expected by the initiators of the concept in 1965, there is a persistent and innovative vitality to the concept particularly in the northeast United States.

HEALTH MAINTENANCE ORGANIZATIONS

This is essentially a prepaid group practice form of medical service delivery which has been the latest "innovation" suggested to bring about more efficient delivery of medical care services. It is based on the experience of the large, industry-based programs such as Kaiser-Permanente Plan and the Health Insurance Plan of New York City which service municipal employees and others. The capability of the HMO to meet the medical care needs of an elderly population has not been determined.

EXTENDED CARE FACILITIES AND SKILLED NURSING HOMES

There is an increasing emphasis on the provision of continuing physician, nursing, and allied health professional services in extended care facilities and specialized nursing homes. This is a promising area particularly when the services are innovative (physician assistants) and joined to other community medical care programs particularly in provision of day-care services.

HOUSING HEALTH PROGRAMS

There are a variety of programs that have sought to develop medical care services directly in large housing projects which have predominantly elderly tenants. The concept of health education and promotion, easy accessibility to care, and some form of continuing health surveillance for groups of elderly is an attractive one but there has so far been very few medical care programs in housing areas for the elderly.

INFORMATION REFERRAL AGENCY

Community sponsored projects which involve voluntary agencies, state offices for the elderly, and various church service groups are making medical care information and occasionally limited home aide-health visitor services available to elderly and their families.

HOME HEALTH SERVICES

Home care is the missing element to keep more of the elderly ill out of institutions. A 1972 report of a Special Committee on Aging of the U.S. Senate on Home Health Services stated the problem of home medical services.

> Despite lipservice to the need for home health services, Medicare and Medicaid have actually fashioned serious roadblocks to the development of such services.
>
> At a time when the "alternatives to institutionalization" psychology is becoming more and more ingrained, the number of home health service agencies is actually *declining,* and many more seem to be in deepening financial jeopardy.
>
> Less than 1 percent of Medicare expenditures now go to home health care, and even that small portion appears to be declining.

The need for innovative home care programs is specifically recognized and supported in proposed amendments to the pending social security legislation (H.R.1) and in major legislative proposals. Home health services will undoubtedly be increased but the present need is real, and totally unmet.

DAY-CARE CENTERS

The development of day-care centers for the elderly for health care, nutritional and social including recreational needs has been demonstrated by Cosin in Oxford, England to be an excellent means to support and involve both the elderly and their families in guided programs of care. The use of suitable nursing homes and other halfway settings for such service is receiving attention.

Medical Care Personnel

The development of physician alternatives such as nurse practitioners and various forms of physician assistants increases medical care availability without lowering quality of service. The nurse practitioner has already developed an independent and highly qualified role, particularly in maternity and pediatric services. There are numerous examples in the private practice of medicine where physician assistants have supplemented physician care. The use of new medical care personnel has developed most readily in structured programs such as neighborhood health centers and some group practices. The legislation that governs the delivery of medical care in some states restricts medical care to physicians and strictly certified professionals. There has also been resistance in some geographic areas and practice arrangements to the delegation of authority or assumption of new responsibilities by nonphysicians.

Training programs for nursing home administrators and continuing education for nursing personnel should accompany implementation of improved standards for the institutional and programmatic care of the elderly. The most important practical need by far is the identification, development, and coordination of homemaker and health aide services for home care of those elderly individuals with varying degrees of incapacity who do not need, or indeed cannot do well in, an institutional setting. What is needed is a friend and not another impersonal assistant.

Self-Help

Since most aged individuals are not in institutions there is need to balance an understandable concern for inadequate institutional care with a more positive approach to maintenance of the elderly in their own homes. Despite other pressures and constraints, members of families have repeatedly demonstrated strongly supportive attitudes to the care of their elderly relatives. A major effort should be made to assist existing caretaker systems.

One aged person may be the major support of another elderly individual, spouse, relative, or friend. In many instances, this may appear to be "the frail helping the frail" but the relationship exists as a form of self-help which should be maintained and strengthened.

Independence through self-help should be the goal of all medical care. Self-help assistance begins with the consideration and attitudes of others. While admitting to the increased incapacity which accompanies much of aging, there should be a balanced and optimistic view of residual capacity. Our negative concerns with our own aging and fear of mortality should not be visited on others. In no way should the elderly be treated as a group.

The essence of the self-help approach has been admirably set forth by Caplan:

> The characteristic attribute of those social aggregates that act as a buffer against disease is that in such relationships the person is dealt with as a unique individual. The other people are interested in him in a personalized way. They speak his language. They tell him what is expected of him and guide him in what to do. They watch what he does and they judge his performance. They let him know how well he has

> done. They reward him for success and punish or support and comfort him if he fails. Above all, they are sensitive to his personal needs, which they deem worthy of respect and satisfaction (Caplan 1974).

Prospects

In his book *The Lost Reform, The Campaign for Compulsory Health Insurance in the United States from 1932 to 1943,* Daniel S. Hirshfield reviews the roles of competing agencies in the Public Health Service, administrators of small hospitals, labor leaders including Samuel Gompers, and the private insurance representatives in blocking national health insurance and illustrating the political maxim that the politically right and left will defeat social reform legislation if such change would result in a loss of power or money. The lack of public education and support for inclusion of medical care in the Social Security legislation was also evident.

> With the emergence of the New Deal, and especially with the acceptance in 1935 of the Social Security system, final victory for the reformers appeared sure. The politicians and the public seemed to accept the reformers' ideas on individual security and social responsibility and to adopt their programs and solutions. Old age assistance and insurance, unemployment insurance, and aid to the blind and dependent children were passed with strong public endorsement.
>
> But while the reformers and their programs seemed to triumph in most areas during the early New Deal, one important reform was defeated. Government insurance against sickness (health insurance) was not achieved despite the best and most determined efforts of the reformers. Health insurance, together with the other reforms, had been an early interest of the reformers in the progressive period; it has been supported by various reformers and reform associations in the 1920's and had been included among the proposals considered by those who helped shape the Social Security Act. But although it was proposed and advocated in the same ways as the other, successful reforms, the political climate and the particular conditions found in the system of medical care in the United States helped to exclude health insurance from the 1935 legislation.

The American Medical Association was not in clear opposition to the extension of federal health insurance in the 1930's. The AMA became vigorously opposed to national health insurance when there were renewed efforts to develop such a program in the late 1940's. The American Medical Association, working together with the private insurance industry and the American Hospital Association, is generally credited (Harris 1966) with directing the very effective lobbying activity against national health insurance throughout the 1950's.

There were few developments in either national health insurance or social insurance for the aged until the first White House Conference on

Aging in 1961. This conference recommended, for the first time in a broadly representative meeting including AMA representatives, that the social security mechanism be utilized for payment of costs of hospital and medical care services for elderly Americans. The issue was bitterly debated but the policy was accepted and formalized in legislation in the Medicare Act of 1965.

The Second White House Conference on Aging, 1971, made specific recommendations for medical services for the aged and a National Health Program.

1. Health care for the aging must be provided as an integral part of a coordinated system that provides comprehensive health services to the total population; but immediate and special consideration and emphasis must be given to the problems of, and services for, the aging.
2. A coordinated delivery system for comprehensive health services must be developed, legislated, and financed to ensure continuity of both short- and long-term care for the aged.

The prospects are for these recommendations to be gradually implemented since both political parties have recognized the need for a "public/private partnership in the delivery of services and for federal financing and quality control" in medical care. The form of the National Health Program will be determined by Congress and the Bureau of the Budget. The financial burden of a National Health Program for the United States is variously estimated as between 40 and 80 billion dollars with a variable amount recoverable from the approximately $70 billion presently being expended for medical care services in both private payments and federal subsidies.

Summary

Medical care for the aged should be:

1. At home with support from community day-care centers and appropriate back-up institutions as needed.
2. Funded by a National Health Program.
3. Interim planning should be through public/private sponsorship on a regional basis with community review including the aged and legislative jurisdiction of standards for all services.
4. Through new forms of health service delivery since financing is not enough as Medicare has shown.
5. Through augmented community services and family supports to maintain the elderly at home with purpose and dignity.

The following publications, entitled "Working with Older People: A Guide to Practice" (1969-1971) of the U.S. Public Health Service were prepared from materials developed by the Gerontological Society. They comprise a comprehensive resource for those directly involved with the varied aspects of medical care for the elderly. The individual volumes and subject matter are described by the PHS as follows:

> Volume I, "The Practitioner and the Elderly," focuses on aging and the world of practice related to aging. The publication puts into perspective the changing character and needs of the aging population and the implications of these changes for required programs and services. The many interdependent needs of the elderly are identified and correlated with areas of the interdependence among practitioners who seek to meet these needs.
>
> Volume II, "Biological Psychological, and Sociological Aspects of Aging," is devoted to the basic sciences most directly related to the process of aging and the aged individual. *Biological aspects of aging* are discussed in terms of those physical characteristics which are affected by time and determined largely by genetic and environmental influences brought to bear on the individual. *Psychological aspects of aging* are discussed in terms of those functions used by the indivudual in adapting to his environment—his senses and perception, his ability to learn and remember, his responses, and his personality. *Sociological aspects of aging* are discussed in terms of the adjustment of the aged individual to society, with consideration given to the degree to which he is, or can be influenced by family, friends and community.
>
> Volume III, "The Aging Person: Needs and Services," deals with the many facets of social welfare as these related to health status of the elderly. Included are sections on such problems as: Food, clothing, and shelter; environmental safety; mobility; leisure activities; legal protection; security and supportive services; and religion and attitudes toward death.
>
> Volume IV, "Clinical Aspects of Aging," is written by specialists for the general practitioner and is comprised of three sections: Diseases and disorders most relevant to single organ systems; clinical problems closely related to multiple organ systems; and aspects special to allied health professions.

The volumes are available as Publication #1459 from the U.S. Government Printing Office.

"Health in the Later Years of Life" is a publication of the National Center for Health Statistics of the U.S. Public Health Service which graphically illustrates the effect of age on (a) outlook for life and death, (b) health problems and their impact, and (c) use of health services. It is available as +1722-0178 from the U.S. Government Printing Office.

References

Berg RL, Browning FE, Hill JG, Wenkert W: Assessing the health care needs of the aged. Health Serv Res, p 36, 1970

Bodenheimer T: Patterns of American ambulatory care. Inquiry 7:26, 1970
Caplan G: Support Systems and Community Mental Health. New York, Behavioral Publications, 1974, pp 5–6
Harris R: A Sacred Trust. New York, New American Library, 1966
Hirshfield DS: The Lost Reform: The Campaign for Compulsory Health Insurance in the United States from 1932 to 1943. Cambridge, Harvard Univ Press, 1970
National Center for Health Statistics: Characteristics of Residents in Institutions for the Aged and Chronically Ill—United States. PHS Publication No. 1000, Series 12-No. 2, U.S. Govt Ptg Office, 1965
Proger S: Doctor of primary medicine (PMD). JAMA 220:410, 1972
Proger S: The education of different types of physicians for different types of health care. The Pharos of Alpha Omega Alpha 35:53, 1972
U.S. Dept. HEW, 1961: The Nation and Its Older People. Report of the White House Conference on Aging. No. 0–588–720, U.S. Govt Ptg Office, April, 1961
U.S. Dept. HEW, Public Health Service: Working with older people: A guide to practice. Volume I, The Practitioner and the Elderly No. 72–6005, revised May, 1972; Volume II, Biological, Psychological and Sociological Aspects of Aging No. 72–6006, May, 1972; Volume III, The Aging Person: Needs and Services No. 72–6007, May, 1972
U.S. Senate Special Committee on Aging, 1972: Home Health Services in the U.S., U.S. Govt Ptg Office, 1972
U.S. Senate Special Committee on Aging, 1972: Evaluation of Administration on Aging and Conduct of White House Conference on Aging. No. 60-215 0, U.S. Govt Ptg Office, 1972
U.S. Senate Special Committee on Aging, 1971: Trends in Long-Term Care. No. 62–264, U.S. Govt Ptg Office, 1972
White House Conference on Aging, Washington, D.C., 1971: Background and Issues: Physical and Mental Health. No. 5247–0021, U.S. Govt Ptg Office, 1971

11
MENTAL HEALTH AND AGING

Benedict J. Duffy, Jr., M.D.

> The usual image of an old person is of one who is weak, infirm, feeble, and afflicted with recent memory defects; he is helpless, dependent, and emotionally useless in a youth-oriented, achievement-oriented, and action-oriented culture such as ours seems to be. This stereotype is incorrect and is a serious misconception. The truth is that less than five percent of persons over the age of 65 require some degree of custodial care, a figure that is applicable throughout the world. We are left then with the consideration of the 95 percent of the aged population who do not conform to these stereotyped notions. However, it does not follow that the 95 percent are all healthy, both physically and mentally. Rather, this population, like any population group, should be viewed over a broad spectrum of health and disorder (Berezin 1972, p 33).

The mental health of the elderly is remarkably good considering the difficulties associated with physical disability, poverty, malnutrition, loneliness, lack of purpose, loss of friends, and a public attitude toward aging of uninformed aversion.* The fact remains that less than 5 percent of all elderly are in medical care institutions and for predominantly physical reasons. A study of the institutionalized aged in a state mental institution (Berg 1970) indicated that 94 percent did not require such hospitalization. It is also apparent from a consideration of data on mental institu-

* *"Aging paints every action gray, lies heavy on every movement, imprisons every thought. It governs each decision with a ruthless and single-minded perversity. To age is to learn the feeling of no longer growing, of struggling to do old tasks, to remember familiar actions. The cells of the brain are destroyed with thousands of unfelt tiny strokes, little pockets of clotted blood wiping out memories and abilities without warning. The body seems slowly to give up, randomly stopping, sometimes starting again as if to torture and tease with the memory of lost strength. Hands become clumsy, frail transparencies, held together with knotted blue veins"* (Curtin 1972).

tions (Figures 1 and 2) that psychosis and alcoholism account for relatively few new admissions of those over the age of 65 although the total mental hospital populations do include many elderly with preexistent, long-standing cases of such disorders. There are few patients over 65 years of age who develop specific psychiatric disorders requiring hospitalization.

The mental impairment of the elderly living either at home or in the community was also evaluated in the Rochester study (Berg 1970) where it was found that 84.1 percent of aged persons were fully normal mentally. A slightly higher incidence of mental impairment was derived from data of the American Psychiatric Association (Aring 1972) in which 25 percent of persons over 65 and living in the community were "significantly impaired psychiatrically." The definition of psychiatric disability is important in such studies since a well-known survey of a metropolitan community (The Mid-town Manhattan Study, Srole 1962) showed an even higher prevalence of psychiatric disorders in the nonelderly. Although the overwhelming majority of elderly people have to be judged to be in normal mental health, elderly with some degree of mental impairment present a major problem in maintenance and home medical care.

The neuropsychiatric disorders of the elderly are characteristically secondary to psychologic stress, other disease states, malnutrition, and particularly institutionalization. There is less occurrence of disorders such as schizophrenia and manic-depressive reaction in the elderly and a corresponding increase in less specific entities as senility.

There is no question that mental and emotional impairment may follow a stroke or other disorder of the brain which can also be localized in many cases to a precise area of the brain structure. The more frequent problem is in attempting to correlate senile behavior with brain damage either by techniques of neurologic diagnosis or later examination of the brain tissue. The use of such terminology as "generalized cerebral arteriosclerosis" or "senile brain" has developed more for convenience than for any understanding of mental illness of the elderly. The fact that there is little relationship between erratic behavior of the elderly and any demonstrated pathology of brain tissue has not discouraged "generalized cerebral arteriosclerosis" as a convenient all-purpose explanation for the confusion, withdrawal, depression, and other behavior disturbances of old age. Admittedly brain damage can result from a number of diseases and disabilities including medical treatment. For example, administration of some of the tranquilizer and sedative drugs to elderly patients may be poorly tolerated. An average safe adult dose may be overdosage for some elderly and cause a sudden drop in blood pressure. This temporary cutoff of blood circulation on top of an already compromised blood supply to the brain may lead to irreversible brain damage.

Since it is impossible to say in the usual case what contribution brain damage makes to "senile brain" or "chronic brain syndrome," it would be more useful in such patients to consider senility of "brain syndrome"

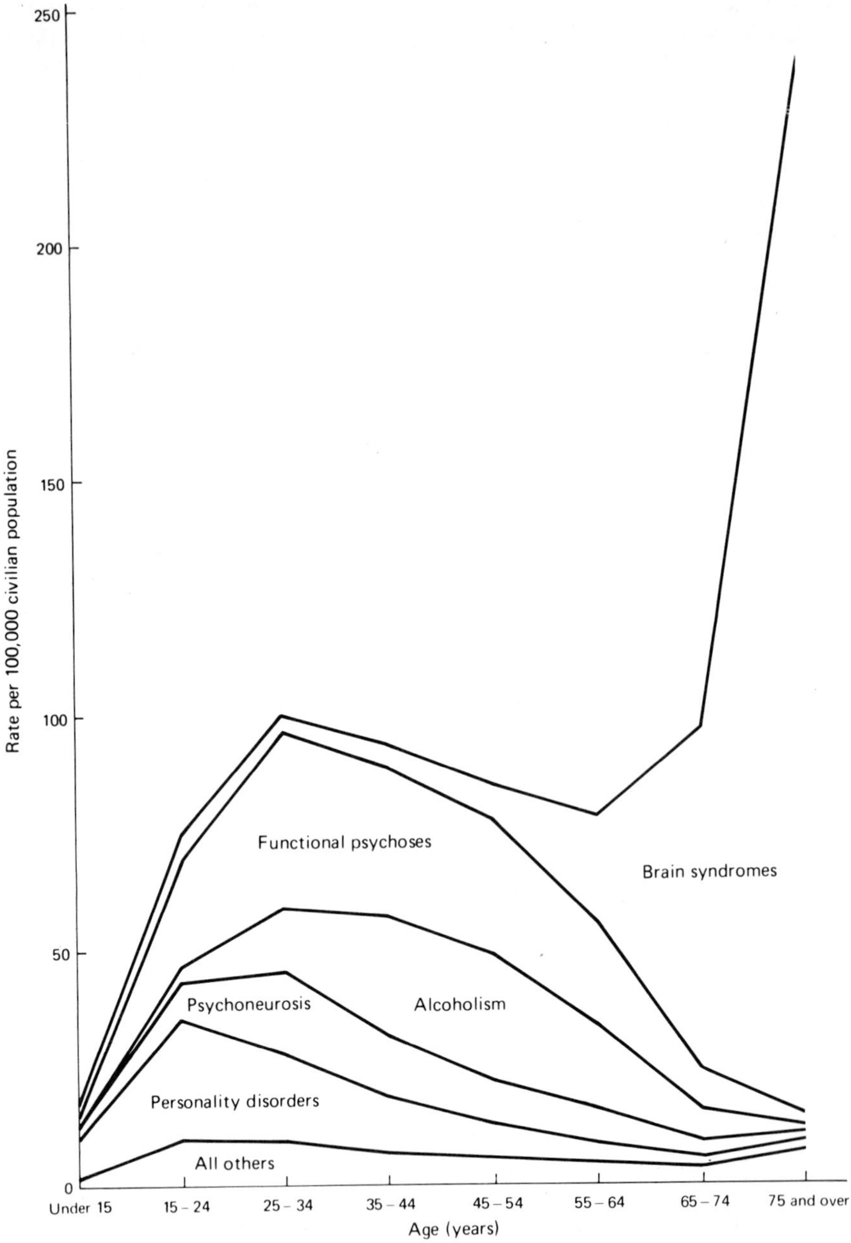

FIG. 1. First admission rates to state and county mental hospitals, by diagnosis and age, United States, 1963. (Source: U.S. Department of Health, Education, and Welfare. Patients in Mental Institutions. Part II—State and County Mental Hospitals, 1963. Washington, D.C.: U.S. Government Printing Office.)

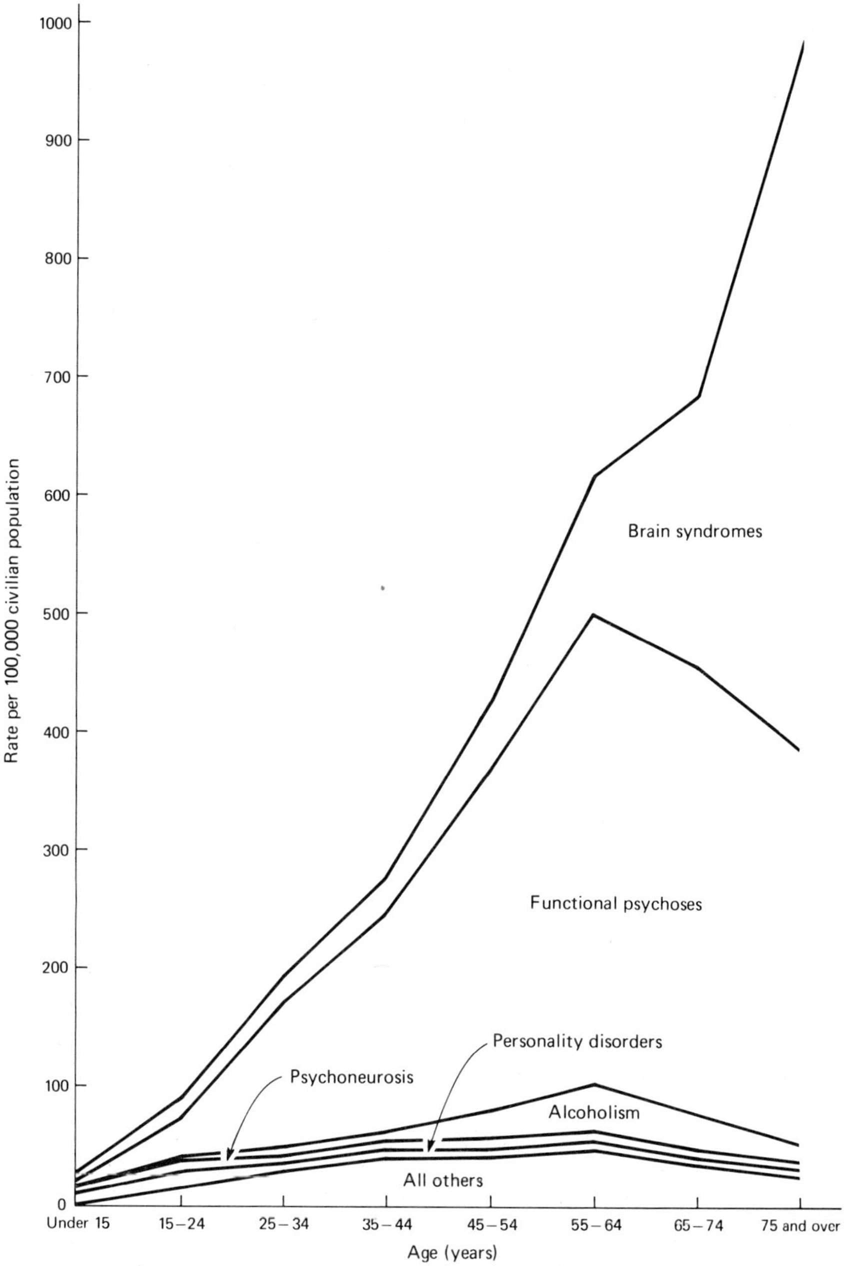

FIG. 2. Resident patient rates in state and county mental hospitals, by diagnosis and age, United States, 1963. (Source: U.S. Department of Health, Education, and Welfare. Patients in Mental Institutions. Part II—State and County Mental Hospitals, 1963. Washington, D.C.: U.S. Government Printing Office.)

secondary to emotional difficulties instead of being solely the consequence of brain damage. The distinction has great importance in the approach to the patient and the development of programs to maintain identity, support purpose and improve mental well-being of those elderly who are subjected to unusual amounts of stress at a time when their physical and psychological resources are limited.

Health, Stress, and Aging

The World Health Organization definition of health as a state of "complete physical, mental and social well-being" has the virtue of indicating the holistic nature of health including its social component but the definition otherwise lacks some understanding of the human condition. A British clinical teacher has noted that "the normal state of most people is to feel faintly tired, harrassed, slightly under the weather. My clinical observations lead me to believe that an abounding sensation of positive health usually presages either a cardiac infarction or incipient hypomania" (Miller 1971).

Stress and adaptation to stress are necessary parts of living, and meeting difficulties of daily living is essential to a healthy view of life. From a dynamic point of view, health is measured by ability to cope with stress. Successful adaptation leads to an increase in self-confidence and mental well-being. The individual's capacity to deal with stress and resolve crisis is quite different at various parts of the life cycle. The decreased physical capacities of age put a heavy burden on psychologic resources and point up the importance of programs for the elderly involving a variety of supports: social, medical, psychologic, interpersonal, economic, and even legal. The goal is to assist the elderly person to deal with stressful situations and to avoid much of the emotional disability, mental confusion and retreat into senility.

Senility Revisited

The development of a positive approach to the problem of senility is emphasized by Oberleder.

> Many of us who work with elderly people believe that senility, as it is commonly called, actually represents an emotional breakdown in elderly people. Its structure, its course, its causes, and its results are very similar to a breakdown at any age. We all agree that loneliness, ill health, retirement, and all the deficits associated with old age cause unhappiness in the elderly, but I think we overlook the obvious fact that those things actually cause mental breakdown. Were we to restore the normal props of living to elderly people, we might very well do away with senility.

> We have been brainwashed into thinking that there are very erudite and definite explanations for senility. We speak freely of arteriosclerosis of the brain and chronic brain syndrome. We are told that we lose millions of neurons every day from our brain cells, so that our brain shrinks in measurable proportion to our years, and for that reason alone we must expect irreversible changes in old age. Those ideas are so fixed that even when dramatic studies indicate there is no relationship between actual, visible brain changes and function in elderly people, we tend to overlook those results.
>
> We also tend to overlook the dangerous implications of what appear to be very common and ordinary situations. For instance, when an old person loses his teeth and must face people and eat without his dentures, we do not realize how intensely traumatic that is for him, perhaps even to the point of bringing on senility almost overnight. Instant senility might also occur when a person is advised to wear a hearing aid. Any of the harbingers of old age can cause a radical breakdown in some people, particularly those who have prided themselves on being intact and healthy (Oberleder 1969).

Oberleder goes on to discuss the importance of sexual repression as a factor in senile breakdown with particular commentary on the Rorschach interpretations by the elderly as symbolic of frustrated needs for sexual satisfaction or at least some physical contact. If one adopts the concept of senility as a curable mental disease secondary to severe emotional stress, it is possible to develop a positive attitude toward a therapeutic program rather than a fatalistic dead-end concept of the irreversibility of the brain change secondary to some unidentified and likely nonexistent organic brain change.

Reality Orientation

The therapeutic program advanced by Oberleder (1969) and by Folsom (1972) is that of "reality orientation." The first requirement is to develop the belief among the medical care staff and family members that something *can* be done with the "senile" patient and thus overcome an almost total negativism of those whose training and experience are as limited as their fears are real. Folsom has achieved rather remarkable reversals of "senility" with VA hospital patients. He quotes a favorite case of a man aged 77 who had had two heart attacks and several strokes.

> "When we got him," recalled Folsom, "his family was convinced he would die. In three months, they had taken away all of his bodily functions (by enemas and the injection of a catheter) except breathing and eating. He had no purpose in living and was in a desperate state.
>
> "First we threw away the pages of instructions from the family. Then we started to bombard him with facts: his name, the date, time, his room number. We showed him the bathroom and started him on exercises. Two months later he was able to go home. But the family had ruled out

> his return psychologically. So he had furloughs at home until they got used to him again.
>
> "He subsequently got back to his vegetable gardening again and keeps the freezers of two families well-stocked" (Boston Sunday Globe, November 26, 1972).

Oberleder is associated with the Albert Einstein College of Medicine and the Bronx State Hospital as a clinical psychologist. She describes a potentially "senile" group as "lonely people who never said a cross word . . . who hated their children for having to worry so much, or were jealous of youth having fun. But they didn't dare express negative feelings. They didn't build up defenses against fear and anger. Senility comes to a crucial head in middle age. It occurs in those who earlier in life were uncompromising, demanding, resentful, and possessive. It won't hurt you to know you hate your husband or your boss or that your children disappoint you."

At the Bronx State Hospital, older persons are taught to practice anger in group therapy sessions. Dr. Oberleder emphasizes that the treatment of senility is a two-way system since "in solving the problems of the aged we are solving our own problems. And if we can keep our aged counterparts out of state mental hospitals, we have removed one of the most terrifying nightmares we all share about growing old: the nightmare of being 'put away'."

Social Dependence

Susser and Watson have emphasized the types of dependence of the elderly and the need to consider special groups of the elderly as having special risks of dependency. "Social dependence is a condition in which the individual is in varying degrees unable to perform social roles and individual functions that will insure for him the means of subsistence. The incidence and the effects of social dependency vary with the type of dependence as well as with the social setting. Inability to continue as a wage-earner may cause financial dependence; in the home, bodily incapacity may cause domestic dependence and, according to the severity of the disability, require assistance from others for such basic activities as dressing, bathing, feeding, and evacuation. In the extreme, the individual may sink into dependence on medical services for the continued physiological function for his cardiovascular, respiratory or renal system" (Susser and Watson 1971, p 414). Noting that information about the distribution of the various forms of dependence is scarce, Susser and Watson suggest that "not only sickness and disability but also retirement, social isolation, bereavement and the availability of social support are circumstances in old age that can be critical for continued function. These circumstances might serve to mark out persons who require help in retaining independence and avoiding the further crisis of admission to institutional care (Susser and Watson 1971).

Preventive mental health in the elderly should center attention on those with remediable physical disorders, problems of recent retirement, bereavement over the loss of a loved one, and the socially isolated elderly. The identification of elderly with major dependence on one other frequently impaired elderly person enables the provision of some assistance before the incapacity of the remaining caretaker brings on forced institutionalization for both (Fig. 3).

Home, Family, and Community

U.S. Senate Special Committee on Aging heard eloquent testimony on the need for home services for the elderly:

> We are warehousing thousands of functioning human beings because they need some relatively inexpensive health care; they can't change their own bed linen; carry the groceries upstairs; wash their own hair; occasionally need a little help getting in and out of the bathtub and aren't able to take a bus ride to the doctor. The same fragile, but psychologi-

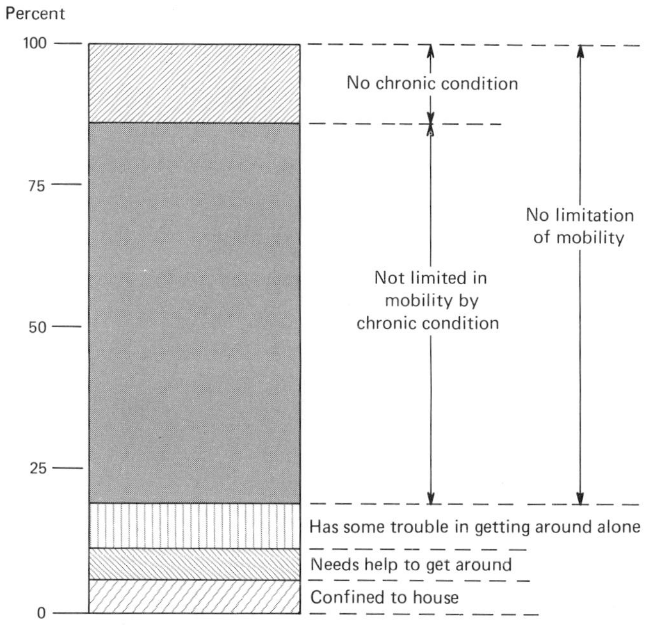

FIG. 3. Effect of chronic conditions on mobility of noninstitutionalized older people, July 1965–June 1967. Chronic conditions are conditions or impairments that have lasted for more than three months or those with an onset more recent which appear on lists of medically determined long-lasting conditions. They range from visual impairments corrected by eyeglasses to a completely disabling stroke.

> cally and socially functioning individual who is lucky enough to have a good doctor, a family and friends, or is able to buy a little help for himself doesn't have to give everything up to share a hole in the wall with a stranger, become a vegetable because nobody there is much interested in doing those things for him either. And the worst of it is, there's no return (U.S. Senate Special Committee on Aging 1972).

The discussion in Chapter 10 on home medical care indicates some of the present difficulties in funding such services (Fig. 4). The development of community-based organizations to provide home services for elderly people has been proposed (Kistin and Morris 1972). A Personal Care Organization could be developed by "a visiting nurse association, a senior citizens organization, a health maintenance organization, or some other public and private agency. Services could be further subcontracted through the PCO for 'Meals on Wheels' and transportation" (Kistin and Morris 1972). The key distinguishing features of the proposal by Kistin and Morris are:

> (1) development of a program appropriate to meet the needs of the total population of elderly and disabled; (2) the feasibility of diverting some current public assistance expenditures from institutional home and community care; (3) freedom of the contracting organization to provide a flexible range of needed services, with emphasis on output rather than input; and (4) concentration on increasing provision of the less professional services such as home helper (Kistin and Morris 1972).

The program is being tested in Massachusetts.

The role of the family in the care of the aged has not received the attention it requires. In an otherwise excellent symposium on "The Family and Its Future" (CIBA 1970), there was an almost total lack of reference to the role of the family in terms of its aged members. The chairman of the CIBA Conference commented in his summary remarks:

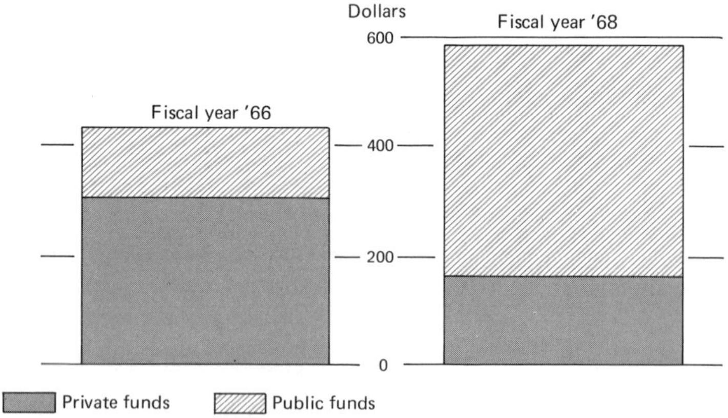

FIG. 4. Per capita personal health care expenditures for persons 65 and over before and after Medicare.

> I notice a very striking orientation towards youth in all our discussions and nobody here has behaved as if people age or said much about the fact that when old they continue to have needs. I think this neglect tells us something about our own preconceptions—preconceptions that will have to change (CIBA 1970).

The Medical Care Unit of the London School of Hygiene has inaugurated a series of studies on the family and community roles in the care of the aged. Pasker and Ashley have commented on the need "to obtain more information about the strains and stresses on relatives which may be caused by looking after High Care patients. Similarly it will become essential to explore what types of services would help to relieve these strains and stresses. For it may well be that the social services provided for families as a unit may be as important as the direct nursing services provided to the dependent patients themselves" (Pasker and Ashley 1971). The need for intensive study of family and community supports which maintain and improve the well-being of the elderly has not received similar attention in the United States.

Death and Dying

Bibring and Kahanna have emphasized the importance of attitudes toward death and dying:

> Any consideration of aging, as of the entire course of life, is incomplete without attention to the fact of death, of the individual's consciousness of it, its impact, and the ways in which it is approached. We know that it has different meanings for different individuals. Thoughts of death are avoided or faced in a variety of ways. We see evidence of its ultimate importance in many older persons in their increased interest in religion, in their desire to have a coherent view of life, to pay ceremonial attention to its station, to gain compensation for their personal losses, to deny the finality of death, and to find some form of explanation of the unknown in the universe (Bibring and Kahanna 1968).

Marcuse has suggested two contrasting ethics that may be derived from an interpretation of death in the history of Western thought. "On the one hand the attitude towards death is the stoic or sceptic acceptance of the inevitable, or even the repression of the thought of death by life; on the other hand, the idealistic glorification of death is that which gives 'meaning' to life or is the precondition of the 'true' life of man" (Marcuse 1959).

Role of Religion

Simone de Beauvoir (1972) has written a rather stark catalogue of aging and the aged which suggests that the general expectation is for a relentless decline and despair except for those fortunate few who can transcend circumstance. de Beauvoir is a dedicated Marxist but she does not have any commendations for social programs for the elderly in either capitalist or socialist countries.*

What is clearly missing from de Beauvoir's book is any reference to the role of religion. This is a singular omission since the effect of religion in support of the aged is quite evident to those who work with the aged (Bibring and Kahanna 1968). Janeway has also commented on this omission.

> I would like to suggest that what religion does (leaving aside what it is, i.e. true or not true) is project an alternative reality to that figured forth in our daily lives. Religion tells us that every day reality is indeed untrue and invalid, a swindle unless it is invaded and transfigured by the sacred. Faith in another reality offers an alternative framework of values to which the self may be attached (Janeway 1972).

This deep-seated need for an "alternative reality" for those living in otherwise hopeless circumstances has been described by Robert Coles in his study of the rural poor in America. Coles has some moving things to say about the need for faith by those whose lives are otherwise quite desperate. "They (the rural poor) sometimes wonder whether they are now, right now, in Hell. Heaven is to them a constant vision. Poor rural people find in their churches a real chance to escape, for haven, for respite from a tough daily life" (Coles 1971, p 594).

The poet W. B. Yeats was not concerned with the "truth" of credal religion when he spoke of the need of the aged for an "artifice of eternity" and summoned up the role of the religion of the aged in the following hopeful verse:

> *An aged man is but a paltry thing,*
> *A tattered coat upon a stick, unless*
> *Soul clap its hands and sing, and louder sing*
> *For every tatter in its mortal dress.*

William Butler Yeats
"Sailing to Byzantium"†

Crisis and Values

Our contemporary experience of living with recurrent crises or a sustained "crisis of crises" is analyzed by Platt (1969) on a scale classify-

**Sidel and Sidel (1972) noted participation of the elderly in political discussions associated with programs of human services in the Peoples Republic of China.*

†From Collected Poems of William Butler Yeats. Copyright 1928 by Macmillan Publishing Co., renewed 1956 by Georgie Yeats. Reprinted with permission of Macmillan Publishing Co., Inc.

ing United States and world problems as to individual severity and potential danger to our future survival. With "total annihilation" as the grade 1 crisis, health problems appear well down the scale of crises after administrative management, slums, participatory democracy, racial conflict, transportation, neighborhood ugliness, and crime. Such a ranking, incidentally, is generally borne out in community surveys of elderly individuals (Castle Square 1972) with health care generally less important than security, recreation, and other needs.

Williams, in an analysis of the effect of sustained crisis on our devaluation in value judgments, questions whether we may have lost our concern for the individual in the process of dealing with crises. "Because of the pressures of the nuclear threat, population, pollution, the 'ugly American war,' civil violence, and youthful defiance, has our democratic society reached a time when it wishes to abandon its most fundamental value: the individual's right to live? Is it ready to agree with totalitarian ideologies that a given life is relatively cheap and meaningless? Should we bother to try to save every baby and old person when we so obviously have more than we can love or support?" (Williams 1970).

Cornely has also been concerned with the role of crisis in determining health care and human services.

> Ours is a crisis-oriented societal organism which does not respond until a powerful irritant appears, and then it reacts in terms of the environment in which this interaction occurs. This has become the operational technique for the kind of political or governmental structure which has developed in this country. No one can contradict the statement that over the past 40 years a variety of studies and reports have suggested priorities and outlined extensive plans by which health care goals can be reached but at no time have they been put into operation. Crisis orientation is much more profitable to a society which is more concerned about profits and political power than about the health and welfare of its people. It is possible for the seekers of power to use this to their advantage and achieve the ends which they desire. So that one year it is regional medical programs, in another it is Medicare and Medicaid, yesterday it was comprehensive neighborhood health centers, today it is HMO's and tomorrow it is the family health center (Cornely 1972).

Elderly Leadership

In the final analysis, the social well-being and mental health needs of elderly Americans will be met only by organizations of the elderly, by the elderly, and for the elderly. The assumption by the elderly of the primary role in directing this society back to some degree of national purpose and program for the elderly is absolutely essential. Toynbee has said that "a society can be measured in its greatness by the care it takes for its elderly." The elderly themselves must determine the greatness of such measures.

References

Aring CD: On aging, senescence, and senility. Ann Inter Med 77:137, 1972
Berezin MA: Psychodynamic considerations of aging and the aged: an overview. Am J Psychiatry 128:33, 1972
Bibring G, Kahanna R: Aging and Old Age. Lectures in Medical Psychology. New York, International Univ Press, 1968, Chap 12, p 204
Castle Square: A coordinated service delivery system for the elderly in public housing. (Monograph) Boston, United Community Service, 1972
Coles R: Migrants, Sharecroppers, Mountaineers. Children in Trouble. New York, Atlantic, Little, Brown, 1971
Cornely PB: Overview of the New Types of Health Care Delivery Systems. Section Address given at Howard University School of Medicine, Dept. of Community Health Practice, Washington, D.C.
Curtin S: Aging in the land of the young. Atlantic Monthly, 230:68, July 1972
De Beauvoir S: The Coming of Age. New York, Putnam, 1972
Elliot K (ed): Symposium on the Family and its Future: A CIBA Foundation Symposium. London, Churchill, 1970
Folsom JC: Simple physical activities for the elderly. Hosp Community Psychiatry 31:377–378, 1972
Janeway E: Review of *The Coming of Age*. Atlantic Monthly, 229:94–98, 1972
Kistin H, Morris R: Alternatives to institutional care for the elderly and disabled. Gerontologist 12:139, 1972
Marcuse H: The Ideology of Death in the Meaning of Death by H. Feifel. New York, McGraw-Hill, 1959, p 64
Miller H: A contemporary view of the historical influences on medicine. In McLachlan G, McKeown T (eds): Medical History and Medical Care: A Symposium of Perspectives. London, Oxford University Press, 1971, p 223
Oberleder M: Emotional breakdowns in elderly people. Hosp Community Psychiatry 20:21, 1969
Pasker P, Ashley JSA: Inter-relationship of different sectors of the total health and social services systems. Community Med 126:272, 1971
Platt J: What we must do. Science 166:1115, 1969
Sidel R, Sidel V: The human services in China. Social Policy 2:25, 1972
Srole L, Langner TS, Michael ST, Opler MK, Rennie TAC: Mental health in the metropolis: the midtown Manhattan study. Int J Psychiatry 1:64, 1965
Susser MW, Watson W: Sociology in Medicine, 2nd ed. London, Oxford Univ Press, 1971
U.S. Senate Special Committee on Aging, 1972: Home Health Services in the U.S. Govt Ptg Office, 1972
Williams G: Needed: a health consumers' organization. Bull NY Acad Med 46:532, 1970

12

SPIRITUAL CRISES AMONG THE AGING

Walter L. Holcomb, Ed.D.

We call them the "Golden Years," and for many of our senior citizens they are just that—years rich in enjoyment, wide-ranging creativity, warm and treasured human contacts, meaningful volunteer services, schedules made in keeping with one's needs, interests, and energy levels, or days left completely unscheduled, "just to do what feels like doing, or to do nothing—just to *be!*" Many senior citizens profess that these are the best years of their lives: "I'm having a ball!"

But for many others these are the desolate and dreary years. Dull gray, they are marked by declining health, below poverty level finances, soaring inflation, mounting medical bills only partially covered by Medicare and other social services, retirement postponed beyond the usual and hoped-for norm, part-time and low-paying work at often degrading tasks, unwilling reliance on others for the most basic services, strained relations in subhuman living conditions, the dehumanizing climate of institutionalized ghettos for the aging—for many persons facing such conditions: "Old age is hell!"

To those in both the golden and the desolate years, and to all persons in between, inevitably come crises of a deeply personal, spiritual, and religious nature. This chapter is about these crises, how we may better understand them, and the people who are facing them. Above all, it is a chapter about how we who work with the aging may help make these the Golden Years for as many senior citizens as possible. It is their right.

Crises: Spiritual and Religious

Spiritual crises occur in the life of a person when one feels or perceives that significant meanings or values are threatened or are being lost, or that important new meaning or values might or might not be gained. The crisis may be short, lasting only a moment if one sees that the threat is unfounded or is passing, or that one has sufficient resources to meet and master the threat or loss, or to achieve a gain. On the other hand, a situation that would normally not be a crisis for a person might become one by the fact that it is prolonged to the point where one's hopes are undermined and one's resources are exhausted. Thus a rather minor chronic illness might be borne with only moderate pain and with modest restrictions on one's routines. Yet the illness might assume crisis proportions if one is led to believe that there is little hope of improvement or recovery.

The seriousness of a spiritual crisis which a person may face will be determined by the significance of the meanings or values to the person, the seriousness of the threat of loss or actual loss, and how one sees one's ability and resources to deal with the threat or loss. How one perceives a chronic illness may be far more important than the seriousness of the illness itself. One person, with considerable emotional maturity and spiritual resources, might endure the pain and restrictions of an illness with equanimity, while another might find that the bearing of the pain and the living with the modest restrictions exacts so great a price that life is robbed of much of its meaning.

Most adults in our culture live in a rich network of meanings and values. The childhood, adolescent, and early-to-middle adult years are invested in building up a rich and significant tapestry of skills, habits, attitudes, human relationships, possessions, status, plans, self-images, commitments, responsibilities, ego-ideals, and dreams—in short, a whole life style. Aging involves centering down, letting go, disengaging from less important aspects and elements of one's life without "losing one's self." The loss, threat of loss, or giving up of many elements from a life style will not cause a spiritual crisis, as the concept is used here. But when significant elements in one's life style are threatened or lost, then one is involved in a spiritual crisis.

In medicine the word "crisis" refers to the turning point in the course of a disease, when it becomes fairly clear whether a patient will recover or die. We have no such limited focus here, but refer to crucial or decisive times, events, situations, or conditions whose outcomes will determine one's life style for good or ill.

However, it must not be forgotten that one's own view of things determines whether or not a situation will become a spiritual crisis. Let us suppose that Mr. Jones unknowingly has a malignant tumor (cancer) in a vital organ, such as the liver. Mr. Jones does not understand the nature of his symptoms which are as yet mild and not very distressing. Neither does he sense the danger lurking behind the symptoms. He makes an appointment for his annual physical check-up with his personal physician, Dr. Friendly. The routine examination arouses Dr. Friendly's suspicions that all is not right, and he suggests a series of tests be made at the hospital, "just to be more thorough than usual." The tests confirm Dr. Friendly's tentative diagnosis. Dr. Friendly never tells Mr. Jones precisely what the diagnosis is; he belongs to the medical "school of thought" that it is better to protect the patient from the anxieties that might be caused by precise knowledge of a critical illness. Mr. Jones is told that an operation is needed, and one is scheduled and performed. Mr. Jones is effectively reassured at each step, and thus never really worries or feels much anxiety. After the operation, he is told that a growth was removed, everything went well, complete recovery is expected, and that he will soon be back home and in a few weeks back at work.

Yet the doctors involved are reasonably sure that had Mr. Jones skipped his annual check-up, or failed to see his physician until the symptoms became really distressing, the cancer might have become inoperable, thus leading in all probability to an early and untimely death. From an objective medical point of view there was potentially a real crisis. But Mr. Jones, blithely ignorant of the real danger, of how close he came to death, experienced little of what is meant by a spiritual crisis. He never personally understood or felt that his life was in danger. The threat, or loss, must be personally and knowingly experienced for it to be a spiritual crisis, regardless of the objective reality.

On the other hand, misinformation, misunderstanding, unfounded fears, or unnecessary worry may bring on a "subjective" or spiritual crisis where none would seem warranted from the perspective of an objective observer. It is what one sees or feels, and the meaning of what is seen and felt, that is crucial in determining whether or not a spiritual crisis occurs.

No sharp distinction is drawn between a spiritual and a religious crisis, as the terms are used here; yet the two are not the same. They have much in common, and a few critical differences. All religious crises are spiritual crises, but not all spiritual crises are religious ones. Hence, spiritual is the more inclusive term, and refers to the thinking, motivating, feeling part of man's existence, especially when centered on important meanings and values of a moral or an ethical nature. Most normal persons' lives are permeated with a network of moral and spiritual meanings and values, ranging from the least to the most significant ones, and from the crude and most self-centered to the most exalted and altruistic. Some are urgent, demanding immedate and total attention at least for the moment; others make small and infrequent claims on one's time and attention.

The term "religious" is used to refer to those meanings and values considered *by the person* to be of ultimate importance and concern. Such meanings and values are literally matters of life and death. They center in the meaning of one's existence, in the faith that one's existence has meaning, in the integrity of one's life, in the acceptance of one's own life style as having more than transitory value in the cycle of the generations and the longer flow of history. The meanings and values regarded as religious may or may not be related to and grounded in concepts of a personal God, or some other theistic frame of reference. The meanings and values may or may not be expressed in the symbols, ceremonies, and other cultic practices commonly associated with one or another of the established religious institutions. The use of such "religious" symbols and the participation in such ceremonies may not have any truly religious significance for a person; that is, the symbols and ceremonies may not even touch what is of ultimate meaning and value, as seen and felt by that person.

From the perspective used here, most adults are religious—*incurably religious*. One might be tempted to say that *all* "normal" adults are religious, except that one would then face the very difficult task of defining what is meant by "normal." In any case, an individual personality or style of life is developed with some sort of meaning and value hierarchy. Among all of the meanings and values, some are seen and felt by each person as more important than others. A few become central and ultimate. Without some such ordering of meanings and values we would quickly become insane, pulled or driven equally in all directions at once, and all the time. When one is revaluing and reordering a meaning or value in relation to one's central and ultimate meaning-value cluster, then one is being religious. Unless one's life style has become totally static, one must keep alive the process of such revaluing and reordering. Thus the being-religious process is lifelong.

That some live more superficial, more driven, less free and less integrated lives than others is obvious even to the casual observer. That some have centered their lives on values and meanings that are crude and crass is equally obvious. But such facts do not stand as a challenge to the adequacy of the definition of the religious as used here. It only means that the religious dimensions for such persons is superficial, crude, self-centered. It does not mean that when the religious center of personally ultimate values is challenged one is not in a religious crisis. It may mean, however, that one has fewer and less powerful resources at one's command with which to meet the crisis.

The religious is not limited to the few meainings and values that a person has made central and ultimate. All those events, situations, habits, attitudes, values, functions, relationships, possessions, hopes and fears, commitments and intentions which the person sees and feels to be tied in with or directly related to the central and ultimate meanings and values are also religious in nature. Therefore, when any of the events, situations, and so forth are so threatened that the core of meanings and values is threatened, then one undergoes a religious crisis.

Types of Spiritual Crises Faced by the Aging in the United States

Some of the spiritual crises faced by the aging in our society are not necessarily native to or inherent in the aging process itself. They may be culturally engendered or conditioned. Two examples should suggest others, and also should alert us to the possibility that most, if not all, spiritual crises of the aging have important cultural components.

It is a common observation that many aging persons suffer from more frequent and more intense aches and pains than are usually experienced by younger persons. Our culture has an antipain norm. Pain is to be avoided if possible; if such is not possible, then pain is to be overcome through quick and frequent trips to the medicine chest, the local pharmacy, and/or the physician. We avoid seeing and participating in the pain of others. Countless television commercials promoting one pain reliever or another are to be endured—as painlessly as possible—in the course of an evening's viewing. On the other hand, in some European nations the cultural norm is the opposite. Pain is not viewed as an unmixed evil to be avoided at all costs, but sometimes even a blessing essential to human welfare. It is not something to be quickly bufferined or narcoticized away, but a natural part of human life, to be born with equanimity and serenity. It is regarded as a mark of strong character to be able to bear pain with tranquility.

The second example of cultural differences relating to the spiritual crises of the elderly centers in attitudes toward the aging process itself. Ours is a youth-oriented culture. We worship at the shrine of youth, with much of the symbolic, ceremonial, and other cultic practices common to the organized religions. In America we spend many billions of dollars annually on cosmetics, clothing styles, dieting fads, surgical procedures, and many other materials and processes designed to maintain and/or restore youthful appearances. References to growing older tend to be socially taboo. The aging process itself is commonly regarded as undesirable, if not inherently evil, and the fact of death is perceived as making all men losers.

By contrast, in many societies aging is both accepted and respected as natural to life itself. There may be recurring fantasy patterns of utopian situations where persons remain perpetually young and vigorous in a mythical Shangri-la, or retreat from old age through periodic visits to a fountain of youth. But the fantasies tend to remain such, and make only minor invasions into the world of reality. In that world, the older child is favored over younger siblings through possession of increased power, status, responsibility, and first claim on the family inheritance. Signs of aging are readily accepted, and terms such as "old woman" and "old man" are commonly used as expressions of endearment. The elders of both sexes are revered, their wisdom respected, their advice and counsel sought on many matters. Tales of the ancestors permeate the folklore, and oncoming generations take pride and share the prestige of place, name, and fame of the forebears. In such ways many cultures actually support and nurture the process of aging as something desired and revered in life. Finally, at life's end, one joins the shrine of one's ancestors, in turn to become venerated by succeeding generations.

These two examples of cultural contrast are not intended as simplistic cross-cultural evaluations, with the implication that one culture is better than another. For such evaluative comparisons to be made with any fairness at all, many important elements from each culture would need to be held in balance—an exceedingly difficult and precarious task. The examples are only intended to suggest that aging in our society is in *some* ways made more difficult than in other cultures. Perhaps our culture has enough positive elements regarding aging at least to balance the scales.

Old age with its complex of crises does not arrive suddenly. Some persons seem to believe that the aging process begins in late middle age, and then develops rapidly. Not so! The aging process apparently begins with most people in their very early twenties, speeds up a bit in the thirties, gains considerable momentum in the forties, while in the mid fifties one may joke about being "in the advanced stages of presenility." Nor does the struggle with the aging process get delayed until the retirement years. Much of it goes on with little fuss or bother, while in other areas the crisis is not acute, but tends to be "low grade, chronic," like a persistent temperature of 100.5 F; it does not kill a person, but it won't go away.

Thus in the early twenties one may "eat like a hog" without putting on much weight; in the thirties one may avoid calories like they were the plague, without losing weight. An extra ten pounds around the waist may bother one at forty, and bring a frown from one's spouse and the family physician; they do not radically threaten one's life style or self-image. At fifty-five the ten pounds may have increased to twenty-five, and the physician's frown may change to a firm warning: "Take off twenty, or you are apt to end up in the hospital with a heart attack!" The crises to both life style and self-image are increased to a level of "medium-grade, chronic."

Certain aspects of the aging process may be observed in an organ of the body, such as the eye. In childhood and adolescence the fluid in the lens of the normal eye is crystal clear, and all the world is bright and shiny. In the early twenties the color of this fluid begins to change from clear to amber, very slowly, very imperceptibly if a year-by-year comparison is made—and oh, so irreversibly! But if decade-by-decade comparisons are made we are aware of differences, at least in how well we see. By the mid-forties it is as though we constantly wore medium-density amber-colored sunglasses. Without knowing why, we change the bulbs in our favorite reading lamps from 75 to 100 watts "in order to see as well as we used to." There is no special crisis here for most people, unless one refuses to recognize the need for more eye care, and for taking more time when going from a brightly lighted room at night into a dimly lighted street. If we refuse to allow our eyes the increased few seconds needed for shifting to night vision we may have a bad fall and a broken bone.

But at 75 or 80 the fluid in the lens may be such a deep amber that vision is seriously impaired, even in good light. Thus staff attendants and some members at a home for the elderly may complain and scold that a few of the men have lost all sense of propriety and social custom by urinating on the flowers in the men's room. Not so! They just can no longer see the difference between a potted geranium and a male urinal. Such a "deliberate disregard for social custom" can lead to the crisis of an attack on one's morals, cruel social ostracism, and a serious threat to one's self-image.

The solution is very simple, once the staff know the cause of the problem—remove potted geraniums from the men's room.

Some of the crises relating to the aging process are usually encountered in middle rather than in old age. An example is the level or strength of the sex drive, especially in men. Kinsey discovered through extensive research more than three decades ago that the average sixteen-year-old boy is four times the "sexual athlete" that his thirty-six-year-old happily married father is, if all sexual outlets are counted, including masturbation and nocturnal emissions. Probably most men do not understand the biologic nature of the aging process in the sex drive. Masculine folklore is filled with dietary remedies for a lowered sex drive. To recover one's sexual vigor one should eat lots of eggs and raw meat, and especially "Rocky Mountain Oysters" (beef testicles). Of course, none of the diets work, notwithstanding the tall stories.

Research indicates that the aging factor for the masculine sex drive is not really located in the reproductive organs, but in the cells of the pituitary gland, located at the base of the brain. This gland secretes hormones which regulate growth, the sex drive, metabolism, and other important functions. In the early adult years the pituitary gland begins very slowly to take on a "grainy" cell structure. The increase of the degree of the grainy structure seems to be directly correlated with the decrease of the hormone secreted by the pituitary, which in turn directly influences the rate of hormone secretion by the glands in the reproductive system; in turn the latter determines the level of the sex drive.

Decreasing sexual prowess in the middle-aged man strikes very directly at a common American stereotype of masculinity. In comparing his sexual vigor with the stereotype, a middle-aged man's masculine identity or self-image may come in for some rude jolts. Seeking to maintain what sexual vigor he has, or even to increase it—and feeling less stimulated by his wife than in former years—he may become easy prey for any passing young skirt that is both "seductive and willing to be seduced." Much marital discord no doubt arises from triangles based in part on such inadequate masculine stereotypes and misinformation about sexual biology.

We have looked briefly at only three of many possible illustrations of the aging process: the increased tendency to add weight; the change from clear to amber of the fluid in the lens of the eyes; and the decreasing level of the masculine sex drive. The main point is not that the aging process begins rather early in life, or that it begins slowly but gradually speeds up, or that little can be done in terms of our present knowledge to slow down or reverse the process. The main point is that the illustrations point to nature's way of preparing us for older age, when the effects of aging are so much more numerous and so much more intense. If all the many effects of the aging process came upon us suddenly in later life, with no preparation for them or experience with them, they would probably be overwhelming for most of us. There would seem to be much wisdom in nature's ways, if we will but learn from her.

The kinds of lessons we need to learn from nature in the early and middle years of adulthood about the aging process are suggested in a couple of stories. Some years ago, a radio announcer was talking about the many ways that middle-aged men use to try to fool themselves and others about how young they look and are. He mentioned such things as jogging, learning the latest dances of the young, wearing sport shirts, slacks, and so forth. "But," he concluded, "you can't fool a long flight of stairs!" Precisely! If we will stop fooling ourselves *about* growing older we will be better prepared *for* growing older.

The second story is one that a happily married but perplexed middle-aged man tells on himself. He had been concerned about his decreasing sex drive, what it was doing to his marriage, to his masculine self-image, what he should or could do about it, and so on. Then he learned the true biologic base for the aging of the sex drive in men. He reported that shortly thereafter "I was lying in bed one night, thinking about what I had just learned. And it seemed that I could hear tiny grains of sand dropping one by one from heaven and lodging in my head, in my pituitary gland. Each grain meant that much less sex. At first it was like the awful, steady drip of a leaky faucet, drip, drip, drip, eroding away an important source of pleasure and happiness. Then I realized there was absolutely nothing I could do about it, except have a good laugh, accept it as a fact, and go on living as normal a life as I could."

It is good that the lengthy and slowly increasing aging process gives most persons several decades to prepare for the onrush of clusters of new situations and conditions which many face at about the time of retirement and shortly afterward. At least five rather distinctive types of clusters of changes may be identified as common to persons in the years from 60 to 70 or 75: (1) diminution or loss of a wide range of physical and intellectual functions; (2) diminution or loss of roles and status in society; (3) increasing fears about poverty, illness, and death; (4) increasing frequency of loss of family members and friends through little contact or death, resulting in bereavement and grief; and (5) feelings of being abandoned and/or rejected, with associated feelings of loneliness, meaninglessness, and despair.

Not every occurrence of one of the above clusters of changes will necessarily result in a spiritual crisis for all persons. Yet any one of the clusters can produce such a spiritual crisis. However, two or more of the clusters occurring at the same time or in close succession are apt to create in a person a type of crisis that is by nature spiritual—the crisis of "identity-in-aging." Many of the types of problems of the aging, and resources and methods for handling them, are dealt with in other chapters of this book, and in standard references in gerontology. These include finances, retraining for part-time employment, nutrition, health care, problems of housing, avocational interests and leisure time activities, and a host of others. The focus here is on how such problems, commonly occurring in clusters, create spiritual crises for the aging, and especially the identity-in-aging crisis.

The Identity-in-Aging Crisis and the Recovery of Meaning

It has been suggested that retirement for the man is equivalent to a divorce for the woman. Perhaps—yet this comparison may rest on two concepts that have already become obsolete, or are rapidly becoming so: first, that the home-and-family is the only real center of the woman's life and identity; and the second, that the job market is the nearly exclusive domain of men, and one from which few women are forced by retirement into an identity crisis. Therefore, another analogy may offer comparative elements that are more nearly representative of reality.

In the "Dark Ages," lepers were pronounced dead as soon as their infection was identified and certified. They were then forced to attend one last Requiem Mass of the Church to hear the "Office of the Dead" recited over them. In the period between their ecclesiastical death and their physical death, they were forever banished from the company of the living. They were linked together in a new company with a chain that is stronger than life—Death. Of course, there was a limited, shadowy kind of commerce and communication with the living, but that was largely limited to the begging of alms.

Perhaps in the 21st century, historians, sociologists, and theologians will look back at our current cultural patterns in dealing with the aging and regard ours as the "Dark Ages of Technology." For we tend to identify our economic-cultural lepers by birth certificate and social security number. We know in advance when they will enter the company of the economically dead. Lack of flexible and humane policies regarding the age of retirement may take company executives off the hook, relieving them of hard decision making based on ethical, psychologic, and humane norms or principles. It can all be done in an impersonal, routine manner based on numbers and by policies based on the numbers. Thus is life, with its uniqueness and unrepeatability, reduced to rational control, with major decisions affecting the lives of so many made with a galling impersonality, with efforts to locate the responsible person behind a policy decision doomed to frustration in a Kafkaesque sense. More importantly, the impersonality of the decision making deals with life interchangeably—one life for another, one job for another—all the while denying that each life is utterly singular, unique, and meaningful.

When the numbers dictate that retirement time has come, we have the modern equivalent of the Requiem Mass and its "Office for the Dead"—the retirement party, with its liturgy of speeches and the giving of a gift or gifts, such as an engraved watch, a portable tape recorder, or a gold-plated ashtray. Then banishment from the world of work!

For those who want to retire and who are economically, socially, and psychologically ready for retirement at the time when the numbers dictate it anyway, such parties can be meaningful and wonderful ceremonies. In some ways, they are appropriate "rites of passage" from the adult world of responsible work into the world of leisure, easy loafing, or just being. Yet even such fortunate ones may be vaguely or even acutely aware that their good fortune is more the result of their individual planning than of any wisdom resident in the numbers policy regarding retirement. And even the more fortunate ones may also sense that the retirement party symbolizes more than the end of one's period of productive work. In a culture in which one's status and one's identity is largely determined by what one does, the occasion of retirement may mean a greater loss to one's sense of identity than it means to one's economic condition. For the retirement party may symbolize not only "you have done a good and an important job," and "we'll miss you—for a while," but also "you are no longer needed." Perhaps nothing is more important to a healthy sense of identity than a sense of being needed, at least in an active, "doing-oriented" culture.

Erik Erikson and others have helped us to understand the often prolonged and intensive psychologic pain involved in the adolescent's struggle to achieve an adult identity. It is a struggle which for many in modern industrialized nations is extended into the late twenties or even later. Many youth attempt to solve the problem, or at least to end the pain of being involved in a prolonged "identity diffusion." by developing a negative identity, such as that of a juvenile delinquent, a radical drop-out, or a violent revolutionary. As one youth put the matter: "I would rather be a Nobody in the gutter than an almost somebody up on the curb." Our culture has become very conscious—perhaps overly conscious—of the identity problems of adolescents.

But we seem to have remained far too insensitive to the identity problems centered in the transition period around retirement and the decade or so following. The adolescent tries to become somebody—a Somebody of worth, integrity, and meaning, both to himself and to the significant others in his or her life. The elderly strive to keep from becoming a has-been-nobody, or another form of negative identity—a burdensome, bothersome somebody. Our culture seems to conspire in countless ways against the elderly in their struggles to find a new identity, with meaning and integrity, with a focus radically different than the one that, through four decades or more, centered in doing productive work.

It may seem that too much has been made of the crisis of retirement. But retirement is not an isolated event—one storm in an otherwise tranquil voyage. It is for many only the bottom of the trough of a period of continuing disenchantment which begins in late middle age. Sociologists may call it the beginning of the period of disengagement. But from the perspective of mental health it may better be understood as the beginning of a period of involution, the folding in upon oneself. There may be periods of more or less serious depression, when even those who were formerly marked by high spirits now sense life as gloomy and foreboding. They now worry, feel anxious, are unable to sleep, become preoccupied with what's wrong with the body, are increasingly concerned with periods and instances of forgetfulness. One's life seems to be running downhill.

In any historic period many individuals in late middle age may face a career crisis that might be called an "Is that all there is in life?" syndrome. Not only may there seem to be no new worlds to conquer; one may now sense that one's own dreams and aspirations will never be realized, that one has gone as high up the achievement and success ladder as one ever will. Worse, one sees others, younger, more gifted perhaps, or more suited for the emerging age, beginning to pass one by. Perhaps most devastating of all, saddest of all, is a growing sense that one's life has not only been somewhat unhappy and unsatisfying, falling far short of adolescent hopes and dreams, but also that many others may view it as a life without worth or integrity. The middle aged and elderly cannot hear with impunity and tranquility the oft-repeated charges from the young that "you can't trust any one over thirty," that middle class values are suspect, that our materialistic culture is bankrupt, that our moralistic virtues are repressive and "square," that the generation gap is widening, and that the youth are increasingly alienated from the culture in which their elders are still deeply involved, which they still defend, and upon whose values their own identity is still based.

The Germans have a word for the deeply troubling condition in which many later middle aged and elderly persons find themselves. It is *thorschlusspanic*, the panic of the closing of the doors. It may be that *thorschlusspanic* in some degree, on some occasions, is a rather natural hazard of growing older. Our western, industrailized, materialistic culture in our particular moment in history seems to have created a *Zeitgeist* which produces acute and prolonged psychologic and spiritual *thorschlusspanic* for an increasing proportion of the aging, while at the same time creating an increasing range of programs, agencies, and situations to care for physical and financial needs and problems of the aging.

It is obvious that a problem so pervasive, so complex, and so persistent cannot be easily brought to a solution. Nor will any simplistic, one cause-one remedy approach yield really helpful results. In the final analysis, only a reordering of national priorities and the recovery of a new and far more humane spirit will move us forward in significant ways. Our crass materialism and dehumanizing competition must yield to a new centering of humanism, a new respect for persons, and new life styles which both espouse and demonstrate personal and group integrity and a pervasive respect for life.

America has long been known as "The Promised Land." But it has been turned into the land of promises—unkept promises. Such a state of affairs inevitably leads to cynicism, cynicism to despair, and despair to revolt. Only a new birth of meaning, of purpose, of integrity in personal and national life can turn us from destructive revolution into constructive reform. It will not be necessary to arrive at some utopian state in order to restore new purpose, hope, meaning, and integrity to life. But as a people we need to feel that we are on the way, making real progress toward worthwhile goals. The progress must be present and visible. A famous American jurist once said: "Justice must not only be done—it must be *seen* to be done!" In like manner, respect for the value and worth of persons as central and ultimate must not only be affirmed verbally—such respect must be *seen* as being lived out in ever-expanding aspects of a responsible and humane society.

The perversion and prostitution of human meanings and values needs to be confronted and challenged at many points, in many ways, by all the elements in our culture which affirm the centrality of persons. For example, the common pattern of perverting youth, beauty, and sex for the profit motive in advertising for cigarettes, liquor, automobiles, clothing, appliances, and countless other products needs to be unmasked as unworthy, unethical, dehumanizing, and a cancerous growth in our culture. If we continue in a national life style which celebrates profits over persons and their meaning and integrity, and if the celebration is symbolized and acted our through the whole range of our mass media, it will be difficult or impossible to convince our aging persons that they have meaning and value that is central in our culture. In like manner, the rape of our natural resources, again for the profit motive, needs to the challenged and halted in a manner that we have only started in the recent stress on ecology. If we can learn to conserve and to use our natural resources with reverence and stewardship for all, then the aging can believe that their culture also has respect and reverence for their lives. New and concerted efforts in these new directions need to be undertaken especially in the educational and religious institutions of our society.

Countless specific suggestions could be made that might in both individual and group cases help to regain new meaning and integrity for the aging, especially in their postproductive years. Such might include the following general types of programs and emphases: (1) extending and humanizing social security benefits, with the elimination of economic penalties for part-time or even full-time remunerative work through as many years as such has meaning and value for the person, with concerted efforts to interpret such benefits as basic human rights, and not as charity or welfare; (2) extension, coordination, and humanizating of health care services, from Medicare and Medicaid to the reforming of patterns and styles of life available for the enfeebled elderly in retirement centers and nursing homes; (3) the development of new styles of life for the aging which will bring them out of their ghettos and keep them in the mainstream of life, at least in terms of interpersonal communities, with special emphasis upon developing new and viable forms of multigenerational living situations; (4) improved, extended, and coordinated services of visitation, interpersonal relations, shared experiences in leisure time activities, communal dining, and the like in cross-generational patterns; (5) concerted efforts to interpret to ourselves and to each other the meaning of a new life style, especially for the aging, based on being, rather than doing; and (6) new and creative patterns of celebrating the full range of human experiences throughout the entire life span, including birth and death.

The last two of the above clusters cannot be overemphasized. They cannot be faked if they are to have meaning. They must be real, and must be seen and felt by the elderly as authentic to the life style of both the young and those in the productive years of middle life. We have scarcely asked ourselves how it might be done; we have only limited and halting experiments in finding out how it might be done. But a clue to the spirit of the new life style may be seen in the revolt of many youth against the productive and competitive orientation of our materialistic culture as the only *raison d'etre* for living. They have turned around the frequently heard command of their elders, "Don't just stand there—do something!" into "Don't just do something—stand there!"

No one of the above approaches or attacks on the problem, or others equally important, will be sufficient if pursued alone. To recognize the complexity of the problem, the need for concerted attacks on many fronts, the marshalling of the maximum of resources, and the persistence of the struggle over a prolonged period of time, should save us from being too easily and quickly discouraged. Indeed, we should see that all of the above together will not be sufficient if we do not in the process create a new cultural climate, a new *Zeitgeist*, which is deeply human and humane. But there is hope that all of the above, done with persistent determination and wise, concerted effort, will create a spirit for the new age for persons of all ages. It would be a *Zeitgeist* in which all of the above and more would be done in the normal course of life. It would be an age in which an increasing proportion of the aging could gladly join in the affirmation of Robert Browning:

Grow old along with me!
The best is yet to be
The last of life for which the first is made
Our times are in His hands.

Robert Browning, "Rabbi ben Ezra"*

Spiritual Resources and the Process of Grief Work

Bereavement and its associated condition of grief is a common and probably a near-universal experience of persons who live beyond the earliest years of childhood. Some persons will experience in a lifetime only a few occasions of bereavement which result in a deep personal crisis; others will undergo many such occasions. For most persons in the retirement years and following, it seems that the occasions of bereavement are far more numerous than in the earlier years of life.

We have already noted that the earlier years of life are invested in building, doing, possessing, and becoming all of those things that make up a life style and a personal identity. During the middle-adult years the building process reaches a sort of plateau; soon the process is slowly reversed, as persons experience the loss of or disengagement from some of

**From The Complete Poetical Works of Robert Browning. Courtesy of Houghton Mifflin Co.*

the functions, status, possessions, relationships, and persons that have become significant elements in their life style. Usually at about the time of retirement, the process is speeded up a great deal.

THE NATURE AND SOME OCCASIONS OF BEREAVEMENT

If any of the elements that are lost or surrendered from a life style and identity are significant enough to a person that such loss or surrender brings acute psychic pain, the person is involved in bereavement. Bereavement is often viewed from a rather narrow perspective, as the death of a person who is "loved, highly prized, and held very dear." Such a narrow perspective excludes many types of experience causing a response of grief which psychologically can scarcely be distinguished from the typical reactions of persons who have lost a significant loved one through death. Nor need the loss be due to death. A young professional woman kept her appointment for early in the week. Her appearance suggested that something important and rather devastating had recently happened to her. Her eyes and face were red and puffy, her posture seated or walking communicated a sense of defeat, or of being worn out and emotionally drained; her voice was flabby, and suggested many hours of recent crying. She excused her condition by telling of the previous weekend during which she broke an engagement which she sensed as leading toward a marriage that could only have ended in personal defeat and perhaps tragedy for both persons involved. She really loved her fiance, but the growing depth of their relationship revealed to her certain elements that seemed sure to cause an increasing state of psychic warfare between them, producing a "civil war" in marriage. She had knowingly chosen the intense and prolonged pain of the bereavement associated with the broken engagement, rather than enter what seemed sure to be a bad marriage.

The loss associated with bereavement need not be of something "real" or actually existing as a part of one's life style and personal identity. Most of us have known gifted persons of quite unusual drive and creativity who have *almost* won an election to some important position, or appointment to a significant and well-paying job—but they just failed to "make it." Their ego-image or "ideal-self" seemed to depend upon securing such a job or winning such a position. The failure shatters the self-image at some crucial point, then the drive, motivation, and creativity are lost or are so seriously diminished that for the person, living changes into a pointless existence. Such persons may fail to recognize that they are in the process of bereavement—for a lost dream! Indeed, the dream need not be for oneself personally. It can center in the hope that a son will be accepted in an "Ivy League" college, or enter a high-status profession such as medicine or law, or carry on one's business, or fulfill one's childhood ambition to be a concert artist, or that one's daughter will marry a "man of distinction." Here the failure of a son or daughter to live up to one's dream for them may undermine one's self-image as a "good" or "sucessful" parent.

Furthermore, the loss need not be of some prized thing, position, or function, or of a loved person. Rather, the loss need only be of something or someone that is significant. Thus, persons grieve over jobs that they have held for many years yet hated every day. Retirement, with the ending of the hated job, leaves a tremendous vacuum in their life style; they find no easy way to fill the hours that the job formerly consumed at however boring a pace; neither do they find new human relationships to replace the network of former, detested employee relations which are now ended.

However, the most important distinction to be made is that the occasion for bereavement for a person need not be for one who is "loved, highly prized, and held very dear." The *only* requirement is that the person lost be significant in the life style and personal identity. Some husbands and wives fight like "cats and dogs" for many years. Their marriages are marked by anger, bitterness, and recrimination; there are few signs of love, or even the most basic respect. Yet when either spouse in such a marriage dies, it is common for the other to have genuine grief symptoms as intense as those experienced by a surviving spouse whose marriage has been characterized by love, open and healthy communication, deep sharing, and mutual trust and self-giving.

Again, our treatment of elderly parents may mask our real feelings and motives, as well as the significant role they still play in our life style. Thus, two middle-aged men were overheard in a hospital corridor, discussing the rapidly approaching hour of death of their elderly father. They had experienced him as a wealthy, self-centered, authoritarian, and hateful old tyrant. Only half understanding what they were doing, they instructed the hospital staff to spare no pains or costs in prolonging their father's life—a procedure carried out with the usual oxygen tents, blood transfusions, intravenous feedings, operations, tubes—"the works." As death drew near, one son said to the other: "They really gave it to the s.o.b. this time, didn't they." Whatever love they may have had for their father was swallowed up by their hatred of him, and they had "used" (misused?) the staff and the procedures of the hospital to vent their hatred of their father. Yet if he were still a significant, even though hated, object in their lives, one could nevertheless anticipate that they would undergo a type of grief, perhaps marked by an unusual amount of guilt and half-conscious self-recrimination. The loss of their "hate-object" would leave a different kind of vacuum in their life style and network of meanings and values. For example, for years they might have blamed the father for all sorts of personal failures, shortcomings, disappointments; they might easily have projected onto the father some of the character flaws they only dimly recognized in themselves. He was a ready-made and convenient scapegoat. Now that he is dead, whom could they so easily blame?

The wide range of illustrations of the occasions of bereavement should open up our perspective and our sensitivity to the fact that the occasions of bereavement are much more extensive than we commonly recognize, especially for the elderly. Grief wears many masks, so that it may go unnoticed even by close friends. As we shall see, unresolved grief can lead to chronic despair, and despair can be lethal.

To help us sense the prevalence of grief, especially in the aging, let us look at the major types of occasions of bereavement:

1. The loss of a significant (loved or hated) person by death;
2. The anticipated loss of a significant person through approaching death;
3. The feared loss of a significant person, for example, a son or husband reported as missing in action in time of war;
4. The anticipated loss of one's own life, through approaching death;
5. The anticipated or actual loss of a bodily function, such as sight, hearing, or sexual potency, or the loss of an organ, such as a hand or foot, a lung or kidney. Some persons even seem to suffer a mild, prolonged grief reaction over the loss of youthful vigor or physical beauty;
6. The loss of a vocational or professional position, through retirement, economic conditions forcing unemployment, and similar conditions;
7. The loss of social, economic, or political status, closely tied in with a person's self-image;
8. The loss of significant interpersonal functions, such as that occasioned by the maturing and growing independence of children, so that one no longer feels needed;
9. The loss of a significant relationship, as through broken engagements, a divorce or separation, or members of the primary family (parents, children, siblings) or very close friends who, through circumstances, become completely alienated.
10. The loss of a significant possession, such as a home, financial reserves, and the like.

Certainly not all persons experience grief over all the types of loss listed above. A person's response to a given loss will be determined by many factors. The situations that bring about a serious grief reaction in one may at most only cause mild sorrow or a brief disappointment in another. For example, young children may go into an intensive but short grief episode over the unexpected death of a family pet. Sensitive parents will not make light of the deep feelings of anguish that children tend to express on such occasions, but will help them talk and work through their grief feelings. The fact of death will not be avoided, nor should we try to suppress the anxieties children may experience regarding the possibility of their own death, or that of their parents, brought to the level of consciousness by the death of the pet.

On the other hand, it is not uncommon to learn of a very elderly person who, with full understanding and approval of middle-aged sons and daughters, make arrangements with the attending physician and the other members of the medical team for an "appropriate death." The family request that the medical staff not prolong a life already rich and full, but now nearing an end through a terminal illness. Medical procedures are limited to those that will insure as much comfort and freedom from pain as possible, but death is permitted to come naturally and with dignity, in its own time. This is not to say that euthanasia, which is a medical procedure employed to cause death, painlessly and to end suffering, should be employed. Rather, we are talking here of dysthanasia, which involves withholding medical procedures that could prolong life for a time—perhaps with much suffering by the patient, and with a sense of agonizing fellow-suffering and great financial drain on the part of family members. To be sure, there are indications of some grief among members of the surviving family—one cannot lose someone as significant as a parent without some sense of loss. But the grief work is commonly less intense and is facilitated by gratitude for a long, rich, and full life, a deep love, and a thankfulness that the last days of the deceased were relatively free from unnecessary suffering and dehumanizing medical procedures.

Thus, one needs to examine not only the significance of a loss for a person, as viewed externally by another, but the inner dynamics of the person, his ego strength, his life style and personal identity, the depth of emotional attachments to that which has been lost, the place the lost one or thing had in the network of meanings and values, and the earlier experiences in coping with occasions of loss.

THE NATURE AND SOME FORMS OF GRIEF

We have seen that there are many forms of serious loss that may involve bereavement, especially in the elderly. Such losses provoke a greater or lesser degree of spiritual crisis, especially when the response is one of grief. If bereavement is the occasion of loss of something or someone of significance, then grief is the response of mourning for that which has been lost, or which one fears will be lost. No simple definition of grief seems to be adequate, for grief is a form of illness that has psychologic, physiologic, and existential (or spiritual) elements or dimensions, which interpenetrate with each other. Different elements or dimensions will seem to dominate in different forms of grief, or at different stages of grief work. Grief work is the process of working through the disengaging process, becoming freed from the relationship that existed, and reinvesting emotional capital, plans, and energy in new dimensions of life. Most forms of grief will involve working through a complex of deep and distressing emotions, and learning to cope with ongoing life without the presence of the person, thing, function, or relationship that no longer exists.

The main categories of grief and grief work would seem to include the following: anticipatory grief and grief work; present grief and continuing grief work over a recent bereavement, and delayed grief work. One may also view grief and grief work as either normal or pathologic. We will examine these in some detail.

ANTICIPATORY GRIEF WORK

Unlike animals, we can anticipate something of the future and symbolize for ourselves its meaning for our lives. Thus, we can "foresee" many occasions of bereavement and "forefeel" the associated experience of grief. That is, through imagination we can project ourselves into the future and experience emotionally something of the impact of anticipated events. The young may tend to push such foreknowledge of dreaded events out of consciousness, but this is increasingly difficult for the middle-aged and elderly. As one grows older, one's circle of friends is diminished through death; members of one's own family die; the passage of time brings about a diminution of one's physical and mental powers, functions, and responsibilities. It becomes increasingly difficult to assume that one can long escape bereavement and grief, or that the end of one's own life can be indefinitely postponed into the future. The march into the future will not be stopped, and the voice of anxiety and dread cannot forever be stilled.

While such foreknowledge or anticipation of coming bereavements and grief may bring to some deep anxiety, depression, or even acute shock when the coming reality is suddenly and forcefully thrust upon one, on the whole anticipatory grief work seems to be a useful process. It enables the person to prepare himself for bereavement when it does occur, and to do some of the grief work in advance in measured doses, to experience in part what life will be like following the significant anticipated loss, and to do some prebereavement planning. If part of one's grief work is done prior to bereavement, it seems realistic to assume that grief following bereavement will be more easily managed, less of a shock, involve less anxiety, and lead to a more rapid recovery.

We may do persons a real disservice by playing on false hopes, attempting to hide the truth from them, or engaging in Pollyanna cliches, such as "All will turn out for the best," or "While there is life there is hope," or "God knows best—His will be done." Such a disservice may involve not only a terminally ill person, but the whole interpersonal network of family members and very close friends. Members of the helping professions, such as doctors, nurses, ministers, often assume that they are being kind by being tactful in avoiding the truth. Such evasions may be self-centered rationalizations, for withholding the truth may mainly reflect the doctor's point of view rather than what best fits the patient or his or her family. It is seldom easy to be the bearer of bad news, so the evasions common to the helping professionals may be practiced for their own comfort. Dr. Thomas P. Hackett, Chief of Psychiatric Consultation Service, Massachusetts General Hospital, Boston, presented an address in April of 1971 to the Dean's Council Seminar at the Episcopal Theological School in Cambridge. Entitled "A Matter of Life and Death," the address set forth conclusions reached by many investigators working independently with terminally ill patients, in many parts of the world. They cut through many strong, arrogant opinions and myths regarding death and dying:

1. Most terminally ill patients know that they are dying no matter what they may have been told. Whether or not they have been told what the diagnosis is tends to be medically irrelevant.
2. The process of dying is feared far more than death itself.
3. Those individuals who have been told the truth about their condition have fewer and less emotional and psychiatric complications than those from whom the truth has been withheld. For example, the incidence of suicidal depression in a dying population is not much greater than in a general population. When suicide does occur, it usually does so in cases where pain has gone out of control or where the patient has no one to whom he can turn for emotional support.

Critically ill as well as terminally ill persons and their families need to be able to trust the truthfulness of the helping professionals in matters of life and death, so that with the truth they can better deal with matters of life and death. The last few days and hours before the death of a loved one are difficult enough without becoming involved in painful and awkward charade. It is a poor time for falsehood and the alienation that comes from broken communications and the feeling that each cannot trust the other in this final event in the relationship—dying and death.

Thus, a coordinated professional team including doctors, nurses, and clergy may best help in dealing with the family in which one member has what is diagnosed as terminal illness. The attending physician, in consultation with such medical specialists as may be needed, would make the diagnosis and prognosis and prescribe such medical procedures as may be appropriate, including those to insure maximum comfort and minimum pain. He might choose to tell the patient and/or the members of the family what the diagnosis is, and the expected progress of the disease, that is, about how long it might be before death occurs. Or he might choose to report such matters to the clergyman and have him be responsible for relaying the information to both the patient and family. The nursing staff would not only be responsible for such medical procedures as the physician assigned to them; they might also try to follow with unusual diligence the counsel of the French surgeon, Paré, who wrote more than 400 years ago: "To cure sometimes, to relieve often, to comfort always." Unfortunately, hospitals do not always follow such counsel. Studies have shown that once a diagnosis of a terminal illness has been made, the attending physician sees the patient much less frequently and his examinations tend to be brief and perfunctory. Other studies show that in such cases, the nursing staff take much longer to respond to the patient's calls than they do with those for whom there is hope of recovery.

If the members of the professional team, the patient, and the family can recognize the communicate about the fact of impending death, then the anticipatory grief work process can be greatly facilitated for both patient and family members. Certain matters of a more formal nature may need to be cared for—talking about important financial matters, the location and condition of important papers, unfulfilled responsibilities or unfinished plans that can be brought to fruition by a member of the family, and so forth. Dealing with less personal matters may then make it more easy and natural to discuss deeply interpersonal matters—to recall old times together, to laugh again over old family jokes, to cry again together over some of the disappointments and failures, to live again in memory and perhaps in some appropriate form of ceremony or other symbolizing way some of the most cherished events of the past, to seek and give forgiveness again or for the first time for hurts of omission and/or commission, to say again and to celebrate by saying what each means to the other, to laugh and cry and hold hands together for the last times, and slowly or quickly as the need may be to say a final farewell and give a last blessing to each other while consciousness lasts! Precious moments these may and should be. How foolish that a lack of candor about the reality of impending death should rob both the living and the dying of such. How much better to risk some physical tiredness to gain emotional catharsis and spiritual refreshment. For these can be a part of the process of disengagement involved in anticipatory grief work for both the living and the dying. How much better, no matter how difficult, that they should be done mutually, together, rather than in desolate sadness, alone!

The above might be called the interpersonal or psychologic dimensions of anticipatory grief work. Such processes, relationships, events, and celebrations may be facilitated by a sensitive and trusted clergyman. If the situation seems appropriate, he may also help in the planning of the funeral or memorial service before death occurs. Special efforts might be made to learn of wishes of the dying person regarding the service—favorite hymns, scriptural passages, and so on that might be used in the final celebration of one's life and death. Important items might be listed for preparing the obituary notices. How frequently clergymen have to deal with family members who have little or no idea about the wishes of the deceased for his or her own funeral or memorial service. How poignant the expressions of regret by family members that the matter had never been discussed! How common the expression: "If we had only known!" (One might add that this is one aspect of the "American way of death" that Jessica Mitford seems to have missed, namely, our pattern of *under*emphasizing death before the fact, and *over*emphasizing it after the fact.)

In addition to dealing with the unfinished business of interpersonal relations centering around the terminally ill person (and perhaps primarily because they are dealt with openly and honestly), a trusted clergyman or some sensitive friend or member of the family may help deal with the deepest existential and religious concerns relating to dying and death.

The reality of one's own impending death may bring to consciousness some of the deepest religious questions and personal anxieties—questions and anxieties that may have had their genesis in traumatic experience of early infancy, but which have been largely repressed or held at some vague semiconscious state of awareness. Now they cannot and will not be put off any longer, because one's personal history is running out of future. Unless we are sensitive we can cause the dying person to suppress them again, or we can too easily dismiss them with superficial cliches that are nonanswers. Dealing with these questions and anxieties may be a normal part of a seldom-recognized phenomena, anticipatory self-grief, or the bereavement over the impending loss of one's own life. Here, bereavement is to be clearly distinguished from the fear of dying, or death itself.

Such fear is most commonly centered in unfounded assumptions that the act of dying is extremely painful;* or that one will be abandoned by others at the time of death, so that death comes in a desperate state of aloneness; or that there may be final medical procedures that will further dehumanize oneself by being turned into a sort of "plumbing shop"; or that with diminished control over one's body one may do things that are shameful or embarrassing.

Much of the fear of dying is a fear of the unknown. Much of the fear that death will be extremely painful can be relieved by sharing with the terminal patient our knowledge regarding pain-relieving procedures and processes. Persons can be helped by knowing, in advance, that the process of dying is probably never pleasant but it is rarely as unpleasant or painful as it is imagined to be.

Some of the fear of dying may be related to the psychologic rather than the physiologic unknown. The ministrations to the person in the process of dying involves the conquest of four symptoms, three of which are physiologic: pain, nausea, difficulty in breathing, and loneliness. Pain is the most easily and most successfully treated of the three; loneliness is less easily dealt with, although suggestions have already been given as to how the community of family and close friends can, in the context of the known and accepted truth about the reality of impending death, through frequent short visits, open communication, and the assurance that the dying person is not abandoned, thus help to dispense with much of the loneliness, and ease that which remains.

However, loneliness is not the only psychologic stress factor relating to the process of dying. Anxieties may center in the unknowns relating to the psychologic process of dying. What is it like to "lose onself?" Is it a horrible

* *It is true that terminal illness or accident* may *bring extreme pain, at least for a time. However, the range of painkillers available is sufficiently potent to control such pain. Further, the body has a built-in self-anaesthetizing process, whereby extreme pain tends to be blocked from the diminishing consciousness of the dying person. Indeed, it is not uncommon for persons who have been in extreme pain (or who would have been without anaesthetics) to experience a near-total release from pain in the last hours–who "die in peace."*

nightmarelike experience, filled with psychologic suffering? Until recently, we have had little information upon which to base answers to such questions, for it was quite rare that persons experienced dying to the end of the process, and then were brought back to life, with memories of the dying process relatively intact. Such experiences are becoming increasingly common with the advent of modern emergency trauma centers in many well-equipped hospitals. Many such persons have now reported their psychologic journey into death. They tell us that there is less terror in the moment of demise than most of us have been led to believe. In not a few cases, there may be bliss and even ectasy!

A case was reported in the *American Journal of Psychiatry* in 1967. A woman was revived from the moment of death, occasioned by a violent allergic reaction to penicillin administered by her dentist for an abscessed tooth. Her recorded account of her experience shows that dying may begin with much that is mundane, something very much a part of everyday life, and then move toward the ecstatic.

In the car when her breathing began to become difficult, she realized what was happening and she experienced frantic fear which soon passed. She next felt intense sympathy for her husband and felt guilty for what she was putting him through. Her last violent reaction was fighting against the sense of dying, even though she was no longer afraid. She then gave in, knowing that she wanted it, death! Next she witnessed in rapid succession a great many scenes from her life. They began around the age of five, and were marked by vivid impressions of color. She had the sense of a beloved doll and was impressed by how bright blue the glass eyes were. She also had a picture of herself on a bright red bicycle on an equally bright green lawn. Other scenes followed, not of her whole life, but of her early childhood, and she emphasized that the death scenes all made her ecstatically happy.

Her final memories of her dying state was of a picture of the Taj Mahal in which she was deeply, idyllically engrossed. But this vision was interrupted by the sense that people were working over her and trying to awaken her; she became resentful and irritated. She wanted to be left alone with the beautiful dream of the Taj Mahal—and then she finally came to. (The Taj Mahal may have been an appropriate image in her case, for it is a monument erected by a doting husband to his beloved wife, and this wife had felt neglected in her marriage to a busy doctor. It may have been her final effort to achieve a sense of reconciliation and fulfillment in marriage, before death.)

Other dying experiences may be somewhere between ecstasy and nightmare, involving both humor and struggle. Dr. Hackett tells of a young male teacher who had a heart attack outside the Boston Public Library. Taken to the Massachusetts General Hospital, he began to feel much better and wanted to leave, against the doctor's advice. While everyone around was trying to dissuade him from leaving, he suddenly passed out. His heart stopped beating and he was physiologically dead. In this state he had the following dream. He found himself in an immense supermarket. Trussed up like a roast, he was on a conveyor belt headed toward the check-out counter. There was an ominous quality about the check-out counter, and he began to say to himself: "Oh no, oh no! They are not going to check me out!" Whereupon he suddenly came to, looked around and found himself surrounded by doctors in white. Startled, he exclaimed, "Christ, there are a lot of clerks in this meat market!" Every one broke out in laughter, and then he was told what had happened. Otherwise he would not have known that his heart had stopped beating and that he was essentially dead. He would probably have recalled only that he passed out and then regained consciousness; but he would never have known how close to the great abyss he had come and from which he could not have returned had his heart not been defibrillated.

ANTICIPATORY SELF-GRIEF WORK

We have seen that fears of the physiologic and psychologic unknowns are common; that they may be largely relieved through sharing knowledge available to the professional health team, and through the supporting presence of a caring family, close friends, and an understanding and supporting clergyman; and that the pains and physical discomforts of dying can largely be relieved or even controlled completely by modern medical practices. However, while all may be related to or directly involved in dying, none of these distress factors or fears are properly related to the process of anticipatory self-grief work as such. Such anticipatory self-grief work seems to be of two quite different kinds.

First, there may be the kind of normal anticipatory self-grief related to the sense of incompleteness in one's own life, foreshortened by an earlier impending death than one might have hoped (or even planned) for. There may be a cluster of small and large unfinished tasks, a sense of unfulfilled responsibilities to family members, a desire to pursue avocational interests, to learn how certain current affairs in community, nation, or world will turn out. Most difficult of all is the process of the final letting go of the significant others in one's life. It is hard to let go of all such persons, tasks, responsibilities, commitments, interests, and values, and there is grieving in both the process of letting go of others, and in the suffering of "being let go" by others.

However, the grieving can be eased and shared by the *expressed* concern of family and friends, of intent to carry on with unfinished work, of assurances that the family will manage to hold together and to cope with life in the future as they have coped, differently, with the full presence of the (now) terminally ill person. Here again, the experiences of sharing and celebrating memories of the past, of symbolizing the network of love and values which has given meaning to the past, will make the present disengagement from life itself more bearable. The mutuality of suffering in letting go and being let go, by both the dying and the living, can ease the pain of each. Perhaps most helpful of all can be the assurance that those meanings and values that were central to the life style of the dying person will be continued and enhanced in the lives of those near and dear.

The other form of anticipatory self-grief work may be at one and the same time the most common, the most commonly unrecognized, and the most difficult to cope with at all effectively. It is the self-grief associated with the unwillingness, indeed, the psychologic inability, to let go of one's life, of oneself, when the life, the life style, the self, all seem unacceptable, to lack integrity, to be unworthy of a departing blessing. The person is unable to bless, and thus to say "goodbye" to oneself. Here it is critical to understand that it is not the acceptability, the integrity, the worth of a life from *any* objective frame of reference that counts—*it is how one subjectively feels about oneself, one's life, one's life style.*

Some persons do live rather or even quite disgusting lives, perhaps for reasons or causes not of their own making. Along the way there may have been countless self-promises to reform and do better, be better, live better—but self-promises have receded into the future without being fulfilled, until there is no more personal future. How can such a person give a final blessing to self, and then let go of self with integrity and tranquility?

Others have lived normal and mundane, or even exemplary lives. Yet their days have been marked by an unrest, a compulsion, a driven-ness appropriately described as the "tyranny of the should." The norms and sanctions of parents, teachers, and other well-meaning significant power figures in the young person's life make it difficult or impossible to accept (not necessarily approve!) oneself in one's present stage of development. Rather, the measurement is commonly against externally imposed and frequently impossible ideals. Thus the pervasive feelings common to childhood—"I should be a better boy/girl than I am, or indeed can be!"—become in adulthood the all-pervasive "I *should* be a better husband/wife, father/mother, employer/employee, citizen, church member, and all the rest, than I am or ever can be." The passing of days and years give no real peace, no self-acceptance, no esteem income, for the "tyranny of the should" imposes ideal standards always at least one step beyond and above what one can do, or be, or become. Unable to accept oneself, one's life, as measured by the "*shoulds*," it becomes difficult or impossible to accept anyone else's unqualified acceptance, much less any positive evaluations from others.

Such a person cannot accept his or her own unique life cycle, life style, and personal identity with integrity, either because there is much of disgust within its fabric, or because however good and noble it may have been, it always fell short of a punishing self-ideal, or more commonly, because it was a complex combination of both of these. Such persons commonly enter the final years with the feeling that life is now too short for any attempt to start another life and find alternate paths to a new life style that would have integrity. Such persons tend to cringe in despair before the idea and the fact of approaching death. It is a despair that hides disgust, if only in the form of a thousand little disgusts about oneself of which the total does not add up to one big remorse, but only to a vague irritation or petty annoyance. ("*mille petits degouts de soi, dont le total ne fait pas un remords, vais un gene obscure.*"—Rostand) We often think of such elderly persons as "cantankerous," and fail to recognize the storm in the sea of disgusts under the surface ripples of "vague irritations."

In a real sense such a person *cannot* grieve over the impending loss of one's own life, nor accept the reality that the end *is* near, because there is the pervasive sense that *it is a life not worth grieving for*. There may be much grieving over lost opportunities, or unfulfilled hopes and dreams, with a deep anger at a sense of being "cheated" by life. But such tends to be grieving for the unrealities of what life was not, and not for the realities of what life was. Grief work is the process of letting go. Letting go always involves trust! If one cannot grieve over one's own life and its approaching end, then one cannot trustingly let go of life. Since life cannot be lived over, and true anticipatory self-grief work cannot be undertaken, then death *is* the ultimate victor; life is snatched away rather than trustfully let go. The person feels that the whole of life, and especially its ending, is a defeat.

Perhaps this is the ultimate spiritual and religious crisis of aging. It may stir—but only to the subconscious or preconscious level of "vague irritation" or "petty annoyance"—deep anxieties that may have had their genesis in the early months of infancy, and which may have been fended off (but only at a terrible price) by keeping them below the level of consciousness through all the years of life. We have no better term for them than "existential anxieties." In order to deal with them better in the aging, it is worth a moment to set forth what they are, and how they may get started in life.

In the normally developing infant at about the age of eight months, strong attachments are being formed to specific mothering persons. Earlier (at about six months) the attachment was not specific, but only to anyone who performed mothering functions; and there seems to be little anxiety about the comings and goings of one or more nonspecific persons performing such mothering functions. But when the attachment becomes specific, then the goings (leaving the room, and so on) of that person tend to produce what is called "eighth month anxiety." The child does not yet have the verbal tools or experience for even the most rudimentary symbolic thinking, and cannot yet understand that things and persons can exist beyond the range of vision. To be out of sight means, for such a child, not to exist. So the departing mothering person seems to have ceased to exist (died) and thus to have abandoned the child. The child does not *think* abandoned with its head, but feels abandoned in its muscles and glands and "guts." It senses its total dependence for its survival upon the mothering person. Its anxieties are overwhelming, for the mother's "assumed" nonbeing could mean nonbeing for the infant. It screams in panic. If the screams are ignored by a nonreturning mothering figure, or are punished by a returning mothering figure—"you spoiled child!"—screams of anxiety are turned into screams of rage, then more punishment, then even more feelings of utter abandonment. All of this process leads to the sensorimotor "assumption" or "conclusion" that one has been abandoned, punished, rejected, because one is bad, unworthy, unacceptable. But expression of anger at the mothering figure, who goes away but returns to punish, is not a possible solution for the infant. Its need for the mothering person is still total. Thus the anger is and must be turned inward against the self. The self is thus rejected as unworthy, and the deepest feeling level of disgust and despair may become a part of a lifelong life style, imprinted in an indelible manner into one's guts and glands.

Of course, the deep existential anxieties may be angered by many other types of experience, different from that given in the illustration above. The important point is that these anxieties are largely "visceral learnings" which tend to persist over long periods of time, especially if reinforced by a succession of threatening and punishing experiences. Furthermore, the patterns of self-rejection which center in the feeling that one is unworthy and unacceptable may and commonly do receive a "religious" reinforcement. That is, in countless ways the young child may be assured that "God loves *good* little boys and girls—so you should be one." But the child who already feels unworthy and unaccepted tends to convert such intended assurances into "God hates and punishes *bad* little boys and girls—and that's what I am."

Such religiously reinforced patterns of psychologic and spiritual masochism may become masked by the developing ego defenses such as denial, projection, rationalization, as they are built up, layer upon layer, in later childhood and on into adulthood. Tragically, these very ego defenses which preserve and enhance the self also prevent or at least make difficult the purging of the bad self-image and especially the bad self-feelings. The defenses prevent the mounting of one "big remorse" which would lead to a healthy self-acceptance and the acceptance of one's acceptance by God and by others. Thus, one could escape from the compulsive "tyranny of the should." Instead, such persons commonly enter upon a path of endless moralisms, trying to be good enough to be loved and worthy of love. It is not enough for such persons to try "to be a better boy/girl than I am in order to be loved." Rather it becomes "I must be a perfect boy/girl in order even to be accepted." The impossible standard thus set by the negative self-image and the rejecting self-feelings *compel* one to use the various ego defenses to avoid overwhelming depression and despair. Overwhelming despair is lethal, commonly ending in suicide. The mechanisms of the ego defenses permit one to escape overwhelming despair, but at the price of a sentence of lifelong chronic depression.*

* *However, depression can be lethal too, perhaps through less direct and dramatic ways than suicide. Many seek escape by becoming acute alcoholics and "killing" themselves more slowly. Others become "accident-prone" and "let death happen" through automobile accidents and the like. Perhaps the more dramatic form of mind-body relationship is suggested by a recent research in one of the Boston hospitals. Precardiac (open-heart) surgery patients were carefully studied through psychiatric interviews to determine which were depressed and which were optimistic about their condition. Borderline cases with mild depression were excluded from the study, and the remaining two groups were matched as carefully as possible in terms of general health and so forth, so the primary variable was the presence or absence of acute depression. About 90 percent of the depressed patients died during or very soon after open-heart surgery, while only about 10 percent of the nondepressed patients died during the same period.*

It may seem that such a life style, with a psychic core of self-rejection, is its own trap from which there is no escape. However, some persons do manage to outgrow, to overcome, or to work through at least the most debilitating and painfully tragic elements of masochistic self-rejection. Some do it through extensive therapy with a professional counselor; other through self-analysis. Some accomplish self-acceptance in therapy groups; other through changes in the situations which become more accepting and supporting so that there is adequate reinforcement of a growing positive self-image. Still others achieve a new self-hood in many ways that remain a mystery to the most astute students of human nature. However, many have not yet escaped from their own psychic traps as they enter the last days of life. Is there any hope that such may gain a release from masochistic self-rejection, and thus engage in enough self-grief work to die in peace?

Erik Erikson has suggested that while many things occur in the earliest developmental stages of an individual's life that need never have happened, few things happen that cannot be overcome. Although Erikson's conclusion seems to be directed mostly toward therapy or reeducation of children, adolescents, or young adults, it would seem to apply, perhaps in unsuspected ways, even to the person in the stages of dying. But how?

It is a well-known fact that in the aged person there is a diminishing of intellectual powers. The memory process is involved in a sort of reversal, with perplexing forgetfulness regarding the most recent events, and a regaining of memories of very early childhood, many of which have long been dormant, but now are present with surprising vividness and a sense that they happened very recently. This "memory reversal" seems to be coupled with a shedding or sloughing off of layer after layer of ego defenses, so that the very primordial fears which first generated the existential anxieties now emerge with an uncomplicated freshness. Thus the loneliness of the terminally ill aged person, and especially the fear of being left alone in the dying process, would seem to be "of a piece" with the infant's anxiety of being abandoned in its helplessness.

It might seem that the lowering of ego defenses would leave the psyche especially vulnerable to a final attack of self-rejecting feelings. The late stages of the dying process, therefore, would seem the least likely time for the "thousand little disgusts about oneself" to add up to "one big remorse," for such would seem to leave the dying person standing psychically naked before the unacceptable self, placing the ultimate stamp of defeat and failure upon one's own life style and life cycle. Yet it seems that something like this is just what does occur with some persons, followed by a sense of self-acceptance, of psychic and spiritual catharsis, or release from a lifelong tyrannical burden, then a short period of self-grief work, and finally the letting go of life with some measure of tranquility.

Our culture, especially in somewhat earlier times, is replete with reports of last hour repentances and "death-bed conversions." To be sure, such experiences may have been culturally conditioned, for not only was there the hope and expectation that such might take place but there were also many pressures placed upon the dying person by family, friends, and especially clergymen, to be "saved while there is yet time." The language may be regarded as obsolete by some; yet there may be more that is psychologically sound and spiritually authentic in such concepts and experiences than at first appears to be the case.

Into the stones over the main entrance of a major hospital in New York City are carved the words: "Of The Most High Cometh Healing." Here is an affirmation by the medical profession that they do not heal—they only help set the conditions for God's healing processes to work. Are we to conclude that such healing processes are limited to bones and glands and muscles? "Is there no balm in Gilead? Is there no physician there?" (Jeremiah 8:22)

An American folk hymn turns Jeremiah's anguishing question into a strong and comforting confirmation: "There is a balm in Gilead, to make the wounded whole; There is a balm in Gilead, to heal the sin-sick soul." How is the balm received, when there has been a failure through the years to trust processes of spiritual healing?

Perhaps the answer sounds oversimplistic in view of the tremendously complicated nature of the human personality. Yet it may be its ultimate simplicity that causes the answer to be so commonly ignored. When the elements are all put together, unadorned, they do make sense!

The intellecutal powers are decreasing. The ego defenses are slipping away. Early childhood memories take precedence over recent events. With little future left of the person's total life cycle, there is little need to strive any longer to be perfect, or even better! As one's strength and bodily functions ebb away, there is increasing dependence on others for the most basic help. How childlike is one at the end of life, as at the beginning. And it is the very nature of a child to trust, if given half a chance.

So an authentic word of acceptance by doctor, nurse, clergyman, friend, or family member can brush aside the final resistances, lead to the acceptance of one as one is, and help gain a sense of the authentic integrity of one's unique life cycle as something that *had to be* as the accidental coincidence of but one life cycle and one segment of history, and which, of necessity, permitted no substitutions. Thus can come a release from the "tyranny of the should," and counsels of perfection are seen at last in their true light, as appropriate for the gods, but poor spiritual diet for mortal humans. Thus, a whole new perspective can be gained (received—or accepted) on one's life as having integrity, as being worth grieving for, and as fit and ready for a final self-blessing at the end.

THE PROCESSES OF "NORMAL" GRIEF WORK

We turn now to a consideration of the processes and psychodynamics of normal grief work, occasioned by a present or recent bereavement. The focus is narrowed to an examination of the stages in acute grief associated with the loss through death of a significant person, keeping in mind that the symptoms of such grief, and the processes of grief work that follow differ in length and degree more than in kind from other and less serious forms of bereavement.

For purposes of simplicity, our treatment of a very complex phenomenon will be of a sudden, unexpected loss by death of one who is a significant person to a normal adult in the retirement years who is capable of coping with life in a reasonably effective manner. Throughout, it should be kept in mind that grief is one of the most deeply disturbing emotional states a human may endure, and that most persons have ambivalent feelings toward the significant persons, relationships, functions, and responsibilities of life. This ambivalent quality adds to the complexity of the emotions of grief itself.

Even when the death of a significant person is not entirely unexpected, the first reaction is commonly one of denial. We hear such expressions as: "Oh, no, this couldn't happen to me;" "You must be mistaken, it is someone else who died;" "Oh, God, say it isn't so;" "It all seems so unreal. I knew this might happen, but I never really thought it would." Even though the denial is not expressed verbally, there is commonly the effort to avoid the thrust of reality, to ward off the blow by denying its existence. In its extreme form, this denial may last only a brief moment, to be repeated a number of times in the next hours in the form of a hope or wish, but coupled with the beginning of the acceptance of reality. However, fresh memories of the deceased may continue to populate the fantasy life with such vividness that the reality of death may seem most unreal in the presence of such memories. So denial and reaffirmation of the reality of the death may continue for relatively long periods in the waking fantasy life and in the dreams of the grieving person.

Following the first shock of denial and then acceptance of the reality of death, the person usually experiences a definite syndrome of somatic disturbances, lasting from twenty minutes to an hour or two in their more extreme form, and for several hours or even a few days in less severe manifestations. These include: tightness of the throat, choking and shortness of breath, need for sighing, an empty feeling in the abdomen, lack of power in the muscles, chills, loneliness, mental pain, dull headaches, a tactile sense as though one were being pricked by pins and needles, especially along the spine. The earliest symptoms will usually be followed by feelings of weakness and tiredness. Things feel too heavy, food tastes like sawdust, saliva will not flow, events seem unreal, the sensory responses seem disorganized and undependable, and there may be fear of loss of sanity. One may almost stagger as though drunk when trying to walk, and feel as though one were walking on another person's legs, rather than on one's own.

The early psychologic syndrome commonly includes the following symptoms: general irritability, whether expressed verbally or not; a feeling of hostility, often expressed toward the deceased in such statements as: "Why did he do this to me?" or "Why did God do this to me?"—really two ways of saying the same thing—"I'm damned mad at my husband/wife (or whomever) and at God for leaving me alone." There may be a time of questioning one's own responsibility in the events leading to the death of the significant person, perhaps with a tendency to assign self-blame even when nothing could have been done by the mourner or anybody else to prevent the death; a desire to talk considerably and especially about the deceased, often in an unconscious effort to "fix" in one's memory the events of the last hours of the deceased's life; a restlessness that seems to keep one going through motions with no zest or meaning; loss of the capacity to initiate activity; and a marked disability to make even minor decisions about trivial matters. Often there will be repeated expressions of bewilderment and aloneness, as in "What is going to happen to me?" or "What do you think I should do?" There may also be efforts to secure reassurance from others, through such questions as "There wasn't anything more I could have done, was there?"

Early physiologic and psychologic manifestations of grief give way to new patterns as the earliest shock wears off. Bodily functions begin to return to normal, although the bereaved will still show tiredness, little appetite, continued expressions of irritability and hostility, coupled with feelings of guilt about these, as seen in efforts to portray the deceased in the most favorable light. Very often there will be lingering expressions of self-pity and self-blame. These may seem to be neurotic rather than normal, but acute grief brings such a severe blow to one's psychic organization that a temporary situational neurosis is to be expected even in the most healthy persons. We must remember, too, that grief triggers the most ambivalent and often unconscious emotions held toward the deceased; healthy grief work requires that there be catharsis for both positive and negative feelings, as well as the working out of one's guilt feelings over past negative feelings and past actions—or failure to act, such as withholding expressions of affection and tenderness.

Someone has called the work of normal grief "the illness that heals itself." When that is the case, it is pain with a purpose. The mourner is forced gradually to renounce his longing for the lost person and to accept a new life without the loved one. This emotional renunciation requires a painful orientation to all details of the world of reality. At first, the bereaved person must concentrate on every object, every process and function, every habit and attitude, every relationship carrying associations with the lost person, until these can be accepted emotionally without reawakening the intense longings that mark the early stages of grief work. Furthermore, the grieving person may feel that it is actually disloyal to the dead person to go through the very process of disengagement and becoming emotionally detached from that dead person, which is required in coming to grips with the new realities of life.

Confronted with such losses and shifting loyalties, the grieving person is torn between uncontrollable desires for the loved one and a recognition and acceptance of the fact that the loved person no longer exists. Grief is the expression of painful conflicts between the inner world of memories, needs, drives, instincts, and fantasies and the claims of the outer world of reality. Only with the passage of considerable time can the grieving person give up his longing for the deceased person and reorder his style of life so that it is based on the new realities.

Commonly the most intense period in the spiritual crisis of bereavement follows rather immediately after the news is received that a significant person has died. However, two more intense periods are yet to be confronted, during which the mourner will need to call upon all available ego strength, and in which much emotional support and spiritual help will be needed from others. These are the preparation for and participation in the funeral service or memorial ceremony, and the return home from the funeral or memorial service.

Unless some of the major decisions and plans have already been made for the commitment of the remains of the deceased, the bereaved person may be led into making many snap judgments under extreme emotional stress, rather than considered decisions which will continue to merit approval in succeeding months: cremation or burial? a funeral service or a memorial service with no casket? if a funeral service, should the casket be opened or kept closed? services in a church or synagogue, or in a "funeral chapel?" a small, private service for family members and closest friends only, or a larger, more inclusive service? flowers, or suggestions that memorial gifts be sent to a favorite charity? a wake? a committal service at the cemetery? the content of obituary notices? a eulogy for the deceased in the funeral or memorial service? For a person in emotional and spiritual shock, the painful price extracted in making so many decisions so soon may seem to be more than can be borne.

Perhaps the mourner is most vulnerable when confronted by the American way of death (Mitford 1963, Chaps. 2,3), with its embalming and cosmetic procedures to suggest the unreality of death ("Didn't Father/Mother look so peaceful, so natural, just as though he/she might wake up any moment!"), its expensive caskets, burial vaults, cemetery plots, marble monuments or bronze plaques, attendants in formal dress, long lines of limousines, and all the rest. The mourner often yields to the temptation to endanger his/her own and other's financial future and to deplete meager savings, already seriously strained by medical and hospital bills, when faced with the nagging question, "What's the right thing to do?" A combination of the pain of grief, guilt feelings regarding relations with the deceased, uncertainty about the wishes of the deceased regarding many or most aspects of the funeral, what is "expected" by the family and one's community of friends and associates, the general ignorance of the practices, procedures, and costs relative to the funeral, the desire not to be "cheap" or cut corners in this final act for the deceased, leaves most mourners very vulnerable to the exploitation of their bereavement!

To help avoid turning crisis into tragedy, a trusted friend, a close member of the family who is less involved in grief, or a sensitive minister or other professional may greatly assist by bringing to the mourner's attention the major items that must be considered relative to the funeral or memorial service and the committal of the dead. Various options can be suggested, with gentle inquiry as to which would be most satisfactory. Here the helper must "play it by ear," trying to sense just how much the bereaved can do, what the mental and emotional reserves are, how much others might share of the decision-making process, how many of the details can be decided by and planned by the bereaved, and whether or not there is a need to suggest postponing decisions for a bit until the mourner is able to make those kinds of decisions which will be regarded as appropriate in later months and years. Again and again the bereaved may seek assurance that the choices he is making are appropriate for his circumstances. Such assurance should be offered, but never forced on the bereaved.

The funeral service itself too often adds to, rather than assists in, the crisis of bereavement. In a day when much of society seems to conspire to keep the reality of personal death from becoming a part of conscious thought, the church as an institution and the funeral as a ceremonial can serve important functions in keeping the basic realities of life and death in clear perspective. In addition, the funeral or memorial service should and can be a comfort and a help to the mourners in their suffering, provide an occasion for the catharsis of deep feelings, develop a "beloved community" which establishes the right and a helpful climate for appropriate mourning and celebration, aid in recalling rich memories of the deceased, tap rich resources for personal integration or reintegration and the stabilizing of the self, and point to the future in hope and trust.

An examination of the crisis of returning home following the funeral will bring into focus some of the important differences in the psychodynamics of grief in the aging and in the younger person. It has already been suggested that grief is a more common or frequent experience of the elderly than of the young, though such experiences may "peak" in the late middle-age. Thus for the aging one grief experience may occur before the major grief work from an earlier bereavment has been completed, and so reactivate the earlier wounds, result in cumulative grief, and therefore place additional emotional strains on already overtaxed reserves.

Before and during the funeral, family and friends commonly surround both older and younger mourners, and attention given to the responsibilities of the moment tend to divert consciousness away from the sense of hurt and loss, at least for brief but helpful periods of time. However, when the responsibilities of the funeral are over, the younger person commonly returns to a continuing circle of family and friends, again faces the common tasks of the day, the need to return to the world of work, and so forth. However, when the aged bereaved returns from the funeral there may be little left except an empty house and haunting memories. A new wave of loneliness is apt to come crashing in, making new demands on already exhausted emotions, bringing again the shock of hurt nearly as intense as in the first moments of bereavement. Many elderly persons report that the return home, and the first night alone following the funeral, is the most painful of all to endure. A concerned and caring community will find ways to insure that a knowledgeable and sensitive person, or persons, will be present through the first day and night or so with the bereaved person who has no close members of a household left.

Normal grief work requires the reinvestment of interest and of emotion, and commitments of time and energy in the world of work, in social activities, community projects, human interactions, and the like. This reinvestment of interest, emotions, and energy by the elderly combine to make grief work difficult and prolonged, for to many of them it does not seem worthwhile for the small time that remains to them. However, the full course of grief work seems to require not only the completion of the disengagement from, the letting go of, the deceased significant person; it also requires the reinvestment of oneself into a reordered or reintegrated life cycle with its new realities. Indeed, it would seem to be impossible fully to *let go of* without *reinvesting in!* One does not have to seek far, therefore, for probable causes of the common feelings of depression, uselessness, aimlessness, severe loneliness, morbid self-pity, thoughts of suicide, and the like, which the perceptive person finds among many of the elderly bereaved.

Although the hardest blows of normal grief may have passed within a day or two or at most a week following the funeral or memorial service, much yet remains to be done in working the grief through to the end. If the deceased was a close family member, there may be a rather long succession of decisions and responsibilities that the grieving person or persons must face. There may be bank accounts to close, bills to pay, a will to get through probate court, accounts to settle, personal property to dispose of or to distribute among the survivors, unfinished tasks to complete for the deceased person, cards and letters to write, and on and on. Each such decision or responsibility may seem only to open the wounds of bereavement, bring fresh suffering, drive home even deeper the loss and the loneliness. What one must or should do *for* the deceased hurts less than what one now cannot do *with* the deceased—the simple chores of life, talking together, holding hands, and a hundred and one things that together gave life meaning.

Now there is a sudden lack of any meaning in simple routines like doing up one's hair or shaving, because the meaning came in large part because they were done for or with the loved one. Yet it is these very activities, now done alone and largely for oneself, that help the person to accept the finality of the death and loss of the loved one, to understand in new depth the true meaning of the deceased person's life, to celebrate that meaning in various private or public rituals, and to complete the process of becoming disengaged from the deceased. Painful though the process may be, it is the pain itself that helps the wound to heal. It has been said that grief is the only illness that heals itself. If we are wise, we will let grief do its healing work.

One aspect of grief work that may be surprising to persons who have not gone through the process is the awkwardness of meeting friends and associates who do not know how to relate easily and naturally to a person in bereavement. C. S. Lewis, writing under the pseudonym of N. W. Clerk, describes such encounters following the death of his wife, as related in his very insightful book, *A Grief Observed:*

> ... An odd by-product of my loss is that I'm aware of being an embarrassment to everyone I meet. At work, at the club, in the street, I see people, as they approach me, trying to make up their minds whether they'll say something about it or not. I hate it if they do, and if they don't. Some funk it altogether. R. has been avoiding me for a week. I like best the well-brought-up young men, almost boys, who walk up to me as if I were a dentist, turn very red, get it over, and then edge away to the bar as quickly as they decently can. Perhaps the bereaved ought to be isolated in special settlements like lepers.
>
> To some I'm worse than an embarrassment. I am a death's head. Whenever I meet a happily married pair I can feel them both thinking. 'One or other of us must some day be as he is now' (Clerk 1963, pp 12, 13).

C. S. Lewis' experience during bereavement with embarrassed friends underscores again the prevalent failure to come to any reasonable terms with death. To die seems indecent, inconsiderate, immoral, "un-American." We continue in vanity to attempt to denude death of its meaning. Thus, our pretenses about death strengthen its power to destroy us while we live. Death is a vital part of life, and to reject death is to reject the life that includes death. In the very degree that we strip death of its meaning and dignity, we strip life of meaning and dignity. Some of the dignity of both life and death can be restored by honoring the processes of grief work in ourselves and in others, by understanding its various stages, by a growing willingness to bear the price of pain to be endured through each stage, and by achieving in the process something of the spiritual transcendence that triumphs over both the finitude of life and the infinitude of death.

PATHOLOGIC FORMS OF GRIEF WORK

Failure to avail ourselves of the spiritual insights and resources within ourselves and within a concerned community may lead to various pathologic forms of grief work.

A person does not need to be basically neurotic for grief work to assume pathologic forms, at least for brief periods of time. Grief itself is usually an intense emotional illness, frequently accompanied by various physiologic symptoms. Feelings of loss, anger, and guilt may be so intense and overwhelming when death strikes down a deeply significant person that only very healthy persons may manage grief work through to its conclusion without being plunged into periods of neurotic response.

Most persons have ambivalent feelings toward all significant loved ones while they are living. The occasion of bereavement tends to stir up and even to amplify strong feelings of anger or guilt, or more commonly, both in combination. The deeper the sense of loss the greater the degree of anger that is likely to be experienced, and the anger in turn generates an increased sense of guilt. However, the anger is commonly at least partially repressed, for the object of anger is usually: first, the deceased loved one—for abandoning one and leaving one to face life alone; second, God—for permitting the death to happen; third, oneself—for various real or imagined faults or sins of omission or commission that one may regard as factors leading to the death of the loved one; and fourth, one or more members of the helping professions, such as a doctor—for not preventing the death—or a clergyman—as God's representative, and one toward whom anger at God can more conveniently and more safely be expressed. Whatever the object of anger, it is threatening to express it directly and openly, for the anger seems so inappropriate and so immoral at such times. Generally it must be largely repressed, for if it could all emerge to the level of full consciousness, it would engender such guilt feelings as to shatter the ego-image.

Where the anger is too strong and too threatening, it makes the pain of grief work too great to bear, and grief cannot thus heal itself. Rather, the processes of normal grief work become diverted into delayed grief work, or masochistic self-punishment, or sadistic aggression toward others.

Delayed grief work takes many forms, wears many masks. As already indicated, our culture seems to conspire to make normal grief work very unnatural and very difficult. In countless ways it tends to sweep the harsh realities of personal death under the cultural rug. In many ways our culture has so placed its dirty paws on persons in this area of life that when they experience their first serious bereavement they have already become incapable of normal grief work. For example, some years ago a woman in her mid-thirties lost her mother. She was deeply attached to and overdependent upon her mother in many ways. She complained during the first hours and days that she could not weep for her mother, although she wanted to do so. It is quite possible that she has never knowingly shed a single tear for the loss of her mother—to shed one tear would bring on an incontrollable flood. Yet for years she broke into tears over the slightest frustration or disappointment.

This is a case of neurotic grief work, and primarily of character neurosis. But many times quite healthy persons are led into situational neurosis triggered by bereavement, with the situational neurosis being fostered primarily by cultural patterns of anxiety regarding death, and by well-meaning but bungling friends, ministers, or other associates, rather than by a weak ego or character structure. Three types of factors need to be mentioned, which may contribute to the situational neurosis of delayed grief work.

1. The "buck-up," "be brave, don't cry," "have faith in God—He will see you through," type of psychology-

theology so prevalent in our misguided attempts to comfort the bereaved that they are made to feel that grieving is cowardly, indecent, and shows a lack of trust in God.

2. The types of escapist funerals that operate as though death were a lovely but bittersweet affair, a nonreality, and that what really counts is the "sweet bye and bye" when we will all gather at the river, God will wipe away all tears, and we will be eternally reunited in a state of bliss. Here no argument against personal immortality is intended or implied, but rather the evasion of the realities of physical death and the pain and suffering such brings to the survivors, such evasion being a strong causal factor in the onset of delayed grief work.
3. The more pervasive factors in our culture, such as the "Forest Lawn Memorial Parks," and the general hush-hush, roundabout manner of avoiding a confrontation with the realities of death—even in hospitals, where so much of our dying occurs.

But death is very real, and it is commonly a very dirty business, as seen in the emotional price it exacts from both the dying and the living. Our poor ways of handling it combine to prevent many normal persons of all ages from entering into normal grief work, and thus cause them to suffer a horrible and needless price as they enter into this condition called delayed grief work. Thus, they may be brave, choke back the tears, swallow their racking sobs, keep the stiff upper lip, play-act as though all were well or soon would be—and then for years wonder what is wrong with them, why they are so irritable, so hostile at things they formerly took in stride, why life has lost its zest and thrust. Then, five or ten years later such persons may engage in long-postponed grief work over the death of a loved one, as they go into mourning over the loss of a trinket, a pet, or a memento of the long-departed loved one.

When the pain of loss or fear of loss-related pain predominates in the experience of bereavement, a delayed grief work may not be unusual. But when guilt is the dominant emotional response in bereavement the grief may be worked out through various forms of masochistic self-punishment. Guilt feelings may be caused by: (1) real moral culpability, such as careless or drunken driving which results in the death of a loved one; (2) the failure to take certain actions in time which *might* have yielded different results, such as waiting too long to obtain medical care for an illness or accident; (3) a morbid conscience or superego, which tends to ascribe guilt to oneself rather indiscriminately; or (4) the strange emergence in later life of a childlike magical thinking, as when in the prerational years one assumed that "wishing makes it so." Thus in a state of strong ambivalence toward a significant person, one might wish for, fantasize about, or dream of the death of that person. The death actually occurs, and by assigning magical powers to one's wish or fantasy life the person wrongly concludes that he or she is guilty of causing the death. Even conscious recognition of the death wish or death fantasy for the significant other person may be enough to engender strong guilt feelings.

Persons who may be particularly prone to such guilt feelings are those who tend to take literally such teachings ascribed to Jesus as "... whosoever is angry with his brother without a cause shall be in danger of the judgment ..." and "... whosoever looketh on a woman to lust after her hath committed adultery with her already in his heart" (Matthew 5:22, 28). Here, fantasy is wrongly identified with intent; there is also the failure to recognize that in our fantasy and dream life, both the best and the worst of us, and all in between, have committed every sin in the book! However, the guilt feelings may not be related to the death or cause of death of the significant person, but may be extended to real or imagined failures or sins of omission or commission during the life together with the significant person. Not infrequently, guilt-prone persons reach another illogical and ill-founded conclusion: because they feel guilty, they assume that God willed the death of the significant other person in order to punish them.

Whatever the cause or the justification, or absence of either, for the guilt-grief syndrome, persons involved in it undergo acute and prolonged suffering. Unlike normal grief which tends to heal itself, guilt-grief tends to be both self-perpetuating and self-intensifying. One's fantasies, feelings, actions, ego, indeed, the entire self are subjected to repeated accusations and condemnations. If only the deceased person could be recalled to life, so that restitution might be made for real or imagined hurts and wrongs! If only life could be relived! But all the self-condemnations, all the wishful thinking, will not recall one moment of the past for reliving. So one's emotional and ego reserves tend to become exhausted, and in more extreme cases depression results, the will to live is seriously diminished, and overt or covert suicide attempts, or actual suicide, may result. Or one may unexpectedly succumb to what would otherwise not be a lethal accident or illness.

If anger is the dominant emotional response in bereavement, then grief may be worked out in aggressive and punishing relations with others. The following illustration may seem extreme, yet in less obvious form is roughly duplicated countless times.

A highly intelligent, professionally trained and happily married mother of two young adolescents lost her husband, a professional executive, through a sudden and unexpected death. The psychologic blow left her angry at her husband in particular and at life in general. The financial blow forced her to change her whole life style, and to assume a full-time and highly responsible executive position in order to support herself and her two children through the most expensive time of their dependent years. She became a compulsively competent and demanding executive. Within the agency of her employment, all men and especially all healthy and happily married men, and all married women, became potential targets for her scathing criticisms and "meat grinder" personal attacks. Probably, she was never fully aware of the depth or the object of her real anger—her husband who died in midlife and left her alone to carry an unwanted financial burden, and God, who had permitted the death to occur. It seemed that her anger toward her deceased husband and toward God was so intense that she could not permit it to emerge into consciousness in full strength and undistorted. She could only displace it upon married women—who had what she wanted and that which had been taken from her in the death of her husband—or upon married men—who reminded her of her husband who had "deserted" her. That she had never been able to forgive God for taking her husband, as she felt that God had done, would have been a truth too horrible for her to acknowledge or to permit to emerge into full consciousness.

We have thus seen in summary fashion three different forms of pathologic or neurotic grief work: delayed or repressed grief work, self-punishing or masochistic grief work, and aggressive-sadistic grief work. Normal grief work may be very difficult and painful to bear, and may take several months or even a year or two to work through. However, in pathologic grief work, the price exacted in pain, frustration, punishing guilt feelings, or displaced rage are much greater than in normal grief work. Furthermore, they may extend the period of grief unduly and thus multiply the total amount of pain the person experiences. The pathologic forms of grief do not heal the wounds of bereavement, but tend only to keep them alive, open, and hurting, although often in disguised forms.

It may seem as though all persons caught in pathologic forms of grief work need lengthy and intensive professional counseling or therapy. The aging might seem to have special needs for such help, since their emotional reserves may be diminishing, they may be faced with more frequent occasions of bereavement than younger persons, and they more commonly live alone than do persons through the broad ranges of middle years. Even those who live out their final years in a retirement center or nursing home may and commonly do feel alone, rejected, and abandoned.

However, in many cases only one or two or at most a half-dozen sessions with a professional counselor are sufficient to help normal persons work through the stages and aspects of grief work that are most painful and most threatening to mental health. More intensive and more extended help may be indicated for those who become involved in pathologic forms of grief work. Of course, many persons—including the elderly and not a few of those with some neurotic tendencies—work through intense grief without any professional help. But many who do need such help and could profit from it simply cannot afford it, or it is not available to them. There are far too few professional counselors and therapists to assist all those who seriously need help. Furthermore, many persons in bereavement do not recognize their need for professional help, or are resistive toward seeking and using it. Must all of these who need help suffer on, enduring their psychologic and spiritual pain in isolation, feeling rejected, abandoned, and punished?

SPIRITUAL RESOURCES, MINISTRIES, AND CEREMONIALS

If the solution is left entirely in the hands of trained professionals, there would seem to be little hope of closing the gap between needs and resources. However, an approach similar to that now being developed in the allied health fields with the recruiting and training of a wide range of "paramedics" would offer much hope. The common "myth," held by both lay and professional persons, must be unmasked as false that only such professionals as ministers and psychiatrists can properly counsel and otherwise help persons caught in bereavement, grief work, the identity-in-aging crisis, and many other major and minor crises and problems of adjustment. Emotionally mature and sensitive laymen, experienced in coping with a wide range of problems and crises, given a reasonable amount of training and ongoing supervision, often prove to be more helpful to persons in crisis than professionals. For one thing, they are perceived more frequently as functioning out of genuine concern for others, rather than for some monetary reward. Thus, they ascribe worth to the persons they serve, and help those served ascribe worth to themselves. When lay counselors and group leaders are selected in part because they have faced and lived through such crises as grief work with a sense of spiritual triumph over the worst that life can deal out, they offer unusual promise as lay counselors-ministers.

It is evident that ministers, psychiatrists, group therapists, and other professionals must find new ways out of the dilemma of too few and too costly professionals and too many persons in acute and chronic spiritual crises without any margins of financial resources. The most promising resource—paramedics and lay ministers—has been suggested, if the professionals will work through their own power and status problems, so that they become team members with laymen, rather than competitors with them. The emerging new role of the professionals will center more in training and supervising and supporting laymen for an ever-widening range of ministries of comfort, interpretation, support, intervention, referrals, and many more forms of service on a volunteer or part-time paid basis. Working through professional jealousy and pride, and discarding obsolete and inadequate layman-professional stereotypes, may be the biggest hurdle for the professionals.

The spiritual resources and untapped services and ministries among lay persons are beyond imagination. There is no reason to believe that they are inadequate in numbers or resourcefulness for the giant tasks that confront us. The most appropriate and promising resources for services and ministries to the aging are to be found among the aging themselves. As we have seen, many of them have felt rejected as useless by their culture following their years of productive employment; many have also felt from early years that they were under the mandate of service as one of the highest and most central tenants of the Judeo-Christian heritage. Yet many have also felt relegated to rather insignificant chores of a housekeeping nature in church or synagogue, or they have themselves felt inadequate for the interpersonal tasks of ministry. Given the time, opportunity, an adequate organizational and communication network, and a modest amount of training and supervision from a professional, they find nothing more significant in their new life style than ministering to peer members and others in moments of loneliness, periods of adjustment to new situations, crises of bereavement, and so on. They do not have to have all the answers to be helpful. They need to be genuinely concerned for others, able to listen and equally able to share long silences, to let happen what needs to happen in meaningful relationships. Again and again, they discover that in being of service to others and in ministering to them, they find their own deepest meaning and value. Thus, they cease to be and to feel useless, alone, and rejected, bored with their existence in the backeddies of life. In having to reach deep into their own spiritual being to help another in distress, if only to suffer meaningfully in silence alongside a fellow human, they find and develop those spiritual resources needed to meet their own needs in times of stress and distress.

But what of the final, the ultimate crisis of the spiritual life—the facing of the reality of one's own mortality and approaching death? For death not only sets the limits within which all ethical and spiritual considerations must take place. There is also, as Karl Rahner (1961, pp 77f) has suggested, an "axiological presence" of death throughout the whole of life, which rules life from within. The awareness of the reality and physical finality of death colors all decisions in life and freights them with moral and spiritual seriousness. It is this axiological presence of death in all of life that resides at the core of our existential anxiety. Evasion of the fact of death is flight from moral seriousness into triviality or compulsive preoccupation with the self.

It has been suggested in many ways throughout this chapter that the spiritual crises of aging are intensified and prolonged because in our culture persons tend to avoid developing an adequate thanatology, or philosophy of death. Careful analysis indicates that an adequate philosophy of life must include a philosophy of death.

Instead of an adequate thanatology, we have developed in our culture a pornography of death (Gorer 1965, App. 4, pp 192-199). The chief feature of pornography is an obsession with the sex act abstracted from its normal human emotion which is love. When the sex act is abstracted from love, it becomes repetitive and dull. Pornographic literature must therefore rescue the reader from boredom by creating vivid fantasies, with the sex act performed in an endless variety of ways, with each more elaborate or intense than the last. A prudish culture in which personal sex is taboo is likely to develop simultaneously a pronographic obsession with sex. The taboo subject includes both the unmentionable event and a compulsive obsession with the techniques of the act.

Gorer argues that the personal event of death has replaced sex as the major taboo subject in our culture. Concealment and obsession go together in the same culture. *Personal* death has replaced copulation and birth as the unmentionable subject, while obsession with violence and the techniques of violent death is dominating our age. As in the pornography of sex, where obsession with technique dominates, so in the pornography of death it is difficult to maintain interest unless violence is done in a variety of ways, with the need for each new act to surpass all former acts in cruelty, fiendish ingenuity, and stark reality.

It is quite unlikely that we would be so involved in the pornography of death if we had developed an adequate thanatology. A strong case could be made that the church, second only to the medical profession, has been a major contributing agency in the development of the pornography of death, rather than an adequate thanatology. Pastors rarely deal with the gravely ill without noticing immediately and becoming involved themselves in the silences, evasions, and brave lies that surround the dying. Neither the doctor nor the clergyman may be villains in the plot by intention or design. Both have seen too many men and women avoid asking the big question, or have heard them asking the question whithout really wanting an answer. But the evasions, silence, and big lies have their origin in the awesomeness and the mystery of death itself. Not only do our philosophies and our moralities and our professional competencies desert us in the face of death; so also do our religious ceremonies and rituals and assurances. Often in our words about death we are caught up in a massive, verbose, uneasy flight from death and its reality; we have nothing left to say except to "say it with flowers."

In the springtime we think of new beginnings. Each autumn reminds us, or ought to, that everything in the world comes to an end. When we think about nature we can usually regard each of the four seasons as good, or at least as not evil. "Oh to be in Devon, now that April's there" has its nostalgic counterpart in "When the frost is on the pumpkin and the fodder's in the shock." Endings are not necessarily regarded as inferior to beginnings. We commonly begin our meals with soup and end them with dessert, saving "the best to the last." Every poem and novel written, every symphony composed and played, every task undertaken has an ending. How terrible, how unendurable life would be if it were not so.

Except when it is the end of a human life—my life—that is considered. Yet the claims of mortality must be met. In the face of those claims all men seem to be losers, for death is recognized as some sort of sacred power that confounds every effort of man to understand or to master it. Before that power all human efforts seem impotent, human longings are of no avail. It is a reality that has inspired theologians and philosophers and poets to meditate, yet brings all those meditations and meditators to an end. It is a reality that drags into oblivion those whom life has made into heroes. It reaches into the deepest course of human life, gripping the heart with love and hope and fear and worry—and flight from an end from which there is no escape. Sometimes its victory is won in frontal attacks; sometimes it lies in ambush and strikes unexpectedly from the side as it claims the young, the innocent, the high-minded, and the frivolous. Its ultimate victory is in persuading us that the good God of all beginnings, whose steadfast loving kindness is seen in all His creation, is turned by the power of death into what James Joyce in *Ulysses* called the "Dio Boia," the "Hangman God," and what C. S. Lewis in *A Grief Observed* called the "Cosmic Vivisectionist."

Somehow or other, we have let ourselves be convinced that personal death is too horrible to face. We have been afraid that our fears would overcome our trust. We have believed that we do not have the spiritual resources to look death in the face, unflinching. *We have been persuaded that death robs life of its meaning, and that therefore death is evil.* And we have believed that faith in some form of personal immortality is the only positive answer to physical death. So we have argued for immortality as the only option that is adequate—and to some it has seemed that the only thing that is adequate about this option is the volume used in trying to convince oneself and others of that which is not fully believed, nor could it be understood if it were known to be true.

Religious ceremonials need to gather up and celebrate through symbolic, musical, and dramatic reenactment the full range of the important events, relationships, meanings, and feelings we experience in life. Those ceremonials must ring true to life, else they become farcical substitutes for the real life and death, joy and sorrow, success and failure, aloneness and togetherness, alienation and reconciliation drama that is native to the human story.

So what should be the nature of our religious ceremonials when we confront and—yes—celebrate death? How do we form and reform and shape them so that they minister in deep and meaningful ways to the whole human community, and especially to the aging and the dying?

Whether public or private, for a few or for many, they should be real, authentic, honest! They should affirm the reality of both life and death. They should recognize both the certainty and the uncertainty of birth and death, and all in between. They should affirm that death draws both its meaning and its mystery from life, as life draws much of its meaning from death, and would be dull and far less meaningful without death. They should reveal to us and help us to reaffirm and reenact the full range of our deepest emotions—joy and sorrow, love and hate, doubt and trust, hurt and hope, aspiration and despair, blessings and cursings. They should help us to understand that we do not really know joy until we have tasted deeply of sorrow; that if we love deeply we also hate deeply; that we cannot trust in depth until we have taken our spiritual pilgrimage through the depths of doubting; that we never reach peak spiritual experiences without enduring the dark night of the soul; that when our knowledge trails out into a thin line of truth disappearing in mystery it is still given to us to trust.

But is it still true that death makes all men losers?

No!

In trust and in gratitude we can celebrate life, whether its length between birth and death be two score, or four score and ten, or a hundred score years. The quality of life is not determined by its length nor the time of its ending. Whether short or long, it can participate in and possess qualities of the ageless and eternal which transcend the birth-death time and space boundaries of a single life.

In trust and gratitude we also celebrate the reality and the mystery of death.

Suggested Readings

Berezin MA, Cath SH: Geriatric Psychiatry: Grief, Loss, and Emotional Disorders in the Aging Process. New York, International Universities Press, 1965
Birren JE: The Psychology of Aging. Englewood Cliffs, NJ, Prentice-Hall, 1964
Bowers MK, Jackson EN, Knight JA, LeShan L.: Counseling the Dying. New York, Thomas Nelson, 1964
Clerk NW (a pseudonym for CS Lewis): A Grief Observed. Greenwich, Conn, Seabury Press, 1963, pp 12, 13
Erikson E: Identity, Youth and Crisis. New York, Norton, 1968
———: Childhood and Society, 2nd ed. New York, Norton, 1963
———: Identity and the Life Cycle. Psychological Issues, Vol. 1, No. 1, Monograph 1. New York, International Universities Press, 1960
Feifel H (ed): The Meaning of Death. New York, McGraw-Hill, 1959
Fulton L: Death and Identity. New York, John Wiley, 1965
Gorer G: Death, Grief, and Mourning. Garden City, NY, Doubleday, 1965
Jackson EN: Understanding Grief. New York, Abingdon Press, 1957
Kastenbaum R: New Thoughts on Old Age. New York, Springer, 1964
Kubler-Ross E: On Death and Dying. New York, Macmillan, 1969
Levin S, Kahana, RJ: Psychodynamic Studies on Aging: Creativity, Reminiscing, and Dying. New York, International Universities Press, 1967
Mills LO (ed): Perspectives on Death. Nashville, Abingdon Press, 1969
Mitford J: The American Way of Death. New York, Simon and Schuster, 1963, Chaps. 2,3
Rahner K: On the Theology of Death. New York, Herder and Herder, 1961
Spitz RA: The First Year of Life: A Psychoanalytic Study of Normal and Deviant Development of Object Relations. New York, The International Universities Press, 1965
Standard S, Nathan H (eds): Should the Patient Know the Truth? New York, Springer, 1955
Tibbits C, Donahue W: Aging in Today's Society. Englewood Cliffs, NJ, Prentice-Hall, 1960
Verwoerdt A: Communication with the Fatally Ill. Springfield, Ill, C. C. Thomas, 1966
Weisman AD: On Dying and Denying: A Psychiatric Study of Terminality. New York, Behavioral Publications, 1972

CASSETTE TAPES

A series of 18 cassette tapes programs entitled "Death, Grief, and Bereavement," available from The Center for Death Education and Research, University of Minnesota, Minneapolis, Minnesota. The persons and titles of addresses are:

1. Robert Fulton, "Dialogue on Death," (With Dr. John Brantner, Prof. Robert Slater)
2. Delphie Fredlund, "Death and the Family: From the Caring Professions' Point of View"
3. Elisabeth Kubler-Ross: "Stages of Dying"
4. Herman Feifel: "The Meaning of Death in American Society"
5. Jeannette Folta: "Social Reconstruction after Death"
6. Glenn Griffin: "Today's Funeral Director—His Responsibilities and Challenges"
7. Robert Fulton: "A Psycho-social Aspect of Terminal Care: Anticipatory Grief"
8. Vincent Hung: "Facing Death with the Patient—an Ongoing Contract"
9. Daniel Leviton: "The Role of the Schools in Death Education"
10. John Brantner: "Death and the Self"
11. Carl Nighwonger: "Religious Faith and Death: Implications in Work with the Dying Patient and His Family"
12. Paul E. Irion: "Bereavement and the Process of Mourning"
13. Helena Lopata: "The Widow in America: A Study of the Older Widow"
14. A Documentary: "Crib Death: A Sudden Infant Death Syndrome"
15. Connie Goldman: "Conversation with a Dying Friend"
16. George E. Williams: "Talking to Children about Death"
17. Edgar N. Jackson: "Death and the Child"
18. Norman Farberow: "Adolescent Suicide: A Documentary"

INDEX